MURDER INCORPORATED

empire \ genocide \ manifest destiny

A Three Book Series

BOOK THREE:

"Perfecting Tyranny"

BOOK ONE: **"Dreaming of Empire"**

BOOK TWO: **"America's Favorite Pastime"**

Mumia Abu-Jamal & Stephen Vittoria

PRISON RADIO
San Francisco
2020

Published by Prison Radio
San Francisco

First Published in 2020

Prison Radio, P.O. Box 411074, San Francisco, CA 94141

Edited by Justin Lebanowski

Cover Design by Robert Guillory

Interior Design by Rocco Melillo

First Edition Hardcover / September 2020
First Edition Softcover / September 2020

LIBRARY OF CONGRESS CATALOGING-IN-PUBLICATION DATA

Abu-Jamal, Mumia – Vittoria, Stephen. Murder Incorporated: Empire, Genocide, and Manifest Destiny/Book Three—1st ed. p. cm.

Includes bibliographical references and index.

1. History—American Empire.
2. History—War.
3.History—Manifest Destiny.

ISBN: 978-1-7346489-0-4 (Hardcover)
ISBN: 978-1-7346489-1-1 (Softcover)

Printed in the USA

People Talk, People Write

About
Mumia Abu-Jamal

"They have moved heaven and earth to stop his voice being heard in the United States. If there were any justice in the world, they would award him the Nobel Peace Prize next year, but I'm prepared to bet you that they won't."

—Tariq Ali
Author, Journalist, Historian, Public Intellectual

"Everyone interested in justice should read the words of this innocent man."

—William M. Kunstler
Attorney, Civil Rights Activist

"Like the most powerful critics in our society—Herman Melville to Eugene O'Neill—Mumia Abu-Jamal forces us to grapple with the most fundamental question facing this country: what does it profit a nation to conquer the whole world and lose its soul?"

—Cornel West
Professor, Author, Public Intellectual

"His voice is vital and strong. . . rooted in his defiance of those determined to silence him. If Mumia Abu-Jamal has nothing important to say, why are so many powerful people trying to kill him and shut him up?

—John Edgar Wideman
Author, Professor, Rhodes Scholar

"Abu-Jamal. . . His writings are dangerous."

—Village Voice

"A brilliant... prophetic writer. Mumia refuses to allow his spirit to be broken by the forces of injustice; his language glows with an affirming flame."

—Jonathan Kozol
Author, Activist, Educator

"The system is threatened by someone like Mumia Abu-Jamal. A voice as strong and as truthful as his—the repression against him is intensified."

—Sister Helen Prejean
Author of *Dead Man Walking*

"Abu-Jamal's words flow like the sap of trees, pulsing with energy and capturing the essence of life."

—Library Journal

"We join with Amnesty International in demanding a new trial for Mumia Abu-Jamal. We will not allow his voice to be silenced."

—Tom Morello

Musician, *Rage Against the Machine, Audioslave*

"The first time I heard a tape of one of Mumia's radio broadcasts, it was the first time I fully understood why the government was so intent on putting him to death."

—Assata Shakur

Author, Former Member of the Black Liberation Army

"A rare and courageous voice speaking from a place we fear to know: Mumia Abu-Jamal must be heard. Losing his voice would be like losing a color from the rainbow."

—Alice Walker

Social Activist, Pulitzer Prize-winning author of *The Color Purple*

"I find him to be a tremendous thinker about sports and society in the world today."

—Dave Zirin

Journalist, Sports Editor for *The Nation*

"He's such a threat—the only person I can think of that represented the same threat to this country was Paul Robeson."

—Frances Goldin

Human Rights Activist, Literary Agent

"The voice of America is a fraud. One day we will find out that he was the voice of America."

—Dick Gregory

Civil Rights Activist, Author, Comedian

About
Stephen Vittoria

About his film *Long Distance Revolutionary: A Journey with Mumia Abu-Jamal*—

"I've sat through many documentaries in my life and this is one of the finest. I was riveted by the film. It was as if Mumia was in the room speaking directly to us. *Long Distance Revolutionary* is a gripping film."

—Albert Maysles
Legendary Filmmaker

"A compelling and powerful documentary."

—The Washington Post

"A powerful indictment of the hypocrisy inherent in the American Dream. A must-see."

—Huffington Post

"A blistering indictment of institutionalized racism... a sensitive picture of a fascinating human being."

—The Oregonian

"Tracing the path of a brilliant journalist whose message cannot be silenced... Vittoria triumphantly heralds Abu-Jamal's return to the political scene."

—Variety

"Fascinating and persuasive... not unlike Oliver Stone's rewrite of U.S. history."

—Seattle Times

"Vittoria's impassioned feature goes past the headlines... This is truly an eye-opening experience."

—Leonard Maltin
Indiewire

"I absolutely love this documentary."

—Faiza Ahmed
PressTV

"Long Distance Revolutionary, a documentary by Stephen Vittoria, is proof that there are still outspoken champions of views too radicalized to qualify as left-wing: people distrustful of law enforcement, the political system, the justice system, the news media, and the very notion that America is at heart the land of the free… this film is certainly a bracing change from the usual back-and-forth of the evening news."

—Neil Genzlinger
The New York Times

About his film *One Bright Shining Moment: The Forgotten Summer of George McGovern*—

★★★★ "Essential viewing!"

—CBS Radio

★★★★ *Grade:* **A+**

"Lively documentary about McGovern's disastrous run for the US presidency. The interviews with him are worth the price of admission."

—David Sterritt
Christian Science Monitor

"A riveting tales of idealism vs. cynicism."

—NY Daily News

"An elegant homage."

—Minneapolis City Pages

"Of the many political documentaries that have recently emerged, *One Bright Shining Moment* resounds perhaps more strongly than any other."

***—Variety* (at the Hamptons Film Festival)**

"Too decent to be president was the label stuck to former senator and 1972 presidential candidate George McGovern, the self-effacing subject of Stephen Vittoria's *One Bright Shining Moment.* If 'decent' means 'polite,' then the movie makes no effort to emulate its subject: Its ferocity about the state of American politics could earn it substantial numbers among doc, arthouse, and politically progressive audiences. Helmer-scribe Vittoria finds bookends everywhere—the political rise of McGovern running from "Tet to Nixon," his public life essentially spanning "Huey P. Long to Huey P. Newton." It's an affectionate portrait of a man once described by Robert F. Kennedy as the most decent man in the Senate… Narrated with heat by Amy Goodman, pic gains poignancy amid speculation about the kind of world that would have existed had he won."

—John Anderson
Variety

WINNER—"Best Documentary Feature," Sarasota Film Festival (2005)

About
Murder Incorporated: Empire, Genocide, and Manifest Destiny

"This is an angry book. The anger is unsparing, incisive and often eloquent. The recasting of rampant American power as that of a world Mafioso is long overdue, and Mumia Abu-Jamal and Stephen Vittoria speak for so many with this bracing counterattack. Read and mark what they say; it is urgent."

—John Pilger
Award-Winning Journalist & Filmmaker

"In book three of *Murder Incorporated,* 'Perfecting Tyranny,' the authors reveal the truth in Tocqueville's prediction of democracy devolving into despotism. What else can be expected from a society seeded by sociopaths and motivated by avarice—the desire for treasure and free labor. In fact, the descendants of the founding sociopaths—from Christopher Columbus to Presidents Andrew Jackson and James Polk—carry on their traditions.

Abu-Jamal and Vittoria make the case that 'we are all enemies of the state' and treated as such. They point out the corporatocracy is complicit with the state in stripping us of our rights. While J. Edgar Hoover's COINTELPRO program was nominally ended in 1971, its policies linger on in the increasing militarization of local police. If a city government can drop a C-4 plastique bomb on a residential neighborhood in Philadelphia on Mother's Day— killing eleven men, women, and children—can domestic weaponized drone strikes be far behind?"

—Martha Conley
Pittsburgh Attorney, Co-Chair of Pennsylvanians for Alternatives to the Death Penalty (Pittsburgh), Official Visitor of the Pennsylvania Prison Society

"Murder Incorporated is a searing, *must-read* for anyone wanting to know the roots, guts, and machinery of the American Empire Project from its very beginning. Having reported from the front-lines of empire in Iraq for more than a year and seen first-hand the blood-thirsty, rapacious nature of this insidious project of global conquest, this book pulls no punches in truth-telling that we need today, more than ever before. I cannot recommend it highly enough."

—Dahr Jamail
Journalist & Author of *Beyond the Green Zone: Dispatches from an Unembedded Journalist in Occupied Iraq*

"Mumia Abu-Jamal and Stephen Vittoria have crafted a bold and fierce analysis of history for those who are ready to see US empire without the rose-colored glasses of 'Manifest Destiny.' Racism and war relies on ignorance and a sanitizing of our past and *Murder Incorporated* is a brutal but honest understanding of American power. With rising levels of white supremacy and presidential bombast, there is no better time than now to read a book such as this."

—Sonali Kolhatkar
Journalist, Author, Host of *Rising Up with Sonali*

"For four decades, Mumia Abu-Jamal has been in prison and loving us enough to offer his ideas about the threads that keep systems of domination intact—from inside the belly of an institution designed to rip apart our communities. In this moment of unprecedented uncertainty and opportunity, we owe it to him and to each other to re-invigorate our fight for a different world from a place of clarity, compassion, and conscience, but most of all, from a commitment to win what our communities deserve. This is our time to move closer to what we care about, closer to the vision that can free much of the world from the chains of domination that are choking so many of us in a myriad of ways."

—Alicia Garza
Co-Founder of Black Lives Matter

"*Murder Incorporated* lays bare the myth of American Exceptionalism, a synonym for U.S. imperialism. Military interventions by the United States have killed millions of people, the result of capitalist expansion based on extermination. Racism embedded in the DNA of the USA also fueled the genocide against Native Americans and enslavement of Africans. But, as Mumia Abu-Jamal and Stephen Vittoria warn, empires contain the seeds of their own destruction. This book pulls no punches. It is a must-read for all who seek the unvarnished, albeit painful, truth about the history of the United States."

—Marjorie Cohn
Professor Emerita, Thomas Jefferson School of Law,
Author of *Cowboy Republic: Six Ways the Bush Gang Has Defied the Law*

"Why does a caged bird sing? Well, this one sings with a warning shriek to wake the walking brain-dead. Mumia writes, from his life-without-parole cage, that we are all imprisoned by a myth that kills: American's self-claimed exceptionalism that chews on the bodies and souls of those in the way of a greed-maddened imperial elite.

Weirdly, it's lots of fun.

Co-authored with Stephen Vittoria, the stories jump from Pocahontas to Richard Pryor, Allen Ginsberg to Nat Turner's rebellion, with tons of *oh-shit!* revelations, quotes you want to underline, descriptions that combine jive poetry with erudite historical analytics, stuff you didn't know and you now want *everyone* to know.

The book's construction is insanely original, like nothing you've ever read, devoid of Lefty cant. Five-hundred years of America is a dive into a roaring flow of long quotes from voices of deranged despots and their academic quislings and words of impossibly courageous truth-tellers.

It's excruciating—as the authors simply let America embarrass itself. But then we are redeemed by Harriett Tubman, as a child slave, hiding four days in a pig-sty, fighting with a mama pig over the scraps and swill, a little girl starved for freedom—an image placed to foreshadow new cruelties set on Tubman's children today.

What a story! Events and eras are gouged open and revealed, sometimes in just one or two sentences. But that's all that's needed to give you what the authors call, 'the grim, black and white meat-hook of reality.' Wow. Read it."

—Greg Palast
Puffin Foundation Fellow in investigative reporting and author of
The New York Times bestseller *The Best Democracy Money Can Buy*

"Authors Abu-Jamal and Vittoria surgically excise the layers of mythology designed to obscure the horrors of racism, sexism and classism in which our country is so deeply rooted. Conveyed with poetic rhythm and soulful shouts their thorough research grabs us and reminds us that we can only go forward if we debride the festering wounds slashed into this land by greed and a false sense of white, male superiority."

—Jewelle Gomez
Author & Activist

"A powerful and profoundly illuminating analysis of the myth and the reality of American history, a story of expansion through murder. Well-written and persuasively argued. I strongly recommend it."

—(the late) **Dr. James H. Cone**
Bill & Judith Moyers Distinguished Professor of Systematic Theology,
Union Theological Seminary

"Mumia and Stephen have mastered the art of communicating clearly and in depth the essence of the American Decadent Empire. *Murder Incorporated* tells the truth and nothing but the truth."

—Emory Douglas
Political & Social Justice Artist

"Poetic, biting, fiery, accessible, and utterly undeniable, *Murder Incorporated* roots this nation in its true history of empire, revealing the Dorian Gray portrait America has worked so hard to hide away.

Continuing the work Abu-Jamal has done for decades under the worst conditions imaginable, this book (co-authored with Stephen Vittoria) reframes American history in terms as brutal as the oppression suffered. But more than just detailing the extent of the evil empire, *Murder Incorporated* highlights resistance to the behemoth, inciting all of us to join the real-world rebel alliance. Reading this book and its framework is literally a matter of life or death."

—Walidah Imarisha
Co-editor of *Octavia's Brood: Science Fiction Stories from Social Justice Movements,* and author of *Angels with Dirty Faces: Three Stories of Crime, Prison, and Redemption*

We dedicated *Book One: Dreaming of Empire* to Reverend Malcolm Boyd and his fiery spirit, one that was honed in an America where revolution soaked the countryside.

We dedicated *Book Two: America's Favorite Pastime* to the innocent victims of America's bloody wars, punch-drunk affairs of imperial vanity and outright genocide—all at the behest of capitalism's insatiable appetite.

Book Three: Perfecting Tyranny.

We could have subtitled this volume *Toward an American Dystopia,* or *The Handmaid's Tale,* or even *The Man in the High Castle,* but we're pretty sure the last two titles are taken.

Where are we going as we hurdle through space? Does anything ever really change? Well sure it does. Kind of, sort of... but in favor of the People and their welfare and against the oppressors and their devastating greed? For peace and against war? A bright day when schools and teachers get all the funding they need and the Air Force has to hold a goddamn bake sale? Look around, not so much. More equitable healthcare and education for all? The list of never-ending mountains to climb is daunting and demoralizingly long.

But change is an odd thing. A quandary. A Joseph Heller Catch-22. On some mornings it seems like change might be underway, in locomotion—

numerous examples come to mind. For instance, 5 November 2008... a black man was elected supreme leader in a country fanatically racist, a country that joyfully celebrates the myths of its gruesome past—one defined by the very real and horrific realities of extermination, slavery, predatory capitalism, and of course non-stop imperial war. Ultimately, a country founded and nurtured in racial terrorism and murder. So here comes Barack Hussein Obama claiming presidential victory. Tears were in our eyes. It's okay, admit it. (Did we REALLY think it would happen in our time, our kid's time, their kid's time?)

But alas, the fairytale quickly unraveled—bamboozled again. *The kids WERE NOT ALRIGHT as they took a giant gulp of red-white-and-blue Kool-Aid.* Here's your hope and change: The Wall Street pigs at the trough were forgiven... the Bush Murder Goons walked away Scott Free with George W. snuggling up close to the new First Lady... the black man in the white house bombed the shit out of—oh hell—a lot of places, including Africa (and wasn't that a real paradox)... mass surveillance grew by leaps and bounds... the Espionage Act of goddamn 1917 was enforced with a vengeance against allegedly protected whistleblowers... deportations skyrocketed... and how about that Orwellian healthcare scheme written by the insurance thugs and jammed down the throat of a desperate populace? And, as the intrepid Chris Hedges reminds us, "It was the Obama administration that delivered a record-setting military aid package to the apartheid state of Israel (including refusal to sanction Israel for its brutal attack on Palestinian people in 2014)."

Hope and change? Maybe if you're delusional or stone-cold drunk.

The American Empire marched on and Mr. Obama lived up to the moniker we suggested for him in Book One: *the white-coated waiter on the Pullman car of empire.*

And why did we think this man would alter the course of history? Were we racially profiling the dude? *He's black! Praise be to Allah, he must be the Black Jesus! An amalgamation of Malcolm X, Dr. King, Frederick Douglass, Angela Davis, Nat Turner, Ralph Nader, Cesar Chavez, Sojourner Truth, Philip and Daniel Berrigan, Fred Hampton, Thomas Paine, Celia Sánchez, Kathleen Cleaver, Gil Scott-Heron, and The Beatles.* Chomsky was right: Obama was a marketing platform with a giant blank slate—and progressive liberals wrote whatever they wanted on this magical mystery tour blackboard.

Obama: better than some, not as good as others. Just another tool fighting for and representing the avarice and violence of empire... another CEO of the Corporation... a shiny gizmo on the road to Kingdom Come.

Then comes the toxic atrocity. The reincarnation of Agent Orange. In the flesh. The expected Caligula afterbirth of an empire run amok. The reckless son returneth—proof-positive that the so-called REVOLUTION failed. Toss the hippies and yippies on the trash heap of history; the baby boomers, them too. Glorious, enlightened, and compassionate ideas—and the needle of change moved a bit but nothing near the reality necessary: change that demanded a tectonic shift in, well, just about everything. Why the failure? Not nearly enough fight and way too much compromise (read: sellout). *Hey, guys, what about the Black, Chicano/Xicana, and LGBTQ movements? Don't go sideways on those!*

We're not. In fact, these groups made the largest impact and dent into the corrupt white power structure—and ironically enough, they had the most going against them: the sledgehammer of state oppression (money + corruption + violence + masterful lies and propaganda) was leveled at these groups with extreme prejudice... and yet these groups somehow managed (and continue to manage) to pressure the power paradigm—but it's not enough. The hippies, yippies, and boomers retreated back to the safe confines of Pleasantville and they even brought some of their black and brown brethren with them, promising picket fences, iPads, and a lifetime supply of cappuccino or avocados (your choice). Author Margaret Atwood reminds us that "when power is scarce, a little of it is tempting."

C'mon, look closely at the ignominious condition of the American State—education, healthcare, poverty and homelessness, the prison industrial complex, police beatings and killings, militarized robo cops locked and loaded, the obscene income and wealth gap, an absolute corrupt and rigged electoral process, brutality at the southern border—all of it ignored, downplayed, or manipulated by a bought and sold AWOL media that facilitates abject debasement right down to the toxic drinking water (take a bogus sip, Mr. Obama). All of these alarms in various red-hot stages of "extreme danger" to human life. And you know what's not on the list? *THE REALLY BAD STUFF...*

(1) indecent and sickening military spending
(2) the proliferation of species-ending nuclear weapons

And then finally, drum roll, please...

(3) climate change and eco-fascism.

Good morning, America... you're fucked.

Oh, right, dedicating *Book Three: Perfecting Tyranny.* We almost forgot. Okay, we've tossed away the soapbox and here we go.

Since power concedes nothing, there needs to be a fight—a knockdown, drag-out *Thrilla in Manila* revolution. One that makes the first American Revolution look like a schoolyard tussle. AOC is cool, but we need a thousand points of AOC light... and then multiply that by a million. Some folks will tell you to calm down and that "things could be worse." Well, friend, "things could also be better." Professor Howard Zinn famously warned that our problem was an overabundance of civil *obedience*—when in reality we are in dire need of copious amounts of civil DIS-obedience. And we're not talking about violence, unless of course we anticipate the expected behavior of the United States government's chainsaw, one they will use in defense of the elite status quo and its hammerlock on Draconian power. Abbie Hoffman knew this well when he wrote:

> *This is the United States, 1968, remember? If you're afraid of violence, you shouldn't have crossed the border.*

Finally, our dedication. To young people... possibly the last bastion of civilized defense, the last great hope before the vice grip of tyranny finishes the job and the planet swings into oblivion. Remember the dinosaurs?

We wrote this entire three-volume tome for you: those closer to their innocence, closer to their maker, closer to the beauty of existence, those inheriting the Earth right now. Forget about us. These past few generations, and the shit that came before that, have left you high and dry. They've adopted the unthinkable and called it normal. They've embraced corruption and called it right (and if this is *right* what the hell is *left* to be called wrong?).

You
How can we fight city hall? Give us a hint, some clues—is there a manifesto we could read? How about a podcast? Is there an app?

Mumia
Yo, Steverino, it's gotta be for the kids, the students, the younger ones... from the old heads to the new ones.

Steve
Right on, boss.

From the very beginning of our process, it's been about exposing pervasive corruption, shining a bright light into the darkness—for young people. Look at *Murder Incorporated,* share *Murder Incorporated*—as well as the many books and revolutionaries like it as your trusty, ever-expanding "bullshit detectors." Believe nothing unless you have vetted the hell out of it. Gather with others, many others... we outnumber the bastards by tens of millions... share, plan, march, topple, and then do it again. And again. And then again. Lather-rinse-repeat.

Plain and simple: *don't do what was done before.* That's how we got here—by doing the same thing over and over and then expecting different results. Insanity.

We mentioned Abbie Hoffman. Look into this revolutionary. Study how he proposed to change public policy. Everyone thinks Abbie was a loudmouthed rabble rouser. He was. But more importantly, Abbie was truly about laying the functional groundwork for change—policy change. Look into a guy named Saul Alinsky. Read about Tom Hayden and something called the *Port Huron Statement.* Study the brilliance and courage of the Black Panther Party for Self Defense—a shooting star of robust revolution that scared the bejesus out of the old white men. Carbon copy Black Lives Matter. Embrace Cesar Chavez. Ernesto Guevara. Emma Goldman. Greta Thunberg. Edward Snowden. Rosa Luxemburg. Harvey Milk. Dick Gregory. Frantz Fanon. John Trudell.

Mary Harris "Mother" Jones. The Student Nonviolent Coordinating Committee (SNCC). Ella Baker. Huey Percy Newton. Naomi Klein. Helen Keller. Arundhati Roy. These freedom fighters will undoubtedly turn you on to hundreds more. In fact, all three volumes of *Murder Incorporated* offer a who's who list of heroes and villains. Go deep. Go deeper. Dig in. There's so much help out there. Support the progressive and radical independent press—they will open up a world that will seem like news from a distant planet. It's not. It's your home. Simply unvarnished, more accurate, and so very close to the truth. If you see a commercial for BMW on a media outlet, look elsewhere. If it feels like they're in bed with Washington powerbrokers (i.e., *The New York Times, Washington Post,* CNN, MSNBC, PBS/NPR, etc.), they probably are, look elsewhere. *The Intercept* is a good place to start. So is *Fairness & Accuracy in Reporting.*

And for now, we leave young people, the ones we've passionately dedicated this volume to, with a final piece of advice... and no one said it better than Glinda the Good Witch to Dorothy:

> *You've always had the power to go back to Kansas.*

The bastards just don't want you to know it.

> "Freedom is a heavy load, a great and strange burden for the spirit to undertake. It is not easy. It is not a gift given, but a choice made, and the choice may be a hard one. The road goes upward towards the light; but the laden traveler may never reach the end of it."
>
> —Ursula K. LeGuin, *The Tombs of Atuan*

ACKNOWLEDGMENTS

Who births a book? Who gives it blood, sinews, limbs, brain, and spine? Books are born, more often than not, by other books, which light flames in the psyche, passing light to those flung far into the river of time.

When I think of great books, it is hardly or ever the official Canon. It is often little known people who wrote against the storm, their minds ablaze by fires from another era—like J.A. Rogers, a self-taught historian who appeared in a slew of Black newspapers, like the *Pittsburgh Courier*, the *Afro American*, and who also wrote numerous books, filled not only with texts, but photographs to affirm his theories. He traveled across continents to salvage some tidbit, some morsel of knowledge that would amaze readers, of Black names, Black nations, Black princes who emerged in worlds we had never known.

This work, therefore, was sparked when a curious teenager found more fun in a bookstore than on a baseball diamond. For, there he read Yosef Ben-Jochannon, Ivan Van Sertima, Herbert Aptheker, C.L.R. James, George Nash, Ishakamusa Barashango, Runoko Rashidi, Ward Churchill, Du Bois, et al.

Often the works of these historians were emblazoned with deftly drawn dark figures in majestic poses, speaking to us across eons, saying softly, almost imperceptibly: "I am Here. I am Here."

Many, if not most of these historians were (a term few would use themselves) "outlaw" historians—rebels, who turned their backs on the Guild, for their work was so disruptive of the accepted Canon.

They searched and searched and unearthed Canons from Antiquity that preceded the works of Europe by centuries. For example, who knows that the phrase "Black is Beautiful!" so evocative of the proverbial '60s, was echoed in spirit more than a thousand years before that era? As a man of that era (really, a teen), I thought we were breaking new ground, speaking thoughts that bubbled in our breasts for the first time.

Well, Dr. Ben (as Yochannon was affectionately known by his students) certainly knew, for in many of his typewritten texts, he cited Al-Jahiz's *Book of the Glory of the Black Race*, written by a Black Arab of Basra, Iraq, decades after Islam's founding. This work, written between 776–868 A.D., reads as if it were written at the height of the Black Power Movement, circa 1968!

These writers dared to break new ground, and to not only learn new things, but to unlearn old canonical verities that were as traditional as they were misleading.

Of course, this work is inspired by the remarkable Howard Zinn, who, burned by the savagery of World War II, and inspired by the true courage of civil rights activists (many of whom were his students, like the acclaimed novelist, Alice Walker), learned not from the classics, but from his students, among them men and women who marched on the front lines of history.

This work is dedicated to all of them, who, by their works, made this one possible.

Mumia Abu-Jamal

The idea for this project emerged from dust during a late evening conversation I had with Gore Vidal in the parlor of his home in the Hollywood Hills. His grasp of history, all history, was only surpassed by his grasp of the evils unleashed by the ruling elite that he knew so well, the robber barons who own the club—own it lock, stock, and smoking barrel. Our back and forth tête-à-tête jumped from TR to FDR, Caesar to Camelot, Foggy Bottom to Langley, and of course from Italian to California wine. And in the crevices and fissures, feeling wholly out of my league with this legendary mind, I stumbled upon the genesis of *Murder Incorporated*—some rudimentary concept that I actually verbalized aloud (thinking, of course, what gibberish did I just set free). But to my great surprise Gore acknowledged the idea with that devious twinkle he sometimes offered and then consecrated my embryonic suggestion by pronouncing "Exactly." That's all I needed.

This project started as a feature documentary film. But after thirty-plus hours of filmed interviews, I slowly realized that it was near insanity to try and tell the five-hundred-year saga of the American Empire in an hour and a half. That's when I turned to my brother with an amazing mind and rock solid will to tell the truth, the whole truth, and nothing but the truth, Mumia Abu-Jamal, and said, "Mu, whaddaya say we..." His immediate fire jettisoned our ship into orbit.

There are a few other writers and soothsayers that delivered me to that night with Mr. Vidal, starting with Dick Gregory (a prophet), Muhammad Ali (the people's champion), Jim Bouton (fire-balling right-hander and unheralded revolutionary), Hunter S. Thompson (with those "right kind of eyes"), Arthur George Rust, Jr., Howard Zinn and Noam Chomsky, Norman Mailer and Bob Dylan, Stanley Kubrick and Dalton Trumbo, George Carlin and Lenny Bruce, the Man in Black, as well as the man wearing white linens and seersucker, Samuel Langhorne Clemens.

There are some folks who helped immensely with stewarding this project along the way: our savage editor Justin Lebanowski, who I still feel like punching every now and then (and then hugging because he was usually right); literary agent Morty Mint who never stopped supporting this project; Jim Kelch who read every word and offered invaluable counsel; Robert Guillory remains a constant pillar of strength and designed killer covers; Rocco Melillo and Julia Sarno-Melillo for their inspired hand and eye designing the interior of these books; Riva Enteen for her tireless work clearing all the potent voices we weaved throughout;

proofreader Jennifer Grubba for making sure everything was punctuated and sppellled correctly, and that at least something from our grade school teachers/grammaticians sunk in to Messrs. Abu-Jamal and Vittoria; and to Catherine Murphy for her invaluable help on Che and Cuba.

And, of course, to Noelle Hanrahan of Prison Radio for her ongoing heroic and Herculean efforts of producing thousands of broadcasts, delivering Mumia Abu-Jamal's voice around the world... and for embracing this book series and the authors with unbridled enthusiasm.

And finally, to a mother and father who didn't teach their son hate... to my daughter Shannon, art historian extraordinaire and a woman who continues to amaze me every moment of every day, offering great hope for the future... and to my lifelong partner and BFF, Ellen Mary Vittoria, whose love keeps my blood pumping for all these sunrises.

Stephen Vittoria

EDITOR'S NOTE

The book series you have in your hand, be it paper or pixels, is the result of an unusual collaboration between two men who met in unusual fashion, but who communed as we always have, since the origin of thought yielded not only "like-mindedness" but the deeper affinities of friendship, solidarity, and love. When filmmaker Stephen Vittoria set out to make a documentary about the "500 year Euro-American march of Empire," he made two valuable discoveries: first, that such a story could not be properly told in a feature-length film; second, that one of his interviewees could be, in fact would be, the subject of his next film. *Long Distance Revolutionary* (2013) tells the life story of journalist and imprisoned dissident Mumia Abu-Jamal, whose fascinating life both before and after incarceration had been largely backgrounded by the publicity of his case and its connection to the Death Penalty debate that raged in the late 1990s.

The kinship kindled during the making of that film has yielded this book, written collaboratively through correspondence between Vittoria and Abu-Jamal, the former composing on a MacBook in Los Angeles and the latter composing on a Swintec clear cabinet electronic typewriter (manufactured especially for prisoners) in the Pennsylvania State Correctional Facility at Mahanoy. (*Murder Incorporated: Empire, Genocide, and Manifest Destiny*—book three, will in fact be the twelfth volume penned solely or in collaboration by Abu-Jamal from within prison.) It's worth noting that since the life of this book began as a film, a number of interviews were already conducted (with the likes of Gore Vidal, Noam Chomsky, Tariq Ali, Michael Parenti, and others), excerpts of which you'll find peppered throughout. And much like a documentary film, this book includes a colorful choir of trenchant voices, many of them an inspiration to the authors, underscoring that history must be told by the many and, often, the many unheard, and not by the few armed with bullhorn and bully pulpit.

Some readers may take affront at this book, as they might others like it that seek to stridently criticize the American nation, or perhaps more pointedly, the

American government and its position and conduct in the world, throughout its brief and productive history. But for the muted and muffled to be heard, their gestures must be bold and their voices loud. Some may take affront at the ironic humor and fiery, sometimes vulgar characterizations. But what is a vulgar word employed to describe vulgar acts of treachery, thievery, slavery, and murder? And ultimately, this book is intended to be informative, insightful, inspiring, and compelling. And if it pisses you off, I can tell you—it's meant to.

J. Alan Lebanowski, Editor

Fall, 2017
New York City

Book Three Note:

If a belief in divine destiny and racial superiority fueled the origins of the American Empire, as detailed in *Book One: Dreaming of Empire;* and if those beliefs were hardened in the crucibles of expansionist war and expansionist capitalism into the myth of American exceptionalism and the grim meat-hook reality of the world's first global superpower, as described in *Book Two: America's Favorite Pastime;* then it should come as no surprise that this Empire would manufacture mechanisms to sustain and maintain itself—its wealth, its power, and its myths.

In *Book Three: Perfecting Tyranny,* Abu-Jamal and Vittoria continue their epic recounting of the history—and present reality—of America. This volume challenges the acceptance of some of the most heralded features of American superiority—a free press, an independent judiciary, individual liberty, equal rights for women and minorities—and shows how these are often myths bent to the will of the Empire.

As with the previous two volumes, the authors recount not only the onslaught of the American Empire, but the fearless persistence of a resistant American People who refuse to acquiesce. Although this concludes *Murder Incorporated* the trilogy, the Corporation—and the resistance against it—carries on.

J.A.L., Editor

Spring, 2020
New York City

PUBLISHER'S INTRODUCTORY NOTE

The Power of Truth is Final[1]

Conventional wisdom would have us believe that it is insane to resist this, the mightiest of empires, but what history really shows is that today's empire is tomorrow's ashes; that nothing lasts forever, and that to not resist is to acquiesce in your own oppression. The greatest form of sanity that anyone can exercise is to resist that force that is trying to repress, oppress, and fight down the human spirit.
—Mumia Abu-Jamal

As we witness every day, the brave truthtellers of the current age are ridiculed, scorned, and marginalized as "raving lunatics." Some are eliminated. When the Empire is questioned or undressed, the noise machine beholden to the elite cries "conspiracy theorist... traitor... apostate"—all of which quickly smears and deprecates this newly crowned "public enemy," one who is unafraid to speak the unspeakable truth.
—Stephen Vittoria

Mumia Abu-Jamal once famously opined, "The state would rather give me an Uzi than a microphone."[2] More than five decades of intense surveillance, harassment, confinement, repression, and torture levelled against him by Frank Rizzo's Philadelphia Police Department, the Department of Corrections, and the Federal Bureau of Investigation have graphically illustrated the truth of those words. The United States government is terrified of what Mumia has to say. And with good reason. See, there is a reason slaves were never supposed to learn to read or write. A reason prisoners are best kept muted, retained hidden behind walls, unheeded. People like us are not supposed to tell these troublesome truths. The truth, Ramona Africa reminds us, is always dangerous to those pushing the lie.[3]

Mumia tells the truth. He has always told the truth, and he does it again here, writing alongside Stephen Vittoria in this third and final installment of their magnum opus *Murder Incorporated.* These three books—*Dreaming of Empire, America's Favorite Pastime,* and *Perfecting Tyranny*—deconstruct and lay bare the United States experiment in imperialism. Co-authored by a captive rebel living under the hostile eye of the state, this historical trilogy exposes the continuous and deadly hypocrisy of empire. *Murder Incorporated* builds on the work of Howard Zinn's landmark *A People's History of the United States.* This work aims to expand the telling of the story of the United States from the front-line perspective of those dispossessed and discarded by the treachery of U.S. imperialist expansion.

It is important to recognize and respect the conditions under which this opus was written. Unlike other twenty-first century scholars, Mumia writes, researches, and publishes having no contact with a university library and no access to the Internet. He has never surfed the world wide web and has no quick access to books, essays, journal articles, or interview subjects. He is only permitted to have seven books in his cell at a time; any more than that are considered contraband.

In researching *Murder Incorporated,* Mumia had to constantly cull his stash of written material, absorbing all he could from each book before getting rid of it to make space for a new one. As has been his process since he first started publishing from prison, he took precise, careful, and scrupulously detailed notes of every book and article he read, along with page numbers and citation information. He wrote as small as possible, to fit as much material as he could into his limited number of notebooks.

At what other time and place has a history of this scope—a thoroughly detailed overview of a nation's crimes of colonization from its inception to the present day—been crafted under such draconian measures? When has such a record of the crimes of a state been created by one of the state's own victims, with every word penned under the state's pretense of control? Consider the barriers placed in the way of Abu-Jamal's and Vittoria's intellectual collaboration. Mumia's access to visitation is strictly limited, and he can only speak on the telephone for fifteen minutes at a time, once a day. Just one fifteen-minute call, *if* he can get the guard to put in a slip for it. He is permitted two visits a week, to which he cannot bring even a pencil or piece of paper. He endures a full-body cavity strip search before and after every single visit. For nearly a decade he was denied visits and phone calls. For two decades, and the first nine of his books, he wrote everything by hand with the mere cartridge of a ballpoint pen. All visits are supervised, all phone calls recorded and surveilled, and all his mail is read by prison staff. Letters, books, or papers deemed "inappropriate" by the mailroom censors are discarded before they reach him.

In order to build the intellectual partnership that created *Murder Incorporated,* Vittoria and Abu-Jamal had to overcome the state's exhaustive efforts to limit Mumia's contact with the outside world. These are some of the constraints under which *Murder Incorporated* was researched and written. Abu-Jamal and Vittoria's success is a testimony to their will, determination, and bond as writing partners.

The book you hold in your hands today is an act of protest and dissent. Its very existence defies the repression of the state. So does its content. While *Murder Incorporated* can and should be used in the polished hallways of academia, it is deeply rooted in the proud tradition of American protest literature. Vittoria and Abu-Jamal seek to advance the interests of the exploited, evicted, imprisoned, and marginalized working class people by telling a history that does not flinch from the truth. In this project, *Murder Incorporated* positions itself alongside Eduardo Galeano's *Open Veins of Latin America,* Vincent Harding's *There is a River,* and Robert Fisk's *The Great War for Civilisation* by embracing the historic imperative of truth telling. Like those great works, Murder Incorporated makes an intergenerationally significant contribution to the bank of historical political thought and social movement theory.

It is no accident that *Murder Incorporated* was co-written by a man in prison, a man who has spent the lion's share of his life on death row. Scholar Joy James suggests that prisons function as political and intellectual sites that are largely hidden from our mainstream discourse.[4] Those warehoused within write with "unique and controversial insights into idealism, warfare, and social justice."[5] Thus, the prisoner, who is denied access to any of the privileges and protections afforded to citizens of the state, who is subjected instead to indignity and deprivations, is uniquely empowered to criticize the state. Moreover, because the prison writer typically has no access to editors or publishers, and writes with no expectation of receiving remuneration from their writing, they are able to write what they know to be true. Their words are uncompromised. In this regard the prisoner is free in a way that no one else is free.

Mumia has nothing to lose from telling the truth. The state has already done everything in its power to silence him. There are no remaining threats that can be leveled against him. There is no tactic of abuse or control left in the state's arsenal that has not already been inflicted on him. He has withstood beatings, torture, and near-fatal gunshot wounds. From the time he was fourteen years old, working as a young organizer for the Black Panther Party, he had already earned security index status from J. Edgar Hoover's FBI.[6] He spent his teen years and early twenties under unyielding police surveillance and harassment. Since his arrest and framing in 1981, he has weathered forty years of incarceration—separated from friends, family, and community. Twenty-eight of those years he spent in solitary confinement with a pending execution. He survived two death warrants, each of which gave him thirty days to live. He survived a life-threatening battle with complications from Hepatitis C, dragging himself back from the brink of death after the prison's vicious and deliberate medical neglect sent him into a coma. He won court battles to overturn laws written and passed by the Pennsylvania legislature with the express specific purpose of forbidding him from publishing his writing.[7] Similar laws were discussed at the federal level, on the Senate floor.[8]

None of it has stopped him. He is perhaps the world's most prolific imprisoned radical. *Perfecting Tyranny* is his twelfth published book, and he has authored thousands of radio commentaries. Within a month after being shot and arrested in 1981, he wrote a pamphlet from Holmesburg Prison.[9] When warrants were issued for his death in 1995 and 1999 while he sat awaiting execution, Mumia *still* continued to write. Recovering from near death in the prison infirmary in 2015, Mumia continued to write. And why not? The state has already made up its mind to kill him. He is alive because he, and the movement behind him, have fought the state at every turn, sometimes winning extraordinary victories—like the overturning of his death sentence—and sometimes grinding into a bitter stalemate, but never giving up ground. The state has not *refrained* from killing Mumia: it has *failed* to kill Mumia. What possible incentive could he have to flinch from the truth?

Given the forces arrayed against Mumia, it may appear as a miracle that this book—or any of Mumia's twelve previous books—was published at all. It was no miracle. It was the hard work of a movement. Mumia's relentless courage and resilience, and Stephen Vittoria's triumphant accompaniment, created an intellectual bond that would not be denied. This, combined with the dedication and unswerving solidarity of hundreds of thousands of activists and artists and lawyers across the country and the globe, have *forced* this book through the bars of the prison into printing presses and into bookstores. This book is a reminder of our individual and collective power.

The great Howard Zinn once remarked that to be hopeful in catastrophic times is not naive. Rather, it reflects an understanding that history is as much about courage and sacrifice as it is about cruelty.[10] Abu-Jamal and Vittoria teach us the same lesson. Mumia Abu-Jamal, relegated to a carceral underworld, has funneled his harrowing experience of captivity into an extraordinary act of truth-telling that benefits our common survival. Stephen Vittoria imparts his searing analysis, poignant honesty, and tremendous tenacity to craft this labor of courage and love and get it past the censors so that this vital work could be in our hands.

Mumia cautions us to remember that "What history really shows us is that today's empire is tomorrow's ashes, that nothing lasts forever." It is humbling to be taught this lesson from one of our nation's most famous political prisoners, who is also a scholar, a revolutionary, and an educator. A gift to us, and a labor of love, this final book in the remarkable trilogy *Murder Incorporated* is the result of unwavering and courageous commitment. It elevates our human spirits and encourages us to have full faith in our ability to change the world.

Again we recall the wisdom of Ramona Africa: the truth is dangerous to those whose power depends on the lie. This book is dangerous. This is why slaves were never taught to write. This is what happens when prisoners contribute to the bank of political thought. Empires hold their power through the silence of their victims; by breaking that silence, Mumia deals a devastating blow to the empire that cages him. *Murder Incorporated* exposes all the dirty, vulgar, shameful actions of the United States—hundreds of pages of the state's blunt secrets revealed, exposing the continuous and deadly hypocrisy of the empire. This historic collaboration between Stephen Vittoria and Mumia Abu-Jamal stands amid the pantheon of social dissent against tyranny and despotism. Its hope and optimism stand as testimony to the unstoppable resilience of the human spirit.

Jennifer Black and Miranda Hanrahan
June 2020
Prison Radio
Pennsylvania & San Francisco

To Frances Goldin (1924–2020)
Housing activist, socialist and literary agent,
who, in her own way, made this work possible
by opening a door in 1995... that no man can close.

—m.a.j. / s.v.

CHAPTERS

FOREWORD

MUMIA ABU-JAMAL IS UNRELENTING in his efforts to encourage us to think more critically about the conditions surrounding our lives. Those of us who treasure his words are forever grateful to Prison Radio for delivering them to receptive ears throughout the world. I am truly impressed whenever I think about the long list of books that have taken shape in his prison cell over the last decades—which was, for almost twenty-nine years, located on death row. His work has offered us illuminating analyses of racism, poverty, the prison industrial complex, and other issues about which we must be cognizant if we wish to continue building movements for justice, even against impossible odds. The collaborative three-volume work he has written with filmmaker Stephen Vittoria, *Murder Incorporated: Empire, Genocide, and Manifest Destiny,* is both edifying and provocative, channeling the spirits of insurgent intellectuals like Howard Zinn, Noam Chomsky, and people's journalist Amy Goodman, and inciting us to action before it is too late.

As with the two previous volumes, *Perfecting Tyranny* also methodically mines the underside of U.S. history. The authors cover a range of themes such as ideology and the media; the role of the opium trade in the production of British and U.S. wealth; women as a political force and feminist analyses of reproductive labor; the unceasing war against Black freedom; law, politics, and empire; and pervasive surveillance and the rise of the security state. This book does not hold back. Even those of us who consider ourselves knowledgeable about the hidden histories of the U.S. have no doubt, like myself, reacted in shock to certain revelations. In this sense the trilogy is clearly a wake-up call. I do remember that millions of Vietnamese people were killed in the war. (Noam Chomsky points out that most Americans assume that the number is closer to 100,000, and he asks how we might evaluate German political culture if the average German estimated that several hundred thousand Jews died during the Holocaust.) But the true horror of Vietnam is that the utter destruction of life during the war is only revealed when considered alongside the vast inventory of similar attacks that constitute the unacknowledged history of the U.S. It is depressing indeed and we ask ourselves, as do the authors in their prologue: What do we do now? "So, this diatribe, this final invective by Messrs. Abu-Jamal and Vittoria begs the question: *Where do we go from here?* Hopefully as a people and a nation, we don't go from here to eternity."

These books do not simply lament the governmental and corporate embrace of violence, racism, and genocide. They also offer us a history of evolving social consciousness and of unyielding struggle. We are reminded of I.F. Stone's Newsletter, which I read as a teenager in New York just as religiously as I follow Amy Goodman's DemocracyNow today. We are reminded of indigenous resistance and of centuries of Black Freedom movements. Reading this book reinforces the idea that those who are the greatest defenders of democracy conceptualize it not as a given but as an ideal, an imagined future, a state of affairs to come. If we wish to lift the curtain behind which "democracy" has been hidden, we can think of democracy as inscribed, instead, in the collective aspirations of those who have been excluded.

Perfecting Tyranny shows us how the assumption that democracy was already generated by white "forefathers"—who spoke not for workers, not for indigenous people, not for enslaved and putatively free people of African descent, not even for white women—ideologically overshadows the true defenders of a just political order, of democracy as a future to be generated by struggle. In our current political times, those who were ignored by the "forefathers" are dismissed as participating in "identity politics," even as the white majority is seen as representative of universal democratic interests. In the aftermath of the most recent U.S. election, Linda Burnham addressed this in her article "No Plans to Abandon Our Freedom Dreams!"

> In my experience, advocates and organizers for racial justice don't think of themselves as purveyors of "identity politics." Nor do immigrant rights organizers, advocates for LGBTQ rights or women's rights activists. Rather, in fighting for the expansion of democracy for particular groups they rev the motor for the renewal and expansion of democracy for the whole. And they know from experience that purportedly universalistic solutions often work to make already embedded inequalities even more rigid.[1]

Moreover, she points out, the "...fusion of white identity and American identity, the bedrock of white nationalism, has such a long history that it has been internalized and naturalized." On the other hand, Black, indigenous, Latinx, feminist, LGBTQ, and other movements have constituted the "spark and spur" of democracy. They are forging ways of disrupting the ultimate perfection of tyranny.

Angela Davis
San Francisco, California
Spring, 2020

PROLOGUE

"the bright and tender flowers of the imagination shall all be crushed beneath its iron tramp"

Thomas Cole's (1801–1848) short life spanned the first half of the 19th century. Born in Bolton, Lancashire, England—a former mill town that urbanized and developed into a textile manufacturing boomtown tethered neatly to the Industrial Revolution—Cole emigrated with his family to the United States as a young man in 1818. After brief stops in Ohio and Philadelphia, he settled in Catskill, New York, the heart of the Hudson River Valley. It is here that Cole, arguably the greatest American landscape painter of his generation, flourished. Widely regarded as establishing America's first national school of landscape painting—later known as the Hudson River School—Cole portrayed the Hudson River Valley and landscapes surrounding the Adirondack, Catskill, and White Mountains with a great passion for the imperative preservation of nature, standing in horror at the onslaught of the Industrial Age rolling hard and angry across the American continent, fueled by tectonic shifts in U.S. economic, political, as well as ecological policy.

Throughout his creative life, Cole celebrated the sacred force of nature. "[H]is fascination with the life cycle of civilizations was informed by deep anxieties about the ecological danger presented by the rise of modern industry, the growth of cities, and the worship of money," writes Tim Barringer, a professor of art history at Yale University. "Cole asks us: Will the ruinous fate of past empires befall modern America?"[1] As the artist himself poetically wrote in his "Essay on American Scenery"—

> ...a meager utilitarianism seems ready to absorb every feeling and sentiment, and what is sometimes called improvement in its march makes us fear that the bright and tender flowers of the imagination shall all be crushed beneath its iron tramp.[2]

Between 1834 and 1836, Cole created his magnum opus—a five-painting series that traces the rise, decline, and inevitable fall of a great civilization. "Widely popular among nineteenth-century audiences," writes Shannon Vittoria of The Metropolitan Museum of Art, "the series has also inspired artists working in the twentieth and twenty-first centuries, many of whom continue to grapple with the prescient themes in Cole's work—from empire building and human avarice to ecological destruction and environmental preservation."[3] Sound familiar?

Give Peace a Chance

In fact, the themes pulsing through Cole's *The Course of Empire* echoed prevalent attitudes among the American populace at the time, the idea that balance and peace with the environment was the ideal system for human existence. (Kind of what the Indigenous peoples of so-called North and South America were trying before they were summarily slaughtered by those who wanted to give peace a chance *their way.*) As evidenced by Cole's stunning work, he heartily believed that roaring empire would lead America to gluttony, greed, and the inevitable and final perish. In fact, as Cole was creating *The Course of Empire,* guess who was sitting in the White House salivating over his massive and destructive land grab while joyfully butchering Injuns westward ho? "The artist addressed the dangers that the young nation faced under the expansionist policies of President Andrew Jackson, which led to drastic ecological, social, and economic change," writes Elizabeth Kornhauser, a Curator of American Paintings and Sculpture at The Metropolitan Museum of Art.[4] The barbaric Andrew Jackson, the über white supremacist who fought so hard in favor of slavery and trigged the murderous Trail of Tears.

When renowned American pop artist Ed Ruscha first glimpsed Cole's dramatic series, the sheer power of it caught him off guard:

> I stumbled across these five paintings in the New-York Historical Society, maybe in the eighties... and I got stopped in my tracks when I realized what they were and what they meant as a narration, as a series... I would go back and visit these things every time I came to New York and each time I would go there, I'd find something a little different and new. But finding the progression of the passage of civilization seemed really profound.[5]

Profound indeed—and prescient in a very real and scary, albeit predictable way. Cole's depiction of this imaginary city-state unmistakably mirrors the excruciating course of the American Empire—from its stolen "savage" beginnings through its current spiraling state of planetary militarism and rapacious capitalism, insanity driving toward the cliffs of destruction—in the crosshairs of nuclear madness trembling in the silos and ecological destruction going on all around us.

The Course of Empire series consists of these five works:

The Savage State
The Arcadian or Pastoral State
The Consummation of Empire
Destruction
Desolation

[We offer the progression here with black and white plates. Please also view online to experience the beauty and power of his work in living color. You can also see them in person at the New-York Historical Society.]

The Savage State

The Arcadian or Pastoral State

The Consummation of Empire

Destruction

Desolation

Clearly, for Cole, the narrative he offers in this panoramic pentalogy has its roots in the rise and fall of the Roman Empire, and at the time he created *The Course of Empire* (1834-36), the works underscored his own tangible reality—the evolution and looming fall of the British Empire. And, of course, there's no doubt, as a burgeoning American artist, the work was a trenchant warning for what was afoot in the United States: the heavy march of Manifest Destiny—behold, a new empire... one founded in genocide, nurtured and built by slavery, and then driven to the brink of *Destruction and Desolation* by insatiable economic corruption, obscene military expenditures to satisfy a voracious appetite for imperial war, and then, finally, worldwide ecological suicide that will make Cole's final paintings look like the good old days.

Unfortunately, his cautionary tale and alarm, like so many others, have gone unheeded. "The artist may have been trying to warn his peers of such political perils so 19th-century American society could correct its course," writes Margaret Carrigan in the *Observer.* "Yet, in the 21st century, the allegory he presents seems more a prophetic vision, especially since the final painting, *Desolation,* reveals a large lunar orb—a super moon, perhaps?—rising over a crumbling, deserted city devoid of citizens, poor immigrants and enterprising millionaires alike."[6]

When we view Cole's third entry in his brilliant parable of empire, *The Consummation of Empire*—the seemingly bright setting in which opulence reigns supreme and the all-powerful are in total authoritarian control of society from their shining city on a hill—we are unfortunately reminded of our third entry in *Murder Incorporated,* the one in your hand titled "Perfecting Tyranny." This is the stage when the mandarins in charge of the runaway train go even further; they go for broke. Complete and utter pig conquest.

"Rooted in his own time"

While Thomas Cole's series dramatically calls into question the march of empire, visualizing the unadulterated pursuit of power and plunder, it's important to acknowledge that Cole's political and moral evocation is not comprehensive. Although Cole was driven by environmental concerns, Professor Barringer has noted that the artist's "views on slavery and indigeneity are firmly rooted in his own time and world view and have no place in our world."[7] No doubt. In fact, Cole typically included Indigenous figures in his landscapes—as many of his contemporaries did—as nostalgic emblems of the past—of the "Savage State," as he termed it—existing apart from the modern world. Nevertheless, Cole's revelatory missive to America remains, leaving us to wonder, as Barringer writes, "Can a nation asphyxiated by 'copper-hearted barbarians' (Cole's words) find its better self?"[8]

Political Sleight of Hand

Princeton University political theorist, the late Sheldon Wolin, powerfully defined how democracy (so-called) in the United States is on the fast track to completely devolve into authoritarianism. He called it "inverted totalitarianism." Say what?

Here's the jam:

In the mid-1930s, at the height of fascism in Europe, Sinclair Lewis wrote the political novel *It Can't Happen Here*—like Cole, he offered the public a cautionary tale, one that warned of a storm front coming, the very real possibility of fascism and authoritarianism eating America alive. "[It] was a frightening book written for frightening times,"[9] exclaims Alexander Nazaryan in *The New Yorker.* Lewis' main character beats FDR for the presidency vowing to restore the nation's prosperity and greatness. Once elected, President Buzz Windrip incarcerates political enemies in concentration camps, outlaws dissent, curtails women's and minority rights, attacks the press, and then establishes and arms "The Minute Men"—a paramilitary goon squad that enforces the wants and desires of the "Corpo" government (corporatist).

To some Americans this sounds far-fetched, the brand of tropes explored on television, in film, and on pages in novels like Lewis' eerily familiar narrative from many decades ago. And then came Trump and his Minute Men-like followers. Not so fucking far-fetched, is it? To other Americans, this type of Draconian totalitarian action by the government is alive and well and has been since 1776 (and before): ask some Indigenous people, ask the descendants of slaves and Jim Crow, ask Japanese Americans who were busy working and living and minding their business around nineteen hundred and forty one... women in every decade-year-and-minute of the republic... the enemies list goes on and on.

If you stop an average American on the streets of Any Town, USA and ask them about their government, they will spit back the myths they memorized in grade school, high school, and college—myths (read: lies) simultaneously made gospel by the mainstream media as well as propagandized by Hollywood and also consecrated by organized religion. (Well-orchestrated and no accident.) Their answers will include words like freedom, democracy, and liberty and will all inherently embody the idea that the citizens, the body politic, are in charge of the store... not like in Russia or the old Soviet Union, or China, or back in Nazi Germany, Mussolini's Italy, or any other obvious totalitarian state. Not us, we're free, we have rights, we are the United States of America, that shining beacon of individual liberties, a free press, and the land where all men are created equal.

"Inverted totalitarianism is different from classical forms of totalitarianism," posits journalist and author Chris Hedges. "Our inverted totalitarianism pays outward fealty to the facade of electoral politics, the Constitution, civil liberties, freedom of the press, the independence of the judiciary, and the iconography, traditions and language of American patriotism, but it has effectively seized all of the mechanisms of power to render the citizen impotent."[10] Just ask Harry Houdini or Doug Henning or any great magician how they make us believe in magic—diversion and distraction... in our current America it is political sleight of hand—then add in lots of shiny objects to buy and become obsessed with and watch liberal democracy fly off to Never Never Land. Upon Wolin's passing, Richard Kreitner, writing in *The Nation,* summarized inverted totalitarianism as "a social and political system in which powerful corporations use sensationalism and mass-consumerization to lull citizens into willfully surrendering their rights and liberties."[11]

This form of a governmental hammerlock doesn't just happen with one election or one event. It evolves over time with painstaking implementation, manipulation, and the godsend of good fortune. It takes hold with scientific precision (NSA), with taking advantage of unforeseen situations (9/11), as well as embracing the weaknesses and inabilities of those the corporate state needs and wants to control. The power structure doesn't need secret society meetings or a Star Chamber conspiracy. Rather, the supremacy is greatly disjointed but moves in one malevolent direction guided by money, power, and a healthy dose of Christendom's white supremacy. Make no mistake about it: a sterilized corporate state is the Holy Grail for the brutes in power. Thomas Cole knew it when he picked up his brush. Chris Hedges knew it when he opened his laptop and wrote this:

> The Trump administration did not rise, prima facie, like Venus on a half shell from the sea. Donald Trump is the result of a long process of political, cultural and social decay. He is a product of our failed democracy. The longer we perpetuate the fiction that we live in a functioning democracy, that Trump and the political

> mutations around him are somehow an aberrant deviation that can be vanquished in the next election, the more we will hurtle toward tyranny.[12]

Hedges deftly underscores the fact that the elites running this failed democracy over the last (at least) half-century, the same robber barons that constructed "the edifice of lies, deceit and corporate pillage,"[13] made a Trump possible—his rise nothing more than the after-birth of the initiation of what Thomas Cole defined as the *Destruction* stage of a crumbling empire, this time around it's the American Empire.

If history (not myth) teaches us anything it's that the evolution of elite American power and control began in 1492 and became codified in a dusty document that begins, "When in the Course of human events it becomes necessary for one people..." Flash-forward... the following summary by Sheldon Wolin of his "inverted totalitarianism"—written in 2003—reads like a report written after the fact:

> The elements are in place [for a quasi-fascist takeover]: a weak legislative body, a legal system that is both compliant and repressive, a party system in which one party, whether in opposition or in the majority, is bent upon reconstituting the existing system so as to permanently favor a ruling class of the wealthy, the well-connected and the corporate, while leaving the poorer citizens with a sense of helplessness and political despair, and, at the same time, keeping the middle classes dangling between fear of unemployment and expectations of fantastic rewards once the new economy recovers. That scheme is abetted by a sycophantic and increasingly concentrated media; by the integration of universities with their corporate benefactors; by a propaganda machine institutionalized in well-funded think tanks and conservative foundations; by the increasingly closer cooperation between local police and national law enforcement agencies aimed at identifying terrorists, suspicious aliens and domestic dissidents.[14]

"We're Going Away"

In 2008, Wolin penned the entire book, *Democracy Incorporated: Managed Democracy and the Specter of Inverted Totalitarianism.* "Like George Orwell's '1984,' Sheldon Wolin's 'Democracy Incorporated' was intended to be a warning not a handbook,"[15] writes Chauncey DeVega at Salon. "Wolin was prescient." Like

Thomas Cole. Like so many others who see the handwriting on the wall and warn of dire consequences only to be marginalized, censured, and admonished by wealthy elites who have so much ill-begotten treasure to lose. Hopefully, the weight of their violent malfeasance and unbridled greed will not clear the planet of humans—***true desolation*** for Cole's world did not include the very real possibilities of nuclear annihilation and catastrophic climate change. Wow that's heavy. Help us out, Mr. Carlin...

> The planet has been through a lot worse than us. Been through earthquakes, volcanoes, plate tectonics, continental drift, solar flares, sun spots, magnetic storms, the magnetic reversal of the poles, hundreds of thousands of years of bombardment by comets and asteroids and meteors, worldwide floods, tidal waves, worldwide fires, erosion, cosmic rays, recurring ice ages... And we think some plastic bags and some aluminum cans are going to make a difference? The planet isn't going anywhere. WE ARE!
>
> We're going away. Pack your shit, folks. We're going away. And we won't leave much of a trace. Maybe a little Styrofoam. The planet will be here and we'll be long gone. Just another failed mutation. Just another closed-end biological mistake. An evolutionary cul-de-sac. The planet will shake us off like a bad case of fleas... and it will heal itself, it will cleanse itself, 'cause that's what it does. It's a self-correcting system. The air and the water will recover, the earth will be renewed.
>
> —George Carlin
> "Jammin' in New York," Paramount Theater,
> Madison Square Garden, 1992, Home Box Office

Like Orwell's *1984,* Cole's *The Course of Empire,* and Wolin's *Democracy Incorporated,* we envision this book, *Perfecting Tyranny* (and all of *Murder Incorporated*) to be a forthright warning in the same vein.

The chapters build a narrative that chronicles the many ways the American nation morphed into the American Empire and has now strategically transformed into a full-blown ironclad corporatocracy—tyranny masquerading as democracy. Each chapter details a mechanism and/or exploitation used by the state, in cahoots with monied interests and powerful barons that paved the final Yellowbrick Road into the heart of a cruel oligarchy.

From Here to Eternity

From the Empire's mass surveillance security state, one in which the citizens are now anesthetized to the entire illegal and depraved out-of-control operation...

To a central myth of America's founding that the villagers are protected by a free press actively questioning authority rather than manufacturing consent...

To the female species that form the numerical majority of humans in this country and the world but have precious little real representation or equality...

To America's fictitious "war on drugs," which in its ruthless reality fueled the FBI and CIA's true-life war on the Black freedom movement, a war that produced the Prison Industrial Complex...

To the purported post-racial America, a myth busted six ways from Sunday as evidenced by a Dodge Challenger flying a Confederate flag plowing into a crowd of peaceful protesters...

To finally a Supreme Court submissively obedient to the power structure rather than the U.S. Constitution set in place to limit the behavior of this thuggish government and their feudal corporate lords, a court that extinguishes the rights of man by judicial fiat, proving time and again that law is politics by other means...

Ordinary, said Aunt Lydia, is what you are used to.
This may not seem ordinary to you now, but after a time it will.
It will become ordinary.

—Margaret Atwood, *The Handmaid's Tale*

So, this diatribe, this final invective by Messrs. Abu-Jamal & Vittoria begs the question: *Where do we go from here?* Hopefully as a people and a nation, we don't go from here to eternity.

But... and it's a big goddamn

BUT...

—with a little luck and a massive heretofore unseen amount of civil disobedience and revolution, we might break these ties that bind. And we, too, one day shall overcome.

MURDER INCORPORATED

empire \ genocide \ manifest destiny

1 Tribune of the People or Servant to Power?

In 1880, John Swinton, former head of *The New York Times* editorial staff and often referred to as the "dean of his profession," spoke to a gathering of fellow journalists in New York City regarding their collective profession:

> ***The business of journalists is to destroy the truth, to lie outright, to pervert, to vilify, to fawn at the feet of Mammon, and to sell this country and his race for his daily bread. You know it, and I know it, and what folly is this, toasting an independent press?***[1]

A central myth of America's founding is that of a protected free press guaranteed by the First Amendment of the U.S. Constitution. The American media has long been thought of as the envy of the world, the jewel in the crown of the "American Exception." Without question, the media is an organ of tremendous importance in any modern society, for it is the medium through which the population perceives itself, projects itself, and delineates its collective narrative. It is also the machinery through which a society lies to itself (and to others) by projecting a face that is as far from the truth as the moon is from the earth.

We are constantly informed that the media constitutes an array of institutions that endows the public with reliable information, accurate analysis, and valuable well-thought-out commentary. And if there is bias and subjectivity, it is within the bounds of acceptability with respect to the basic premise of truth telling and the reportage of facts. Of course, if this is so, it is usually the media itself that says so—a media that is also a *medium,* a body existing between the subjects of stories and those who consume those stories. Such a relationship demands trust, but when is that trust deserved?

The American media, in particular the mainstream corporate media, has evolved into a now-complete vast wasteland of infotainment, scandal, and, beyond all, government-generated agitprop designed to shelter the status quo, promote perpetual war, and, of course, protect the Empire's wealth. This sad state of affairs blankets the print press as well as broadcast and cable television (albeit with glimmers of hope springing up across a wilder, more free Internet).

Man on the street laments: "Oh, if only we could summon back the good old days."

Unfortunately, there were no good old days, only days that weren't so goddamn awful and pathetic. Our poor man on the street conjures fading memories of Uncle Walter and Chet Huntley through sepia-toned glasses—magical lenses that have exchanged myth for reality. But the history of American journalism resembles a protection racket, one that positions the so-called "Fourth Estate" as the Madison Avenue PR firm representing American capital and American exceptionalism. So as we roll through the 21st century, journalist Amy Goodman asks the painful but necessary rhetorical question about the condition of the omnipresent corporate mainstream media: "You have to ask, if this were state media, how would it be any different?"[2]

Amen.

"Fourth Estate" or "Fourth Branch"

The legendary journalist I.F. "Izzy" Stone trumpeted the same candid warning over the course of his remarkable and renegade career, one that spanned the heart of the 20th century. "You've really got to wear a chastity belt in Washington to preserve your journalistic virginity," Izzy opined. "Once the secretary of state invites you to lunch and asks your opinion, you're sunk."[3] Stone biographer, Myra McPherson, writes that, "Government leaks tossed out at private dinner parties were as suspicious as hand grenades to him."[4] Izzy loathed the cozy relationships that existed between Washington wholesalers and their media sycophants. "You can't just sit on their lap and ask them to feed you secrets," Izzy crooned, "they'll just give you a lot of crap."[5]

Here's how it works: the president makes decisions. He's the decider. The press secretary announces those decisions, and you people of the press type those decisions down. Make, announce, type. Just put 'em through a spell check and go home.[6]

—Stephen Colbert

No doubt that the brush we use to disapprovingly paint the establishment press—both historically and in its current feeble state—is unforgiving and all encompassing and may in fact blur the gallant, if too infrequent, work done by great investigative journalists over the years, heroic revelations like Seymour Hersh's exposé on the My Lai massacre or Carl Bernstein's epic *Rolling Stone* critique of the CIA's mass infiltration of America's newsrooms, where even good old Walter Cronkite was targeted for his government love affair. But these intermittent great efforts are obliterated by the mountains of half-truths, misinformation, and cant dumped on the American plate by a dictatorial body determined to ensure the sanctity of its clubhouse, one populated by manipulative government officials and lickspittles banging on Underwoods (or Macs and Dells). And when it comes to the ever-popular world of American cable news, we witness a madhouse of screaming and swollen bloviators feasting on their young, a band of savage misfits and over-caffeinated meat puppets mud-wrestling in a hellish national immorality play.

Immoral indeed for here comes the money.

The media, which functions as a kind of barometer of national and regional morality, possesses no such morality itself. As an omnipresent and time-honored institution, it supports that which is popular—i.e., that which promotes sales of its product. If a certain person, policy, belief, or tendency isn't popular, it will make it so, in furtherance of its bottom line. Thus, wars are forever popular because their reportage makes it so, by the easy demonization of what William Blum refers to as the "officially designated enemy."

English author Thomas Carlyle remarked, in his 1841 work *On Heroes, Hero Worship, and the Heroic in History:* "[Edmund] Burke said there were Three Estates in Parliament; but, in the Reporters' Gallery yonder, there sat a Fourth Estate more important than them all."[7] Such a characterization by Carlyle via Burke succinctly captures the influential role media can play in a society, but it does not determine how or in service to whom the power supports. The press has the potential to serve the People and it has the potential to serve the powerful, the established, and those in positions of influence and wealth. The march of history unequivocally defines it as the latter and has ever done so, except when mass popular movements and broad public opinion pushes the monolith to adopt more enlightened positions. In other words, the media has long been the voice of the repressive status quo, indeed far more often than otherwise. In this context we might say that the Fourth Estate is perhaps more appropriately dubbed the Fourth *Branch,* a close ally of state power and elite wealth.

Manufacturing Consent

Another grand myth passed down through the ages is the myth of press "objectivity." From 18th-century colonial America, a period historians refer to as the "dark ages of journalism" (wrought with vicious and personal ad hominem attacks), through the manufactured and sensationalized "Yellow Journalism" age spearheaded by William Randolph Hearst and Joseph Pulitzer, the idea of objective journalism was nary a thought. Reportage was bare-knuckle no holds barred brawling. Anything goes and it usually did—grandiose melodrama and laughable hyperbole drove the frenzy of war (the Spanish-American War, the Philippines) and sold millions of papers as the U.S. emerged a world power with the press demonstrating their immense influence and clout.

What's more, this new era of increased production and mass circulation of newspapers post-World War I changed the language utilized by elites when discussing the functions and role of the press, but its essential nature, that of a defender—not of the commoner, but of the privileged—remained operative.

In their historic critique of America's mass media propaganda model, Edward Herman and Noam Chomsky document how the elite powerbrokers "manufacture consent" in almost every aspect of American life. They proffer and then go on to document in detail how the main function of mass media is "to amuse, entertain, and inform, and to inculcate individuals with the values, beliefs, and codes of behavior that will integrate them into the institutional structures of the larger society." Herman and Chomsky conclude that, "In a world of concentrated wealth and major conflicts of class interest, to fulfill this role requires systematic propaganda."[8] The propaganda model described in *Manufacturing Consent* underscores the very real and clear-cut truth that power alone determines what is reported, what is discussed, what is revealed, to put it simply, what is "news."

The Chomsky/Herman paradigm emphasizes that dissenting voices as well as the voices of victims being crushed under the weight of various power structures (i.e., governmental, corporate, industrial religion) are afforded near zero air time or column space, while government and military officials, along with their big business corporate collaborators, are provided a colossal bully pulpit to advocate and cement any policy, agenda, or action: war is necessary, poverty has been duly eradicated, police officers never go beyond serving and protecting, and capitalism is Jesus' favorite economic model—the gospel according to God the Father.

Once again, mass media is the "Fourth Branch"—anything but independent, anything but the People's advocate or vigilant watchdog. Rather, it props up a multi-pronged tsunami of predatory capitalism, a devastating state of perpetual war, and presents America as an ultimatum, right or wrong. The rare exception rather than the rule, that of fiercely independent journalism, gritty investigative work by individuals dedicated to revealing the impropriety of unbridled power, comes around far too infrequently, like Halley's Comet.

For her entire life, independent journalist Amy Goodman has epitomized this rare exception. She remains the antithesis to the state propaganda model, dedicated to confronting the Washington Beltway establishment and their Wall Street cronies, all doing their best impression of John Jacob Astor pumped full of Kryptonite. For Goodman, exposing the lies, corruption, and immorality of American corporatocracy means scaring away the dark. Is she successful most of the time? Not even close. But not because she's not trying. Ever try to stem the tide with a small bucket as the Atlantic pounds away? Regardless, journalists like Goodman attempt to give voice to the voiceless. "It really should be the motto of all journalism, all media today," she stresses, "and that is 'the exception to the rulers.'" She explains: "There is a reason why our profession, journalism, is the only one protected by, enshrined in the Constitution, because we are supposed to be the check and balance on government."[9]

The exception to the rulers.

In Bed

A classic and timeless example of the rule rather than the exception is one that illustrates beyond a shadow of a doubt the might and muscle of the propaganda model. When we examine the lead-up to the Iraq Slaughter post 9/11, we witness an astounding display of Pravda-like behavior, especially when we consider the gravity of the situation and the number of human lives that hung in the balance. "Distrust of anti-war views is based on the assumption that the United States is committed to fighting a 'just war' in Iraq," writes author and professor Anthony DiMaggio. "[T]hose who question that 'just' war are 'harming America.'"[10] This all-too-typical critique outlined by DiMaggio, a critique implemented as policy in major American newsrooms leading up to Washington's mugging in the Middle East, implies that those standing in opposition to the invasion of Iraq actually support the Baath regime. We recall CBS News honcho Dan Rather's xenophobic knee-jerk public reaction as the American media beat the drums of war.

> It's not a time to argue... George Bush is the president. He makes the decisions... wherever he wants me to line up, just tell me where.[11]

This is the anchor of the so-called "liberal-biased" *CBS Evening News.* Shortly after 9/11, *New Republic* editor Peter Beinart thumped his chest like Thor, saying, "This nation is now at war. And in such an environment, domestic political dissent is immoral without a prior statement of national solidarity, a choosing of sides."[12]

Immoral?

Then there's the usual nonsense emanating from Thomas Friedman of America's purported "paper of record," *The New York Times,* getting all historical (or is that hysterical?) on us:

> After every major terrorist incident, the excuse makers come out to tell us why imperialism, Zionism, colonialism, or Iraq explains why the terrorists acted. These excuse makers are just a notch less despicable than the terrorists and also deserved to be exposed.[13]

Despicable?

At the time, CNN's Paula Zahn suggested that Scott Ritter, former U.N. weapons inspector and vocal critic of Washington's thirst for war with Baghdad, was in bed with Saddam Hussein, by attacking the veracity of his stance during an on-air interview, yelping, "People out there are accusing you of drinking Saddam Hussein's Kool-Aid."[14]

Opposing the Iraq war = drinking Saddam Hussein's Kool-Aid.

While on MSNBC, Ashleigh Banfield introduced antiwar congressman, Nick Rahall, with this demeaning set-up: "This representative not only opposes attacking Saddam Hussein, he took his message all the way to Baghdad for three days from September 13th through the 16th to support Saddam Hussein and say give peace a chance."[15]

Accuse him of supporting Saddam Hussein... and debase Lennon's peace sentiment with mockery—all in one sentence.

Then there's Judith Miller of *The New York Times.* Where do we start? Where do we end? For Judy's Middle East dispatches, and the subsequent tempest that resulted, could fill volumes. The fuse was ignited with Miller's embedded reporting with the Mobile Exploitation Team (MET) Alpha in Iraq—a military unit desperately trying to find those dastardly weapons of mass destruction that would help sell the Bush/Cheney doomsday narrative. At the core of her story we find an Iraqi scientist who allegedly had all the goods on Saddam Hussein's chemical warfare program. This mysterious scientist knew who, what, where, and when. He also supposedly revealed that Iraq was working in cooperation with Al Qaeda. On the surface, this information amounted to, as Jack Shafer from *Slate* defined, "journalistic bombshells."[16] But well into her story, Judy Miller reveals the deal she made with MET Alpha and the U.S. military for her access:

> Under the terms of her accreditation to report on the activities of MET Alpha, this reporter was not permitted to interview the scientist or visit his home. Nor was she permitted to write about the discovery of the scientist for three days, and the copy was then submitted for a check by military officials.
>
> Those officials asked that details of what chemicals were uncovered be deleted. They said they feared that such information could jeopardize the scientist's safety by identifying the part of the weapons program where he worked.[17]

"Terms of accreditation to report?" Shafer is quick to add that this "is a new piece of journalistic jargon to me." Of course, as an embed, Miller is hiding behind the safe and oft-used shield of concealing any intel that might jeopardize military security or the security of in-country allies. Shafer, clearly agitated by Miller and her newspaper's lack of journalistic integrity (or guts), unloaded on their behavior:

> [I]s Miller implying that she struck a more complex ad hoc deal with MET Alpha? (I think she is.) It's quite a deal when you read the story closely. She agreed not to interview the scientist, visit his home, divulge his identity, write about the MET Alpha for three

> days, or disclose the composition of the chemicals. And, most pungently, she consented to pre-publication review—oh, hell, let's call it censorship!—of her story by military officials.
>
> Did the "military officials" who checked her story *require* her to redact parts of the story, or did she do so on her own accord? Were any other "terms of accreditation" imposed on Miller? Other levels of censorship? Are other *Times* reporters filing dispatches under similar "terms of accreditation"?[18]

As the *Times'* reporting unfolded, Miller's stories were pulled to pieces, savaged, and more dramatically, debunked, discredited, and exposed as, at best disingenuous, and at worst, completely counterfeit (that feels right). Regardless, at the time when it most mattered, her reports became delicious raw meat and cannon fodder for cable news pundits to slam their desks, screaming, "See, see, SEE... *we told you*—THERE ARE mobile biological germ labs, THERE ARE aluminum tubes stuffed with evil oozing goo, and Hitler, er... I mean Hussein, has centrifuges ready to enrich that goddamn yellowcake uranium and then strike the homeland at a moment's notice! (now spitting) Unleash the dogs of war! Of War! Glorious War! USA! USA! USA!"

Damage done. Commercial. Fade to black.

But months earlier, on 8 September 2002 (the eve of the first 9/11 anniversary), the *Times* ran another monster story by Miller and her co-writer, Michael Gordon, entitled "U.S. Says Hussein Intensifies Quest for A-Bomb Parts." This one launched a cinematic co-production between the American media and government that was awe-inspiring in its manipulative force and could not have been duplicated if George Balanchine and Mikhail Baryshnikov were choreographing the "dance" moves—each "pas de deux" a work of totalitarian brilliance. In fact, before the bundles of papers hit the concrete, Bush Administration officials were caterwauling like a pack of frenzied bobcats—and the mainstream corporate media was happy to oblige.

Dick Cheney emerged from his cave to grunt and growl on NBC's *Meet the Press,* dutifully and aggressively confirming Miller's details. Colin Powell cartwheeled into the Fox studios and also confirmed the *Times'* alleged bombshell. Department of War honcho D. Rumsfeld walked right past the ghost of Edward R. Murrow and onto CBS's *Face the Nation,* offering to save America from this Islamic demon seed.

And then there was Condi Rice. When she visited CNN, and the very serious and important Wolf Blitzer, she uttered the famous, now infamous line, "we don't want the smoking gun to be a mushroom cloud." It was a multi-stage performance for the ages. And just like they capitulated thirteen years prior when the elder Bush turned Iraq into a killing field, the American press walked blissfully in lockstep with their government cohorts. *Where to next, boss?*

As we documented in our CIA chapter in Book Two, American journalists in unison with CIA, Inc., shared a very cozy relationship for a very long time during the height of the Cold War. In fact, Frank Wisner, one of the masterminds of this totalitarian liaison between State and Press, said the CIA played the press like a "mighty Wurlitzer"—the press orchestrated like a giant pipe organ broadcasting and circulating any message the boys out in Langley (and by extension the White House, State Department, and Pentagon) wanted or needed disseminated. "While American politicians ridiculed the notion of state-sponsored media in places such as the Soviet Union," write Amy and David Goodman in their media critique, *Static,* "American journalists became willing agents of their own government."[19]

The dismal saga of Judith Miller and her international rostrum at *The New York Times* clearly illustrated that the "Mighty Wurlitzer" is as playable as ever. "These days, the CIA doesn't need to rely on covertly placed and paid reporters," Amy and David Goodman conclude, "It has people such as former *New York Times* national security reporter Judith Miller, who will do the government's bidding for free."[20] In the late 1970s, as the CIA-press relationship was revealed and the CIA was forced to slither back into their hole, one of their senior officials polished his crystal ball:

> The pendulum will swing, and someday we'll be recruiting journalists again... [When that time arrives], I will have no problem recruiting. I see a lot of them, and I know they're ripe for the plucking.[21]

Judith Miller, plucked like a ripe tomato in Grandpa's backyard.

The New York Times also reported widespread opposition in Europe regarding an invasion of Iraq. "[It's] a sentiment the paper describes as 'often virulent,'" reports *Fairness and Accuracy in Reporting (FAIR).* The adjective, they remind us, "is derived, of course, from 'virus,' suggesting that something is seriously wrong with opposing the war."[22]

Peace or antiwar reactions = virus.

Former congressional Democrats, Jim McDermott and David Bonior, who were opposed to the Iraq war, traveled to Baghdad in an attempt to intervene before all hell broke loose. Getting all worked up over their trip, National Public Radio and FOX correspondent Mara Liasson bawled, "These guys are a disgrace. Look, everybody knows it's 101, Politics 101, that you don't go to an adversary country, an enemy country, and bad-mouth the United States, its policies and the president of the United States. I mean, these guys ought to, I don't know, resign."[23]

You're a disgrace... so quit.

[Interesting note: Mara Liasson, "journalist," cut her teeth at the progressive Pacifica Network's Berkeley affiliate KPFA—Hey Mara, what happened? Who got to you? Blink twice if you need help.]

NBC's Tom Brokaw was an anchor who was very practical about American bombs bursting in air. "One of the things we don't want to do," Brokaw warned, "is to destroy the infrastructure of Iraq because in a few days we're going to own that country."[24] Biting journalism, don't you agree? "Listen, while you're blasting these bastards to pieces, don't get blood on the furniture or knock over any vases, we're gonna need that shit."

These pathetic examples could go on and on and on...

The other incredible revelation you might have noticed in Brokaw's statement, along with noticing the exact same detail with nearly every other purported American journalist, is the use of the pronoun—

We

George Carlin used to say that language gives people away, a tool for concealing an inconvenient and uncomfortable truth. Well, the use of the pronoun "we" by American journalists is a drop-dead giveaway that the corporate media has been and remains an airtight extension of the public relations apparatus surrounding the cozy relationship between Washington bureaucrats, the Pentagon, and big business.

By their very nature as large media conglomerates, some segment of multinational giants like General Electric (NBC and Universal until 2013), newsrooms and reporters are part of the club, the country club of passive access and peaceful coexistence with the very institutions and leaders they are charged with watching, scrutinizing, and investigating their dubious behavior. Does the term "fox watching the hen house" grab you where it hurts? "All are tied into the stock market," explains British media critic, David Cromwell. "Wealthy people sit on the boards of these major corporations, many with extensive personal and business contacts in other corporations [like GE and Westinghouse's weapons production and nuclear power development—ed.]. It is difficult to conceive that press neutrality would not be compromised."[25] How else can we explain ABC/ NPR reporter Cokie Roberts, when asked on NPR's *Morning Edition* during the build-up to the Iraq invasion if there were any congressional dissenters to the war and she answered, "None that matter."[26]

None that matter.

To bought and sold journalists, who, for the most part, act as PR pundits for power, the construction of news, the framing of ideas, and the dissemination of "facts" will nearly always be pro-military, pro-government, pro-Wall Street, ultimately pro-American regardless of the history, the circumstances and context, and above all, the victims.

None that matter.

"It's a jaw-dropping statement," wrote a gentleman by the name of David Portorti, who lost his brother James on the 96th floor of the World Trade Center, reports Amy Goodman. "Roberts' flippant dismissal of dissenters," Goodman continues, "inspired Portorti to write a book, *September 11th Families for Peaceful Tomorrows.*"[27] Portorti takes Cokie Roberts' "None that matter" and turns it on its ear:

> It's a handy phrase you can use at home as well... Will network news divisions, owned by defense contractors, give us any useful insights into the workings of the U.S. military? *None that matter.*[28]

"Dissent does matter," stresses Goodman. "It's what makes this country healthy. And the media has a responsibility to go to where the silence is, to present the views of people all over this country and not simply beat the drums for war."[29] And do they ever, especially when you examine the buildup toward the invasion, demolition, and occupation of Iraq beginning in 2003. *FAIR* studied the four major networks' evening broadcasts for two weeks a month before the invasion (CBS, NBC, ABC, PBS). It was clearly a crucial period in the national discussion.

The results define the conveyor belt, factory-like manufacture of consent. Three hundred ninety-three on-air interviews were conducted regarding Washington going to war and only three voices of the almost four hundred were individuals arguing against the invasion.[30] That's less than 1%... or 0.76335878% to be exact. "That is not an independent media," Goodman intones. "That is not a media that is giving voice to this country. That is a media that is hell-bent on war, and it is violating our sacred responsibility to be fair."[31]

This one-sided agitprop avalanche also underscores the mainstream media's reliance on official government and corporate sources to define what is and what is not "news."

- *A Pentagon spokeswoman determined that...*
- *State Department officials made it clear...*
- *The White House Press Secretary clarified the President's position by saying...*
- *General Thaddeus "Thunderbolt" Ross remarked that boots on the ground...*
- *An NYPD spokesperson told reporters that the protestors...*

Official sources pave the way. "What those people say is news. Their perspectives are automatically legitimate," says communications professor Robert McChesney from the University of Illinois. He argues that "if you talk to prisoners, strikers, the homeless, or protesters, you have to paint their perspectives as unreliable, or else you've become an advocate and are no longer a 'neutral' professional journalist."[32] There's the rub and that's the danger: the ongoing narrative roars down a one-way street where dissenting voices and alternative journalistic views challenging the establishment status quo are denounced, dismissed, or just simply ignored. McChesney warns that, "This is precisely the opposite of what a functioning democracy needs, which is a ruthless accounting of the powers that be."[33]

... a ruthless accounting of the powers that be. Amen.

The massive consolidation of the American media is an integral part of the ongoing corporate state takeover. Large conglomerates manage almost every pixel of what Americans watch, listen to, or read. The motive for even owning a news division or media outlet is not about press freedom, investigative journalism, or the ever diligent watchdog soul of the professed Fourth Estate, rather the motives of the owners and management are centered on free market capitalism. These huge conglomerates are all beholden to Wall Street, to the worship of the hallowed bottom-line over any semblance of serious independent journalism dedicated to protecting the general welfare of the People and the planet they inhabit, utilizing the immense power of their pulpit and its incredible reach.

The large mainstream media umbrella tenders homogenized fodder for easy consumption: think this way, walk this way, buy this shit, and above all, don't question authority. "A democracy survives," journalist Chris Hedges stresses, "when its citizens... can discern lies from truth. Take this away and a democracy dies."[34] Clearly, Hedges' words distill down the essence of America's entropy, for that rank smell you detect when watching cable news, network news, listening to the submissive ramblings on NPR or PBS, or when you read the so-called Washington-Wall Street gospel of the nation's leading papers, are the mewlings of a dying republic.

In Bed In Charlottesville

And then the 2016 presidential campaign happened and we watched in horror as the American media sold out their last dying breath... one final last gasp to Donald J. Trump. American journalists—print and broadcast—went all in on the reality TV carnival barker. Like a 3am drunk in Caesar's Palace who pushes his remaining chips, in reality his house and kids' college fund, across the table with reckless abandon toward the dealer and salivating casino. Trump, with his insane racist, misogynist, and fear-mongering gibberish, showed up just at the right time, especially for 24-hour cable news that thrives on crazy shit to fill their news cycle—a baby stuck in a well for three weeks, a Florida alligator eats an entire family from Iowa, and then this orange New York gasbag runs for U.S. president and beats the hell out of every sorry Republican candidate, while defining Mexicans as rapists and murderers, calling predominantly Black cities and neighborhoods "crime-infested hellholes," promising to shut down dangerous Muslim immigration, and then whipping up crowds to lock up Hillary Clinton for conspiring with international bankers a la "The Protocols of the Elders of Zion"—ongoing batshit crazy comments like his infamous:

> I could stand in the middle of Fifth Avenue and shoot somebody and wouldn't lose any voters, okay? (Trump then mimicking firing a gun with his fingers) It's, like, incredible.

And the American press embraced this crude, ignorant, usually disqualifying display because they knew it sold, and sold big—ratings bonanza big. The various news organizations would focus their center camera on an empty rostrum for minutes into hours waiting for the gasbag to show up—building anticipation for their newfangled oddity, the bearded lady, this Wizard of Oz. The press created an absolute frenzy, Trump amassing millions upon millions of dollars of unpaid big time advertising—and by the constant coverage and adulation, they legitimized a completely illegitimate candidate, as well as his dangerous demagoguery. The toxins were on the loose.

The unintended consequence?

The gasbag won (albeit against arguably the worst candidate the Democrats have ever run). The American mainstream media never thought the guy had a chance so why not put on a rollicking moneymaking vaudeville extravaganza. Make a king's ransom on the freak show and then get back to business as usual. But it just kept getting crazier. And uglier. "We replaced a million hours of Trump with a million hours of 'Trump is bad,'" says *Rolling Stone* contributing editor Matt Taibbi. "We took a lot of heat during 2016 for giving him billions [of dollars worth] of free coverage and we had this fork in the road, like, are we going to cover him less, or are we going to cover in the same amount but in a different way? And then we chose Door No. 2."[35]

> Thank you President Trump for your honesty & courage to tell
> the truth about #Charlottesville & condemn the leftist terrorists in
> BLM/Antifa
> —@DrDavidDuke (Twitter)

Trump's victory was hailed by the Ku Klux Klan, the American Nazi Party, as well as every other white supremacist group and individual that crawled out from under a rock. Charlottesville happens and the gasbag offers a clear and clarion call regarding the violent and murderous "Unite the Right" rally: a false equivalency between the sadistic white supremacist protestors trying to ensure that the legacy of oppression continues and the peaceful counter-protestors trying to end the medieval cruelty. Murdered in this purely American melee—one that is a direct descendent of Bull Connor's fire hoses and dogs, the incalculable lynchings, the abject terrorism of slavery, as well as every treacherous act that stretches back to the Great American Slave Trade—was peaceful counter-protestor Heather Heyer, viciously killed by a neo-Nazi tool of America's ugly racist heart.

> "We condemn in the strongest possible terms this egregious display of hatred, bigotry, and violence **on many sides,"** (before adding again) **"on many sides."**
> —Trump (from his private country club in New Jersey)

The neo-Nazis were emboldened—they viewed Trump in the White House as a giant success story, a vindication of their disdain and virulent hatred for "the others"—every group they consider inferior to white Christian Euro-Americans. "Trump's reticence betrays a reactionary bias, which comes as no surprise," writes Shuja Haider in *Jacobin.* "But his rhetoric was not unique to him—the mainstream media and liberal intelligentsia had set the precedent."[36] One of the few, Haider underscored the mainstream media's moral equivocating on Charlottesville (as they do so often and so well). "Looking at circumstances like these and seeing 'many sides,' indistinguishable from each other, is a stance that history has never revealed to be anything but moral cowardice."[37] Identical in spirit with how the U.S. mainstream media covers America's imperial wars ("kill one person call it murder, kill a million call it foreign policy"), they found their so-called "objective, fair & balanced" center and delivered that pablum to their audience and readers. Of course those with a slight right bent stretched one way and those with a slight left bent stretched the other way, but in terms of "moral cowardice" the left is world champion. Some issues simply do not offer two sides, two points of view. And according to Trump's unmasked racist message, "many sides" are not advocating violence and racist hatred—one side clearly owns that game plan lock, stock, and smoking barrel. But the corporate media, as constituted now, drives right down the middle of the highway regardless of what's burning or shaking on either side. Haider calls it "middle-of-the-road tongue-clucking" and it is this ubiquitous trait that runs through newsrooms and networks like a main circuit cable—whether covering war, cops killing at will, women's rights trampled by old white men, or constitutional rights trampled by, well, just about everyone in U.S. power. Count on the media to cower in the safe confines of the middle.

For editors and writers and reporters at these outlets who need good guys and bad guys like they're covering the shootout at the O.K. Corral, Charlottesville (and other actions) provides them with a perfect punching bag, a just what the doctor ordered scapegoat—Antifa aka "the boogeyman." Rather than take on demagogues like Trump and the usual enablers, who are actively pouring gasoline on burning white nationalist matches, they frame Antifa as the antichrist, the bad seed on the so-called left (same strategy used with Dr. King, Malcolm X, the Panthers, the

Young Lords, Black Lives Matter, the women's movement, christ the list is never ending). The American press refuses to reveal with hammer and tong journalism the fact that a racist playbook is being used by the leaders of the U.S. government to retain control and divide opposition to racist hatred and domestic terrorism. As always, they need to retain their passes and credentials to the country club owned and operated by the Washington power structure—can't fuck with that for a myriad of obvious reasons.

And we all know why they use Antifa as the scapegoat: because they can paint Antifa as a violent entity making the situation worse, when in reality Antifa is fighting for survival—defending against the racist violence and oppression perpetrated against people of color and people of peace. Like the Black Panthers were forced to protect black and disenfranchised neighborhoods against state violence and oppression carried out by police departments nationwide—the government gave them no choice. Similarly, Antifa faces off against the Neanderthals in white hoods and Confederate fucking flags and takes no prisoners. This is the job of the FBI, local cops, as well as the U.S. Justice Department. And let's be clear: Trump's actions clearly triggered the exploits of these white supremacists, therefore defining the state-sanctioned violence.

A typical example of the media's standard capitulation on the Charlottesville narrative was written by Sheryl Gay Stolberg at *The New York Times* who reported from Virginia in a Tweet that, "The hard left seemed as hate-filled as alt-right." In one perfect stroke, this reporter leveled the playing field between a stance for obvious justice and an ugly racist terror campaign.

Moral cowardice. The U.S. government slaughters millions—from Hiroshima and Nagasaki in 1945, to Southeast Asia in the 1960s and 1970s, to the Middle East from 1990 on... and now Africa ongoing—as the mainstream media hides behind American exceptionalism, not only skirting its journalistic imperative but helping to bang the drums of war. We also see moral cowardice on the part of the media when it comes to the ongoing battle for racial justice—and the really scary part of this cowardice is the fact that those fighting for right and fighting for love stand in absolute bright and blazing sunshine... and those fighting for wrong and hatred stand in absolute darkness, at the Gates of Hell, and yet the media power brokers have somehow successfully managed to blur the line between good and evil.

When a crisis like racial justice—a 500-year-old crisis—is as clear-cut as it is and the power structure still holds on to the darkness, for whatever reason, there can be only one response:

REPORTERS TAKE HEED

If you turn off your conscience...
turn off your heart...
it's harder to turn it back on...
if you are to remain human.

The Echo Chamber that is NPR (Cheez Whiz vs. Velveeta)

"We don't watch that nonsense on Fox News or CNN. We watch PBS and we absolutely love NPR. By the way, did you hear that terrific piece on *All Things Considered* today? Very insightful, how enhanced interrogation techniques can really be quite useful. More chardonnay please."

Many pseudo-liberals embrace National Public Radio and PBS like the Holy Grail of enlightened thought—or at least they believe it's a viable alternative. Back in the 1990s, long before the late David Koch (of the Koch Brothers song and dance team) and other elite funders held political sway over public broadcasting with their multi-million dollar Park Avenue donations, sociology professor Charlotte Ryan, now from the University of Massachusetts, conducted a major study of NPR, long thought to be the citadel of liberal ideology as well as a bastion of alternative and progressive journalism. "NPR's regular coverage mirrored that of commercial news programming," Ryan determined. "NPR stories focus on the same Washington-centered events and public figures as the commercial news, with the White House and Congress setting much of the political agenda." Ryan concluded that NPR's sources "often paralleled" the networks, with the same embrace of government sources "and politically centrist or conservative think tanks and publications" that dictate their overall narrative. And, of course, the vast majority of individuals quoted are government officials.[38]

Glenn Garvin, in his classic 1993 critique of NPR entitled "How Do I Hate NPR? Let Me Count the Ways," punctures the belief balloon that NPR extols liberal virtues against the right-wing brute machine thumping for war, continued white supremacism, and predatory capitalism. "Instead, it's a house organ of respectable inside-the-Beltway liberalism," Garvin stresses, "news written by and for aging yuppies whose idea of adventuresome politics is telling Dan Quayle jokes."[39]

Besides the anachronistic references, the critique remains dreadfully valid—if not more so—to this day.

> NPR's toughest critics these days come from the left, and they hammer away at this very point. Quoting Democrats instead of Republicans, the critics argue, offers an alternative in roughly the same way that Cheez Whiz is an alternative to Velveeta.[40]

Throughout this book series, we have frequently quoted America's most prolific public intellectual Noam Chomsky. Here's another slice of Professor Chomsky, but this time it's less emphasis on his intellectual side and more light on his visceral side. Guess what gets under Chomsky's skin? NPR.

> I was driving home from work the other day, torturing myself by listening to NPR—kind of a masochistic streak I can't get over. Actually, some day I'm going to sue them. Once they got me so angry that I started speeding and lost control of what I was doing. I was stopped by a cop. I was going like sixty miles an hour in a thirty mile zone—may be a basis for a civil suit if there are any lawyers around here. They had a segment on Barack Obama, "the great new hope." It was very exuberant: "what a fantastic personality he is and a great candidate, thousands of people coming out." It went on for about fifteen minutes of excited rhetoric. There was only one thing missing: they didn't say a word about what his policies were on anything.[41]

Perhaps political commentator, David Sirota, frames it best when he writes, "PBS's behavior, which appears to violate its own disclosure and conflict-of-interest rules, effectively turns the network into just another outlet whose journalism is stealthily shaped by moneyed puppet masters."[42] Running parallel to their advertising-driven counterparts in the for-profit media/infotainment business, PBS has committed slow suicide by removing "public" from its historic calling and has now become "the Plutocrats Broadcasting Service."[43]

How you know you live in an empire:

> *when there's an announcement your govt is about to start*
> *a new 3-year war & it seems barely newsworthy.*[44]
> —Glenn Greenwald

In its current state, the media remains the undisputed heavyweight champion of manipulation and chicanery, and, at the same time, it is possibly the most essential instrument in the arsenal of the Empire. It wields immense power, and for the most part, remains an unmovable monolith.

But sometimes, we witness a crack in empire's breastplate, as evidenced by the recent revelations exposed by, among others, Julian Assange and WikiLeaks, Edward Snowden, and Glenn Greenwald. And sometimes it has to be documented and disseminated by a (semi) fictional account—like a 1976 movie adaptation by screenwriter William Goldman of the Bob Woodward and Carl Bernstein's classic real-life thriller *All the President's Men. Washington Post* editor, Ben Bradlee, played with grace by Jason Robards, sums up the gravity of their 1972 Watergate situation, a summation that could very well characterize the similar critical state of America's current media monster:

> Ben Bradlee:
> You know the results of the latest Gallup Poll? Half the country never even heard of the word Watergate. Nobody gives a shit. You guys are probably pretty tired, right? Well, you should be. Go on home, get a nice hot bath. Rest up... Then get your asses back in gear. We're under a lot of pressure, you know, and you put us there. Nothing's riding on this except the First Amendment to the Constitution, freedom of the press, and maybe the future of the country. Not that any of that matters, but if you guys fuck up again, I'm going to get mad. Goodnight.

It a hopeful and hopeless situation. And it's been this way from the beginning.

The Early Days

The great observer of American democracy, Alexis de Tocqueville, the lawyer, aristocrat, and writer from France, saw enough of America during his 19th century sojourn that he captured something both unflattering and significant about the subject of his study. America's much-ballyhooed freedom of conscience, of mind, and of speech did not find a believer in de Tocqueville, who observed:

> I know of no country in which there is so little true independence of mind and freedom of discussion as in America... In America the majority raises very formidable barriers to the liberty of opinions:

> within these barriers an author may write whatever he pleases, but he will repent it if he ever steps beyond this. Not that he is exposed to the terrors of an auto-da-fé, but he is tormented by the slights and persecutions of daily obloquy. His political career is closed forever, since he has offended the only authority which is able to promote his success. Every sort of compensation, even that of celebrity, is refused to him. Before he published his opinions he imagined that he held them in common with many others; but no sooner has he declared them openly than he is loudly censored by his overbearing opponents, whilst those who think without having the courage to speak, like him, abandon him in silence. He yields at length, oppressed by the daily efforts he has been making, and he subsides into silence, as if he was tormented by remorse for having spoken the truth.[45]

From de Tocqueville, we learn that real freedom of speech and thought is but an illusion—albeit one of long duration. For he wrote these words just over a third of the way through the 1800s, when the promises of the French and American Revolutions were still fresh in memory.

As we have seen in the lofty constitutional promises about "freedom" and "equality" of "citizens" in both the U.S. and French constitutions, the real lives lived by millions of people were rarely, if ever, affected. What de Tocqueville pinpoints is not the "right" of dissent, but the very real cost of dissent in a society that lies to itself about liberty. America was a slave society; and it spread its venom around the world to ensure that it would continue to be so. And the primary vehicle for that venom? The American press—"Get ya papah."

From America's earliest era—as a white, settler nation—the newspaper industry began as local and regional productions, usually the organ of a political party and, of course, wealthy families. This fledgling institution may have been episodic (monthly, bi-weekly, or weekly) but it struggled to be the state's central voice—and somewhat fancifully saw itself as "the voice of the people." Hence, we find that papers from wide geographic, ethnic, and ideological perspectives claimed the name "tribune," from the Roman institution imposed between the plebeians (the common people) and the patricians (the well-to-do), for the protection of the former.

Some notable examples include Benjamin Harris' *Publick Occurrences,* published in New England in 1690—it was later shut down for lack of official permission; in 1704, postmaster John Campbell published the first regular newspaper in the colonies, the *Boston News Letter.* Then in 1732, Benjamin Franklin published his first *Poor Richard's Almanack* in Philadelphia, which continued for twenty-five years. The nation's first daily newspaper, *The Pennsylvania Evening Post,* began publishing in 1783.

Samuel E. Cornish and John B. Russwurm were co-founders of the first Black newspaper, *Freedom's Journal,* in 1827. Cornish would go on to found a number of such papers throughout his life and career. Russwurm would later settle in Liberia, West Africa. Most likely, this was motivated by a controversy sparked when Russwurm announced it was "a waste of words to talk of ever enjoying citizenship in this country."[46] His comments lit a firestorm of recrimination with some calling him a "traitor" for advocating the emigration of free Blacks back to Africa. Russwurm relinquished his post at *Freedom's Journal,* giving us some sense of the actual power of the Black press in expressing Black opinions.

Perhaps the most revered and respected Black journalist of the antebellum period (or any other, for that matter) was Frederick Douglass, the fiery abolitionist and editor of the *North Star,* which began publishing in 1847, the year Lincoln was elected to the U.S. House of Representatives and Jefferson Davis entered the Senate. An escaped captive, Douglass laced the pages of his paper with equal parts fire and brilliance. Before the Civil War, some forty Black newspapers served their communities, among them the *Colored American,* the *Mystery,* and the renamed *Frederick Douglass' Paper.*

Douglass used his paper as a clarion demand for freedom and social justice. There he thundered against slavery, the American invasion of Mexico, and for women's rights. But we must recall that his organ was a work of a Black journalist, writing primarily to a Black reading base in the North. This was true of many Black papers given the great lengths to which the southern governments went to censor and exclude such materials from circulation in their regions, allied with efforts of the U.S. Postmaster-General to ensure they never made it through the mail—so much for freedom of the press!

It is important to note that the early Black press often operated on a shoestring budget or were supported by fraternal organizations (or in Douglass' case, by friends and contributors in the abolitionist community). Unlike their competitors in the white community, these papers did not enjoy the excess wealth of the manufacturing classes or subsidized donations from wealthy families. The majority press was, almost from its infancy, a corporate press, rather than an entity giving voice to common folk. It was, in many ways, the voice of the economic, social, and political elites, and, more often than not, the tribune of segregation, white supremacy, and yes, terrorism. In fact, examining the early American press is like gazing through a looking glass right into the racist roots of America.

Have we overstated the case? Hardly.

"WHITE SUPERIORITY IN FLORIDA"

> *The noble and valiant Anglo-Saxons of Manatee county, Fla., are engaged just now in demonstrating the superiority of the race...* [47]
> —Headline & editorial from the Springfield (Massachusetts)
> *Weekly Republican*
> January 19, 1896

During the early half of the 20th century, local newspapers (that is, *white* newspapers) had a feature that guaranteed not only high interest, but also high sales. They ran pieces editorializing and advertising the lynching of a Black person that, in many instances, were virtually indistinguishable from ads for a picnic or a sporting event. While the bulk of these articles were printed in southern dailies, this was an American feature—and not entirely a southern one. Ralph Ginzburg's unflinching compendium, *100 Years of Lynching,* is chilling in its reportage, for it is a bare-knuckle affair, featuring actual news clippings from virtually every state in the Union, reporting on lynchings and, in some cases, advertising a lynching to come.

For nearly a century, these newspapers played a decisive and supportive public role in normalizing state and private terrorism against Blacks. This facet of American journalism, its intense "Negrophobic" racism, certainly was an important factor in the exclusion of Black journalists from the newsroom of major papers until the height of the Civil Rights and Black Power movements of the 1960s and 1970s. In fact, journalism remains a province of white supremacy, where today Blacks are leaving the profession at an increasing rate (usually for online ventures at Black-owned publications). Thus, the establishment—and now corporate—media has been a disciplinary tool of teaching terror to an undereducated and fearful community by celebrating the ugly traditions of racism and violence in support of the same. But it would be misleading to simply reflect this as a black/white affair.

The American press also has a long history of supporting wars of aggression against indigenous people. It is disconcerting for us, of this generation, to read the coverage of local newspapers overtly agitating and inciting local white communities to attack, destroy, and "exterminate," in the haunting words of the *Rocky Mountain News,* all "the red devils,"[48] both hostile and non-hostile Cheyenne of Sand Creek, Colorado. And exterminate they did: women, children, the infirm, and the elderly. In fact, the tone of the *Rocky Mountain News* was carried by papers such as South Dakota's *Aberdeen Saturday Pioneer* and California's *Humboldt Times,* which praised an 1860 slavery law, designed to exploit the "free labor" (slavery) of Indians in the territory. The paper crowed, "What a pity the provisions of the law do not extend to greasers, Kanakas, and Asiatics. It would be so convenient to carry on a farm or mine, when all the hard and dirty work is performed by apprentices!"[49]

Extermination and Slavery—all endorsed by your friendly neighborhood newspaper: today's media in its swaddling clothes.

War Scribes

There has never been an American war abroad that was not made more easily waged by the support and acquiescence of the corporate press. These "house" scribes for the rulers could be readily counted on to praise the valiant efforts of "our" soldiers, and to denounce the reprehensible nature of the foe. If that were not sufficient, the media would provide, in collusion with their governmental father figures, the ideological framework that justified every invasion, every occupation, and every act of U.S. interference in the business and running of foreign nations, even if the justification presented was completely erroneous—or simply absurd.

If those were the charges in the indictment of the industry, it would suffice to convict, but the rap sheet must lengthen. That's because the industry has worked diligently, not merely to misinform, but to obscure the true interests supporting war, for those individuals and entities are either controlling interests in the media itself, or an important (read: "powerfully rich") entity, which may have advertising interests over the organ itself. But the media also serves a political function, especially when it becomes a megaphone for a specific point of view. This amplification serves to inform and misinform citizens, and makes war far more probable as the fire of emotions are stoked and war mania intensifies. And, as always, this media thunderstorm frames the unthinkable horrors of war as normal. Amy Goodman posits this vision: "If for one week in the United States we saw the true face of war, we saw people's limbs sheared off, we saw kids blown apart, for one week, war would be eradicated. Instead, what we see in the U.S. media is the video war game."[50]

A Yellow Citizen in King Arthur's Court

> KANE: We have no secrets from our readers, Mr. Bernstein...
> Read the cable.
>
> MR. BERNSTEIN: "Girls delightful in Cuba, stop. Could send
> you prose poems about scenery but don't feel right spending your
> money, stop. There is no war in Cuba, signed Wheeler."
> Any answer?
>
> KANE: Yes. "Dear Wheeler, you provide the prose poems,
> I'll provide the War."
>
> *(Citizen Kane,* 1941, screenplay by Herman J. Mankiewicz
> and Orson Welles)

The U.S. invasion of Cuba in 1898, ostensibly to assist the Cuban Liberation Army in their battles against the colonial forces of Spain, was the opening needed to assert U.S. control and, later, domination of the economy and political life of their neighbor to the south. Before the war began, an ambitious politician, Theodore Roosevelt, used the Spain/Cuba conflict to lobby for a role in the Navy administration under newly elected President William McKinley, who expressed interest, albeit with private reservations. McKinley told one of Roosevelt's friends, "I want peace and I am told that your friend Theodore—whom I know only slightly—is always getting into rows with everybody. I am afraid he is too pugnacious."[51]

The president wouldn't have long to discover what kind of man Theodore was and, when T.R. began his blustering, the press was there to create headlines, fan the flames of war—and sell papers. Lots of them. Mere months into his appointment as Assistant Secretary of the Navy, Roosevelt, during a speech at the Naval War College, began the war of words—with words of war. Reporters there counted the word "war" from TR's lips more than 60 times! But rather than be appalled, or at least skeptical, the press greeted his speech with strong praise. *The Washington Post* exalted, "Theodore Roosevelt, you have found your place at last!"

The Baltimore Sun pronounced Roosevelt's speech as "manly, patriotic, intelligent and convincing."[52] Roosevelt must've been buoyed by such reports, for they fit perfectly into his Aryan worldview of absolute Manifest Destiny and American exceptionalism, which also translated war into an exercise of male virtues. (Years later, as you may know, George Carlin called it "America's Bigger Dick Foreign Policy.") In his naval post for less than six months, Roosevelt was taking every opportunity (such as when his boss was out of town) to brief the president on the necessity for war. McKinley, feeling the public (actually, the press') mood, acquiesced.

Years later, a member of the McKinley-era Congress, U.S. Representative Thomas Butler of Pennsylvania, would recall, "Roosevelt came down here [Caribbean] looking for war. He did not care who we fought as long as there was a scrap."[53] In his private correspondence during the pre-war period, Roosevelt virtually echoed the congressman's impression when, writing to a professor at West Point, Roosevelt confided, "In strict confidence… I should welcome almost any war, *for I think this country needs one.*"[54] Here then, was the American press advocating for war without reason, cheerily subservient to a man who wanted a dust-up for personal pleasure, personal gain, and for the advancement of American imperial power.

The movement toward war swelled and all it needed was the right pretext that would engage the people into supporting it. That pretext arrived on the morning of 15 February 1898. The national corporate "yellow press" blared the necessity for war, but none in a more shameless fashion than the Hearst property, *The New York Journal,* which blared in a bold, banner headline: "DESTRUCTION OF THE WAR SHIP MAINE WAS THE WORK OF AN ENEMY." That claim was supported by another huge boldface headline, reading: "ASSISTANT SECRETARY ROOSEVELT CONVINCED THE EXPLOSION OF THE WAR SHIP WAS NOT AN ACCIDENT." This, before a shred of evidence was known. But it mattered little, for Roosevelt had his pretext and Hearst had his headline, one that sold more than a million copies—that day.

Money and War! What could be sweeter?

Nevertheless, President McKinley was terribly reluctant to endorse the endeavor, despite the beckoning headlines. He privately told a confidante, "I have been through one war; I have seen the dead piled up, and I do not want to see another."[55] The war scribes did everything short of calling McKinley a girlie-man for his reticence. *The New York Journal,* which broke the "enemy" story regarding the destruction of the *U.S.S. Maine* (which actually happened because of a ship malfunction not uncommon for steam ships of the period), opined that it sought "any signs, however faint, of manhood in the White House."[56] *The Atlanta Constitution* resorted to ridicule, calling McKinley a "goody-goody man," adding that the nation needed a "declaration of American virility... At this moment here is a great need of a man in the White House... The people need a man—an American—at the helm."[57]

Was not McKinley, a former governor of Ohio, a former congressman, and—for heaven's sake—a veteran of the bloodiest war in the nation's history, "an American?" Apparently, not to the war scribes. Not to be outdone, a competitor to *The New York Journal,* the *New York World,* joined the war cry, with an editorial on manhood that cut McKinley's measure: "There are manly and resolute ways of dealing with treachery and wrong. There are unmanly and irresolute ways."[58]

It is also worthwhile for us to note that the nation's press trumpeting war was in possession of no evidence whatsoever of Spanish involvement in the destruction of the *Maine.* Nor did it need any. It, like Roosevelt, needed a war. If there was treachery afoot, it wasn't from the Spanish. On 20 April 1898, McKinley capitulated and affixed the presidential signature and seal to the war resolution against Spain, and the deed was done. McKinley had to lie to himself. He framed the invasion as an attempt to help the Cuban people in their fight against Spanish tyranny. This same rationale would justify American wars, invasions, and occupations for generations to come. But in the spring of 1898, as the water broke on the birth of the American Empire, the Roosevelt dream and thirst for war became a reality. But without the unconditional collaboration of the war scribes, his plans would have gone for naught.

Within a few months, war would commence in Havana, and Roosevelt would have his splendid little war. But, more importantly to the press, Roosevelt's war sold millions of papers, amassing private fortunes for wealthy American publishing families, like Hearst, building castles high above the clouds over his San Simeon mountaintop on the central coast of California. The former Civil War general, Ulysses S. Grant, famously wrote that "war is hell"—but the press jumped headfirst into the bubbling cauldron, adding this observation, also equally true: "but it's great for business!"

An Immaculate Conception of the News

> *The guns of Dewey in Manila Bay were heard across Asia and Africa, they echoed through the palace at Peking and brought to the Oriental mind a new and potent voice among western nations.*[59]
>
> —U.S. Senator Chauncey DePew, Carnegie Hall, endorsing Theodore Roosevelt for Vice President, 1900

Once the Cuban invasion and occupation was well in hand, Washington turned their sights on one of Spain's other colonial outposts, the Philippine Islands. In fact, toppling Spain was relatively easy. It began with the Battle of Manila Bay on 1 May 1898. Commodore George Dewey destroyed the Spanish Pacific Squadron straightaway. Spanish rule ended three months later. "Recognizing the Filipino people as the real threat," writes Susan Brewer, professor of history at the University of Wisconsin, "the American command worked out a deal with the Spaniards to stage a mock battle,"[60] and this "battle" took place in Manila on 13 August 1898. Both sides agreed to shoot at each other "and then Spain would surrender before the Philippine Army of Liberation could take part."[61] With Spain out of the picture, the bloodshed began. No longer called the Spanish-American War, the new imperial transformation developed into the Philippine-American War.

History suggests that Washington powerbrokers along with their corporate partners were targeting U.S. world dominance through financial and market supremacy rather than employing direct government control over distant populations. The invasion and takeover of the Philippines was a dramatic first step, bolstered by the construction of the Panama Canal, which opened the shipping lanes through Central America, chasing the sun, as always, west, this time en route for all the tea in China.

But the American press failed to notice those little details, which amounts to the core essence and base motivation for America's imperial gallivanting throughout the Pacific. *That* is the story. All the rest—liberty, freedom, Christendom—nothing more than window dressing and public relations, but the press reported it as the gospel truth—and still do.

It didn't take long for the last Civil War veteran who would ever take up residence in the White House, to carry on—and with great zeal—the divine mission of America. McKinley looked to the far Pacific, to the natural resources and financial markets of Asia, as new pots of gold as well as a concurrent giant leap forward toward new imperial prominence. The Washington propaganda machine began chugging away. Roosevelt lit the fuse and then McKinley learned fast. "He compared the Filipinos to Native Americans," Brewer notes, "calling them savage warriors or 'little brown brothers.'" Brewer continues: "Appealing to popular attitudes of the times, he encouraged Americans to fulfill their manly duty to spread Christian civilization. The United States, he asserted, was a liberator, not a conqueror."[62]

When McKinley uttered "little brown brothers" to invoke the dehumanization that must happen to demonize "the Other," he was being presidential. But the soldiers under his command held no pretense of racial manners or gentle euphemisms. Political scientist Noel Kent writes that, "The U.S. military, a white supremacist outfit deeply conscious of its role as the vanguard of Anglo-Saxon superiority, was wholly contemptuous of Filipino 'goo-goos' and 'niggers'"[63]

And the press of the day, as expected, walked arm-in-arm with their government masters, laying the foundation for slaughter and war. The *Boston Herald* offered a prime example:

> Our troops in the field look upon the Filipinos as niggers and entitled to all the contempt and harsh treatment administered by white overlords to the most inferior races.[64]

Harper's Weekly published a story on Filipino soldiers killed by the Santa Cruz River, in which they wrote:

> They die the way a wild animal dies—in such a position as one finds a deer or an antelope which one has shot in the woods.[65]

Kent, a professor at the University of Hawaii (another land, along with Guam, that McKinley co-opted on his way to the Philippines), writes that, "There was a revealing tendency [in the press] to compare Filipinos to animals in the wild. Cartoonists portrayed them as monkey men and naked cannibals."[66]

Instead of recognizing that the Filipino people were struggling for their lives, for their own liberty and independence (something Americans are always pounding their chests about) against imperial western powers, first the Spanish and then the Americans, the press spun the false narrative that Washington was fighting a regrettable but just war—one that rightly wanted to achieve (what Twain mordantly called) "Benevolent Assimilation" for America's distant friend, those "little brown brothers." But the bottom-line lie was clear: these savages are incapable of governing themselves.

As the call for war in the Philippines intensified, McKinley and his administration seamlessly incorporated the pliable press of the day into their party line. The misinformation regarding a necessary war in the Philippines began flowing like fine wine. In fact, ramping up to sell the war, McKinley's staff ballooned from six individuals to eighty. They monitored hundreds of dailies from across America, keeping tabs on how Washington's war talk was being presented and how the message could be crafted and controlled. McKinley was also the first chief executive to employ a secretary to meet with the press every day "for a kind of family talk," recalled muckraking journalist Ida Tarbell. Susan Brewer adds that, "To make sure that reporters accurately conveyed the president's views, his staff issued press releases, timing the distribution so that reporters on deadline filed only the administration's version of the story."[67] Similar to what we witness today, it was an immaculate conception of "the news," one designed to manufacture consent. "Through news management, the McKinley administration disseminated war propaganda based on facts, lies, ideas, patriotic symbols, and emotional appeals,"[68] Brewer concludes.

Typical of the American government, their war scribes, as well as their guild historians, Washington officially declared the hostilities over in 1902—except Philippine resistance lasted another ten years, with the strongest resistance coming from the south, especially on the island of Mindanao. Official U.S. estimates report the casualties as 20,000 Filipino soldiers and approximately 300,000 Filipino civilians killed. It's not surprising that these numbers are low when compared to the Philippine-American War Centennial that calculated 510,000 civilian casualties. "Others have pegged 1,000,000 to 1,500,000 Filipino deaths during that period,"[69] writes Philippine journalist Alejandro Roces.

An ugly and incredibly high death toll, except, on the whole, it went unreported to the American population, and it took a great deal of time for the carnage to find its way into American history books. A few Americans at the time, like the Anti-Imperialist League and Mark Twain, were vociferous dissonance to the patriotic claptrap, but the vast majority of American voices rubber-stamped the company line that drifted back from Southeast Asia.

Four years after Washington claimed that the war was over, a brutal and bloody action on the island of Jolo in the southern Philippines was a precursor to future U.S. military slaughters and joins My Lai in Vietnam and Fallujah in Iraq in the annals of imperial massacres. On 10 March 1906, in the crater of a dormant volcano named Bud Dajo, U.S. Army Major General Leonard Wood led more than 500 American troops on their mission to attack a village of mostly unarmed Muslims, many of whom were women and children. U.S. command thought it was time to clear out the crater. The bombardment and firestorm started. One day later between six hundred and one thousand Filipinos were dead, killed like rats in a barrel. Three days later, TR sent Wood a congratulatory cable:

> I congratulate you and the officers and men of your command upon the brilliant feat of arms wherein you and they so well upheld the honor of the American flag. (Signed) Theodore Roosevelt.[70]

Twain, who remained one of the sane voices crying in the wilderness of American silence, fired back at Roosevelt:

> He knew perfectly well that our uniformed assassins had not upheld the honor of the American flag, but had done as they have been doing continuously for eight years in the Philippines—that is to say, they had dishonored it.[71]

Roll back the tape on Twain: "Uniformed assassins"—indeed, then as now.

Although *The New York Times* acknowledged the gravity of the situation in their headline which read, "WOMEN AND CHILDREN KILLED IN MORO BATTLE... PRESIDENT WIRES CONGRATULATIONS TO TROOPS," nevertheless the article neatly placed the blame for the massacre on the victims (a gambit that is often employed by the custodians of the Holy Grail). Their report out of Manila called the villagers "outlaws," "savages," and "head hunters." The *Times,* as well as Major General Wood's account, framed the killing as inevitable, suggesting that the savages used children as human shields and that the women dressed as men and that "it was impossible to discriminate." (Sound familiar?) The *Times'* story estimated very high casualties for the "savages" but never went into detail of the gore, except they spent a paragraph on First Lieutenant Gordon Johnston, who suffered a slug passing through his right shoulder while performing "a gallant deed." The *Times* concluded by reporting, "that general satisfaction is expressed over the extermination of the outlaws."[72]

Extermination.

Few media outlets or journalists ever go beneath their curatorial guardianship of the establishment's status quo. Rarely do they stand up to the monolith of power and truly buck the prescribed narrative, tendering an alternative account that questions authority, or wealth, our the sanctity of "our troops." Mark Twain did, and did so with fire pulsing through his veins. His ability to throw their language and horrific actions right back in their face, some call it speaking truth to power, is as remarkable to read now as when it was written more than one hundred years ago. His account is the type of journalism and context that the government and corporatocracy fears the most.

> A tribe of Moros, dark-skinned savages, had fortified themselves in the bowl of an extinct crater not many miles from Jolo; and as they were hostiles, and bitter against us because we have been trying for eight years to take their liberties away from them, their presence in that position was a menace.
>
> Our commander, Gen. Leonard Wood, ordered a reconnaissance. It was found that the Moros numbered six hundred, counting women and children; that their crater bowl was in the summit of a peak or mountain twenty-two hundred feet above sea level, and very difficult of access for Christian troops and artillery... Our troops climbed the heights by devious and difficult trails, and even took some artillery with them. The kind of artillery is not specified, but in one place it was hoisted up a sharp acclivity by tackle a distance of some three hundred feet... Our soldiers numbered five hundred and forty. They were assisted by auxiliaries consisting of a detachment of native constabulary in our pay... and by a naval detachment, whose numbers are not stated...
>
> Gen. Wood's order was, "Kill or capture the six hundred."
>
> The battle began—it is officially called by that name—our forces firing down into the crater with their artillery and their deadly small arms of precision; the savages furiously returning the fire, probably with brickbats—though this is merely a surmise of mine, as the weapons used by the savages are not nominated in the cablegram. Heretofore the Moros have used knives and clubs mainly; also, ineffectual trade-muskets when they had any.

> The official report stated that the battle was fought with prodigious energy on both sides during a day and a half, and that it ended with a complete victory for the American arms... The completeness of the victory is established by this fact: that of the six hundred Moros not one was left alive. The brilliancy of the victory is established by this other fact, to wit: that of our six hundred heroes only fifteen lost their lives.
>
> General Wood was present and looking on. His order had been. "Kill *or* capture those savages." Apparently our little army considered that the "or" left them authorized to kill *or* capture according to taste, and that their taste had remained what it has been for eight years, in our army out there—the taste of Christian butchers.[73]

Australian sociologist, Dr. Phillip Ablett, has studied and written extensively on the Philippines. His words underscore the unfortunate reality that unfolded in Southeast Asia at the turn of the 20th century. His words also underscore the same dangerous pattern that continues to exist between the U.S. government and its "free" press:

> The Philippine–American War, which led to the colonial subjugation of the Philippines by the United States for over forty years and the suppression of the first independent republic in South-East Asia, is one of America's forgotten wars. The historical amnesia surrounding this conflict is no accident. It is an enduring legacy of US government and military propaganda, widely disseminated by a largely supportive corporate press, which contributed in no small way to the American victory both at home and abroad.[74]

Lip Service

From 1880, John Swinton (former head of *The New York Times* editorial staff, speaking to his brethren) continues...

> ***There is no such thing, at this date of the world's history, in America, as an independent press. You know it and I know it. There is not one of you, who dares to write your honest opinions, and if you did, you know, beforehand, that it would never appear in print.***

Post-World War I, the American press, for the sake of bigger, more professional owners and staffs, began to give lip service to notions such as "objectivity" and "fairness." In point of fact, these are rather recent innovations, the better to sell ads to commercial entities, and thereby, the hawking of consumer goods to broad markets. Thus we should remember that this new innovation, of objectivity and fairness, was meant to increase circulations of a commercial product; to standardize staffs and editorships; to make the product more amenable to a growing social sector: an educated working and managerial class.

Professional societies began to emerge, purportedly to support and regulate this new codified press, but in truth, their impact on working members of the craft was and is negligible. Consider this: When have you last heard or read of a journalist called out or disciplined by such a body? You probably haven't, for journalists in America are neither licensed nor controlled by such agencies. They need only regard the whims of their bosses—the owners or high managers of their outlet. The rest is but window-dressing. Interestingly, and perhaps best seen in the realm of cable news, we are seeing a return to the sensational and often racist roots of American journalism. Witness the rise of Fox News and its commercial success. *Plus ça change...*

What's more, the post-World War I era of increased production and circulation changed the language utilized by elites when discussing the functions and role of the press, but its essential nature—that of a defender, not of the plebeians, but of the privileged—remained operative, an ally of state power and elite wealth.

In the wake of World War II, the once-rising colonial powers of England and France were left diminished, not only in scope and power, but in reputation and standing in the world—a world grown increasingly connected and self-aware. Aimé Césaire, the acclaimed poet and devoted Africanist, critiqued Europe's failures during the colonial period in the opening pages of *Discourse on Colonialism* (1955):

> Europe is indefensible. Apparently that is what the American strategists are whispering to each other. That in itself is not serious. What is serious is that "Europe" is morally, spiritually indefensible. And today the indictment is brought against it not by the European masses alone, but on a world scale, by tens and tens of millions of men who, from the depths of slavery, set themselves up as judges. The colonialists may kill in Indochina, torture in Madagascar, imprison in Black Africa, crackdown in the West

> Indies. Henceforth, the colonized know that they have an advantage over them. They know that their temporary "masters" are lying. Therefore, that their masters are weak.[75]

The U.S. entered into post-World War II affairs as allies of their weakened brethren, but also as a world power seeking its own manifest interests. The American media, which had heretofore been an overt voice of white supremacy—its right to rule by virtue of its whiteness—had to adopt a new line in light of the horrors of the Nazi regime's Draconian racism and fascism and the results of such ideology. Thus, open, overt, and clear white supremacist writings, which had dominated the American press for well over a century, had to transition to a more democratic, universalist, and less evident language—not only to attract the new, young, post-war generation of readers, but to present its best face to an immense dark world—Africa, Asia, and Latin America.

The American media switched easily, if only on the surface. It would also take up its new imperial mandate with relish by becoming the global megaphone of the State and the amplifier of democracy, of free trade, and something oddly undefined: Americanism.

Defiance

> *I don't want to be buried in this goddamned town.*
> – I.F. "Izzy" Stone on Washington D.C.

A ten-thousand-foot view of the American press, the history of it, is a classic archetype of the good, the bad, and the ugly, and sometimes the very ugly. Press freedom in the United States is still stronger than in most places on this third rock from the sun. And when you dig through the past and present, there are stacks of golden moments, instances when courageous journalists and their newspapers, as well as television news divisions, macheted their way through jungles of corruption and well-orchestrated misinformation, all the while navigating the dire straits of shark-infested waters. Recent fearless and crusading heroes, some unsung, include men and women like Cam Simpson from Bloomberg Businessweek who uncovered the iPhone 5 scandal in Malaysia when more than 1,300 migrants from Nepal were abandoned by Apple, left starving and destitute by the computer giant. Journalist and documentary filmmaker Laura Poitras, who was part of the team awarded the Pulitzer for Public Service for its reporting on the American surveillance state, went to hell and back with the NSA on her film *Citizenfour*—

brilliant investigative journalism revealing the nefarious narrative surrounding Edward Snowden and the NSA spying outrage. (The film won the 2015 Academy Award for Best Documentary Feature.)

Decades before, Australian journalist Wilfred Burchett decided that Hiroshima was where he needed to be just days after the city was turned into an atomic wasteland. Armed with his typewriter, some rations, and an old revolver, Burchett defied General Douglas MacArthur's orders barring the press and delivered the shocking front-page reality in London's *Daily Express* from inside the bowels of hell, out to the world, past American military gatekeepers and dark-shadowed bureaucrats who attempted to control every speck of information regarding the death, destruction, and radiation nightmare gripping the islands of Honshu and Kyushu. Of course, as is the custom, Washington condemned Burchett's revelations, accusing him of being in bed with Japanese agitprop. But no worry—the lapdog press embraced the U.S. cover-up regarding the horrors of radiation (what Burchett called "the atomic plague") and dutifully printed their bullshit coverage. *The New York Times* and their reporter William Laurence bought it (or *sold it* is more like it) with their bogus account of what actually went down—a reality defined as absolute annihilation. In fact their coverage amounted to nothing more than a murderer's bag of lies. The great irony? The "reporting" won William Laurence the Pulitzer Prize. The great almost unbelievable reality? William Laurence was on the payroll of both *The New York Times* and the War Department, writing releases for Truman and War Secretary Henry Stimson, all of it helping to "sell" the positive effects of atomic death and destruction.

Making the unthinkable normal.

But beyond these journalistic atrocities, it's clear that courage does exist and sometimes thrives: Bob Woodward and Carl Bernstein revealing Nixon's crooked presidency and massive Watergate cover-up; Hersh revealing the rape, carnage, and murder of the My Lai Massacre; John Pilger revealing the genocide in Cambodia at the hands of Pol Pot and the Khmer Rouge; documentary filmmaker Joe Berlinger revealing with his film, *Crude,* the "Amazon Chernobyl" at the hands of Chevron in Ecuador's Lago Agrio oil field; *The Boston Globe's* "Spotlight" team's exposé of widespread and systemic child sex abuse by numerous Roman Catholic priests in the Boston Archdiocese; and of course two classic 20th-century muckraking exposés—Upton Sinclair's quintessential 1906 novel revealing the exploitation of immigrants and the grotesque conditions in the meat packing industry; and

George Seldes' long battle with the tobacco industry and their distribution of "legalized poison."

"Advertising signs that con you"

In fact, there are scores of journalists throughout history and scores of journalists banging on laptops right now that have defied and still defy the echo chamber created and protected by the foundational forces of empire. But like a solitary man sent to the water's edge by his village elders to fend off a tidal wave, armed only with a large stick, the ocean will win, it will engulf and devour the chap whole. And so it is with courageous and crusading muckrakers: Lord we desperately need their scrap if we are to breathe free, but the game is so stacked against them, stacked against the truth (and therefore the people) by the elite financial wherewithal of the corporate-controlled airwaves and press outlets. This systemic force, a never-ending avalanche of government, corporate, and Wall Street aegis, remains as a seemingly immovable object.

For a number of reasons. First, the practical, as Swinton's continued denunciation illustrates:

> ***I am paid weekly for keeping any honest opinion, out of the paper, I am connected with. Others of you are paid weekly, similar salaries for similar things, and any of you, who would be so foolish, as to write honest opinions, would be out on the streets, looking for another job.***

One would have had to been living under a rock not to notice the massive consolidation of media companies into a concentrated few elite giants, and this elite cadre of mega-corporations firmly establishes the conceptual framework for what is and is not acceptable coverage. Because intertwined in this titanic battle between the free press and the free market we find giant media moguls selling ad space to aggressive companies who want to sell something—anything—to you, through their Madison Avenue pipedreams, "signs that con you into thinking you're the one, that can do what's never been done, that can win what's never been won, meantime life outside goes on all around you."[76]

Do you think CNN editors, answering to CNN executives, will broadcast raw video of a massacred child's entrails following a drone strike just before a BMW commercial? That's a tough act to follow. In fact when bottom-line fanaticism rules the day, as it now does, newsrooms and news divisions must be advertiser-friendly to survive shareholder venom. If a major multi-million dollar advertiser is concerned with potentially dangerous political coverage that could challenge the status quo and confront country club control, their threat to pull out advertising dollars will most assuredly influence coverage as well as editorial content.

~~Question Authority~~ Acquiescent to Authority

Another practical stranglehold on media freedom is the very real (and normal) career aspirations of journalists, or anyone on a professional path entering any system. "Journalists," Noam Chomsky writes, "are unlikely to make their way unless they conform to these ideological pressures, generally by internalizing the values; it is not easy to say one thing and believe another, and those who fail to conform will tend to be weeded out by familiar mechanisms."[77] Chomsky suggests that class and social status are the bloodline that bonds establishment elites and media elites together: "Those who occupy managerial positions in the media, or gain status within them as commentators, belong to the same privileged elites, and might be expected to share the perceptions, aspirations, and attitudes of their associates, reflecting their own class interests as well."[78]

What about message control and public relations, you ask? Corporations everywhere strategically control their public persona—and the United States government, a massive corporation, is no exception. Messaging is a combination of historical propaganda, known as American exceptionalism, that focuses on the traditional bedrock of liberty and justice for all, and current propaganda, known as all the news that's fit to print, news (read: PR) that has been well-crafted, first by the government itself, and then cemented as gospel by the aforementioned stenographers of power—the corporate media. We've cited here and we witness daily the breathtaking audacity with which the American government will spin, twist, and lie the unthinkable normal—and their pals in the press go along for the ride. Sure, they rub each other like sandpaper along the way, that's the game, but in the end, the mainstream media retains their *access to power* by being civil, amenable, and acquiescent to authority. Quid pro quo.

Imagine a reporter from ABC is granted a sit-down, Rose Garden interview with the president. Of course, beforehand, the White House and ABC run over some ground rules on questions, follow-ups, and talking points. Then during the interview, the journalist takes off the kid gloves and starts throwing bare-fisted hardball questions that everyone wants to ask but seldom if ever do. The kind of visceral inquiry that cuts to the blood and guts of war, the terrorism of class oppression, of poverty, of race, of lopsided heath care coverage, of asymmetrical educational standards, and then a bombshell about the destructive nature of predatory capitalism followed by a query regarding the corruption of Wall Street and robber barons owning this so-called democracy... this journalist would be dumped out on Pennsylvania Avenue in a heartbeat—and then knocked senseless. The closest he or she would ever get to the president again might be on the White House tour.

This never happens. You know why? Most folks don't like to commit career suicide. Civility ensures access, and access is the fodder for which each side yearns. Don't listen to Chomsky, or your authors, listen to Dan Rather, the ultimate mainstream journalist, discuss how the corporate media self-censors:

> There was a time in South Africa that people would put flaming tires around people's necks if they dissented, and in some ways the fear is that you will be necklaced here, you will have a flaming tire of lack of patriotism put around your neck. Now it is that fear that keeps journalists from asking the toughest of the tough questions, and to continue to bore in on the tough questions so often. And again, I am humbled to say, I do not except myself from this criticism.[79]

Homogenized Static

There's another very practical reason why this entrenched system persists. *The People.* For "the People" have been so boozed, bamboozled, and marginalized over time by the elite forces of power, that they are staggeringly unaware, uninformed, or badly informed regarding the myth and reality of their own history, which dictates and transforms their own present day. We interviewed the late Gore Vidal for this book series and asked him about "the People" abdicating their power and responsibility to the powerful, especially since the end of World War II. As always, Mr. Vidal did not mince words:

> We were doing so well people didn't pay attention to politics. But politicians paid attention to the people, how to get control of them, how to get them to buy things they didn't need, how to get them to buy junk. This was a glorious moment for noncreative capitalism and terrorist capitalism. Those in power set out to create a generation and then another generation. I've lived through two or three by now who are trained only by television and terrible

> public education. They're trained to be docile workers who do not question their masters in the shop, as well as eager consumers. That's all—that's all they're taught. Scratch an American's head and you'll find a jingle selling something because that's the first thing they learned as a child. Ask him who Benjamin Franklin was, he won't be able to tell you. And regardless, it's kind of an insult. I know all that stuff. And if I don't know it, it wasn't worth knowing, was it? Because now I have this wonderful, wonderful job at IBM.[80]

Why is Mr. Vidal an expert on the manipulation and domination of "the People?"

> Well, now, you know, I was brought up in the ruling class... and they hate the people. The Bush family, if you gave them Sodium Pentothal and asked them, "And what do you think about the American people?" You will hear such profanity as you've never heard before. The American people are an obstacle. The Constitution stuck us with all these elections... But they've now got the country they wanted.[81]

Not surprisingly, Noam Chomsky concurs. But he illustrates the control of "the People" with startling findings from a University of Massachusetts study during the Iraq invasion post-9/11:

> When you have total control over the media and the educational system and scholarship is conformist, you can get [the "official" government story] across. One indication of it was revealed in a study done at the University of Massachusetts on attitudes toward the current Gulf crisis—a study of beliefs and attitudes in television watching. One of the questions asked in that study was, "How many Vietnamese casualties would you estimate that there were during the Vietnam War?" The average response on the part of Americans today is about 100,000. The official figure is about two million. The actual figure is probably three to four million. The people who conducted the study raised an appropriate question: What would we think about German political culture if, when you asked people today how many Jews died in the Holocaust, they estimated about 300,000? What would that tell us about German political culture?[82]

Chomsky argues that this lack of grasping the truth by the American public is a truism across the board.

> Pick the topic you like: the Middle East, international terrorism, Central America, whatever it is—the picture of the world that's presented to the public has only the remotest relation to reality. The truth of the matter is buried under edifice after edifice of lies upon lies.[83]

The American Empire, along with their media constituents, has achieved incredible success at sustaining the façade of a staunchly independent and vigorous free press. And that's imperative for control of the masses in a society that feigns a vibrant Fourth Estate. The logic is inverted: an autocratic and repressive government can simply control their population and limit their involvement by coercion and brute force. They can freely rule with an iron fist. (Shut up. Whack... and then the upstart disappears for a short time. Or forever. At the very least, he or she will walk funny for some time.) But in a purportedly free and democratic country, containing the threat of mass involvement aimed at revolutionary change means constantly crafting the message, spinning the message when reality doesn't cooperate, and then finally controlling the message in every manner possible.

As the so-called "Reagan Revolution" unfolded in the early 1980s, ninety percent of American media outlets were owned and operated by some fifty companies (90%, 50 companies). Thirty years later, in 2011, six corporations controlled the same ninety percent (90%, 6 companies). In fact, the figures reveal that roughly 230 corporate executives controlled the information choices for almost 280 million Americans. The total revenue for these six companies was just north of $275 billion.[84] By 2019, the six were shaved down to five—the big five giant conglomerates are all household names: Disney, Comcast (via NBCUniversal), Viacom & CBS (both controlled by National Amusements), and AT&T (via WarnerMedia). As well, since the mid-1990s, "four companies have been devouring local TV stations across the United States," reports BillMoyers.com—and these four companies are "using shell companies to dodge the federal ownership rules, consolidate their power and wipe out their competitors." The four companies leading this local buying frenzy: U.S. Gannett, Nexstar, Sinclair, and Tribune. The report continues, noting that, "In many communities, one company controls two, three and even four stations and airs the same news programming on all of these outlets."[85]

Real Time host Bill Maher discussed the same media consolidation narrative with ex-CBS anchor Dan Rather:

BILL MAHER
Corporations have a political agenda. They're anti-regulation, they're anti-tax, they're anti-labor—in that same period, we have seen regulations diminish, taxes go down, union membership go down. Is that a coincidence?

DAN RATHER
No, it's not a coincidence... These large corporations, they have things they need from the power structure in Washington, whether it's Republican or Democrat, and of course the people in Washington have things they want... To put it bluntly, very big business is in bed with very big government in Washington, and [that] has more to do with what the average person sees, hears, and reads than most people know.[86]

Bottom line: there's an extraordinary amount of information shooting off satellite dishes and lighting up electronic gadgetry everywhere, but—and this is a big one—it amounts to homogenized static, giving the illusion of choice.

"Access of Evil"

The quotation marks belong to Amy and David Goodman and the sentiment remains one of the great "coinings of a phrase" in journalistic history. They use it to define the everyday practice by establishment scribes to trade everything in their journalistic arsenal for access. "I am not a fan of partying with the powerful," Amy Goodman explains. "We shouldn't be sipping champagne with Henry Kissinger, Richard Holbrooke, and Donald Rumsfeld. We should be holding those in power accountable."[87]

But that is clearly not taking place in newsrooms in New York, or D.C., or Los Angeles, or anywhere in the mainstream sphere. As discussed, there are, of course, exceptions. The late Helen Thomas is a notable aberration. With any model or standard there are always exceptions. Of course some dissenting voices hurdle the castle walls, but the essence and drive of reportage, the headlines and narratives on the front page reiterate and bolster the Corporation's modus operandi.

If the mainstream media wasn't the royal megaphone, those in the halls of power could never get away with their ongoing corrupt behavior: using other people's children as cannon fodder for endless wars of capital, pushing the species to the brink of nuclear annihilation, and the final suicidal move—destroying the planet's ecosystem for short-term bushels of cash.

But ultimately, for the moneyed press, it's about "playing ball" with those in power. "Access" to the "club" keeps the political theatre revving forward. "Access" is everything. One may ask: "C'mon, the media is everywhere, they're downright ubiquitous. Millions of papers are printed everyday, thousands of web pages launched, 24-hour cable shows pumping news endlessly, reporters running into battle, shoving microphones in power's face... How can you say they aren't covering the stories, questioning authority?"

The boldfaced answer exists when you step outside the aforementioned echo chamber and its concomitant hall of mirrors. The answer exists in a vacuum of what's *not* said, what's *not* defined, what's *not* challenged. "The lie of omission is still a lie," writes veteran reporter Chris Hedges, who has experienced the monster from inside and out. "It is what these news celebrities do not mention that exposes their complicity with corporate power."[88] Reporters and anchors are all reading from the same playbook, one that never questions or challenges the overarching corporate state. They fiddle with surface trifles between ruling factions, or the ever handy sensational, lurid, and melodramatic. It's the silage that fuels the necessary deflection from questioning the genuine precepts and dogma of power. Hedges frames the political theatre:

> The celebrity trolls who currently reign on commercial television, who bill themselves as liberal or conservative, read from the same corporate script. They spin the same court gossip. They ignore what the corporate state wants ignored. They champion what the corporate state wants championed. They do not challenge or acknowledge the structures of corporate power.[89]

In the myth of the "Fourth Estate," the media is said to function as a public trust, diligently standing watch over the police, the military, the intelligence apparatus, elected officials, as well as their corporate masters to ensure that lies are exposed and corruption is revealed, leading to just punishment—a deterrent to those who might one day also embrace the dark side. In the final analysis, the myth of the "Fourth Estate" offers this fundamental and essential commandment: it gives a powerful voice and check to the masses that, without this defense, would have no voice and no recourse against the onslaught of abuse. But journalists cozying up to power and trading their trump cards for an all-access pass nullifies and reverses the myth. Rather than being the voice of the voiceless, and a compelling and prevailing check on unbridled power, they become the amplifier of power.

Hedges describes the descent into journalistic nihilism:

> Their role is to funnel viewer energy back into our dead political system—to make us believe that Democrats or Republicans are not corporate pawns. The cable shows, whose hyperbolic hosts work to make us afraid of self-identified liberals or self-identified conservatives, are part of a rigged political system, one in which it is impossible to vote against the interests of Goldman Sachs, Bank of America, General Electric or ExxonMobil.[90]

A 1999 conversation between former CNN Vice President Frank Sesno and Amy Goodman sums up the sellout nature of America's so-called voice of the voiceless. At the Overseas Press Club banquet, Goodman asks Sesno about CNN's willingness to put U.S. generals on their payroll:

> GOODMAN:
> You can get the Pentagon's point of view for free. Why pay these generals? And have you ever considered putting peace activists on the payroll? Or just inviting them over to the studio to respond to the drumbeat for war?
>
> SESNO
> We've talked about this. But no, we wouldn't do that. Because generals are analysts, and peace activists are advocates.

("I need an analyst to analyze that one," writes Goodman.)

> GOODMAN
> Would you consider interviewing an antiwar scholar like Noam Chomsky?
>
> SESNO
> No. I don't personally know him.[91]

This brief conversation means one of two things: the Frank Sesno-like media rulers are morons, or they're public relations mad men shilling for power, trading their souls for access to the club. We vote for the latter.

CIA: *Communications Industry of America?*

Controlling media influence isn't just a domestic activity for state power. Post World War II, as the U.S. embarked on its globalist, corporatist, Americanization agenda, the American press marched in lockstep with their government cronies, by defining allies and enemies both at home and abroad. Its theme was Americanism and, with the rise of the Soviet Union, it had an enemy: Communism. This despite the fact that the Soviet Union had borne the brunt of the fight against Germany in the war, losing some *twenty million* lives. By contrast, the U.S. lost approximately 400,000—about a third of which were other than combat deaths.[92] Nevertheless, they were the enemy and the American media would happily transpose its once-blatant racism for blatant red-baiting.

It is axiomatic that the essence of a free press isn't merely who owns it, but that the State has little, if any, control over what's reported, printed, broadcast, or aired. While that claim appeared to govern media relations at home (more in myth than in reality) there wasn't even a pretext of such a relationship with media abroad. For that nefarious government agency (chronicled in damning detail in book two of this series), which rose from the fiery cinders of WWII, so committed to stemming the tide of communism, was also poised to get in on the media game. And this was no dalliance. At its peak, the CIA would be operating as a global media institution with the express purpose of controlling American interests abroad through the manipulation of public information.

While the average American might envision the CIA through the lens of spy novels, movies, or television shows, the educated reader will know at least something of the meddling and murdering history of the agency's actual record. What is less known is that the CIA has also been a remarkable publisher of newspapers, magazines, radio programming, and television shows—mostly abroad. This feature of its immense funding, reach, and power has allowed it to utilize information dissemination and control, and to wage war on the minds of the target populace. Albeit unknown by most, this range of its extralegal authority may be the arena of CIA activity that has had the largest impact on the largest audience.

Former foreign service officer turned CIA muckraker, William Blum, has written for decades about the foibles and felonies of the Agency abroad. His writing has provided readers the world over with chapter and verse of the crimes committed by the CIA: the murders, the assassinations, the removals, the purchasing of politicians in every major (and quite a few minor) capitals, the buying off of generals, and the tortures—not to mention the torture-trainings.

In his celebrated book, *Killing Hope,* Blum illustrates how U.S. money in CIA hands paid off the press in other countries to present its chosen perspectives to unsuspecting readers:

> A more direct American intervention into the 1976 [Italian] elections was in the form of propaganda. Inasmuch as political advertising is not allowed on Italian television, the US Ambassador to Switzerland, Nathaniel Davis, arranged for the purchase of large blocks of time on Monte Carlo TV to present a daily "news" commentary by the editorial staff of the Milan newspaper *Il Giornale Nuovo,* which was closely associated with the CIA. It was the newspaper that, in May 1981, set in motion that particular piece of international disinformation known as "The KGB Plot to Kill the Pope."
>
> Another Italian newspaper, the *Daily American* of Rome, for decades the country's leading English-language paper, was for a long period in the 1950s to the '70s partly owned and/or managed by the CIA. "We 'had' at least one newspaper in every foreign capital at any given time," the CIA admitted in 1977, referring to papers owned outright or heavily subsidized, or infiltrated sufficiently to have stories printed which were useful to the Agency or suppress those it found detrimental.[93]

Notice that the Agency said, "at least one" newspaper. The CIA, which has carte blanche to lie even to Congress had, according to Blum, a great deal more than that in its pocket. Blum reports that the CIA was effectively a global communications company—correction—a closeted global communications *industry.* In his chapter on mid-20th century Western Europe, he notes:

> The principal front organization set up by the CIA in this period was the grandly named Congress for Cultural Freedom (CCF). In June 1950, prominent literati and scientists of the United States and Europe assembled in the Titiana Palace Theatre, in the American Zone of Berlin, before a large audience to launch the organization whose purpose was to "defend freedom and democracy against the new tyranny sweeping the world." The CCF was soon reaching out in all directions with seminars, conferences, and a wide program of political and cultural activities in Western Europe as well as India,

Australia, Japan, Africa and elsewhere. It had, moreover, more than 30 periodicals under its financial wing, including, in Europe:

> *Socialist Commentary, Censorship, Science and Freedom, Minerva, Soviet Survey* (or *Survey), China Quarterly,* and *Encounter* in Great Britain; *Preuves, Censure Contre les Artes et la Pensée, Mundo Nuevo,* and *Cuadernos* in France (the last two in Spanish, aimed at Latin America); *Perspektiv* in Denmark, *Argumenten* in Sweden, *Irodalmi Ujsag* in Hungary, *Der Monat* in Germany, *Forum* in Austria, *Tempo Presente* in Italy, and *Vision* in Switzerland.

There were as well CCF links to *The New Leader, Africa Report, East Europe* and *Atlas* in New York.

Generally, the CCF periodicals were well-written political and cultural magazines which, in the words of former CIA executive Ray Cline, "would not have been able to survive financially without CIA funds."[94]

That a nation claiming constitutional fealty to the fundamental notion of free press could essentially subsidize, produce, and distribute press to much of the world attests to the very emptiness of that claim. Examples such as these show us that, for the CIA, the press was little more than an instrument of state, a mechanism to manipulate the illusion of "public opinion." Remember: this is the work of the government that brayed incessantly about the First Amendment and a "free press." There is an old axiom: "Freedom of the press belongs only to he who owns one." Well, perhaps there's a kind of truth in that adage (except the "free" part), for the CIA. They bought it. They owned it. And when a country dared to try to rise up a working-class challenge to the rule of capital, the U.S. government and their CIA henchmen had a ready rejoinder: Purchase foreign media properties and control content by using the newly-bought acquisition to change minds. While preaching democracy, they were liberally buying off and corrupting foreign governments with wild abandon.

By means such as these, the U.S. government created, sustained, and projected American myths of freedom, democracy, and fair dealing, while in fact they were undermining these principles daily by their manipulative activities in foreign countries (not to mention inside their own country).

Blum's informed reporting reveals that the CIA was, in some ways, a more subversive international communications network than a traditional spy agency—all to smear their opponents in the world trade union and labor union movements, or to create a bright, shining, "city on a hill" image of America through the subversion of the world's media outlets. It reveals, in a sense, Washington's fear and insecurity in letting people abroad think their own thoughts, or write their own papers, magazines, and books. The fear of a functioning socialist alternative compelled them to work on a global scale to insure that a working class analysis would not turn the heads of the people of the world.

Policing Dissent

While the CIA pursued its Cold War media manipulations abroad, the American corporate media followed lockstep as a flood of press brought about the post-war Red Scare. Indeed, the press didn't merely report from a fundamentally corporatist slant. It served as a trusted corporate soldier in the great Cold War, playing a powerful and pivotal role in policing dissent in opposition to the Empire. When people dared to say "No!" to war, "No!" to segregation, or most importantly, "No!" to imperial occupation, the media fulfilled its class roles to isolate, ridicule, and slander such figures for daring to dissent—de Toqueville's critique of early America still very much alive and kicking.

How the government has policed dissent in America remains a story largely untold, at least to a mainstream audience. This is largely due to the role of the formal and informal media, for these entities performed a crucial role in the demonization of dissent, for they, by their pro-government slant, helped project the portrayals that served their statist narrative: that dissenters were and are somehow "un-American" for their opposition to the government's actions, both domestically and abroad. As evidenced by hard-boiled historical fact, the nation's federal police were more than just a force chasing counterfeiters, Mafia chieftains, and rogue interstate commerce. They assumed the tactical role of political and race police (thanks in large part to that pillar of American justice, J. Edgar Hoover). State agencies around the country saw as their central duty the protection of white supremacy—and this was true whether one lived and worked in the north or the south.

As de Tocqueville has pointed out, the media prefers "moderate" voices, those that are malleable and not too strident—especially when it comes to Black leaders. But speak outside those "barriers to the liberty of opinions" and the hounds come bearing down. Such a scenario is particularly relevant in the case of Dr. Martin Luther King, Jr., for, if he began his public life as a "moderate" and "responsible" Black leader, his latter years took him along quite a different trajectory, one of radical opposition to the American Empire's triple-headed monster of militarism, capitalism, and racism, one which opened the trap doors of repression and heightened state enmity. But, King didn't just stagnate. He felt compelled to speak out against that which was burning within him—the war in Vietnam, its wild destruction, its mass liquidation of hundreds of thousands of Vietnamese peasants. On 4 April 1967, he took a script worked by the late Rev. Dr. Vincent Harding and delivered it at New York's posh Riverside Church. It was a speech that would mark a turning point in his already storied life. He rose to the ornate pulpit of a church erected by the seemingly endless wealth of the Rockefellers. And then he spoke:

> I come to this magnificent house of worship tonight because my conscience leaves me no other choice. I join you in this meeting because I am in deepest agreement with the aims and work of the organization which has brought us together, Clergy and Laymen Concerned About Vietnam. The recent statements of your executive committee are the sentiments of my own heart, and I found myself in full accord when I read its opening lines: "A time comes when silence is betrayal." That time has come for us in relation to Vietnam.[95]

His polite greeting and generous attribution delivered, he launched into the heart of this brief, yet earth-shaking speech. He said he had been silent in the past, but could be silent no more. He recalled trying to counsel young men in the ghettos, armed with rifles and Molotov cocktails, as he spoke against violence. They silenced him with a question: "What about Vietnam?" they asked. He had no answer for them.

> Their questions hit home, and I knew that I could never again raise my voice against the violence of the oppressed in the ghettos without having first spoken clearly to the greatest purveyor of violence in the world today: my own government.[96]

King's words that day at Riverside Church radiated far and wide beyond the rich marble and ornate altar of this "magnificent house of worship" in New York City. It reached the White House, where a shocked American president, Lyndon Baines

Johnson, felt betrayed and angered by the oration. It reached Wall Street, the nation's home of the "profit motives" and "property." It careened across newsrooms from coast to coast and lit tempers of rage and umbrage. It even echoed among leaders and the passionate in his own Movement, and many—far too many—left him in this lonely hour of righteous need.

And how did the national press react to this performance of prophetic courage, love of man, and heroic call for justice? *The Washington Post* opined that King's words were "sheer fantasy," and "not a sober and responsible comment on the war," but rather "filled with bitter and damaging allegations and inferences that he did not and could not document."[97] The paper's editors went further, with the *Post* declaring that King:

> has done a grave injury to those who are natural allies... and even graver injury to himself. Many who have listened to him with respect will never again accord him the same confidence. He has diminished his usefulness to his cause, to his country and to his people. And that is a great tragedy.[98]

The august State Scribe, *The New York Times,* echoed its brother paper from Washington and rebuked King for "recklessly comparing American military methods to those of the Nazis."[99] Even the Black press was in professional lockstep, as evinced by the *Pittsburgh Courier,* which wrote that Dr. King was "tragically misleading" Black people on matters that were "too complex for simple debate."[100]

Life magazine lamented that King dared go "beyond his personal right to dissent when he connects progress in civil rights here with a proposal that amounts to abject surrender in Vietnam." Then this bare-knuckle punch, calling King's words "demagogic slander that sounded like a script for Radio Hanoi," adding that the civil rights leader "comes close to betraying the cause for which he has worked so long."[101]

His fellow civil rights leaders either hunkered down ("no comment") or outright attacked him. Whitney Young, leader of the National Urban League, and Roy Wilkins, head of the NAACP, disassociated themselves from him.

As is the norm, and reacting on cue, the petulant press was right there, obediently doing the Empire's head-hunting, flogging, and whipping the man they now love to lionize. And their hostility remained vigilant until Martin stepped out onto the balcony of Room 306 at the Lorraine Motel in Memphis a year later.

✓ **Facts Don't Matter**
✓ **Attack the Messenger**
✓ **Media Moguls Decide Who Tells the Story**
✓ **Regurgitate Government Claims**

> *All successful newspapers are ceaselessly querulous and bellicose. They never defend anyone or anything if they can help it; if the job is forced on them, they tackle it by denouncing someone or something else.*
> —H.L. Mencken

> *The press also has a role to play, one that, so far, it has largely ignored. That role is to report on and investigate the whistleblower's revelations of illegality, not on the kind of car he drives, the brand of eyeglasses he wears, where he went to college, or what his next-door neighbor has to say about their childhood.*
> —John Kiriakou (Former CIA analyst and whistleblower)

> *I knew when I began reporting the [NSA] story, that the technique that the U.S. government uses—and its media allies use—against anybody who discloses what they're doing in the dark is to distract attention away from the contents of the revelations.*
> —Glenn Greenwald

Independent journalist Glenn Greenwald could just have easily been referring to the behavior of the press in King's day as he was regarding the media's attacks on his own character as well as the character of NSA whistleblower Edward Snowden, whom Greenwald has covered extensively. When Julian Assange and WikiLeaks released an avalanche of documents revealing the illegal and immoral behavior of the U.S. government and military, the media didn't take the revelations and go all-out hard at the perpetrators, they didn't grab hammer and tongs and hold Washington's feet to the fire, they didn't fly the malfeasance to the top of the flagpole so the American people could hold the guilty parties accountable—*no, they attacked Assange.* From the summit of Mount Parnassus, they questioned Assange's veracity and his credentials as a journalist: "Who the hell are you to expose this story? You're not with *The Times, The Post,* or *CBS Evening News.* You're just an Australian with a goddamn website!" They didn't back up their brethren, a fellow journalist. Instead they marginalized his ability to deliver the truth (that is *your right to know the truth).* They attacked WikiLeaks' release of the so-called stolen documents (documents, by the way, that belong to the American people) as endangering "national security," when in reality what has endangered national security is the imperial hubris revealed in the documentation. This vital information, like the Pentagon Papers a generation earlier, reveals a narrative detailing what the American government is doing in the name—and with the funding—of the American people.

Character assassination is another popular tool used by both government and media. See Secretary of State (and famous discarder of his Vietnam medals) John Kerry ferociously calling Ed Snowden "a traitor" and "a coward," followed by the media obediently running hog wild with the story. Smear attempts are also very effective, like the *New York Daily News* "breaking" a homophobic hatchet job on Glenn Greenwald and his past representation (when then a lawyer) of a gay porn company. Or NBC mouthpiece David Gregory asking Greenwald on the air if he should be prosecuted for "aiding and abetting" Snowden. Greenwald fired back:

> I think it's pretty extraordinary that anybody who would call themselves a journalist would publicly muse about whether or not other journalists should be charged with felonies.

Would Gregory pose the same question to a reporter from *The New York Times,* CNN, or his own network at the time if they broke an international bombshell based on classified information handed over by a source? Again, it's the corporate media deciding who's a credible journalist and who's not. "Who are these people to decide who's a journalist and who isn't?" writes *Rolling Stone's* chief political reporter Matt Taibbi. "Is there anything more obnoxious than a priesthood?"

If we are to extend Gregory's argument, then every investigative journalist who works with inside sources who supply information should also be threatened with prosecution. That's a truly chilling proposition. The fact that mainstream internuncio "journalists" like Gregory even entertain the thought is proof-positive of the unholy alliance between government and media. In an interview with one of your authors, former United States Senator, Jim Abourezk, summed up the diversion this way:

> That's of course the way of the establishment to shut people down—government and the press. You accuse them of criminal activities, of treason. You ridicule dissent. It's an old and very effective game, one that's alive and well in this country.[102]

To the truly courageous and intrepid reporters who do work within this mainstream media paradigm, facts matter. Revealing illegal and immoral behavior is at the heart of their motivation. But the problem—and it's a massive one—is two-fold: first of all, these bold reporters are a small minority, battling against systemic forces dedicated to preserving the status quo (and their jobs), and secondly, when heavy duty facts and stories climb the ladder in American newsrooms, they inevitably reach the editors—sentinels for the political wing of the corporation. Similar to the U.S. Justice Department where you might find crusading lawyers ready to prosecute Wall Street pigs, and BAM—they hit a wall and this wall is the political firing squad, ensuring safe passage for white collar criminals.

In the end, when it counts, facts simply don't matter. But lunch does, as explained by Daniel Ellsberg:

> There are two types of courage involved with what I did. When it comes to picking up a rifle, millions of people are capable of doing that, as we see in Iraq or Vietnam. But when it comes to risking their careers, or risking being invited to lunch by the establishment, it turns out that's remarkably rare.

Behind the Looking Glass: Independent Journalism & New Media

John Swinton concludes:

> ***We are all tools and vassals of rich men, behind the scenes. We are the jumping jacks, they pull the strings and we dance. Our talents, our possibilities, and our lives are all the property of other men. We are intellectual prostitutes.***

We have wondered and indeed speculated on the performance and proclivities of the media. Whom do they serve? The powerful? Or the powerless? But we have not fully identified the depth of what is arguably the root problem, or as the old saying goes—the root of all evil.

Howard Zinn suggested that for just one moment we suppose that all restrictions on free speech and press freedom have been magically eliminated—Supreme Court limitations on the absoluteness of the First Amendment, cops cracking down on free expression, FBI and NSA secret surveillance—all of it gone with the wind. Now, with the shackles smashed, citizens could communicate and make known whatever they want and without fear or consequence. Sounds promising, but here's the glitch—and it's a life or death glitch: As ordinary and caring citizens, how far and wide will our message travel? Fifty people? Five hundred? Or what about ten million? Or more? The answer, of course, is obvious: how much money and resources are available? Zinn elaborates:

> [F]reedom of speech is not simply a yes or no question. It is also a "how much" question. And how much freedom we have depends on how much money we have, what power we have, and what resources we have for reaching large numbers of people. A poor person, however smart, however eloquent, truly has very little freedom of speech. A rich corporation has a great deal of it.[103]

In times of deep distrust of the corporate media, individuals take the leap to create their own media—free of the servility of their corporate cousins. This happened on a grand scale during the 1960s. As antiwar sentiment raged among the nation's youth, Black youth, tired of the Arctic rate of progress seen by the Civil Rights Movement, began shaping their own movement: the Black Liberation Movement, inspired by the martyred Malcolm X, and, as was he, uncompromising and outspoken in their militant rejection of the White Nation. These two social forces swelled and (at least psychologically) sustained each other, until it could be said that a community of interests was beginning to form amongst activist sectors of the young. This kind of community of resistance became the undergirding for the development, production, and support for an alternative press that used hyperbole, ribald humor, and irreverence to sell their new, hip publications.

In cities across the country, alternative papers blossomed into being, with a voice that seemed to resonate with young people tired of the rigors and rigidity of the straight-laced '50s ethos. Papers like *Fed Up* (Tacoma, Washington), *About Face* (Los Angeles), *Last Harass* (Fort Gordon, Georgia), and *Helping Hand* (Mountain Home Air Base, Idaho) appeared on military bases across the country. By 1970, some fifty alternative newspapers circulated among military folk. This mirrored what was happening in the world outside. Papers like *The Berkeley Barb* peppered politicians and the square press in northern California. Philadelphia had its *Drummer,* and the Liberation News Service became a national replacement news service to feed this growing appetite for news from the bottom up. The Black Panther Party published its own weekly, *The Black Panther,* by a committed and motivated staff of high-school dropouts, college dropouts, and Vietnam vets—writing with a bite and sass that was provocative. This journal sold into the hundreds of thousands across the country. *Muhammad Speaks* (a paper founded by Malcolm X) joined this voice as hawkers sold them on the street corners and in Nation of Islam restaurants and businesses. (One of your authors, the white one, remembers taking a lot of flak and hostility for daring to dig *Muhammad Speaks.)* These forms of media were, in a sense, reflections of relief from the mono-cultural, monochromatic news of the turbulent decade.

In the South, activists involved with the Freedom Rides produced a number of newsletters and papers (often made by mimeograph machines) to give voice not only to their movements, but also to the community, and sometimes, the children learning literacy in Freedom Schools. These journals (delightfully referred to as "freedom papers") were published intermittently, and distributed by various nonconventional means (newsboys often refused to sell them), but they provided a window into the curriculum of their schools, offering pieces about Black and African history, and opportunities to write for some of the children.[104] For once, during the entire sad saga of the 20th century, Americans of all stripes had access to a Free Press—they just had to make their own.

Fast forward and enter a new world—one of cyberspace, blogs and vlogs, podcasts, social media platforms galore, indie-media centers, documentary filmmakers, as well as other grassroots media cooperatives and choices offering the body politic a vast new set of eyes to help see and understand their country and the world. Within a surprisingly swift turn of years, a New Media has emerged—one with some ties to the Old Media, to be sure, but also one with a fierce freshness. Irreverent, youthful, informed, and technologically advanced over the mass industrial models. Gone is the bulk distribution of paper products, and in its place, light-signals sent at warp speed across nations and hemispheres. And while we who study history are accustomed to new technologies perceived and projected as threats to the old, this time, the exchange seems to possess a ring of truth. This is partly because this new medium transcended space and time limits of the old technology—for this virtual reality is malleable and theoretically limitless. Not only does this new form reach readers effortlessly, but it produces quantities of material that previously could not have been published and distributed in hyper-speed. This new medium creates new journalists—citizen-journalists—who write without editor or state sanction and disseminate information around the traditional gates of information gathering.

This structural shift in how we communicate has the potential to truly democratize the media playing field and offers new doors encompassing more populist points of view. Narratives and exposés are generated and told by voices considered "below" the traditional elite media outlets perched on pedestals—stories crafted by independent journalists (as well as citizens themselves) and told through the reality of whistleblowers, dissidents, activists, poets, artists, and the all-important victims trampled under the heavy foot of empire and corporate misconduct. And this is exactly why corporate and government power brokers desperately want to control the flow of media, and they especially want to assume control and command of the Internet. It's why the idea of continued "net neutrality" jolts the hell out of them. As the 21st century rolls on, the fight to decentralize control of the media paradigm, one that allows for a host of grassroots voices and articulations flowing freely, will be titanic. Remember, power concedes nothing. Corporate and government gatekeepers will dig in hard before they concede to a more fluid and flourishing independent media equaling a stronger democracy.

The first utterance these dinosaurs in the mainstream will shriek (to the cadence of "the Russians are coming") is "ADVOCACY JOURNALISM! ADVOCACY JOURNALISM!" This outright folly on their part is based on some enchanted folklore about journalistic impartiality. Matt Taibbi asserts that objectivity "is a fairy tale invented purely for the consumption of the credulous public, sort of like the Santa Claus myth." Hunter S. Thompson once quipped to one of your authors: "The only objectivity in journalism are baseball box scores, and even those things don't tell the whole savage truth." Taibbi emphasizes the point:

> *All* journalism is advocacy journalism. No matter how it's presented, every report by every reporter advances someone's point of view. The advocacy can be hidden, as it is in the monotone narration of a news anchor for a big network like CBS or NBC (where the biases of advertisers and corporate backers like GE are disguised in a thousand subtle ways), or it can be out in the open, as it proudly is with [Glenn] Greenwald... or institutionally with a company like Fox. But to pretend there's such a thing as journalism without advocacy is just silly; nobody in this business really takes that concept seriously.[105]

In fact, Taibbi argues that corporate news organizations are "always" passionately caught up in their reporting. "Just ask the citizens of Iraq," Taibbi argues, "who wouldn't have spent the last decade in a war zone had every TV network in

America not credulously cheered the White House on when it blundered and bombed its way into Baghdad on bogus WMD claims."[106]

Independent, alternative, or new media can take on many forms. Flourishing technologies have enabled journalists in the mainstream to break free from the ties that bind, strike out on their own and report on issues without the filter of a corporate overlord or political buddy system. The dramatic results continue to bolster free speech by offering tributaries around the lies, distortion, noise, and overt omissions that distort and disguise what is actually going on—aka the truth.

"Citizen media" (sometimes referred to as "participatory media") is another powerful alternative. These are stories covered and produced by individual citizens and distributed online as well as on community radio and television stations. Clemencia Rodriguez is a professor at Temple University (before that the University of Oklahoma) and a well-known scholar when it comes to models of media. She coined the term "citizen media," and her scholarship and advocacy has significantly pushed the boulder up the hill. "I could see how producing alternative media messages implies much more than simply challenging the mainstream media," she explains. "It implies having the opportunity to create one's own images of self and environment; it implies being able to recodify one's own identity with the signs and codes that one chooses, thereby disrupting the traditional acceptance of those imposed by outside sources."[107] Moreover, stories and media generated by independent sources tend not to be as influenced by national boundaries as are corporate-owned and -operated news entities.

In September of 2011, in the dark shadows of Wall Street, the Occupy Movement burst onto the scene in New York's Zuccotti Park. Initial grassroots victories over corporate attempts (by AT&T) to significantly weaken net neutrality were celebrated at the same time. Both movements challenged conventional wisdom that ordinary people can't brave the corporate stranglehold. The same profound hopelessness exists when the masses believe they can't hold their government accountable. But we are witnessing cracks in what seemed to be an impenetrable citadel. Simply consider the Arab Spring that burst forth in late 2010. Pierre Omidyar did. He's the founder and chairman of eBay:

> I believe that social media is a tool of liberation and empowerment. That may seem fairly audacious when a good portion of the Western world is using Facebook and Twitter to post pictures of what they had for dinner or take quizzes on what TV character they

> may be. But the freedom to communicate openly and honestly is not something to be taken for granted. In countries where traditional media is a tool of control, these new and truly social channels have the power to radically alter our world.[108]

Omidyar is quick to point out that social media, as a global tool to spread news and organizational capability, is in its infancy. "We're in the days of Alexander Graham Bell talking to his assistant Watson across a rudimentary wire," Omidyar contends. "Once we truly learn how to harness this new technology and these new ways of communicating, we will feel the full impacts of social media."[109]

There are numerous "things" governments fear. Near the top of the list are the masses out in droves, in the streets, protesting and demanding change. Controlling the tools that can potentially support mass movements is essential to all governments, whether they're open and supposedly democratic or outright totalitarian—hence the governmental coziness with the massive mainstream media complex as well as the grumblings and grappling with net neutrality, social media, and independent media that are all growing beyond their traditional control. "What the government fails to realize is that people will not stop communicating," writes Omidyar. "They will always find new ways to do so. The power of truth and the reach of social networks can be a threatening combination for those with something to hide."[110]

As we've seen, the corporate news media perpetuates long-established and habitual elite power structures. Together, they share vast economic and ideological ground. They have long been an instrument of empire. New media archetypes challenge this essential control and offer a community discourse that focuses on voices and points of view usually ignored or silenced by the mainstream. These are voices that are counterintuitive to the imperial and authoritative gospel churned out by the corporatocracy that historically (and efficiently) manufactures consent.

Cup of Joe

Some have made the historical connection between a robust alternative media fueled by rapid-fire Internet distribution and the vigorous, full-bodied interactions of the 17th and 18th century coffeehouses that populated Europe. In fact, these coffeehouses—and there were hundreds—offered scientists, writers, politicians, and businessmen a forum for the exchange of ideas and thoughts that energized their interactions. "Collectively," writes *The Economist,* "Europe's interconnected web of coffee-houses formed the internet of the Enlightenment era."[111] This connection through coffeehouses became very influential in the scientific and business worlds, as well as with literary figures, but it was "their potential as centres of political dissent" that grabbed the government's attention. In 1675, England's Charles II officially proclaimed that coffeehouses fostered "Malitious and Scandalous Reports… devised and spread abroad, to the Defamation of His Majestie's Government, and to the Disturbance of the Peace and Quiet of the Realm."[112] Jonathan Swift offered a counterbalance, writing that he was "not yet convinced that any Access to men in Power gives a man more Truth or Light than the Politicks of a Coffee House."[113] In France, the government infiltrated coffeehouses with spies on a regular basis. Frenchmen spouting anti-government views were often dragged off to the Bastille. And it was in Café de Foy, in July of 1789, that radical pamphleteer, Camille Desmoulins, jumped on a table, guns drawn, and implored the patrons: "Aux armes, citoyens!" Scottish historian Thomas Carlyle dramatized the moment:

> But see Camille Desmoulins, from the Café de Foy, rushing out, sibylline in face; his hair streaming, in each hand a pistol! He springs to a table: the Police satellites are eyeing him; alive they shall not take him, not they alive him alive. This time he speaks without stammering:—Friends! shall we die like hunted hares? Like sheep hounded into their pinfold; bleating for mercy, where is no mercy, but only a whetted knife? The hour is come; the supreme hour of Frenchman and Man; when Oppressors are to try conclusions with Oppressed; and the word is, swift Death, or Deliverance forever. Let such hour be well-come! Us, meseems, one cry only befits: To Arms! Let universal Paris, universal France, as with the throat of the whirlwind, sound only: To arms!—"To arms!" yell responsive the innumerable voices.[114]

Desmoulins' rallying cry became a flashpoint and within hours Gay Paree was in chaos. And it's in this moment that we understand why European governments of the day wanted to control the coffeehouses, and why, some 250 years later, governments today want to control cyberspace and the associated means of new media with the same gusto. French historian, Jules Michelet, summed up the power of the French coffeehouses—the participatory media of another day—writing that French citizens "who assembled day after day in the Café de Procope saw, with penetrating glance, in the depths of their black drink, the illumination of the year of the revolution."[115]

It's unreliable!

Independent journalists and new media outlets are constantly being accused of being unreliable, unprofessional, and as previously discussed, advocate journalists—dissidents and activists with an agenda and an axe to grind.

The short answer to these critics is easy—it's two words: Judith Miller.

Big time news organizations present this myth: you can trust us because we don't interject personal opinions and personal agendas; we gather the facts and deliver the story. Period. This inherent agreement with their readers and viewers is the stock-in-trade for news organizations like *The New York Times,* CBS, PBS, and others. "Papers like the *Times* strive to take personal opinions out of the coverage and shoot for a 'Just the facts, Ma'am' style," Matt Taibbi explains. "The value there is that people trust that approach, and readers implicitly enter into a contract with the newspaper or TV station that takes it, assuming that the organization will honestly try to show all points of view dispassionately."[116] Taibbi believes some organizations strive to fulfill that promise but others habitually "violate that contract, and carefully choose which 'Just facts' to present and which ones to ignore, so as to put certain political or financial interests in a better light."[117] Whether journalists openly acknowledge their advocacy or not, Taibbi makes it clear:

> People should be skeptical of everything they read. In fact, people should be more skeptical of reporters who claim not to be advocates, because those people are almost always lying, whether they know it or not.[118]

There should be at least one leak like the Pentagon Papers every year.
—Daniel Ellsberg

What happens when the Gate of Tradition can no longer hold the secret thrust upon them by the powerful? What happens when teens, equipped with the digital dexterity that few of their parents possess enter, at will, any database they seek and remove, not papers, but coded light signals that can be decoded in the blink of an eye?

We have all entered the world of WikiLeaks—an outfit bent on government transparency—one able to monitor the most secretive documents imaginable and then broadcast them on an unimaginable scale. The persons involved with the once little-known group, have become household names, especially as they have become targets of governments, government agencies, as well as the acquiescent media for their hackwork in cracking and releasing a veritable treasure trove of documents from the deepest, darkest recesses of government, national security agencies as well as political parties and corporate giants.

When a relatively low-level U.S. Army computer-ops private began to troll through documents on the behavior of U.S. troops in Iraq, he was shocked by what he learned. He subsequently reached out to WikiLeaks and arranged for transfer of this material. He, (then named) Bradley Manning (since renamed Chelsea), unleashed a whirlwind, revealing the inner voices of American occupation and how they perceived their Iraqi hosts—and more importantly, how they treated them. Manning, as an intelligence analyst, knew what he was looking at in the files. War crimes. U.S. war crimes. William Blum explains:

> It was after seeing American war crimes such as those depicted in the video, *Collateral Murder* and documented in the "Iraq War Logs," made public by Manning and WikiLeaks, that the Iraqis refused to exempt US forces from prosecution for future crimes. The video depicts an American helicopter indiscriminately murdering several non-combatants in addition to two Reuters journalists, and the wounding of two small children, while the helicopter pilots cheer the attacks in a Baghdad suburb like it was the Army-Navy game in Philadelphia.[119]

Manning was indeed an American soldier, and yes, she was also an intelligence analyst, per her training. But she was first and foremost, a human being, one moved to action by what she learned when she viewed and read files reflecting the ferocity and violations inherent in the U.S. occupation of Iraq. In an online chat, Manning describes the things she saw—and how these things impacted her decision to bring them forth:

> If you have free reign [sic] over classified networks… and you saw incredible things, awful things… things that belonged in the public domain, and not on some server stored in a dark room in Washington, D.C.… what would you do? …God knows what happens now. Hopefully worldwide discussion, debates, and reforms… I want people to see the truth… because without information, you cannot make informed decisions as a public.[120]

As soon as Manning unleashed the documents, the wolves pounced. She was arrested and, under military custody, she was stripped—literally—and held naked in a cell for years(!). And as bad as the military treated her, worse was how the media attacked Manning—for essentially doing *their* job. Calling the U.S. the site of the "new Devil's Island," Blum has written that Manning's abominable treatment and subsequent torture has served to "intimidate" those who might have wished to openly support Manning, but were afraid to do so. The U.S. government dusted off and rolled out the Espionage Act of 1917, which exposed the young soldier to 136 years in prison.

Manning was brought before a military tribunal, where "aiding the enemy" was dropped, and Espionage (spying) was sustained, as well as theft of government documents (files). Those six charges of violating the Espionage Act of 1917, and the additional charges, exposed the young soldier to 136 years in prison (her lawyers whittled it down to a mere ninety years).

Photo: Tim Travers Hawkins

Chelsea Manning

Ridiculed as a transgendered person, called "troubled" by her own defense attorneys, the endless subject of pop psychologists to detect her "defect," Manning was attacked, and her files—meant to spark debate among the citizens of "an informed public"—outshone the war crimes of the Empire. Chelsea Manning became the name of infamy—not the slaughters of Iraqis at Haditha, or Fallujah, which melted into a fog of silence. And as Manning was vilified, so too were the recipients of her data, or those who sent it out into the eyes and arms of the wide, wondering world: WikiLeaks founder, Julian Assange, and his primary journalist contact, Glenn Greenwald. Like Manning, both men have had their sexualities flaunted to the world by a leering press, the better to detract and demean men who have demonstrated the highest traditions of whistle-blowing and journalism—standing up to imperial power. Assange was targeted by obscure rape charges, widely seen as Sweden's service to the U.S. Empire, which would serve as a brief way station to an American gulag, where espionage (or worse) charges awaited him. Assange, unwilling to trust his liberty to the U.S. Prisonhouse of Nations, chose instead to enter a friendly embassy, and thus, essentially, to enter another country. Greenwald, who made the files available to leading newspapers on several continents, was attacked by his envious fellow reporters who denied he was actually a journalist. He was a mere "activist," they sniffed.

These WikiLeaked cables sent shock waves around the world and may have sparked the Arab Spring that engulfed the Middle East for a time, before it was brutally crushed to earth. For once, national (and international!) populations saw their political elites in living color—and they didn't like what they saw. They also saw how the Empire, New Rome, did business with the political elites of the world. It fueled dissent from left and right—for once in agreement about the dastardly shit being done behind closed doors and down dark digital corridors.

For this, Manning, a brave person indeed, faced torture by her own government, nakedness, reddening ridicule, solitary confinement—and the ever-present threat of death. For this, Julian Assange faced self-imposed lock-up in an embassy—so as not to face possible torture and life imprisonment (for espionage) in a U.S. federal prison. For this, Glenn Greenwald was denounced by every major media outlet in America—his professional reputation impugned, and his personal life invaded by the minions of the State.

For acts like this, Edward Snowden, a brilliant intelligence analyst, risked losing a life of love and comfort—in the closest thing the world offers as Paradise (Hawaii)—a loving girlfriend, and possibly the probability of ever returning to his homeland, his parents, his chosen profession, all in order to tell the story of how the world really works.

[As of this writing, Snowden's girlfriend/partner moved to Moscow to join him and they are now married.]

[As of this writing, Manning's sentence was commuted by President Barack Obama; she was jailed again in March of 2019 for her continued refusal to testify before a grand jury against Julian Assange and WikiLeaks. In April of 2019, Assange's asylum was withdrawn by Ecuador with British police arresting the WikiLeaks founder for violating the Bail Act and sentenced to fifty weeks in prison; the United States then unsealed an indictment against Assange for computer intrusion linked to information released by Chelsea Manning; the U.S. government again whipped out its Espionage Act and additionally charged Assange with violating this prehistoric and Draconian legislation; and not to be outdone, Swedish prosecutors reopened their rape investigation against Assange. The Empire strikes again.]

Indeed... the Empire, the Law of Planet Earth, does what it wishes when it wishes, by virtue of its unbridled, sheer Power. If you question it, if you challenge it, it will grind you into dust. It will torture you. It will separate you from all that you know and love. It will ridicule you... and then its curs and minions in the media will echo and amplify their curses. You will be isolated, damned, made a man or woman alone against the fury of their foul winds.

As the Empire grows more rapacious to protect their massive corporate campaign to privatize and pillage the nation's treasury, as they bolster war and the militarization of damn near everything in sight, and as they continue to construct and carry out the most exorbitant mass surveillance apparatus ever unleashed, they will do everything in their power to handcuff (literally) and crackdown on journalists while increasing their already authoritarian stranglehold on whistleblowers. During the "liberal" administration of Barack Obama, one of promised transparency, journalists were targeted in dramatic fashion with the F.B.I. spying on journalists' phone records and emails, issuing subpoenas aimed at forcing reporters to reveal sources, even naming one journalist (James Risen) an "aider, abettor" and a criminal co-conspirator of an indicted leak defendant for simply reporting on the case. In fact, the Obama Administration prosecuted at least three times more cases involving whistleblowers than ALL PREVIOUS ADMINISTRATIONS COMBINED, using the aforementioned antediluvian 1917 Espionage Act (a World War I-era commie spy noose) as their tool to generate felony criminal prosecutions against officials who talked with reporters. "The [Obama] administration's war on leaks and other efforts to control information," writes veteran *Washington Post* editor Leonard Downie, Jr., for the Committee to Protect Journalists, "are the most aggressive I've seen since the Nixon administration, when I was one of the editors involved in *The Washington Post's* investigation of Watergate."[121] All of this followed by Donald J. Trump's "Fake News" and labeling the American press, "the enemy of the people."

But, a surety yet exists. No empire lasts forever. No human Power is Eternal. If there is any true lesson of History, there it is. With his own matchless eloquence, with the soft voice of the learned, Christopher Hedges tells that story, one which he urges us to hearken:

> The earth is strewn with the ruins of powerful civilizations that decayed—Egypt, Persia, the Mayan empire, Rome, Byzantium, and

> the Mughal, Ottoman, and Chinese kingdoms. Not all died for the same reasons. Rome, for example, never faced a depletion of natural resources or environmental catastrophe. But they all, at a certain point, were taken over by a bankrupt and corrupt elite. This elite, squandering resources and pillaging the state, was no longer able to muster internal allegiance and cohesiveness. These empires died morally. The leaders, in the final period of decay, increasingly had to rely on armed mercenaries, as we do in Iraq and Afghanistan, because citizens would no longer serve in the military. They descended into orgies of self-indulgence, surrendered their civic and emotional lives to the glitter, excitement, and spectacle of the arena, became politically apathetic, and collapsed.
>
> The more we sever ourselves from a literate, print-based world, a world of complexity and nuance, a world of ideas, for one informed by comforting, reassuring images, fantasies, slogans, celebrities, and the lust for violence, the more we are destined to implode. As the collapse continues and our suffering mounts, we yearn, like World Wrestling Entertainment fans, or those who confuse pornography with love, for the comfort, reassurance, and beauty of illusion. The illusion makes us feel good. It has its own reality. And the lonely Cassandras who speak the truth about our misguided imperial wars, the economic meltdown, or the imminent danger of multiple pollutions and soaring overpopulation, are drowned out by arenas full of excited fans chanting: "Slut! Slut! Slut!" or television audiences chanting, "JER-RY! JER-RY! JER-RY! [122]

Chelsea Manning, Julian Assange, and Edward Snowden have paid a considerable price to awaken the People from their narcoleptic slumber.

Do we but change the channel, and join the chant?

Or, as Henry Louis Mencken suggested in *Prejudices: First Series*—"Every normal man must be tempted, at times, to spit on his hands, hoist the black flag, and begin slitting throats." Do we fight like hell for a changing of the guard?

2 The REAL Drug Warriors

Just mention the word "drugs"—and people go batshit crazy, loopy, nuts.

There is a mania at work here in America that touches the pocket, purse, and prosperity of every American within reach. It is deep in us, seasoned through decades of fear, fire-and-brimstone preaching by politicians, and the mass influence of the screaming media machine. For, as we all know: "drugs are baaaaad."

The Most Drug-addled Peoples on this Planet

There is a method to this madness, for as shocking as it may seem, it was not always thus. There was a time when kings, popes, and presidents freely utilized coke (as in cocaine) as a jolt pick-me-up. In fact, cocaine-infused beverages were quite common in the late 19th and early 20th centuries, along with cocaine tonics, powders, and pills that were believed to cure a variety of ailments. In 1886, John Pemberton, an Atlanta pharmacist, fashioned Coca-Cola after a very popular French drink, coca wine—a mixture of Bordeaux wine and coca-leaf extract. Coke's mad scientist simply used sugar syrup instead of wine, added a kola-nut extract as well and voilà: rocket fuel. Truly, as their ad campaign boomed across the land, "Coca-Cola revives and sustains."

And in early America, when most people traced their origins to small towns, villages, and rural communities (before the urban explosions of the Industrial Age), people grew up with a kind of herbal lore that included what we've conventionally considered fashionable among the neo-hippie hives of San Francisco and Berkeley, and in college dorm rooms from sea to shining sea. (Though the ubiquity of this ancient herb in dispensaries—both recreational and medical—continues to stretch from sea to bong hit and edible sea, legal distribution or decriminalized use, suggesting a growing mainstream acceptance and maturation from the naiveté of recent generations.)

It's also true that when Europeans came to the Americas, they met a people (when they weren't busy exterminating them) who were well versed in the cornucopia of nature.

Their knowledge of herbal pharmacology was extensive. Leaves, roots, bark, mushrooms, and the stems of plants formed their natural healing technology, and the people of pre-Columbian America nourished, healed, and replenished themselves for thousands of years... and could have continued to do so, if they were not invaded, colonized, and/or killed.

Did they use mind-altering drugs? Of course they did. But they used them ritualistically—as tools of perception, to reach beyond their present. To see, feel, and sense that which was beyond their reach. Tobacco was used by Indigenous people during sweat lodges, for example, as a tool to sharpen minds when in heated discussions of matters of great importance. What we call marijuana was also used, but sparingly, as part of this ritual. Was it used daily, as a kind of "food for the head?" This seems unlikely.

But, if so, what of it? The peace, balance, and life-affirming nature of much of Amerindian communal and clan life has been attested to by witnesses whom we expect to be biased. If they used drugs, they certainly didn't establish a national (even international) drug industry that corrupted all it came in contact with. Contemporary evidence of the periods of Amerindian dominance reflect a society that was the envy of both European and neo-European communities. So, if we assume such a tradition or practice, we know, if only by inference, that the materials used contributed to social harmony, as opposed to discord. If we're honest, we would overwhelmingly agree that the drugs of which most Americans partake are largely legal, without a serious consideration of whether these drugs bring societal or personal harm. As independent scholar Richard Lawrence Miller has noted, the most dangerous drugs are those that are the most available to the majority of customers.

As the 1990s began, the National Institute on Drug Abuse found that between 98,293,000 and 107,537,000 Americans were current users of alcohol. Between 50,413,000 and 56,981,000 were current tobacco cigarette smokers. Between

8,918,000 and 11,669,000 were current users of marijuana. Between 307,000 and 798,000 were current crack users. Neither price nor availability accounts for the overwhelming consumer rejection of crack. A drug's appeal depends not on its chemistry but instead on how many needs it satisfies in a person's life.[1]

Who can deny that the extensive usages of alcohol and cigarettes have serious, life-threatening effects on both users and those around them? Yet they are respected (albeit somewhat tarnished) industries that earn significant margins of the nation's capital every year. According to the U.S. Commerce Department's Bureau of Economic Analysis, alcoholic beverages (non-bar, private usage) netted some $49.3 billion dollars in 1990; by 2012 that figure rose to $106.6 billion. Similarly, cigarettes (and other tobacco) sales hit $41 billion in 1990; by 2010 it swelled to $94.4 billion.[2]

To call these drug industries big business is an understatement, and despite the social damage caused by them, they are fully protected by law. Americans clearly learned during the heyday of the 18th Amendment—the congressionally-passed Prohibition Amendment, which forbade the sale, manufacture, transportation, and importation of alcohol "for beverage purposes"—that sometimes the law causes more problems than it purports to cure. The Prohibition Amendment lasted only fourteen years (1919 to 1933) before its death by the repeal process. The so-called Drug War (although not made a constitutional amendment) has had a significantly longer, more brutish life.

Some researchers have argued that the so-called "war" was but a tool of political and social repression—with clear-cut political objectives. International Studies scholar, Vijay Prashad, points the finger at the late President Richard Nixon as the impetus for the 20th-century mania surrounding drugs:

> In 1968, as the world despaired over the US bombardment of Vietnam and Cambodia, President Richard Nixon declared war on drugs. "Within the last decade," he told Congress, "the abuse of drugs has grown from essentially a local police problem into a serious national threat to the personal health and safety of millions of Americans... A national awareness of the gravity of the situation is needed: a new urgency and concerted national policy are needed at the federal level to begin to cope with this growing menace to the general welfare of the United States." Raising the problem of drugs to a "national threat" produced a national panic not over drugs, but

over the imputed criminality of drug users. If Nixon could not get his entire package of anti-drug legislation passed, he set the ball rolling for future administrations to lock the US government into a state of warfare with its own people.

> These are not strong words. In 1989, the number of people under the supervision of the correctional system totaled 1,842,100. In 2001, the number leapt to 6,592,000. In the same period the number of prisoners went from 503,586 to 1,962,220. The US now leads across the globe in per capita incarceration. With nearly two million people behind bars and an additional five million under the surveillance of the criminal justice system, the US far surpasses the rates of incarceration elsewhere. In 1994, the rate was 569 per 100,000 people—40 times the rate in South Africa and 15 times the rate of Japan. Since then, the difference has only increased. In the 1960s, the imprisoned population was but an eighth of its current size.[3]

Not to be outdone, linguist and public intellectual Noam Chomsky has been an outspoken critic on this (and related) issues for some time. Chomsky, too, sees the so-called "Drug War" from a political perspective, but he frames a broader vista, painting it as a replacement war for a nation that was/is addicted to war:

> One substitute for the disappearing Evil Empire [here Chomsky speaks of the Soviet Union] has been the threat of drug traffickers from Latin America. In early September 1989, a major government-media blitz was launched by the president [Bush I]. That month the AP wires carried more stories about drugs than about Latin America, Asia, the Middle East and Africa combined. If you looked at television, every news program had a big section on how drugs were destroying our society, becoming the greatest threat to our national existence, etc.
>
> The effect on public opinion was immediate. When Bush won the 1988 election, people said the budget deficit was the biggest problem facing the country. Only about 3 percent named drugs. After the media blitz, concern over the budget was way down and drugs had soared to about 40 percent or 45 percent, which is highly unusual for an open question (where no specific answers are suggested).

> Now, when some client state complains that the US government isn't sending it enough money, they no longer say, "we need it to stop the Russians"—rather, "we need it to stop drug trafficking." Like the Soviet threat, this enemy provides a good excuse for a US military presence where there's rebel activity or other unrest.
>
> So, internationally, "the war on drugs" provides a cover for intervention. Domestically, *it has little to do with drugs but a lot to do with distracting the population, increasing repression in the inner cities, and building support for the attack on civil liberties.* [Emphasis added]
>
> That's not to say that "substance abuse" isn't a serious problem. At the time the drug war was launched, deaths from tobacco were estimated at about 300,000 a year, with perhaps another 100,000 from alcohol. But these aren't the drugs the Bush Administration targeted. It went after illegal drugs, which had caused fewer deaths—3,500+ a year—according to official figures. One reason for going after these drugs was that their use had been declining for some years, so the Bush administration could safely predict that its drug war would "succeed" in lowering drug use.
>
> The administration also targeted marijuana, which hasn't caused any known deaths among some 60 million users. In fact, that crackdown has exacerbated the drug problem—many marijuana users have turned from this relatively harmless drug to more dangerous drugs like cocaine, which are easier to conceal.[4]

The observations of Miller, Prashad, and Chomsky give us clear evidence that something else is at stake in the so-called "drug wars." Something deeper, and perhaps sinister. There is the unholy confluence of politics, social policy, drugs, and the notion of drugs as not merely "baaaaad"—but evil.

Politics, of course, exploits a false fear ginned up by the corporate and compliant media, but it could only do so if there is something there to exploit: like fear, hatred, loathing, and maybe even something deeper.

But what is that something?

If America is that odd and disjointed convergence of neo-Europe and New Rome, then it brings over from the "Old Country" ideas and ways of looking at the world that may give us precious insight into the underlying thought processes that fuel these movements against not merely alcohol (really—a Constitutional Amendment?), but drugs—almost all drugs (except those many deemed legal and profitable to capital's formal markets).

Europe, especially deep into its Christian conversion phase, brought with it a unique hatred and revulsion against the body—and the very notion of pleasure. Why is that important to our work here? Simple. *Drugs are pleasurable!* And thus, they are to be opposed—not just drugs, or alcohol, but pleasure; and the State will be the vehicle through which this Prohibition will be achieved. Historian David Stannard writes about the deep view of early Christians in Europe who saw all pleasure as intrinsically evil:

> [W]hat distinguished the Christian saint from other men, said the early Church fathers, was the Christian's recognition of the categorical difference and fundamental opposition between things of the spirit and things of the world. The two realms were utterly incompatible, with the result, says the Epistle to Diognetus, that "the flesh hates the soul, and wages war upon it, though it has suffered no evil, because it is prevented from gratifying its pleasures, and the world hates the Christians though it has suffered no evil, because they are opposed to its pleasures."[5]

If pleasure is intrinsically evil (as "of the world"), then those items of nature, which stimulate pleasurable responses, are also evil. What we are suggesting is not that this survived as a discrete religious practice (as the self-flagellating practice among Shia's in Islam) either in Europe or in neo-Europe (America), but it survived in *consciousness,* in a way of looking at and interpreting the world, even when the original rationale is no longer known or understood.

Indeed, early Americans saw themselves as inheritors of an ancient, biblical, and even divine prophecy in which this land was the place of the unveiling of God's will, as the old lands and kingdoms—Europe, England, and Israel—had failed to obey the holy laws of old. Historian Anders Stephanson, in his influential work *Manifest Destiny,* has explored these themes in considerable depth. In this passage, he reveals how old ideas found release and new life in the brave new world called America:

> For Europeans, land not occupied by recognized members of Christendom was theoretically land free to be taken. When practically possible, they did so. The Christian colonizers of the Americas—including the Spanish and the Portuguese—understood theirs as sacred enterprises; but only the New England Puritans conceived the territory itself as sacred, or sacred to be. As the appointed bearers of the true Christian mission, they made it so by being there. To the same degree, England was thereby desacralized. This, then, was the New Canaan, a land promised, to be reconquered and reworked for the glory of God by His select forces, the saving remnant in the wilderness. The Puritan reenactment of the Exodus narrative revolved around a powerful theology of chosenness that was to be decisive for the course of colonization as well as for the later American self-concept.[6]

This view, this self-perception wasn't just the ideas of elites but of the nation's religious figures as well. It lived in a kind of common consciousness that explained and gave divine sanction to the taking of this land and the purposes of that taking. This distinctly Puritan view, that pleasure, as sin, was impure, found a ready site for the later political exploration of those concerns to enact legal prohibitions against various forms of pleasure: alcohol, drugs, sexuality, and perhaps most policed of all: interracial sexuality. In fact, as this was a deeply-held worldview, one informed by a quasi-religious "destinarianism"—or sense of holy destiny (i.e., Manifest Destiny)—it seeped into consciousness, and became a trough of belief, unacknowledged, and largely unarticulated (or, as tacitly approved, unquestioned).

To the astute politician, facing a black, white, brown, and female youth rebellion, opposing the Vietnam War, as well as racism, sexism, and police repression—how powerful a weapon must drugs have seemed, especially when it seemed like most of the ragged, unwashed protestors were smoking that "wacky weed." If he could criminalize the drug—he could simultaneously criminalize *them.* This was precisely the case during the height of the 1960s, when social and mass movements were rejecting the staid, colorless status quo of the '50s. All across the country (and throughout the media), young people were rhetorically, politically, and psychologically rejecting the ways of their parents and those of important political institutions, like the federal, state, and local governments, universities, colleges, even high schools, and of course the military (not to mention the dogma of institutionalized religion). "The System" was seen as corrupt and vile—a monstrous force in the nation's life, waging a maniacal war in Vietnam for base purposes. David Gilbert was a young man during that period, and his recollections, although leavened by later knowledge, reflect the power of generational upheaval and tumult that was the 1960s:

> The exuberance and sense of revolution in the air that came with the cultural upheavals of the 1960s was exhilarating—even if my view today is tempered with an awareness of both the sexism and the tremendous damage drugs have done. Still, coming out of the social conservatism of the 1950s, with its sexual and gender repression, when the government was always right and serious dissent was automatically discredited as "Communist," youth culture was like a giant plow, breaking up that hard, caked ground to open up fertile soil for all kinds of new life. A world of many splendid colors burst out of the preceding drab background, opening up space for a wild range of nonconformity. The flowers of creativity were expressed in art, theatre, and style, but most dramatically in music. By the end of the decade, millions of kids were singing along with a variety of lively, catchy songs that opposed the war and disdained the establishment. I felt we might have a better chance to transform society than the old left, even though they'd had much more developed organizations, because the 1960s rebellious cultural ferment involved a whole generation.[7]

Gilbert, as many others of his generation, grew in radicalism stemming from opposition to the U.S. Empire's murderous role in the Vietnam War, and this broadened and deepened over time to relate to other issues in American life, and subjects of political and cultural contention.

We have written of the so-called "drug war" in almost academic fashion, citing the work of mostly historians (and one antiwar activist) to sculpt the lay of the land. Frankly, we think this is merely the tip of the iceberg for what's needed to fully capture what the so-called "drug war" really means in the lives, fortunes, and peril of everyday people who live under the incessant guns of that "war." The late brilliant writer, playwright, and bon vivant, Gore Vidal, wrote with a voice and clarity that was decidedly rare, not only for one among his class, but among many in his chosen profession (here we refer to his extensive and successful writing career). Vidal, in one of his later works, rips the bandage off of the cancer that is the drug war, with sometimes startling directness:

Nineteen ninety-two. Bridgeport, Connecticut. *The Hartford Courant* reported that the local Tactical Narcotics Team routinely devastated homes and businesses they "searched." Plainclothes policemen burst in on a Jamaican grocer and restaurant owner with the cheery cry "Stick up, niggers. Don't move." Shelves were swept clear. Merchandise ruined. "They never identified themselves as police," the *Courant* noted. Although they found nothing but a registered gun, the owner was arrested and charged with "interfering with an arrest" and so booked. A judge later dismissed the case. [James] Bovard [in *Lost Rights* (1994)] reports, "in 1991, in Garland, Texas, police dressed in black and wearing black ski-masks burst into a trailer, waved guns in the air and kicked down the bedroom door where Kenneth Baulch had been sleeping with his seventeen-month-old son. A policeman claimed that Baulch posed a deadly threat because he held an ashtray in his left hand, which explained why he shot Baulch in the back and killed him. (A police internal investigation found no wrongdoing by the officer.) In March 1992, a police SWAT team killed Robin Pratt, an Everett, Washington mother, in a no-knock raid carrying out an arrest warrant for her husband. (Her husband was later released after the allegations upon which the arrest warrant were based turned out to be false.)"

Incidentally, the KGB tactic—hold someone for a crime, but let him off if he then names someone else for a bigger crime—often leads to false, even random allegations that ought not to be acted upon so murderously, without a bit of homework first. *The Seattle Times* describes Robin Pratt's last moments. She was with her six-year-old daughter and five-year-old niece when the police broke in. As the bravest storm trooper, named Aston, approached her, gun drawn, the other police shouted, "Get down," and she started to crouch on her knees. She looked up at Aston and said, "Please don't hurt my children..." Aston had his gun pointed at her and fired, shooting her in the neck. According to [the Pratt family attorney John] Muenster, she was alive another one to two minutes but could not speak because her throat had been destroyed by the bullet. She was handcuffed, lying face down. Doubtless Aston was fearful of a divine retribution; and vengeance. It is no secret that American police rarely observe the laws of the land when out wilding with each other and as any candid criminal judge will tell you, perjury is often their native tongue in court.[8]

That is the truest face of the "drug war," but it is one we rarely see. For to see that kind of human carnage would force us to question its factual and ethical basis. We would see it as a war on the poor, the Black, and the brown. We would see it for what it is. And that is simply not allowed. That's why the voracious corporate media splashes our eyes and brains with government-initiated anti-drug propaganda, even while Americans are one of the most drug-addled peoples on this planet.

Remember when we noted the growing expenditures for alcohol and cigarette products? It pales beside the vast amounts of money Americans spend for pharmaceutical products (i.e., legal drugs). In 1980, Americans annually spent $59.1 billion on pharmaceuticals and related products. In 2010, we spent $330.6 billion![9]

Opioids: Like Bite-Size Snickers on Halloween

According to the U.S. Department of Health and Human Services (Centers for Disease Control), more than 130 people die EVERY DAY—in the United States alone—from overdosing on opioids (2019), though it actually may be a lot more. The CDC reports that the misuse of and addiction to opioids (including prescription pain relievers, heroin, and synthetic opioids like fentanyl) is an out-of-control national crisis that severely impacts public health as well as social and economic welfare. In fact, according to the Feds and the data disclosed at the heart of the largest civil action in U.S. history, America's major drug manufacturers flooded the market with—wait for it—76 BILLION oxycodone and hydrocodone pain pills from 2006 to 2012. Again, using 2019 figures, the CDC reports that the total economic burden of prescription opioid misuse in the U.S. is estimated at $78.5 billion a year. This includes the costs of healthcare, lost productivity, addiction treatment, and, of course, meandering through a corrupt–inequitable–and–discriminatory criminal justice system.

How did this happen you ask?

Enter Big Pharma. It's the late 1990s and drug companies assured and reassured docs and Big Medical that their patients would not succumb to addiction on prescription opioid pain relievers. So healthcare providers started handing this shit out like bite-size Snickers on Halloween. According to the National Institute on Drug Abuse, this "led to widespread diversion and misuse of these medications before it became clear that these medications could indeed be highly addictive." By 2017, opioid overdose rates began to skyrocket. The CDC reports "more than 47,000 Americans died as a result of an opioid overdose." Also in 2017, they estimate that another "1.7 million people in the United States suffered from substance use disorders related to prescription opioid pain relievers," with still another 652,000 people suffering from heroin use. For context, the opioid death march is now FAR BEYOND the number of American soldiers killed in the Vietnam and Korean wars combined (and it climbs higher every day).

They should be in jail, next to El Chapo.
—Nan Goldin, artist & activist

Of course, we can't type a word about opioids without at least "mentioning" the all-powerful Sackler Family and their pharmaceutical company Purdue Pharma (who might be a tad busy lately with lawsuits dropping like frogs from the sky for their malevolent part in the opioid crisis). You might have heard of or even used the highly addictive OxyContin®, Purdue Pharma's star player. "Rush Limbaugh, c'mon down!" But for the Sacklers, here's the win-win beauty part that they envisioned: profiteering on both sides of the crisis—producing, marketing, and selling the popular painkiller while at the same time also fueling the development and/or acquiring the rights to sell various drugs that fight the addiction and reverse the effects of an overdose to their highly addictive drugs. That's capitalism in a cupcake. And get this, they even had a cute CIA-like name for it: Project Tango.

The Sacklers and Purdue Pharma are far from alone in this diabolical racket. Enter Johnson & Johnson, who "did everything it possibly could to get doctors to prescribe more and more opioids,"[10] said Dr. Andrew Kolodny, as he testified in open court in the first trial where a state (Oklahoma) held a drug maker responsible for contributing to the U.S. opioid epidemic. Kolodny, co-director of opioid policy research at the Heller School for Social Policy and Management at Brandeis University, is a one-man wrecking crew fighting against multinational giants like Johnson & Johnson. Kolodny testified that the pharmaceutical Goliath aggressively pushed doctors to prescribe the painkillers even though they knew full well more than a decade before that the fatally addictive drugs posed a major public health threat. As early as the 1980s, Johnson & Johnson had their eye on the golden goose. They purchased a company in Tasmania that grew and processed poppies and by 2015 Johnson & Johnson became the number one supplier for the raw ingredients necessary in these painkillers. They even developed and produced a rare strain of poppy (named Norman) that was a main ingredient in

OxyContin. Kolodny made clear that "There would have been no OxyContin without J&J ramping up in Tasmania."[11]

Oklahoma sought $13 billion in damages but the judge in this non-jury case talked tough but let the iconic corporation off easy with a $572 million judgment—a drop in the bucket for one of the wealthiest corporations in the world. But Kolodny stressed, "We're getting to a point where I think scapegoating this family (Sackler) and this one company can be counterproductive, because other opioid manufacturers also contributed to the epidemic."[12]

Postscript: Photographer, artist, and activist Nan Goldin (herself having battled addiction, overdosing on heroin and fentanyl) has been shining a bright light of resistance on the Sacklers and those who take their money in the name of charity and philanthropic endeavors—like The Metropolitan Museum of Art with their Sackler Wing that houses the ancient Egyptian "Temple of Dendur" and the adjacent iconic reflecting pool. At 4:10pm on 10 March 2018, Goldin led a throng of activists in a protest. As they hurled prescription drug bottles into the pool, Goldin offered this entreaty: "In the name of the dead. Sackler family. Purdue Pharma. Hear our demands. Use your profits. Save our lives." Then Goldin cried out: "Die!" On cue, fellow protesters fell to the museum floor alongside the pool, chanting "Sacklers lie, people die."

And then a *Washington Post* headline about a year later: "Citing Opioid Ties, The Met Says It Will Stop Accepting Gifts from the Sackler Family"—see, sometimes, there is a god. Good for The Met and thank you Nan Goldin.

So, it would seem that something else is afoot—and it ain't about the drugs. It's like the old saying: "If they say it ain't about the money, it's about the money."

This is enough from the periphery. Let us enter the heart.

From the Inside Out

In the deep and forbidden warrens of the Drug Enforcement Agency (DEA) we find the heart of the U.S. governmental machinery constructed to address (illegal) drug offenses. Mark Levine, like the proverbial cat, has lived quite a few lives in that world: agent, whistleblower, writer, broadcaster, and victim. When Levine writes about the "drug war," he presents his views from the inside of the game, and, to be sure, it ain't no prettier:

> When President Nixon first declared war on drugs in 1971, there were fewer than half a million hard-core addicts in the entire nation, most of whom were addicted to heroin. Most of them lived in larger inner-city areas, with the greatest number residing in New York City. Only two federal agencies were charged with enforcing drug laws back then—the Federal Bureau of Narcotics and U.S. Customs. These two agencies were greater enemies to each other than to any drug cartel. The total drug war budget was less than $100 million.
>
> Three decades later, despite the expenditure of $1 trillion in federal and state tax dollars, the number of hard-core addicts is shortly expected to exceed five million. Our nation has become the supermarket of the drug world, with a wider variety and bigger supply of drugs at cheaper prices than ever before. The problem now not only affects every town and hamlet on the map, but it is difficult to find a family anywhere that is not somehow affected.
>
> Currently, fifty-five federal and military agencies (that we know of) are involved in federal drug enforcement alone (not counting state and municipal budgets) while US military troops are invading South and Central American nations under the banner of "drug war." The federal drug war budget alone is well over $20 billion a year, and my personal quest to find one individual anywhere in the world who could honestly testify that America's trillion-dollar war on drugs has somehow saved him or her from the white menace has thus far been fruitless.[13]

With figures like these known—and coming from an agent of the DEA—how could anyone, anywhere, dare to argue that the so-called "drug war" is anything but a miserable, expensive failure? They could only do so given the mind-altering powers of the corporate press, which lapped up drug fairytales like a kitten on catnip. They—what Levine calls "the shills"—wanted a sexy, go-get-'em crime story. Politicians and their agencies would be only too happy to oblige.

Levine writes that after his 1984 hardship transfer back to New York City, he faced two personal crises. His brother, David, a long-time addict was so despondent by his habit that he committed suicide, leaving a note saying: "I can't stand the drugs anymore." Moreover, his fifteen-year-old daughter also got hooked. Back in his city, he was still in the loop of the DEA-media game, writing of his job in the Big Apple that, "[I] was assigned as the supervisor of an active squad that was constantly being called out to stage raids for television news—CBS, ABC, etc.—all the big players. On a slow news day, the SAC (Special Agent in Charge) would get a call: 'You guys got anything going down we can put on the eleven o'clock news?' We could always come up with something. What was good for their ratings was good for our budget."[14] Hmmm... Back to the money, eh?

What was pitched and sold as an alleged "drug war" by political and media elites, became, through American style politics—voila!—an American drug industry that fueled various sectors of the American economy. Levine wrote about the "drug war" as an inducement to international intervention (in the name of drugs, of course), but, as ever, what happens abroad sooner or later comes home on the tide.

At this point we must return to an event discussed previously in this series so we can explore in more detail what has proven to be one of the most remarkable stories ever to emerge in contemporary media—the breaking of an earth-shattering story from an unknown journalist, Gary Webb, writing for a morning newspaper, the *San Jose Mercury News.* After this story, Webb's relative anonymity would vanish. Webb later compiled his reports into a book, *Dark Alliance,* an account of how the CIA played a nefarious role in the drug industry that surged throughout Black America, causing untold carnage. Of that story, Webb wrote:

> Over the course of three days, *Dark Alliance* [initially the title of his newspaper series] advanced five main arguments: First, that the CIA-created Contras [Spanish for counter-revolutionaries] *had* been selling cocaine to finance their activities. This was something the CIA and the major media had dismissed or denied since the mid-1980s, when a few reporters began writing about Contra drug dealing. Second, that the Contras had sold cocaine in the ghettos of Los Angeles and that their main customer was L.A.'s biggest crack dealer. Third, that elements of the U.S. government knew about this drug ring's activities at the time and did little if anything to stop it. Fourth, that because of the time period and the areas in which it operated, this drug ring played a critical role in fueling and supplying the first mass crack cocaine market in the United States. And fifth, that the profits earned from this crack market allowed the Los Angeles-based Crips and Bloods to expand into other cities

> and spread crack use to other black urban areas, turning a bad local problem into a bad national problem. This led to panicky federal drug laws that were locking up thousands of small-time, black crack dealers for years but never denting the crack trade.
>
> It wasn't so much a conspiracy that I had outlined as it was a chain reaction—bad ideas compounded by stupid political decisions and rotten historical timing.[15]

Webb faced the obdurate antipathy of the major big-city press, which pooh-poohed the story, based largely on nothing more than the CIA's initial rejection of his findings. By the time he was proven right, Webb, an award-winning journalist, was, after his release from the *Mercury News,* shunned by the industry that his fine work distinguished. Webb stepped on the toes of power, for which he was handsomely repaid. Found dead in his home some years later, attributed to suicide, the *Dark Alliance* had finally come full circle. The film starring Jeremy Renner and directed by Michael Cuesta sure did get the title right: *Kill the Messenger.*

This Is Not a Unique or Rare Occurrence

The drug industry, it would seem, was as grimy on the inside as it seemed on the outside. The money was flowing like water, and the industry grew like kudzu in the summer Georgia sun. The State forces assigned to fight it were instead throwing fresh corn to rats; they force-fed the industry into the behemoth that it is today.

There is another side that bears revelation. As Webb has written, the CIA-initiated program had a tremendous impact on the Black community. Black nationalist organizer and activist, Omali Yeshitela, head of the Uhuru Movement (headquartered in St. Petersburg, Florida), delivered a speech that keynoted the destructive role of the drug wars on Black, insurgent life. Yeshitela told his audience how the FBI and CIA played dual roles to damage the African-American freedom movement:

> Immediately after the defeat of the Black Revolution, then-president Richard Milhous Nixon rewarded [William] Sullivan [former deputy chief of the FBI, and architect of the COINTELPRO program that targeted activists and radicals] for destroying our movement by sending him to a post in Southeast Asia. He was supposed to make war against drugs. He was sent to the area of

> Southeast Asia known as the "golden triangle," where most of the world's heroin was grown.
>
> Sullivan was sent to Southeast Asia to fight a war against drugs that we didn't even know existed. Shortly after he got to Southeast Asia, Sullivan recruited people like G. Gordon Liddy, E. Howard Hunt and Richard Secord, who was involved in the drug scandal with Oliver North. They became a part of an organization that he created, the Office of Drug Abuse Law Enforcement (ODALE) that later became the Drug Enforcement Administration (DEA). This agency was the origin of the heroin epidemic that hit our communities as soon as the Panthers and other organizations were taken off the streets. This was during the time when the United States government was involved in a counterinsurgency war against the heroic and courageous people of Viet Nam.
>
> On the one hand, they were making war on the people of Viet Nam. On the other hand, they were making war against the African people here. Inside this country the counterinsurgency took the form of heroin—pumped into our communities by the U.S. government. Heroin was everywhere. There was not a city that was too small or too rural—if African people were there, heroin people would be there. This was around 1971 and 1972, the year of the founding of the African People's Socialist Party. That was the year when, as far as they were concerned, the Black Revolution and revolutionary trend in the world was supposed to be all over.[16]

Yeshitela told his audience that the Vietnam War's end didn't come as the Empire expected, for the little people—those the Americans delighted in calling *gooks*—would emerge victorious over the most mechanized, most destructive army in the history of human warfare: the Americans. The world would marvel at this feat. But it would have other affects. It would even alter the drug war. Yeshitela told those before him:

> When the Sandinistas took over Nicaragua, the strategic counterinsurgency efforts of the United States government shifted from Southeast Asia to Latin America. And guess what? It just so happens that most of the world's cocaine grows in Latin America. All of a sudden, African people supposedly lost our taste for heroin. Suddenly, we got involved in cocaine. Not just cocaine but a cocaine

derivative called "crack." It was something that someone went into a lab and created, so that it would be cheap enough for massive distribution through the African community.

So, there was a counterinsurgency war being initiated against the Nicaraguan people and the Nicaraguan Revolution, and another was being initiated against African people here. Now that the Black Revolution had been destroyed, the counterinsurgency was being waged against the entire African population to try to make sure that we stayed demoralized and powerless and would never again build the Black Revolution. This counterinsurgency takes the form of crack cocaine chemical warfare! This is what the United States government has done to African people.

In August, 1996, Gary Webb, a white guy working for the San Jose Mercury News, kicked off a series of newspaper articles revealing the FBI involvement in creating the crack cocaine epidemic in our communities. This came out of San Jose, California. It just so happens that San Jose is about forty-five minutes away from Oakland, where we waged struggles from the early 1980s up until now exposing the fact that the United States government has imposed drugs in our communities.[17]

Yeshitela cites Webb's extensive reporting and his firing from the *Mercury News.* His remarks make clear that Black activists throughout Black America tied the drugs to the CIA—the U.S. government—as part of its long war against Black people.

Wait a minute. Wait a minute! (We can hear you thinking.) Can we possibly be suggesting—out loud, as it were—that the government, nay, "our" government could possibly—*possibly!*—be involved in (<gasp!!>) drugs? Drug dealing? "Get the fuck outta here." (We can still hear you.)

In point of fact, the government has been involved with drugs—openly!—for years. Michael Levine, whom we've referenced above, a veteran of the DEA, has argued that the U.S. government was instrumental in putting a cocaine-drenched government in power not too long ago. Levine argues that the U.S. was integral in actually creating a narco-state:

On July 17, 1980, for the first time in history, drug traffickers actually took control of a nation. It was not just any nation; it was Bolivia, at the time the source of virtually 100 percent of the cocaine entering the United States. The "Cocaine Coup" was the bloodiest in Bolivia's history. CIA-recruited mercenaries and drug traffickers—collectively called the "Angels of Death"—unseated Bolivia's democratically-elected president, Lidia Gueiler, a leftist (according to the CIA) whom the American government didn't want in power. The drug traffickers also took the opportunity to eliminate their competitors along with all suspected DEA informants so they could consolidate raw materials and production to meet the U.S.'s skyrocketing demand for cocaine. The result was the creation of what came to be known as *La Corporación*—the Corporation—in essence, the General Motors or OPEC of cocaine.

Immediately after the coup, cocaine production increased massively, until, in short time, it outstripped supply. This was the true beginning of the cocaine and crack "plague," as the media and hack politicians never tire of calling it. July 17, 1980, is truly a day that should live in infamy along with December 7, 1941. There are few events in history that have caused more and longer-lasting damage to our nation.

What America was never told—despite the mainstream media having the information as well as a primary inside source who was ready to go public with the story—was that the coup was carried out with the aid and participation of Central Intelligence. The source could also testify and prove that, to carry out the coup, the CIA along with the State and Justice departments had to combine forces to protect their drug dealing assets by destroying a DEA investigation—U.S. v. Roberto Suarez, et al. How do I know? I was that inside source.[18]

Whoa. (Bet you haven't seen that on The History Channel or CNN.) And yet, this is the written work of a retired DEA agent—someone entrenched in the bowels of the drug game. But, as we have hinted above, this is not a unique or rare occurrence. Not by a long shot.

The World's Greatest Drug Dealer

If we were to ask you, the reader, to name the world's largest drug dealer, who would come to mind? Most would mention, almost automatically, the name of the formidable Columbian drug lord, Pablo Escobar. Or perhaps the latest inheritor of that tarnished throne. Yet, it's a virtual certainty that whomever one names, he is either African-American (a la the real "Freeway Rick" Ross, the young man who helped propel the crack industry across the nation), or a Latino male. How could anyone do differently? For, isn't that the image projected to us by the corporate press?

How about if we told you that the world's greatest drug dealer is no secretive, shadowy figure? That he (or she!) is relatively well-known, among the richest people in the history of the world—and well, world famous?

Intrigued?

Well, follow on as we examine what was the biggest, most lucrative, and most-hard-fought drug battle of them all. For this purpose, we must leap back in time, and in space, to when the world was a collection of empires and colonies. And when "the sun never set on the British Empire." We speak of the closing years of the 18th century, when the British Navy ruled the seas fixated on achieving their distant colonial ends.

Their relationship with a massive Asian state such as China, however, proved the limits of such daring, for Sino-Anglo relations were dictated by trade—a commercial conflict that the British were decidedly losing. For, when the British tried to trade in manufactured goods, as opposed to the traditional use of silver, the Chinese emperor, known as the "Son of Heaven," could not be less impressed, writing England's King George III in 1793, "We possess all things, I set no value on objects strange or ingenious, and have no use for your country's manufactures."[19] To say the least, this did not sit well with the English, for the Chinese were saying, in essence, "we don't want your junkyard—if you want to trade, use silver!" In fact, the British Empire, while a wealthy one, had its limits, and silver was a limited resource that the vast Chinese market was swallowing up at an increasing rate. Historian Carl Trocki, in his book, *Opium, Empire and the Global Political Economy,* notes:

> The 1700s were boom times for the Middle Kingdom as English silver flooded into China. China's population over the period tripled from about one hundred million to over three hundred million. The constant importation of Asian products in the European markets caused a permanent drain of gold and silver from Europe towards Asia. Only a small trickle of precious metals must have re-entered Europe... The greater part of gold and silver remained in Asia never to return to Europe.[20]

Such a state of affairs did not bode well for the British or their cunning colonial official, governor-general Warren Hastings, posted in Bengal (today's Bangladesh) in northern India. This region was a long-time producer of opium, which had medicinal and social uses throughout Asia. For quite some time Arab sailors had conducted a profitable Bengal-to-China opium market, which Portuguese sailors in the region wanted in on. So they muscled their way in and, mixing opium with tobacco from their Brazilian colony, created a product more pleasing to the Chinese users. The opium market boomed, becoming incredibly popular in China. Seeing the danger to his realm, the Son of Heaven issued an imperial ban on its sale and use in China. Needless to say, the Foreign Devils of Europe and England ignored imperial edicts, and the British, sensing an opportunity, utilized the vast regions of Bengal and hyped up its farming, harvesting, and production of opium in the region. A million Bengali (and other Indian) farmers were registered to grow the drug to feed this huge market and the British opened factories to systematize production.

In the face of Chinese law, which rendered opium's sale and use illegal, the Brits set up floating warehouses in the Pearl River Delta (if capitalism is one thing it's resourceful)—and, under cover of darkness, sold their booty to Chinese criminals who smuggled the drugs into China where it sold like hot cakes. The India-to-China opium trade brought in so much loot that it became the "world's most valuable single commodity trade of the nineteenth century."[21] In fact, this illegal opium trade netted vast amounts of dough that flowed to European banks, shipping companies, and insurance companies. For the British Empire, the opium trade accounted for some twenty percent of their revenue. Twenty percent. Big business.

"Jesus Opium"

Meanwhile, the opium plague was virtually wrecking China, destroying the vitality of its subjects, and strengthening (through wealth) its growing criminal classes. The Chinese called the drug "Jesus opium," for it was smuggled into the Middle Kingdom by Christians. And while the "Jesus opium" wreaked havoc on the health of the Chinese people, it also posed a real danger to their economy and trade balance, for "[b]etween 1814 and 1850," historian James Bradley writes, "the Jesus-opium trade sucked out 11 percent of China's money supply."[22] Bradley further notes, quite astonishingly, that, "China lost more silver in thirty years than had flowed into the country in the 125 years leading up to the opium trade." [23]

As the money supply contracted, taxes increased and peasants had difficulty paying them. Silver, once abundant throughout the empire, became "unnaturally" scarce. China was the first nation to use paper money (as recorded by Marco Polo in the 1200s), but this crisis forced rising counterfeiting and the economy shook between waves of ebb and flow. Chinese society, so long situated on the basis of Confucian principles of "filial piety" and social harmony, was being ripped apart at the seams because of its economic upheavals and insecurities.

This escalating social disruption and conflict left the Son of Heaven with few options, and in 1839, he sent a royal emissary to Canton to put an end to the Foreign Devil Jesus Opium trade. However, in order to do this, the Son of Heaven had to convince the British to cease and desist in this most profitable of businesses. But this, the most powerful man in the most populous and wealthiest country in the world, could not do, because for the British Empire this was about money—big money. And they had no intention of giving up such a lucrative trade. When the Son of Heaven's edict reached London, a newly crowned, twenty-year-old Queen Victoria paled at the prospect of losing such an income. Indeed, her very empire rested upon the vast wealth flowing from the opium trade in Asia. She sent her Royal Navy to the China Sea to enforce her right to push an illegal drug upon an unwilling, but addicted people. She went to war (two wars, in fact!) to protect her investment. Perhaps the young Queen's sense of entitlement defines her as the original millennial.

The Opium Wars (from 1839 to 1842; and 1856 to 1860) to force China to submit to the "Jesus-opium" were successful. In fact, the great wealth from the drug trade allowed the British forces to wage war on a relative pittance. Once humbled, the Middle Kingdom was forced to cede part of its national territory (Hong Kong) to the Foreign Devils as the spoils of war. As for the opium, it would continue to poison and pollute Chinese people for decades to come, and Hong Kong would become the center of the opium trade, as illustrated by the statement of its governor, Sir John Francis Davis: "Almost every person... not connected with government is employed in the opium trade."[24]

When one considers the sheer scale of these operations, and the enormous global profits netted therein, the escapades of Pablo Escobar and "Freeway" Rick Ross, pale in comparison. For while both men, as drug lords, amassed enormous sums of money ($600 million, according to one estimate for Ross), neither could profit long, for they were up against the forces of the State, and hence, suffered the results of state action—either death or imprisonment.

Queen Victoria

Victoria (1819-1901), Queen of Britain and Ireland, Empress of India, had the longest reign in English history. In imperial terms (to borrow a phrase from France's King Louis XIV) *she was the State.* Her additional title, not often noted, was "The Greatest Drug Dealer in History."

But as this was drug-dealing on an epic scale, a global scale, and there were literally *millions* of customers to hook and therefore profit from, this massive loss of money savaged the Chinese economy for many, many years. However, even the greed and avarice of the British Empire could not hold nor control this immense flow of capital. Money (usually in the form of silver coinage) swelled various circuits of business, and other nations got into the act: most notably, the Americans.

That is the other side of the *real* drug dealers.

Yankee Drug Dealers Go Bowling for Dollars

"Hold up—hold up!" "Yankee drug dealers?!" Who are you guys talking about? The Italian Mafia? The Irish Mafia? The Black Mafia? The Russians? The Puerto Rican Mob? Who?

Nope.

We mean "Yankees"—as in good old American white dudes—not from the ghettos of America, nor from amidst the poor. This story, like that of Queen Victoria, also didn't make its way to The History Channel (to our knowledge), nor to CNN. But here, in these pages, openly, honestly, we share what we've learned, for the story of imperialism is more than a colonial tale of taking, of colossal greed, or state violence.

It is that, to be sure; but it is so much more.

It is global crime: the crime in the *suites,* not the crime in the *streets.* And, as in most "suite crime," it is more lucrative, more socially destructive, more violent—and thus more hidden beneath the awnings of quiet respectability.

In America, there is a class that seldom makes the front page of the daily rags. Their names, if ever recorded, may litter the society pages, but who reads those? They aren't famous in that curiously American-celebrity sort of way. For they are the scions and princes of American industry and wealth. They are the first families. Captains of Industry. They are what is often termed *old money.* Haven't you ever wondered: where did that "old money" come from? We have. And, actually, the answers shouldn't surprise us—for the rich, the well born, the comfortable, rarely, if ever, leave their places of comfort and ease for the treacherous, challenging, and dangerous realms of the unknown. Put quite another way, princes and princesses rarely become immigrants from their lands of birth, place, status, and wealth. Paupers do. Seekers do. Those at the ends of their ropes at home seek new places elsewhere with the hope that it will be better than the "old country."

Thus, many of the people who set sail for this ancient "New World" did so under intense financial pressures, and also social repression and ostracism. They didn't bring any cash with them—they rarely had any! But, after the initial settlement and their most basic needs were satisfied, the social climbing began—the uniquely American drive to "keep up with the Joneses." How did they do this?

One of the most lucrative businesses to ever hit American shores was, as we know, slavery. The other biggie? Drugs. Steven Sora is a writer and researcher who specializes in the history of the Knights Templar, a military religious order that operated during the Crusades (circa 11th through 13th centuries), which, because of its vast wealth, became the bankers of Europe until their suppression and alleged destruction under Philip IV of France. Through this connection, he theorizes that many (or some) survivors of the order made their way, surreptitiously, to America, and played roles in the Colonial Revolution.

This begins to make sense only if one considers that a revolution is, by its very nature, an illegal activity—*until it prevails*—for it opposes the established order. Prior to the American Revolution, the law in the American colonies was what Parliament or Buckingham Palace decided the law was. Sora writes about how the dual industries of slavery and smuggling (including drugs) enriched the mercantile classes in the colonies, and how they grew and prospered:

> While it is not surprising that America's Founding Fathers were mostly slave owners, a legal activity, it may be surprising to discover that they were often smugglers as well. Profits from drug running, smuggling, slave trading and even piracy are directly responsible for the founding of several of the country's most important banks, which are still in operation today. New England's staunch insurance business was born and prospered through profits earned from insuring opium and slave ships. The large railroad system that was built throughout the continental United States in the nineteenth century was funded with profits from illegal drug smuggling. And one of the greatest opium fortunes would provide seed money for the telephone and communications industry.[25]

If the reader recalls the above comments about revolutions, one can perhaps better comprehend Sora's point about how this Revolution was funded, supported, and made possible—via crime and its associated crime syndicate. Sora explains:

> The secret and elite structures that have built America's business empires and family fortunes have concealed their history as well. In an age when the slightest indiscretions sometimes have the potential to disqualify a candidate from public office, the tainted background and family histories of the Founding Fathers of the country and its institutions are remarkable. We have inherited colleges and universities named for slave traders and opium dealers. We honor presidents and other politicians whose families built their fortunes through crime. We patronize businesses founded by men whose fortunes are rooted in illegal activity.
>
> Many of the families regarded as America's blue bloods, our equivalent of aristocracy, have hidden in their ancestral closets men who would make today's organized criminals look cherubic. They were not mere horse thieves and snake-oil salesmen, nor were they con men who were ridden out of town on the rail. These Founding Fathers rose to great wealth. Their legacy was passed on to heirs who still enjoy that wealth—and their power too, which is protected by the institutions they put in place and ensures their participation in the future. The system, thanks to ill-gotten gains and power, perpetuates itself.[26]

In point of fact, the sacralized "founders" used criminal means to wage war against the British throne. Sora writes:

> Piracy was not the only crime on the high seas; the American colonies also prospered through smuggling. John Hancock was a wealthy Mason whose ship *Liberty* would put Boston on the path to the Tea Party and Revolution. With one foot in the elite Masonic lodges where the workingman was accepted, Hancock provided work for one third of Boston. It was Britain's insistence on enforcing its laws against smuggling that precipitated the Revolution. The colonies relied on their smugglers to provide food, arms, and supplies to fight Britain.[27]

Remember: British law was American law, for the laws written in London governed its colonies like America. Until the Revolution, London represented the final say on any law. Sora argues that businesses wanted to smuggle goods into the colonies that were not subject to the taxes placed upon them by London. *Taxes.* Sora reminds us, "Merchants buying even commodities from any of the numerous European possessions in the New World were almost always breaking the law."[28] But this wasn't regarded so much as crime, as it was good business, for it led to larger profits (and less taxes!). And when the British began cracking down, Americans became more and more irate.

Of such forces as these, a Revolution was born.

We have assembled the ingredients in our *mise en place.* We have written about the underlying economic interests, the banks, flush with opium loot, and the British connections, right up to the imperial throne.

Now is the time to serve the dish.

The drug lords of Britain and America were making profits of 1,000 percent off the opium trade. *One thousand percent?* Who could resist such sums? (Definitely not those who believed themselves spiritually, racially, and culturally superior to the plebes.) Millions of Chinese people suffered as drug addicts in order to fund and establish British and American dynasties of wealth, power, and prestige. Sora delves into the American branch of drug lords:

> Thomas Perkins deserves credit for being one of America's first and foremost opium dealers, as well as one of the great drug smugglers in history. His amazing fortune places him ahead, in comparable

> dollars, of even the computer billionaires of the 1990s. Perkins' wealth made him a very influential man in American politics and the power behind the Boston Brahman class. Old reports state that the first families of Boston were from Salem, which implies they made their fortunes in shipping. What is not often understood is that these first families all made their start in the opium trade. The Appletons, Cabots, Endicotts, Hoopers, Higginsons, Jacksons, Lowells, Lawrences, Phillipses, and Saltonstails made their money by being related to Thomas Perkins or by riding on the coattails of the mercantile prince.
>
> Not only did these families create wealth, but also they then created industries that survived and prospered for decades to come. One industry was insurance. The Perkinses understood the value of spreading risk; they would often be financed in part by the first families of New England, who wanted their share of the area's most lucrative trade, and in part by insurance.
>
> Marine insurance is regarded as the grandfather of all modern forms of insurance in America, and it got its start in New England insuring cargo from basic commodities to slaves and opium. Connecticut was home to some of America's first insurance companies. Many have survived intact or as parts of larger companies, though few realize their foundation was insuring the drug and slave traders in the early nineteenth century.[29]

As for us, we must confess, most of the names of the first families are unfamiliar. And that is precisely the point. Given the media predilection for sensationalism and the advancement of narratives that project criminally upon the poor, the marginalized, and the dispossessed, how does it come to be that we know the names of notorious drug lords like Escobar and Freeway Ricky, but not those who are among the wealthiest and well-born in American life? Who do you think owns the media? Activist John Looney reminds us:

> It takes millions of dollars even to think of buying a daily newspaper or starting a television station. (If a license is available). The average group of concerned citizens cannot take on such a financial burden. Furthermore, should financial resources really be the only qualification for starting a newspaper? I can only think of one in

recent years, the new *Washington Times.* Who had money for that? Rev. Moon and his Unification Church known as the "Moonies"![30]

"You can always steal more with a briefcase than you can with a gun"

Perhaps the name of someone who is famous may suffice to give us some insight into the breadth and scope of the drug trade, and its influence upon states and politics. James Bradley, in his exemplary *The Imperial Cruise,* wrote about the rivers of drugs that enriched and replenished America's great families. Some of these families reached the highest rung of political life: The White House. Writes Bradley:

> On March 17 1905, one of the most significant weddings in American history took place in a house in New York City at 8 East 76th Street, between Madison and Fifth Avenue. At 3:30 p.m., Miss Alice Roosevelt—serving as a bridesmaid dressed in a white veil and holding a bouquet of pink roses—opened the ceremony as she proceeded down the wide stairs from the third floor to the second-floor salon. The bride—her cousin Eleanor Roosevelt—followed, and behind her was President Theodore Roosevelt, who would give his niece away to the bridegroom, his fifth cousin Franklin Delano Roosevelt.
>
> Eleanor wore a pearl necklace and diamonds in her hair, gifts from Franklin's rich Delano relatives. Even though Franklin had never made much money himself, Teddy knew that he would be able to care for his new wife: FDR was heir to the huge Delano opium fortune.
>
> Franklin's grandfather Warren Delano had for years skulked around the Pearl River Delta dealing drugs. Delano had run offices in Canton and Hong Kong. During business hours, Chinese criminals would pay him cash and receive an opium chit. At night, Scrambling Crabs—long, sleek heavily armed crafts—rowed out into the Pearl River Delta to Delano's floating warehouses, where they received their Jesus opium under the cover of darkness. The profits were enormous, and at his death Delano left his daughter Sara a fortune that she lavished on her only son.
>
> The Delanos were not alone. Many of New England's great families made their fortunes dealing drugs in China. The Cabot family of

> Boston endowed Harvard with opium money, while Yale's famous Skull and Bones society was funded by the biggest American opium dealers of them all—the Russell family. The most famous landmark on the Columbia University campus is the Low Memorial Library, which honors Abiel Low, a New York City boy who made it big in the Pearl River Delta and bankrolled the first cable across the Atlantic. Princeton University's first big benefactor, John Green, sold opium in the Pearl River Delta with Warren Delano.
>
> The list goes on and on: Boston's John Murray Forbes' opium profits financed the career of transcendentalist Ralph Waldo Emerson and bankrolled the Bell Telephone Company. Thomas Perkins founded America's first commercial railroad and funded the Boston Athenaeum. These wealthy and powerful drug-dealing families combined to create dynasties.[31]

Talk about "the American way!" When next we deign to imagine what a drug dealer looks like, walks like, or sounds like, perhaps now we have a more informed, more well-rounded view than the one usually projected in the corporate media.

We know we do.

3 Women of the World vs. the Empire

For the women of this world, who form the numerical majority of humans, life must seem, to say the least, odd.

For all around them exists the rhetoric of equality, or big-D Democracy—or "Representative Government," or similar such clichés—but what actually exists is precious little real representation. For the Halls of Power are bedecked with MEN—men who often talk a good game, but when faced with the prospect of women's agency, furrow their brows and cross their arms like little boys in tree houses adorned with crayon-lettered signs that read:

Photo: Unknown (circa 1938)

He-Man Womun Haters Club
No Gurlz Alloud!

Darla Hood as "Darla"
Our Gang aka *The Little Rascals*

Indeed, boys will be boys... and big boys love their power more than little boys love their toy soldiers. There are, of course, exceptions to the rule, but those exceptions are, well—exceptions. That deep intransigence to real power-sharing goes beyond the U.S. Empire, and predates it by millennia.

For our present is a reflection of our past, and the War Against Women has had thousands of years of practice... and the annals of history are littered with the bones of women who dared to stand against the sheer misogyny that fills just such chronicles. Those beginnings (or claimed beginnings) still live in our daily consciousness, drilled deep by the ghostlike specters of Religion, Tradition, and Politics.

It was not ever thus.

In the Beginning

Modern industrialized society traces its beginnings to Rome, which, as an empire, had developed a martial, man-centered culture that immortalized those deemed the "manliest" among them. They treasured war, domination, conquest, and of course the spoils of battle. Their greatest general was hailed and laurels were placed around his head. The Senate named him Emperor—the mightiest man in the State, who was, for all intents and purposes, a living god.

The influence this history had on European (or Euro-descended) societies is undeniable. In such a martial environment, women were both sacralized and industrialized as Mothers—they were those who could breed more soldiers for the empire and, among the elites, a son to inherit from the father.

Today, we see and hear much of our legal discourse utilizing Latin to reflect ancient principles of law inherited from Rome. These ideas, carried through legal systems, also found expression in the modern world, especially one in which the reasoning of the fathers were interpreted as precedents from the hoary past, yet lived in the now. Under these precedents women were but the property of a man—lesser than males—beings, to be sure, yet beings of a lesser order.

In law, up until the 20th century, women couldn't own property in their own name, and husbands, under the legal doctrine of coverture, which meant, in a legal sense, a husband "covered" his wife, subsumed her legal rights, and that his signature was sufficient to counteract any legal disability occasioned by the disease or infirmity of womanhood. Even today, women are perceived (especially among business and corporate leaders) as not worthy of the highest wages paid to male executives, who are obviously more in need and deserving of such remuneration.

And while the law has held deeply ingrained prejudices against the female sex, the realm of the sacred did no better.

Women, as we were told in Sunday school (or in the lessons imbibed in catechism) were cursed in the cradle of humankind—the Garden of Eden—for listening to the Snake and not God. Moreover, we were all—all of humankind—borne into being by Adam, who birthed his mate, and all of her progeny. Thus, in much of the world, the realm of the sacred is the offspring of man, as priest, bishop, rabbi, imam, sahib, master—*Father.*

Women, no matter how rich in spirit, are called nuns or sisters, or—if they preside over a collective of such women—Mother Superior.

Nun. None. *No one?*

In antiquity, before Rome became a Christian conclave, male and female deities were worshipped. And for each god, there was a concomitant goddess, where both powers seemed to balance the other. For Jupiter was his sister/wife, Juno; Cupid was the son of Mars and Venus; and the like. Rome took the gods of Greece; and Greece took their gods and goddesses from Kemet (Egypt): only the names were changed. Yet, these ancient goddesses, even the ones that predated Rome, were worshipped throughout Europe.

Before the "City of Lights" or one more vapid and plastic American celebrity, there was another Paris—the legendary Trojan prince from ancient Greece, who abducted the lovely Helen and launched the Trojan War. For his troubles, the great city was named in his honor.

Not so.

Author Ean Begg cites numerous sources for the notion that the name is an abbreviated derivation from the term Par-Isis or "grove," and "barque" (or temple) of the Egyptian goddess called Isis (Auset in Kemetian). Indeed, a temple stood at the western reaches of the city, on the Seine's left bank.[1] Thus, women had public power, as priestesses, oracles, healers, and teachers from the days of antiquity to the rise of the Church.

The Church, as the House of Orthodoxy, suppressed any communal movement that sought to find its own way of celebration and salvation. One of those groups that chose to express its faith in its own way was the Cathars. Their beliefs were at variance with the Church, and their villages, towns, and places of worship were destroyed, not to mention the many thousands of Cathari. Among their doctrinal differences was the spiritual equality between men and women. Begg writes:

> One of the most remarkable and distinctive features of Catharism, which it shared with some early Gnostic groups, was that women were admitted to their priesthood of paffaits and parfaites. A celebrated example is afforded by Esclarmonde of Foix, the owner of Montsegur and inspirer of its resistance, who bore eight children before, with her husband's agreement, she became a parfaite.[2]

Feminist philosopher Marilyn French has written that religion continues, almost unabated, to be a powerful political tool engaged to weaken women's social power:

> Religions are major vehicles for subjugating women. To keep women from having political power—power within churches, a voice on public issues—religions concentrate mainly on women's bodies, treating the female body as if it incarnated the morality of the entire human race. Thus some focus on women's appearances, dress, and habits, as if all human virtue depended upon them (yet men's appearance, dress, and habits are seen as irrelevant to virtue); others focus on women's potential for motherhood, as if women alone had the duty to perpetuate the human species. Religions do not require men to support or reward or help women in this task, but they demand that men control it.[3]

It should be noted that we are not specifically referring to ancient history here. Clearly, these themes still resonate with destructive force against women in our life lived today, in churches and communities across the U.S. and around the world. Time and time again, the religious realm inexorably bleeds into the political realm, for there, power lies.

Image: Gilbert Stuart, National Gallery of Art (1815)

Abigail Adams

Miss Adorable

Do not put such unlimited power into the hands of husbands. Remember all men would be tyrants if they could. —Abigail Adams

At the very inception of the United States of America, one of the most radical (and most ignored) voices of the revolutionary generation was that of Abigail Adams, the wife of John. Perhaps that's because in ages of revolution, minds are opened to the delicious possibilities that rise from the souls of the dispossessed. In papers and letters that have survived, Abigail seems like the truest revolutionary, prodding, pushing, and trying to reason with her husband, to expand the realms of the possible. John Adams, while not completely deaf to her arguments, regards them as unrealistic. But were they?

In 1774, Abigail Adams opined that (Negroes) "have as good a right to freedom as we have."[4] In a series of letters written to her husband, Abigail Adams wrote movingly of the innate worth of women and prevailed upon her husband to prevail upon his fellow convention members to think about American women and their right to rights. In her correspondence, she wrote:

> [I]n the Code of Laws which I suppose it will be necessary for you to make, I desire you would remember the ladies, and be more generous and favourable to them than your ancestors...

She strengthened her appeal by prescribing precisely what she wanted her husband and his confederates to do:

> Do not put such unlimited power into the hands of the husbands. *Remember all men would be tyrants if they could.* If particular care and attention is not paid to the ladies, we are determined to foment a rebellion, and will not hold ourselves bound by any laws in which we have no voice or representation. [Emphasis added]

Imagine that. She is saying, essentially, if we have no part in the making of your laws, we are not bound to obey them. *This is revolutionary stuff.* Abigail next skillfully delivers the coup de grace:

> That your sex are naturally tyrannical is a truth so thoroughly established as to admit of no dispute, but such of you as wish to be happy willingly give up the harsh title of master for the more tender and endearing one of friend. Why then, not put it out of the power of the more vicious and lawless to use us with cruelty and indignity with impunity? Men of sense in all ages abhor those customs which treat us only as the vassals of your sex.[5]

"Naturally tyrannical," are men, according to this woman of the revolutionary age. Was this so? Was she correct?

John Adams was softly dismissive of his wife's concerns, and rallies against what he termed "the despotism of the petticoat." He attempted to use humor to parry Abigail's attacks, by comparing the discontent of women with the many threatening forces that already tore at the seams of the newly hatched republic. Blaming it on the British ministry, which relentlessly tried to drive divisions among the Americans, Adams writes that "[a]fter stirring up Tories, Landjobbers, Trimmers, Bigots, Canadians, Indians, Negroes, Hanoverians, Hessians, Russians, Irish Roman Catholicks, [and] Scotch Renegadoes, at last they have stimulated the [women] to demand new privileges and threaten to rebell."[6]

Abigail could see no humor in such an attempt, and in a letter to a friend, Mercy Warren, says as much. Speaking of John, she wrote, "He is very saucy to me in return for a list of female grievances which I transmitted to him." She suggested a petition be written to move the members of the revolutionary government.

John Adams, like men of his age and men of the present era, could not bring himself to take women seriously. (We must yet recall that even Abigail Adams, of so elevated and forward-thinking a mind, did not mean to include Black women in her equation.) And no, her noble attempt to influence the direction of the nation toward greater democracy failed, for in men's eyes, it wasn't "reasonable." A century and a half would pass (from 1776 to 1920 = 144 years) before women would be allowed to participate in the national franchise, when the 19th Amendment to the Constitution was ratified, granting women the right to vote. Throughout this long drought, the views, insights, and wisdom of women was denied to the nation and its counselors.

The nation had to grow up to the point where it could accept that women had the same faculties as men. In January 1776, during the 3rd Provincial Congress, members actually did debate whether the vote should be extended to women. Several representatives agreed with that proposition, but John Adams wasn't one of them. He argued that neither women nor the property-less deserved to vote, and his way prevailed. Meanwhile, across the Delaware, New Jersey's state constitution did address women; and more interestingly, it passed an article supporting such a practice. UCLA historian Gary Nash writes in his book, *The Unknown American Revolution,* that New Jersey's representatives knew exactly what they were doing in approving the measure, as from 1776 to 1807 women—including single women—were actually allowed to vote. But in 1807, the state legislature actively disenfranchised women by amending the state's constitution, thus bringing it closer in line with its surrounding sister states.[7]

SIDENOTE (just for shits and giggles)
The title for this section is "Miss Adorable"—which is how John Adams addressed his wife in one of his more famous letters. "Portia" was another possibility for the title—Abigail refers to herself as Portia in one of her playful letters to John, a clear reference to a Shakespeare character in *The Merchant of Venice.*

Injuries & Usurpations

As is always the case with revolutionary movements, the vote did not come into being by the good graces emanating from the lords of government. It came by ceaseless and relentless agitation. It came from women organizing all across the country—demanding it. On 19 and 20 July, 1848, women (and some supportive men) gathered at the first Women's Rights Convention in Seneca Falls, N.Y. Some 300 women attended the event. At its close many signed a Declaration of Principles, modeled on the U.S. Declaration of Independence, but with relevant references to the rights of women. A portion of the former document reads thus:

> When in the course of human events, it becomes necessary for one portion of the family of man to assume among the people of the earth a position different from that they have hitherto occupied...
>
> We hold these truths to be self-evident: that all men and women are created equal; that they are endowed by their Creator with certain inalienable rights; that among these are life, liberty and the pursuit of happiness...
>
> The history of mankind is a history of repeated injuries and usurpations on the part of man toward woman, having in direct object the establishment of an absolute tyranny over her. To prove this, let facts be submitted to a candid world...[8]

Among the grievances listed for women of that period were the denial of the vote, denial of rights to her wages or to property, no entry to college, and no equal employment opportunities. The Declaration ended with words again hearkening to the Declaration of Independence: "He had endeavored, in every way that he could, to destroy her confidence in her own powers, to lessen her self-respect and to make her willing to lead a dependent and abject life..."[9]

The Convention made quite an impact, and was replicated by women in different parts of the country. It served as a powerful narrative to let women and men know that these issues were on the minds of women, and some men (albeit a relatively small number).

The gentleman who penned the words, "All men are created equal," Thomas Jefferson, obviously didn't mean Black folks, but neither did he mean the female HALF of the human race. American women, he sniffed, were "too wise to wrinkle their foreheads with politics."[10]

The renowned abolitionist, Frederick Douglass, was among that small class of men who supported the rights of women. He came upon this position by way of his fervent love of freedom, which, as an ex-captive, was deep within his spirit. In the first issue of his newspaper, *The North Star,* was emblazoned the legend:

> *Right is of no sex.*

When the Women's Rights Convention came to Seneca Falls, he was there, and shortly thereafter, wrote in his paper that he fully supported the "grand movement for attaining the civil, social, political, and religious rights of women." He explained in *The North Star* of 28 July 1848 the following:

> Standing as we do upon the watch-tower of human freedom, we can not be deterred from an expression of our approbation of any movement, however humble, to improve and elevate the character of any members of the human family... We are free to say that in respect to political rights, we hold women to be justly entitled to all we claim for man... Our doctrine is that "right is of no sex!" We therefore bid the women engaged in this movement our humble Godspeed.[11]

Helen & Emma

Photo: Unknown (1905)

Helen Keller

Photo: Library of Congress (1908)

Emma Goldman

With an eloquence and nobility often lacking among the founders, Frederick Douglass, the escaped slave, gave voice to a stirring vision of freedom among women. But not all women's voices called for the vote. Women like the famous (and outspoken socialist) Helen Keller, and the anarchist leader, Emma Goldman, decried the allure of voting, and downplayed its real effectiveness in gaining freedom and social justice for women. Keller, writing to a suffragette in 1911 England, noted:

> Our democracy is but a name. We vote? What does that mean? It means that we choose between two bodies of real, though not avowed, autocrats. We choose between Tweedledum and Tweedledee...
>
> You ask for votes for women. What good can votes do when ten-elevenths of the land of Great Britain belongs to 200,000 and only one-eleventh to the rest of the 40,000,000? Have your men with their millions of votes freed themselves from this injustice?[12]

Keller, although physically blind, saw clearly and true. Goldman would set forth a similar critique:

> Our modern fetish is universal suffrage... The women of Australia and New Zealand can vote, and help make the laws. Are the labor conditions better there?
>
> The history of the political activities of men proves that they have given him absolutely nothing that he could not have achieved in a more direct, less costly, and more lasting manner. As a matter of fact, every inch of ground he has gained has been through a constant fight, a ceaseless struggle for self-assertion, and not through suffrage. There is no reason whatever to assume that woman, in her climb to emancipation, has been, or will be, helped by the ballot.[13]

Goldman was an advocate of direct action—not pseudo-representative democracy. These were women steadfastly in opposition to the empire. Keller, a woman blind, deaf—but certainly not dumb—wrote with a fierceness and intensity that has escaped us in the present, in how she is presented in popular media. But, as the words above illustrate, she was a strong and staunch socialist, who questioned the State and capitalism. As for their critiques of the reigning political system, and the emptiness of our politics, who can dare refute it?

As of this writing, the American Congress has an approval rating that hovers below twenty percent, often dipping near ten percent. They are widely seen as a collective tool of the moneyed classes. Are there those who think that wrong?

Yes, there are women in the house of politics in America, but are their voices authentically that of women, or echoes of the interests that can afford them? They preside over a political betrayal of the interests of women (as Emma Goldman said) for dignity, true freedom, and liberation from the stifling chains of tradition. The 2018 U.S. midterm elections ushered in unsullied and vibrant new voices to the stale American landscape—Representatives Rashida Tlaib (D-MI), Ayanna Pressley (D-MA), Ilhan Omar (D-MN), and Alexandria Ocasio-Cortez (D-NY). The predictable knee-jerk reactions to these voices—dynamic female voices offering alternative strategies to the anti-individual, anti-democratic, and anti-equitable policies of the establishment's power structure—was vicious, racist, and above all misogynistic attacks by Republicans and Democrats alike, men and women alike. Is there any doubt that four young (white) men would have been regarded and handled differently?

To most Americans, Helen Keller is long remembered as the little deaf and blind girl who defined courage in the face of overwhelming adversity. This is evidenced by the statue of Helen that stands in the U.S. Capitol building—a young girl standing next to the iconic water pump, the essence of "The Miracle Worker" and her teacher Anne Sullivan. But what most Americans do not know or embrace is the fact that Helen Keller was an outspoken radical activist who greatly supported and participated in the major progressive social movements of her era. It was Keller's work with the blind and the revelations regarding their mistreatment that opened the door to her steadfast involvement fighting for the rights of workers, women, and other oppressed groups. As Keller matured politically, she remained a lifelong pacifist, socialist, and feminist inspiring many to push on. Helen Keller was a true revolutionary force.

Never afraid to loudly speak her mind or fight for unpopular causes, Helen Keller was closely watched by the FBI all of her adult life. From her younger days, when she condemned John D. Rockefeller as a "monster of capitalism" for his involvement in the Ludlow Massacre during which his goon squad slaughtered coal miners and their families in Colorado, through her strong denunciation of the Vietnam

War that raged at the time of her death in 1968, Keller celebrated diversity and deplored injustice. Ruth Shagoury of The Zinn Education Project writes in her piece "Who Stole Helen Keller?" that American educators and textbooks greatly distort Keller's life's work and thereby miss glorious opportunities to inspire young minds.

> [S]he is remembered chiefly as a child who overcame the obstacles of being deaf and blind largely through the efforts of her teacher, Anne Sullivan. While she may be hailed as a "hero" in lesson plans for today's children, the books recount only a fraction of what makes Helen Keller heroic.[14]

In popular American culture, women have value inasmuch as they can be exploited for their sexuality. They are but another commodity to be bought and sold on the streets, in hotels, on television and movie screens, and of course saturating the Internet from a porn industry churning over billions of dollars annually.

We've discussed a group of heroic women, but principally (not totally) these have been elite women, members of wealthy families or wives of men of power, position, and social rank. We should acknowledge that these voices in no way represent the majority of women in America—for the vast majority of women lived, died, and went largely forgotten from the ranks of the poor, the workers, and those from oppressed societies of African or First Peoples origins. As many of these women did not have wealth as the foundation of their families, there remains little evidence of their passage through the foibles and feuds of American life.

Little. But there is some.

The dogged research of historian Gary Nash has unearthed the lives and, on occasion, the voices of some of these women, many of whom remain little remembered as the "Founding Mothers" of the American Revolution. In truth, they fought a revolution from below, often against the very men whom we now certify as Founding Fathers. Inevitably, as a response to their very real and serious life challenges of near-starvation, they looked with considerable disfavor at the rich among them, especially the merchants who gouged them with exorbitantly high prices for foodstuffs. Nash's account of many of these women who led and staged food riots is a sobering portrait that rarely makes its way into our modern renderings of the period. He writes:

> On the home front, female militancy revolved around obtaining subsistence commodities. While their husbands and sons fought the British, the women and children had to eat. Almost by definition, the war between the Americans and England dislocated the market economy. The prolonged clash of arms cut off avenues of trade to the West Indies and continental Europe, created shortages as marauding American and British armies requisitioned food and livestock, forced the Americans to rely on paper currency (which soon led to rampant inflation), and offered unusual opportunities for unscrupulous merchants, retailers, and even farmers to manipulate the price of foodstuffs.
>
> Many [of these women] were managing their families, farms, and urban shops in the absence of men. Trying to cope with a disordered economy, women became involved in a majority of these food riots and often were the principal organizers. Striding onto the public stage, they became arbiters of what was fair, what was patriotic, and what was necessary to serve the needs of the whole community. Fighting for ethical marketplace conduct was consonant with supporting "the glorious cause"; conversely, men like Thomas Boylston displayed antipatriotism by contributing to the misery of middle- and lower-class families—those who bore the brunt of battlefield blood sacrifices.[15]

(The Thomas Boylston referenced here was a prominent Boston merchant, who was on the British blacklist, as a "vehement" patriot, but also resented by Boston women who regarded him as "miserly" and "stingy.")

Price gouging during the anti-British war sent women into rages of protest, and they gathered to let the greedy merchants know of their ire. Some resolved to sell at prices set by the populace. Some, not surprisingly, did not agree to such protests, and they were met with the organized fury of the locals. In Beverly, Massachusetts, some 60 women (and a "handful" of men) seized sugar from a merchant charging exorbitant prices, forced other merchants to surrender *their* sugar—and appointed a woman shopkeeper to sell this product at a fair price!

Such an action as this would have been embraced by a woman like Emma Goldman, a committed anarchist. The word anarchy comes from the Greek term, *anarchos,* which literally means "no ruler." As Howard Zinn explains, "It's called direct action. That's what anarchists believe in. You don't sign petitions. You don't lobby. You don't visit your legislator. You take direct action against the source of your problem."[16] That's what the women of the pre-revolutionary and revolutionary period did. They needed bread, rice, and meat... so they organized and then they demanded it of the merchants. When that didn't succeed, they took it, and sold it, at a fair price, to the people and families of the city.

Goldman was following in their footsteps. In fact, she held a special place in Zinn's heart. Her spirit, of pure unadulterated rebellion, appealed to his sense of justice. But there was also another reason, as Zinn explained:

> I had vaguely been aware of Emma Goldman. It was interesting—here I was with a PhD in history, and what could be higher than that? But here I was with a doctorate from Columbia, and Emma Goldman had never been mentioned in any of my classes, and none of her writings had ever appeared on my reading lists, and it's just that I vaguely remembered reading a chapter about her in an old book called *Critics and Crusaders*. There's a chapter on Emma Goldman. So I had this vague notion about Goldman, but I didn't know anything about her.[17]

Born in Russia in 1869, Goldman was brought to the U.S. as a child and raised in the aura of American democracy, free speech, and justice. Those lessons paled in 1886, in what came to be known as the Haymarket Affair, when eight anarchists were charged in the bombing of workers and cops involved in a major labor protest in central Chicago. There was a mass demonstration to strike for an eight-hour workday. The demonstration mobilized some three thousand workers in support of the measure. As storm clouds rolled over the city, the crowd diminished considerably, and when there were several hundred left a phalanx of cops came on the scene, advanced to the speakers' platform, and ordered them to disperse. The speaker said that the meeting was almost over. Almost immediately, a bomb went off in the midst of the cops, wounding more than sixty of them. In response, the cops opened fire on the crowd, killing several workers, and wounding two hundred people.

With absolutely no evidence to show who tossed the bomb, the police later seized eight known anarchists, and charged them all. A major Chicago newspaper called for a quick and "short" trial for the eight accused. And so it was—the eight men were charged as accomplices to murder that none of them committed, and their only guilt was their political belief in anarchism.

In the heat, passion, and prejudice of the era, to be an anarchist was tantamount to being a communist a generation later. None of the men were even proven to be present at Haymarket Square, except the speaker at the podium. A year after the trial, five of the men were hanged, and one, Louis Lingg, a 21-year-old carpenter, smuggled an explosive into the prison and set it off, killing himself.

The executions electrified the nation, and 25,000 people attended a funeral march in Chicago. To a teenaged factory worker named Emma, it marked her political awakening and radicalization. She began to study and practice anarchism and to oppose the State with all of her youthful gusto. Sixty thousand citizens signed petitions that went to the new Governor of Illinois, John Peter Altgeld, who, after an investigation into the case, not only denounced the trial, but also pardoned the three remaining anarchists. But the damage was done, for the trial largely achieved many of its objectives: to frighten working people and to enhance the power of the State (in defense of capital, of course). And while the memory of the Haymarket Martyrs has since faded, it was a powerful lesson to the young people of the time—and it transformed both Emma and her lover, Alexander Berkman, into revolutionaries. Truth be told, the State's bold attack on the movement created more radicals and revolutionaries than we can now know.

For this was the era of life after the Civil War—a time of triumph for the capitalist powers of the North and their concomitant captains of industry. Labor struggles were raging coast to coast, from big cities to small towns, as workers fought for better lives outside of the feudal factories. Often, the woman "manning" the barricade, the speaker lifting the spirits of the working men and women, was Emma Goldman. If there was a struggle against the forces of wealth and power, Emma took the lead, practicing the freedom of speech that she learned as a child.

She condemned the robber barons.
She lambasted the corporate press.
She blasted the judiciary.
She spat against capitalist war.

Ah. That was it. That was the proverbial straw that cracked the camel's back: her opposition to war.

Specifically World War I—the war that began between European states and deepened into a vast carnival of murder involving some thirty-two nations. A war that cost more than ten million lives on the field—and double that—twenty million people from disease, starvation, and want. It was a war to secure capitalist control over lands, colonies, and territories—on both sides of the ledger. At the very beginning, Americans opposed it virtually en masse. They wanted no part in Europe's wars. But to create the grounds for U.S. entry, the President, the Attorney General, and the Congress came together to outlaw both words and ideas. To speak out against war was patently "unpatriotic." Worse, it was criminal. And the U.S. government targeted Goldman, the woman activist, for speaking out against supporting another capitalist war. She would be convicted of violating the Espionage Act for opposing the draft and she was sentenced to two years in a state penitentiary in Missouri. Her lover and comrade, Alexander Berkman, would also be convicted and sent to the federal joint in Atlanta.

When they emerged in December of 1919, they entered into a new mix of state repression, occasioned by the alleged anarchist attempted bombing at the home of A. Mitchell Palmer, the U.S. Attorney General who later launched the infamous "Palmer Raids"—attacks on aliens who were arrested, deported, and shipped to the countries of their birth. For Emma and Alexander, this meant the Soviet Union. When Emma was an infant, Russia was the hereditary lands of the Czar. The Soviet Union did not exist. For her and Berkman, they were deported to a country that was just as much an enemy as the United States. "They soon found themselves in Russia at odds with the new Bolshevik regime because they were anarchists," recalls Howard Zinn, who also points out that as anarchists they were essentially antistatist and railed against any authority. "Maxim Gorky was putting out a little dissident newspaper and it didn't last long because they were rounding up dissidents," Zinn continues. "So as opponents of the regime, they soon left the Soviet Union (and) settled in Western Europe."[18] They lived modestly on the coast of France and remained somewhat plugged in to the political scene through the end of their lives. Berkman died in 1936 and Goldman died in Canada in 1940 on a rare return visit to North America.

Goldman, by taking the side of the poor, the oppressed, the workers, and the opponents of war, remained a lifelong exemplar of a radical, indeed, revolutionary life. In fact, Zinn was so moved by her life that he wrote a play entitled: *Emma: A Play in Two Acts about Emma Goldman, American Anarchist.*

Goldman is presented here not merely because of her singular rebellious personality, but because she represented a generation of revolutionary people who shared her basic worldview of an America at war with a greedy elite that strived to grind workers into dust to make another buck. That America is not really known to us today because of the massive shift in perspective from that defiant time to the current capitulation to power. That is so in part because capitalism has triumphed in the contest between the United States and the former Soviet Union and, as such, economic royalty seized the ideological high ground, which positions the reign of capital as not only reasonable, but inevitable.

This perspective has become normative and is projected from every major organ of American capitalism's vast reach and power. Thus, any other idea is attacked as not only "radical" but wholly irrational. Generations ago, in the days of Helen Keller and Emma Goldman, this business sense did not permeate popular consciousness, and there was a broad, deep sense of workers as an embattled populace, fighting for their lives against the rapacious forces of greed.

War is the MOTHER of all things

In the bottom of the 19th and the top of the 20th centuries, rich corporate giants, in a rush to make more wealth, killed workers by the thousands through dangerous working conditions and, when workers dared strike for labor protections or better wages, the captains of industry paid platoons of armed men to mow them down like wheat in a field.

The year 1893 marked the worst economic season yet in the American republic. More than six hundred banks shut their doors and thousands of businesses shut down completely. Millions of people were unemployed and neither the state nor businesses made any provision for the hungry mouths that wept for food. Emma Goldman gave a speech at Union Square in New York City where she told the assembled throng that if any unemployed worker couldn't feed their family, they had every right to go into the stores—and take it. She was arrested, charged with "incitement to riot," and given two years in prison. This was a woman who spent her life's energies fighting against the empire. She was not alone.

Remember the old axiom: "War is the mother of all things."

Putting aside the ugliness of pairing the creative act of motherhood with the genocidal instincts at the heart of war, it is a fact that war brings change to societies engulfed therein. When the Great War raged across Europe, many people fought against American intervention. As we have seen, Emma Goldman was tossed into jail for daring to oppose the military draft.

Before a generation had come and gone, another war would burn across the world—World War II—and its arrival sent ripples of change in a society desperately trying to hold on to the traditions of the not-so-distant past. But the forces of capitalism required workers to do the jobs that kept the American factory running, and in search of workers—it recruited and employed women. Lots of women.

As Zinn tells us, the growth of female workers during this period expanded significantly:

> World War II had brought more women than ever before out of the home into work. By 1960, 36 percent of all women sixteen and older—23 million women—worked for paid wages. But although 43 percent of women with school-age children worked, there were nursery schools for only 2 percent—the rest had to work things out themselves. Women were 50 percent of the voters—but (even by 1967) they held 4 percent of the state legislative seats, and 2 percent of the judgeships. The median income of the working woman was about one-third that of the man. And attitudes toward women did not seem to have changed much since the twenties.[19]

Put into position by the exigencies of imperial war, women tasted lives outside the home, in positions of responsibility, and supported their families with increased returns in wages. By the 1970s and '80s, more and more women were forced to find work because of the rapidly expanding costs of living, which required two (and sometimes three) incomes. But, still, things were not as peachy keen as they seemed. For, in a capitalist state, one dominated by the stranglehold of corporations, increased work doesn't necessarily mean increased wages. Philosopher Marilyn French, in her book *The War Against Women,* illustrates precisely how more is less, especially when it comes to women's economic and social power:

> Elite men kept seeking ways to defeat organized labor, moving their factories to regions, and, later, countries where labor was not organized. Forming transnational corporations, they built factories in countries without protective laws where they could also buy cheap raw materials. Corporations huge enough to control governments (some of which, notably in England and the United States, tried to wreck unions) set out to bring labor to its knees. After World War II in the United States, wages and working conditions improved for blue-collar men, whose average earnings leaped from $15,056 to $24,621 in 1973. But by 1987 their average wage, adjusted for inflation was $19,859, a 19 percent decline. By the 1980s, many married women had entered the work force to raise family incomes, but in 1988 salaries brought in only 6 percent more than one in 1973. Business policies are gradually eradicating well-paid jobs protected by union contracts. As one economist puts it, "One well-paid smokestack job with health insurance has been replaced by two service jobs without benefits."[20]

To protect corporate profits, corporations waged an outright assault against the wages won by union power, and then hired women—paid them less for essentially the same (or similar) jobs—and watched their ill-gotten profits soar. Greatly facilitated by bought-and-paid-for feeble and duplicitous politicians, this discriminatory practice (read: game plan) changed the very foundation of American life.

NYPD mugshot, Antiwar Protest (1965)

Andrea Dworkin

Okay, Abu-Jamal wanted to include this Dworkin quote as a transition:

Feminism is hated because women are hated. Anti-feminism is a direct expression of misogyny; it is the political defense of women hating.
—Andrea Dworkin

Vittoria this one:

"I want to see man beaten to a bloody pulp with a high-heel shoved in his mouth, like an apple in the mouth of a pig."
—Andrea Dworkin

Witness the obvious difference between your authors, Butch & Sundance.

"She dances for dimes and dollars on poles"

We have explored some examples of women fighting against the empire. This has been (to use a popular phrase) "A long hard slog." Yet, as Dr. Marilyn French's book title suggests, there has been an ongoing and brutal imperial war waged against women.

What are the features of this war? How is it fought? Who are the combatants? Who's winning? And who's losing?

As we quoted earlier in the chapter, Dr. French's work gives us significant insight into these questions, which goes a long way toward explaining the dynamics and parameters of this ages-long conflict, for war comes in various forms and utilizes various fronts to attack its targets. Dr. French argues that one of the earliest weapons employed against women was in the realm of religion.

Dr. French further illustrates the interplay between religion and the guttural world of politics. Both, she argues, are forms of governance and control over female bodies and, perhaps more importantly, female psyches:

> The discussion of religious war against women moves on to state efforts to dominate women by passing laws governing female bodies, either in alliance with a religion or independent of it. Tied to religion and to the notion that women bear the burdens of

> human sexual morals is a practice promoted under the aegis of many religions, genital mutilation of women, which an estimated twenty million women in the world today have undergone.[21]

It is more than interesting that religions would serve as a "major vehicle" for the subjugation of women, for, in most instances, religions are supported, undergirded, and peopled by women. Women are celebrants in almost every conceivable religion—yet, in most of the major, universalist, Abrahamic religions, women wield very little power in these spiritual formations, per tradition.

French further examines another front in this war: labor and its fair return to the worker. French writes that the world of work is one in which women play a predominant role: that of workers. Yet, when it comes to a fair return for that labor, they are famously underpaid:

> The statistics presented at the United Nations Conference of Women in Copenhagen in 1980 remain true today: women do between two-thirds and three-quarters of the work in the world. They also produce 45 percent of the world's food. But they are still granted only 10 percent of the world's income and 1% of the world's property—and part of that 1 percent masks male ownership hidden for tax purposes. (In the United States, property ownership is murky because most people own only a residence, usually placed in the names of both husband and wife. But the U.S. Census Bureau estimates that 16 percent of the property in this country is owned by women in their own right as female heads of household.) And women's situation is worsening because a new world order created by the new economic system puts men in power everywhere, even in places where women had some voice until recent decades.[22]

The societal, social, and economic contributions of women are, without question, pivotal to the very continuation of the human species, especially in the realm of human re-production. Feminists from the early 20th century (and before) have argued that women, given the centrality of their role, should be compensated for the work that makes all other work possible, i.e., a living wage.

Back in 1972, two feminists and socialists, Mariarosa Dalla Costa and Selma James, published *The Power of Women and the Subversion of the Community,* a 79-page pamphlet detailing the contribution of women to society in its re-production. As students of Marx, they delved deeply into the meaning of production (the heart of Marxist analysis) and uncovered something quite remarkable. They wrote:

> Marx's analysis of capitalist production was not a meditation on how the society "ticked." It was a tool to find the way to overthrow it, to find the social forces who, exploited by capital, were subversive to it. Yet it was because he was looking for the force that would inevitably overthrow capital that he would describe capital's social relations, which are pregnant with working class subversion. It is because we were looking for women's lever of social power among those forces that we were able to uncover that even when women do not work outside their homes, they are vital producers.
>
> The commodity they produce, unlike all other commodities, is unique to capitalism: the living human being—"the laborer himself."[23]

In sum, women recreate the world—one being at a time. In fact, James and Dalla Costa use this insight to advance the next phase in their freedom movement: the campaign for the state to pay for housework. This was, to be sure, an attack against the Empire (of capital), and, as such, challenged the primacy of capital for the irreducible primacy of Life itself. The very fact that this essential centrality of woman is largely invisible is part of the war against women: to marginalize the very necessity of them for any human activity. But war has many forms, among them political and allegorical. We have referenced so-called "wars" against poverty, drugs, cavities, and the common cold. They are not wars in the most common of senses. The best that can be said is that they are "wars" of words.

But in real war—man's grandest endeavor—here too women are deeply involved, with the result of which being women's antipathy for war. Dr French continues:

> In the twentieth century alone, the world has fought at least 207 wars that killed 70 million people. And while states glorify the soldiers who fight the wars, most of those killed in them are women and children. In each minute that passes, thirty children die from want of food or inexpensive vaccines; in that same minute, the world's governments spend $1.3 million of wealth produced by the public (between two-thirds and three-quarters of it by women) on military expenditures.[24]

We can be sure that no statues or medals are awarded to these casualties. Yet even other forms of violation and violence are directed at women, under the apparent rubric of desire. Here, capital appropriates sex as merely another commodity, where women are but bodies to be used, and virtually discarded. Marilyn French explains:

> The most blatantly exploitative form of development is what is called sexploitation or sex-tourism, a new business, tours for men to Third World countries to visit brothels created specifically for them, womaned by virtual slaves—girls, often just children, sold into bondage by poor peasant fathers. Sex-tourism was proposed as a development strategy by international aid agencies. Maria Mies writes that the sex industry was first planned and supported by the World Bank, the IMF [International Monetary Fund] and the United States Agency for International Development. Thailand, the Philippines, and South Korea are the present centers of Asian sex-tourism. Parties of Japanese businessmen are flown to one of these centers by their companies as a reward. American workers at a construction site in Saudi Arabia, totally fenced off from the culture around them, were flown to Bangkok every two weeks to be serviced by Thai women working in massage parlors. Another part of the sex industry is marriage brokerage; private companies, most in what used to be West Germany, sell Asian or Latin American women as wives, openly advertising them as "submissive, nonemancipated, and docile." Both industries are maintained by a support network of multinational tourist enterprises, hotel chains, airlines, and their subsidiary industries and services.[25]

To speak of war, especially in a nation that often imbibes from the bloody fountain of war, is an easy thing. For, it is the very essence of our speech, the stuff of our dreams, and the substance of our hopes.

American history is defined by an orgy of war. ***America loves war.***

America loves it with unbridled passion. It is the broken water that attended the birth of America. It is the germ of the very notion of nationality—it is "us vs. them" (no matter who "they" are). And these passions have been unleashed from the dawn of so-called civilization to dethrone women from the vault of heaven, and down to the hovels and huts of the earth.

In antiquity, the female essence was idealized as goddesses who granted humans the boon of a fertile, giving earth. She blessed marriage, brought fecundity, and bore the names of ancient Mothers of the mind and the heart. Now, she is fallen into a commodity. She dances for dimes and dollars on poles, adorned with the modern form of misogyny—plastic breasts instead of foot-binding; or works two jobs to make ends meet.

She is the "collateral damage" of war (along with her children); her work is devalued on the factory floor; she is the unshaven lass bound by chains of shame and fear to the profits of a porn palace in Asia... or a porn palace in sunny Southern California, down San Fernando Valley way; she is the last and least-paid. Women are at war, and have been so long, that they flee the implications of that reality, in the pews of the church, in the burdens of work, in the lonely walk through life with "companions" who look down upon them, as rapists view their carnal prey.

Because war is terrifying. Organized, mechanized terror.

Stupid Spoiled Whore

War is a male conspiracy against the bodies, minds, souls, psyches, and sexuality of women—in which the very victims are so unaware that they love the victimizers!

They are conditioned to see themselves as "free" in a culture that binds them in gilded cages, with their eyes moist from movies that project them as whores with golden hearts, in that their only worth is their sex (*Pretty Woman* storyline), filling teenage minds (and younger) with the fantasy of hooking for a living until they luck up and marry a millionaire—instead of building an enterprise to make their own wealth, or create their own businesses.

Sometimes we find truth in the damndest of places—like the South Park Mall, a fictitious hell born in the absurdist yet truth-seeking minds of Trey Parker and Matt Stone. Their *South Park* episode, "Stupid Spoiled Whore Video Playset," holds an unfortunate mirror up to American society:

> A LARGE GROUP OF KIDS HAVE GATHERED AT THE GRAND OPENING OF A NEW STORE AT THE SOUTH PARK MALL.
>
> 4th Grader #1: *Come on Wendy, we're gonna miss it!*
> Wendy: *We're gonna miss what?*
> 4th Grader #1: *Paris Hilton is making an appearance at the mall.*
> Wendy: *Who's Paris Hilton?*

4th Grader #2: *Who's Paris Hilton?!?!?*
4th Grader #3: *You don't know?!?!?*

MC (onstage): *Hello everyone. The Guess Clothing Company is pleased to have as its new spokesperson and model, a woman all you young ones can look up to, Miss Paris Hilton.*

(cheers and applause)

Wendy: *I don't get it. What does she do?*
4th Grader #3: *She's super-rich.*
Wendy: *But what does she do?*
4th Grader #2: *She's totally spoiled and snobby.*
Wendy: *WHAT DOES SHE DO?*
Adult Male: *She's a whore!*

Paris (onstage): *Hey everyone. Sorry if I'm a little spent. I did a whole lot of partying last night with a lot of different guys (coughs up a misspent night). Anyway, I'm pleased to be here in Gouth Dark to announce the opening of my brand-new store. A store where girls can buy everything they need to be just like me!*

(reveal storefront) STUPID SPOILED WHORE!

(more cheers and applause)

But there's one voice of reason...

Wendy: *You guys, don't buy this stuff. Why do you want to be like Paris Hilton?*

4th Grader #3: *It's not just Paris. It's Britney Spears, Christina Aguilera, Tara Reid... they're all stupid spoiled whores.*

Wendy: *But the idea that we'll be whorish for money is belittling to our gender.*

This dark comedy of a cartoon is more chilling than absurd as it frames an undeniable truth—twisted values and manipulated dreams rule the American day. And when the storm clouds part, it becomes clear as we glimpse the truth: Capitalism is killing them and their only empty joy is in the narcotic of shopping.

Erich Fromm, the psychoanalyst, coined a term to describe modern man (and, by extension, and perhaps more fitting, modern woman): *homo consumens.* Shopping [Hu]Man. Thus, our worth is determined only by what we have to spend to feed the capitalist beast. This is who we are. This is what we are. Tools. Walking tools to be exploited.

"Three generations of imbeciles are enough"

And yet there is more that Dr. French has to teach us. There is another feature of the state misogyny that has destabilized and oppressed women that we have not yet addressed. Indeed, it has a long history in the United States that reaches deep into the 20th century as the U.S. government framed the state practice of sterilizing women, ostensibly because of their poor mental faculties. Putting aside the fact that for much of the history of the United States, women—here we speak of white women—were not allowed to enter or practice the supposedly male professions of law, medicine, or politics. It was this purported disability of mental development and growth that was utilized to keep women in check—and this vile practice of sterilization was one of the most powerful ways to curb women: render them infertile "for the good of society."

Of course, no one questions which society, for it is assumed that the alleged interest of whites is the very essence of society. Dr. French notes:

> Before the church-driven campaign to criminalize abortion penetrated government, the United States quietly worked to sterilize populations it considered undesirable—mainly Southern black (especially in North Carolina), Native American and Hispanic women. In 1972 alone, clinics used federal funds to sterilize 100,000 to 200,000 people in the United States (Hitler managed to sterilize only 250,000 in his entire regime). Over 35 percent of Puerto Rican women of childbearing age were sterilized in the 1970s, and 24 percent of Native American women of childbearing age by 1976.[26]

In the beginning of the second quarter of the 20th century, a woman in Lynchburg, Virginia, named Carrie Buck, brought suit against the forced sterilization of her (and other women) held at the State colony for Epileptics and Feeble-Minded, citing a violation of the constitution's protections of equal protection.

In 1927, in an 8-to-1 opinion dubbed *Buck v. Bell,*[27] the court, per the highly regarded jurist, Oliver Wendell Holmes, writing for the court majority (there was no dissenting opinion, although Justice Pierce Butler refused to join the opinion), returned with a line that has echoed loudly down the corridors of history. In turning down Ms. Buck's petition, Holmes wrote, pithily, "three generations of imbeciles are enough."[28]

Sterilization was important, he reasoned, because people such as Buck would "sap the strength" of society. Ms. Buck was forcibly sterilized later in the year of the *Buck v. Bell* decision, which became the law of the land, and before long, most American states had laws authorizing forced sterilization. It stood as legal until the 1942 decision, *Skinner v. Oklahoma,*[29] which outlawed sterilization without due process (or a hearing).

Photo: M.E. Grenander Special Collections and Archives, University at Albany

Carrie Buck, left, with her mother Emma in Virginia (1924), was one of 60,000 poor or disabled people in 32 states who were forcibly and "legally" sterilized to prevent reproduction; on the list were women diagnosed as insane, feeble-minded, suffering from epilepsy, or determined to be an idiot or imbecile.

It should be noted that this practice, once legalized by the U.S. Supreme Court, was used on a national scale to sterilize both males and females. But the deep societal bias against the intellectual capabilities of women certainly made it easier for the majority of the Court to rule against a family described in the case as "shiftless, ignorant, and [a] worthless class of anti-social whites."

These déclassé whites were but the door to the destruction of hundreds of thousands—perhaps millions—of potential lives that were denied existence by way of state-supported sterilizations. And given the deep white (not to mention, male) supremacy that dominated state policy during the period, it should not surprise us that the majority of the sufferers of this state program of eugenics were people of color: Black, brown, yellow, and red.

As we have seen, capitalism requires a sinister hierarchy of oppression, where people are individualized—the better to be oppressed—and oppressive forces are consolidated under the power of the State (or religion, tradition, even corporation). Under such a regime as this—one flavored by the intricate barriers of race and class—people are broken apart and separated from one another: the better to weaken them before the storm of corporate and state power.

Women, who are the majority of the people of this nation and the world, are given the rhetoric of equality, fed the thin gruel of democracy, and assuaged with the illusion of sexual liberty, all the while kept under the roving eyes and ears of the State and, perhaps worse, kept unwittingly under the many and varied weapons of war. And yet, women, those vessels of life, hope, overcoming and eternity, continue to bring forth living miracles of resistance, resilience and, when the day dawns, revolution.

Ella Baker: "I was not a person to be enamored of anyone"

Photo: Afro Newspaper (1941)

Ella Baker

It is said that Mother is the first teacher, and her lessons last lifetimes. It is often through this edification that struggles survive despite monstrous and unrelenting oppression.

At the half-point of the 20th century, a movement arose that poised itself against an ocean of white hatred and contempt. It came to be called the U.S. Civil Rights Movement and its icons, to this day, are far too often the men who led them. To be sure, more often than not, in various stages and platforms of the Movement, it was a matter of which man women allowed to lead them.

Why is that so? Because if the vast majority, or even the working majority, of the followers of a movement are (were) women, where would the "leader" be without the led?

The U.S. Civil Rights Movement was, in fact, a proxy of the Black activist church movement—a body that is peopled, more often than not, by women and girls. In fact, as shocking as it may seem, the vast majority of Black churches and churchmen (especially of the Baptist variety, that which claimed Rev. Dr. Martin Luther King, Jr., as a member) did not participate in the civil rights movement, for its leaders, mainly conservative male ministers, could not accept the notion of protest and civil disobedience. In many instances, people—female people—moved by their conscience and their deep discontent with the status quo, left their churches and joined others, which allowed them to join a movement that found the echo in their hearts.

If one examines the newsreels of the early Civil Rights Movement in the South, one cannot fail to see a predominance of women and children. One such woman who refused to bow to male preachers, yet managed to teach, to organize, and to have a deep and profound impact on Black youth of the period was Ella Baker—a skillful and committed intellectual, activist, organizer, and teacher.

Baker, working through a New York-based group (In Friendship), was the brains behind the inception of the Southern Christian Leadership Conference (Rev. King's group), a branch director of the NAACP, a grassroots voting rights activist, and she helped found the vibrant activist group known as SNCC (Student Nonviolent Coordinating Committee—pronounced "Snick"). Dr. King had problems relating to her, for he and his (male) colleagues thought her haughty and aloof, for she rarely deigned to defer to the men. Said Baker, "I was not a person to be enamored of anyone."

Smart, insightful, determined, and feeling fully able, she felt if she couldn't be talked to as an equal, then she had no use for the offices offered to her, despite it being widely known that she was by far the best organizer they ever encountered. So, why wasn't this able, educated woman given the posts she deserved? Baker herself explains:

> There would never be a role for me in a leadership capacity with SCLC. Why? First, I'm a woman. Also, I'm not a minister. And second... I knew that my penchant for speaking honestly... would not be well tolerated. The combination of the basic attitude of men, and especially ministers, as to what the role of women in these church setups is—that of taking orders, not providing leadership—and the... ego problems involved in having to feel that there is someone who... had more information about a lot of things than they possessed at the time... This would never have lent itself to my being a leader in the movement there.[30]

Baker, although not long in leadership positions of the major (or minor) organizations of the civil rights era, exercised inordinate influence over the lives, leadership styles, and political development of many activists—as well as a significant number of radicals and revolutionaries. As a founder and inspiration for the formation of SNCC, she exercised considerable influence over developing youth, who were encouraged to speak their minds and to make important decisions to act, or not to act, on issues of importance to them—without regard to the views of the elders (shall we say, the adults?) of the movement.

She encouraged independence and urged her younger activists to question, and when appropriate, disagree with those who were widely perceived as the leaders of the Movement. It was in that spirit that we witness SNCC people standing out as activists who were unafraid of either disagreements, or taking stands that were, frankly, quite dangerous to them and their fellows. They worked for voter registration and citizen education in counties and states where such acts attracted, not just death threats—but death itself.

Some of the SNCC founders went on to establish and build other movements and organizations—always building on the lessons learned and practices embraced while in SNCC. The late Kwame Ture (the activist-formerly-known-as Stokely Carmichael) comes to mind. Former District of Columbia mayor Marion Barry led SNCC briefly, before his foray into politics. The venerable U.S. Representative John Lewis of Georgia was also a major leader; he was succeeded by Ture (née Carmichael) as head of SNCC.

Kathleen Neal Cleaver, who became Communications Secretary and central committee member of the Black Panther Party, cut her eyeteeth as a SNCC member. Scholar and historian Clayborne Carson was a member of SNCC. Each of these people, directly or indirectly, felt the force of Ella Baker's brilliant spirit, her relentless drive, and her refusal to bow to unworthy idols.

Born in 1903, Baker was an activist-intellectual when many of the civil rights icons she would later work with (albeit with difficulty) were wearing short pants. Our comrade, historian Howard Zinn, in his masterpiece, *A People's History of the United States,* has (regrettably) a sole reference to the remarkable organizer, and it dates from the middle of the 1930s!

Citing an issue of the *Crisis* (a journal of the NAACP), Zinn notes how a 32-year-old Baker, and her colleague, Marvel Cooke, wrote about the modern-day (early 20th century) "slave marts" that dotted northern communities, particularly the "Bronx Slave Mart" in New York City during the hard times of the 1930s—at a time, we should add, when Little Marty King (Jr.) was a precocious 6-year-old! Baker and Cooke wrote in 1935 in Crisis:

> Not only is human labor bartered and sold for the slave wage, but human love is also a marketable commodity. Whether it is labor or love, the women arrive as early as eight a.m. and remain as late as one p.m. or until they are hired. In rain or shine, hot or cold, they wait to work for ten, fifteen, and twenty cents per hour.[31]

This is not just fine, evocative prose; it is a political and radical (from the roots) perspective of two fine minds at work, telling the story of the lives, humiliations, and struggles of women in 1930s America. This gives us some perspective, too, on the life and work of a brilliant organizer and movement worker—who did some of her best organizing in her sixties! That alone should qualify her for one who worked against the white empire, without respite, for a lifetime.

Yet, there is more. For she mentored a woman who went on to become an unforgettable figure on the big stage.

Postscript:
Angela Davis spoke at the Women's March on Washington in January 2017. In front of a crowd numbering hundreds of thousands of people, mostly women, there to protest the incoming demented, racist, and sexist administration, Davis, in her incomparable voice, offered this:

> *Those who still defend the supremacy of white male hetero-patriarchy had better watch out... This is just the beginning and in the words of the inimitable Ella Baker, "We who believe in freedom cannot rest until it comes."*

"I consider Rosa Parks a radical woman, a revolutionary woman..."
— Ericka Huggins, Director,
Black Panther Party's Oakland Community School

Photo: Unknown

Rosa Parks being fingerprinted by
Deputy Sheriff D.H. Lackey
Montgomery, Alabama (1956)

Rosa Parks is one of the very few women (besides the saintly projection of Coretta Scott King—and perhaps, Dr. Betty Shabazz) who achieved some renown during the highlights of the American Civil Rights Movement. It might be said that the Mississippian organizer and speaker, Fannie Lou Hamer, achieved some degree of prominence, but, in all honesty, Parks presented a profile that brought a kind of comfort and ease (among whites, mind you!) that Hamer never projected. This may be so because Parks was lighter-skinned, had less nappy hair, and was thus less frightening to millions of Negrophobic whites than her darker, more rootsy sister, Hamer.

But, projection is one thing; truth another.

We have spoken of Baker, but what we may not know is that the person we misremember as Rosa Parks might not have come into being without Ella Baker's influence. According to political scientist Jeanne Theoharis, Baker's impact on Parks was "profound," stemming from a meeting of NAACP leaders in the mid-1940s. Citing the work of historian Barbara Ransby,[32] Theoharis writes:

> A second organizer who saw local activists as the key to the work of the organization, Ella Baker was then serving as the NAACP's Director of Branches. Baker shunned the hierarchy and class leanings of many in the organization. In the mid-1940s, Baker sought to develop the NAACP's local chapters and the grassroots leadership within them. She instituted a series of conferences (like the one Parks attended) to train local leaders in developing ways to attack community problems and encourage them to see local issues as part of larger systemic problems. Baker left the director of Branches position in 1946, in part because she had grown disappointed by the ways the national office did not adequately support the work and vision of the local chapters. Baker later became branch president of the Harlem NAACP, helped found In Friendship to support the emerging Montgomery protest, served as the first acting executive director of the Southern Christian Leadership Conference (SCLC), and then helped to establish the Student Nonviolent Coordinating Committee (SNCC).[33]

Theoharis reports that Parks saw Baker as a "beautiful mentor"—a woman "smart and funny and strong," who instilled great inspiration in her work to come.

While the media (as well as the political classes) have portrayed Rosa Parks as a "quiet, dignified lady" who didn't want to get up from her bus seat on a segregated bus, Theoharis sets the record straight: that Parks was a woman enamored of Black folks, and as such supported groups like the Republic of New Afrika, the Black reparations movement, as well as the Black Panther Party—groups projected as the unwelcome stepchildren of the Black freedom movement. When Professor Theoharis spoke about her biography of Parks (*The Rebellious Life of Mrs. Rosa Parks*) on the *DemocracyNow* news hour, she stressed that "This is the story of a life history of activism, a life history that she would put it, as being 'rebellious,' that starts decades before her famous bus stand and ends decades after." In Theoharis' view, Parks was "a race woman"—and wherever Black people struggled, she sought to add her quiet presence.[34]

Also, think about this: Rosa Parks' meeting with Baker takes place almost a decade before the famous refusal to leave her seat on a Montgomery bus on 5 December 1955. Clearly, she was a trained organizer, and as Black revolutionary nationalist, Muhammad Ahmed has opined, Parks and the other women activists were "more progressive than the men."[35] (Why are we surprised?)

Bottom line? The women of the civil rights era were "more progressive" than their male "leaders" or peers. They felt deeper. They worked harder. Parks worked against the Vietnam War. Her hero? Malcolm X. In her seventies, decades after she remained seated and said "No," she attended anti-apartheid protests in Washington, D.C. in the mid-1980s at a time when Nelson Mandela was firmly planted on the United States' Terrorist Watch List (until 2008!), an act strongly supported by media-darling Margaret Thatcher, who infamously called the African National Congress a "typical terrorist organization." (The Reagan administration, still drunk on the elixir of the Cold War, surmised that there might be COMMUNISTS in the ranks of the ANC—"communists, I tell ya... red communist moles indebted to the Kremlin!")

Parks, like her mentor Ella Baker, knew better and fought against the Empire and their sycophants. They fought with brilliance and they fought with bravery. Theoharis paints a portrait of Parks that never made its way into national newspapers nor the Empire's history books. She recounts how Parks went to Oakland, California, to both visit and support the Black Panther Party's school, an award-winning institution. Theoharis relates the meeting between these two, iconic entities:

> During the 1979/1980 school year, Parks paid a visit to the Black Panther Party's Oakland Community School, an independent black elementary school started to address the deficits in Oakland's public educational system and the Party's longest-running survival program. The students performed a play they had written in her honor, which included a reenactment of her bus stand, and then she answered questions. "It didn't matter if they asked the question again and again, she answered them," according to the school's director, Ericka Huggins, who recalled how much Parks loved it. "She just kept thanking me and the instructors and the Black

> Panther Party for doing what we are doing." The students and entire staff were "touched," according to Huggins that Parks "came all the way" and talked about it for weeks afterwards. Huggins recalled her own delight at Parks' visit. "I consider Rosa Parks a radical woman, a revolutionary woman, showing up in real time at an elementary school run by the Black Panther Party."[36]

Rosa Parks—mentored by Ella Baker, admired by Panther women like Ericka Huggins—women all standing steadfast against the Empire, fighting on the fields where they found themselves, struggling, against monstrous odds, yet struggling still, to bring forth change to the American way of apartheid.

They were living avatars for a struggle that moved through the rivers of time.

Women of the Party

The Black Panther Party was, perhaps, the high (and low) point of the revolutionary movement that came into being when the civil rights movement failed to address and make whole the hopes and fears of the Black Nation. By turns, nationalist, then internationalist, revolutionary and (in a term coined by BPP co-founder, Dr. Huey P. Newton) "Intercommunalist," the Black Panther Party attracted militants from all areas of the nation, to found, lead, and organize chapters and branches in more than forty American cities.[37] This soon-to-be national formation attracted both male and female militants and revolutionaries, and despite its internal contradictions of sexism among the men, women struggled and sometimes prevailed in their struggle for power and parity among members.

Unlike most organizations of the movement period, women found openings to become section leaders, squad leaders, lieutenants, and captains of chapters and branches across the country. They were influential members of the organization's central committee, and after the "exile" of Newton, they assumed command of the entire party structure—both above and underground.

Neither in the civil rights-oriented movement, the antiwar movement, nor the student movement did we see such transformation. BPP member, scholar, and activist Angela Davis told us, "We've lost the memory of the fact that it was, by and large, women who ran virtually every chapter in the country."

Formally, Panthers were instructed not to characterize Party activities as either male or female work; one was defined as either a Panther or a revolutionary, and all were expected to fulfill the requirements of these roles, without regard to one's gender. But, of course, these formal rules and orders too often suffered in the breach of reality lived by individual Panthers. Brothers behaved in the only way they'd ever known—in sexist and chauvinistic ways. Sisters sometimes filed charges with chapter leaders; some complaints got "lost" in the system.

Who can deny this? Yet, these efforts represented the challenge of trying to build a non-sexist formation in a profoundly sexist social, cultural, economic, and political structure. That said, sexism became a self-defeating challenge and barrier to the presence of women in the Party structure, and women fought inter-organizationally to pull down such walls. They spoke openly about what the organization and the party needed to do to make way for a strong female presence, one with power. Scholar Tracye Matthews writes that 1969 became a pivotal year of that struggle:

> In July 1969, Panther Roberta Alexander spoke on a panel on women in the struggle of the BPP-sponsored United Front Against Fascism (UFAF) Conference. In her speech, she confirms there indeed is "a struggle going on right now" within the Panther party and that people are "confused about the Black Panther Party on the woman question." She observed that "Black women are oppressed as a class... They are oppressed because they are workers and oppressed because they are Black. In addition, Black women are oppressed by Black men... The problem of male supremacy can't be overcome unless it's a two-way street. Men must struggle too."[38]

As we have noted, those discussions continued within the organization, and had some degree of impact, the significance of which we cannot adequately ascertain. For some Panther women, it was the women who struggled in other movements for Black liberation before them, who inspired them to play the roles they did in the BPP. Scholar Angela D. LeBlanc-Ernest writes of that long, glorious historical chain:

> Women who joined the Black Panther Party were a part of a long tradition of African American women steeped in social service and political activities. During the 19th century, African American women in northern states, such as Pennsylvania and New York, participated in the Free African Societies. Historian Shirley Yee notes the central role of African American female abolitionists in

the anti-slavery campaign. Similarly, Paula Giddings documents the activities of Black women during the late-nineteenth and early-twentieth centuries. African American women believed in collective work and therefore formed organizations such as the National Federation of Colored Women. Individual women like Ida B. Wells and Mary Church Terrell, inspired by their race devotion, combated the lynching of African American males and advocated women's suffrage through public speaking, journalism, and agitation. Other Black women such as Anna J. Cooper and Mary McLeod Bethune advanced the interest of the race through education. Bethune founded Bethune-Cookman College, a historically Black college. Amy Jacques Garvey, prolific writer, leader, and historian of the Universal Negro Improvement Association (UNIA); Claudia Jones, a Communist Party activist and political prisoner; Fannie Lou Hamer, a tireless grassroots organizer; and Ella Baker, indefatigable union and community activist, Southern Christian Leadership Council (SCLC) member, and mother of the Student Nonviolent Coordinating Committee (SNCC), are but a few examples of women of African descent who were the forerunners and torchbearers to the women in the Black Panther Party.[39]

The women named in LeBlanc-Ernest's reference above aren't mere filler. They were each and all women of extraordinary commitment and will.

Photo: Mary Garrity (1893)

Ida B. Wells

Ida B. Wells was born in Holly Springs, Mississippi in 1862. Orphaned as a child, she attended Fisk University and Rust University and then soared into the role of crusading journalist after a relatively brief period teaching. In 1895 she published *The Red Record,* a path-breaking work on lynching. According to her research, some ten thousand Blacks were lynched between 1878 and 1898.

In May of 1884, Wells bought a first-class train ticket for a quick trip from Memphis to Nashville. The train crew ordered her to move to the car "reserved" for colored passengers. Outraged, she refused to move and was ushered off the train by brute force. Wells sued the railroad, won the judgment in a Circuit Court, which was swiftly overturned by the good old boys sitting on the Tennessee Supreme Court. This all-too-familiar racist bullshit motivated Wells to pick up a pen as her mighty weapon and challenge the chauvinistic and bigoted status quo.

Her star rose quickly—journalist, publisher, as well as teacher in the segregated Memphis public school system. Wells fought tough battles against the appalling conditions for Black children in the Memphis system. She was then summarily fired from her job. A true revolutionary, Wells kept on swinging.

Tommie Moss and ten other local Black men owned a small cooperative grocery store in the mixed-race neighborhood of Curve outside Memphis. Called "The People's Grocery," the store was attracting white customers from another area white store and that's when the vicious southern race "activities" began in earnest—leading to fights and defensive shootouts between angry mobs and Moss along with two of his store co-owners, Will Stewart and Calvin McDowell. The men were arrested and placed in the Shelby County Jail. They never made it to trial. The jail was surrounded by a lynch mob who dragged the three men from their cells to a railroad yard just outside of Memphis where Moss, Stewart, and McDowell were viciously lynched and murdered. Moss' dying words still echo today: "Tell my people to go west—there is no justice for them here." In fact, Moss' warning prompted an exodus of Blacks from the Memphis area to the western territories. Today, the historic marker on the site ends with this statement:

> This lynching prompted Ida B. Wells, editor of the Memphis
> Free Speech, to begin her anti-lynching campaign in this
> country and abroad.

Wells almost single-handedly raised the issue of racist lynching to such a pitch that her office was later ransacked by yet another mob—southern white thugs enraged by her stirring editorials. Visiting New York City at the time of the break-in, Wells was threatened with violent death if she ever returned to Memphis.

Ida B. Wells set her sights on organizing civil rights groups dedicated to carrying out action-based initiatives. She co-founded the National Association of Colored Women in 1896 (along with Harriet Tubman and March Church Terrell) and then was a founding member of the National Association for the Advancement of Colored People, along with others including W.E.B. Du Bois, Mary Church Terrell, and Mary White Ovington.

Ida B. Wells once wrote:

> I felt that one had better die fighting against injustice than to die like a dog or a rat in a trap.

> Dear Miss Wells:
> Let me give you thanks for your faithful paper on the lynch abomination now generally practiced against colored people in the South. There has been no word equal to it in convincing power. I have spoken, but my word is feeble in comparison... Brave woman!
> —Frederick Douglass (1895)

Photo: National Park Service (late 19th century)

Mary Church Terrell

Mary Church Terrell was both an activist and a professional of the late 19th and early 20th centuries. She was co-founder and president of the National Association of Colored Women, the principal of the Washington Colored High School, and then appointed to the District of Columbia school board—the first Black woman to sit on a major U.S. city school board. The NACW acted as a female corollary of the National Afro-American Council, a mostly-male group that attracted the leading Negro activists of the later 19th and early 20th century.

Terrell's ninety-one years on earth touched two seminal moments in racial history: she was born in 1863, just months after the Emancipation Proclamation, and she died in 1954, just two months after *Brown v. Board of Education* affirmed segregation in American schools unconstitutional. She was one of the first Black women in America to graduate college (Oberlin in 1884).

In the fall of 1906, Terrell spoke at the United Women's Club in Washington, D.C. The speech, entitled "What it Means to be Colored in the Capital of the United States," examined how racism permeated her everyday life. Terrell eloquently wrote:

> "Surely nowhere in the world do oppression and persecution based solely on the color of the skin appear more hateful and hideous than in the capital of the United States, because the chasm between the

> principles upon which this Government was founded, in which it still professes to believe, and those which are daily practiced under the protection of the flag, yawn so wide and deep."

Her little known but remarkable speech was forever cemented in history in her 1940 autobiography, *A Colored Woman in a White World.*

Photo: Unknown (circa 1960)

Claudia Jones

Claudia Jones was a radical's radical—a Trinidadian-born feminist, communist, and Black Nationalist. Some called her a visionary and an audacious freedom fighter. Others called her an enemy of the state. Decades after her death, a September 2017 headline in Black Agenda Report underscored her impact and importance on true revolutionary politics: *Why Claudia Jones Will Always Be More Relevant than Ta-Nehisi Coates.*

In 1949, Claudia Jones wrote and published an essay in the magazine *Public Affairs.* The piece is considered a cornerstone in her body of work and an early example of what UCLA and Columbia Law School Professor, Kimberlé Williams Crenshaw, developed as "intersectionality"—the landscape where political and social discrimination intersects with gender discrimination. Here is a short segment from the beginning of Jones' essay entitled, "An End to the Neglect of the Problems of the Negro Woman!"

> The bourgeoisie is fearful of the militancy of the Negro woman, and for good reason. The capitalists know, far better than many progressives seem to know, that once Negro women begin to take action, the militancy of the whole Negro people, and thus of the anti-imperialist coalition, is greatly enhanced.
>
> Historically, the Negro woman has been the guardian, the protector, of the Negro family.... As mother, as Negro, and as worker, the Negro woman fights against the wiping out of the Negro family, against the Jim Crow ghetto existence which destroys the health, morale, and very life of millions of her sisters, brothers, and children.

> Viewed in this light, it is not accidental that the American bourgeoisie has intensified its oppression, not only of the Negro people in general, but of Negro women in particular. Nothing so exposes the drive to fascization in the nation as the callous attitude which the bourgeoisie displays and cultivates toward Negro women.

A constant thorn in the side of U.S. imperialism and an elected member of the National Committee of the Communist Party USA, Jones experienced the full thuggery of the U.S. government, knee-deep at the time in Joe McCarthy's red menace cesspool. After various stints in prison, Jones was convicted with eleven others of violating the Smith Act—the statute used to persecute, err… prosecute those (mostly members of the Communist Party USA) advocating the violent overthrow of the U.S. government, even though the defendants argued their peaceful First Amendment guarantees regarding speech and assembly. In the end, the Feds determined she was an "illegal alien" under the McCarran Act and she was deported in 1955, taking up residency in Great Britain. It was here that Claudia Jones evolved into the journalist, editor, and courageous activist whose legacy still motivates many today. And it was here, long before it was popular or chic, that she vociferously rallied Londoners in support of then-imprisoned Nelson Mandela.

Claudia Jones, née Claudia Vera Cumberbatch, died in 1964 at only 49 years old of a massive heart attack. She is buried in North London's Highgate Cemetery, just to the left (geographically and politically) of Karl Marx.

These women, and so many others, were engaged in the long struggle against the aforementioned and very real American way of apartheid, and as such, were considered enemies of the Empire. They labored mightily against the Leviathan that America was and what it later became.

Hallelujah:
The Might and Power of the People is Beginning to Show

By: Emory Douglas

Of Women Born

In the beginning of this chapter, we referenced both the Adamic story that is the origin tale of many world religions, and the beginning of male usurpation of female power. It is integral not just to the formation of the West (i.e., the European realms), and the foundation it built under modern societies subsequently developed, but also as a tool of Western (and Middle Eastern) traditions that assigned subordination to those born female. It is so deep in Western consciousness that it needs no reiteration here; for we are all familiar with it, are we not?

But what if, in the realm of the sciences, we can find another origin tale, one that consigns such founding myths to the attics and basements of antiquity?

Photo: Unknown (circa 1968)
Huey P. Newton

Dr. Huey P. Newton, one of the two founders of the Black Panther Party, had occasion to think out and write of the formative period of the human species, and reveals something startling (at least to men). Citing the latest science at the time of his writing, Newton posits the rather remarkable biological fact that *all* humans are born female. *ALL.*

In Newton's 1974 article, "Eve, the mother of all living," he wrote:

> The psycho-biologist Mary Jane Sherfrey made two startling discoveries in the mid-1950s. The first was that biological research had clear evidence that life in the uterus begins as female; the fetus was defined by a rudimentary phallus. The surprising irony of Dr. Sherfey's discovery was that this elementary fact had been totally ignored, or rather repressed, by biology as it existed under the spell of the "male bias"—and that is the second discovery. The two discoveries are of equal importance: to begin with, that life begins female, and second, that science has repressed and suppressed this twentieth-century heresy.[40]

This, on its face, is dangerous knowledge, for it upends millennia of doctrine, and shows the primary role of females in human generation (not to mention re-generation, eh?). Men erected male-centered religious structures to wrest the once universal worship of Mother from the People. This deep, almost intuitive mother-worship still finds expression, though hidden under Marianism—or the veneration of Mary (especially in Catholic belief) as the virgin mother of a god.

Envy, jealousy, and fear led to this usurpation—which was accomplished by profound, mind-numbing violence throughout Europe (and in the Euro-Americas). Women had to be disciplined. They had to be cowed into playing a role of submission, rather than mastery and wisdom-bearers.

They had to be beaten down.

But as we have seen, they continued to rebel, from the earliest days of this republic, to the present. They rebel still. The French feminist intellectual, Simone de Beauvoir, in her 1949 book, *The Second Sex,* wrote: "This has always been a man's world, and none of the reasons hitherto brought forward in explanation of this fact has seemed adequate." In point of fact, studies of antiquity have taught us that primal human societies, especially those led by worship of the divine feminine, colored the world in different shades of being.

Second Wave Feminism

I suspected... there was some relationship between the maleness of God and male domination.

—Carol Patrice Christ

Feminist historian and theologian

As we touched on earlier in this chapter, and we've regrettably witnessed throughout history, the women of the world have not only suffered greatly under the oppression of a patriarchal paradigm but have also diligently rebelled against these dark forces—this male fury ingrained since time immemorial, meticulously sustained by guardian lords stationed at every mile marker along the way. One emblematic case in point of how patriarchal oppression was sustained by so-called male "giants" involves influential Catholic theologian, Thomas Aquinas, who embraced Aristotle as "the philosopher" and attempted to synthesize Aristotelian philosophy with Christianity. When the abovementioned Carol P. Christ was at Yale University studying for her PhD, she delved deeply into the works of Swiss theologian Karl Barth and St. Thomas Aquinas to explore their disquisitions on women, "hoping to gain insight into why I was being treated as if I did not have a mind in my body." Her findings weren't surprising but were sobering nonetheless:

> What I found was that "the great" theologians of Roman Catholicism and Protestantism agreed that woman was created to be obedient to and subordinate to man. Aquinas followed Aristotle in proclaiming that females had a lesser rational capacity than males. No wonder my rational mind was not being taken seriously by my colleagues![41]

Barth, who Pope Pius XII called "the greatest theologian since Thomas Aquinas," maintained "that God created 'man' to have 'initiative, precedence, and authority' in relation to 'woman,' just as God had in relation to man,"[42] writes Christ (Carol not Jesus).

As the revolutionary women's rights movement of the 1960s and 70s fought for equality on numerous fronts ("Women's Lib"), a second wave women's spirituality movement sprang to life from the prolific political bounty that was Berkeley in the 1970s. This movement, a spiritual tributary, was aimed at the reconceptualization of traditional and powerful patriarchal Judeo-Christian religions. Identified as the "women's spirituality movement" (aka feminist or goddess spirituality), this grassroots effort was taking its rightful place at the religious table, one that underscored a female divinity. At the time, Lydia Ruyle, scholar and artist whose feminist/activist art has been exhibited in more than forty countries, recognized a personal and political crossroad, writing "nothing in the socio-political realm would change until the spiritual story of women changed."[43]

Historians believe that this radical event has never been given the important attention it deserves—the mass exodus of women abandoning the religions of their upbringing, in that moment "woke" to the extent of institutionalized sexism, racism, and homophobia propagated by their churches. Poet and author, Mary Mackey, describes her journey:

> In the mid-to-late 1960s and early 1970s, I became involved, first in the Civil Rights Movement, then in the Anti-Vietnam-War Movement. Rebelling against the male domination of both, I joined the emerging Women's Movement which is now generally known as Second Wave Feminism.[44]

Historians of the movement also cite a major unintended consequence: that this spontaneous movement—composed of white middle class women, enjoying the riches of white privilege—did not speak for or represent women of color or women in poverty suffering from economic hardship. Author, scholar, and a main cog in the movement's viability, Vicki Noble writes, "We can understand now, in hindsight, the power of white privilege and the many ways that the movement did not (could not) speak to most women of color at the time." Noble acknowledges that the movement's "blindness to racial and class issues" were at the core. This second wave movement "can still be given credit for the courageous act of leaving organized patriarchal religion and inventing a new spirituality with Goddess at the center."[45]

Every so often, privilege can be used for good.

Author, activist, and teacher, Luisah Teish, remembers a personal moment in the movement as she questioned her nuns as well as the Bible by challenging male/female segregation in the church:

> In a Consciousness-Raising '70s moment I realized that "Eve was Framed." She had been accused of bringing all evil into the world, and because of her I was "destined" to share that burden. I realized that my own future and that of generations to come depended on changing the impact this mythology and its images had on the lives of real women, particularly women of color.[46]

Glinda the Good

Sitting on her mother's lap and listening to her read from *The Wonderful Wizard of Oz* and its sequels, Mary Mackey recalls that childhood moment as her flashpoint into the movement, even if it was years away. It's not surprising. The popular OZ book series was written by L. Frank Baum—his wife was Maud Gage, daughter of the eminent abolitionist and women's suffrage activist, Matilda Joslyn Gage. Under the heading of "the acorn doesn't fall far from the tree," the Gage influence is heavy throughout Baum's work. Mackey writes:

> As I grew from child to woman, I carried the talisman of Glinda The Good Witch in my mind and heart as I struggled to survive in an America that was deeply hostile to the idea that anything divine could be female.[47]

"Glinda Searches the Records"
From L. Frank Baum's
The Marvelous Land of Oz (1904)

In Sojourner Truth We Trust

In the beginning of our individual beings as bodies in utero, we were female, until the riverine rush of androgens floods the body, influencing and producing an external drop of the testes, and the emergence of a rudimentary phallus. Similarly, the human race came into being from the dark flesh of an African Eve—not Adam. In this sense, de Beauvoir actually gets it backward. For males, it seems, are truly the Second Sex. This lesson was perhaps so destabilizing, so disturbing to the male psyche, that he had to rebel against Female Power, and set Adam aside as the Mother, under the pantheon of Male God(s), with a minor infertile goddess giving birth to one of them.

A man's world was taken first in fantasy, and later in fact, using the age-old hosts of a fictitious tradition as the basis for the taking of an ancient power from the Mothers of the Race of Humanity. War, cruel and brutal, was waged—for centuries, to dim the bright eyes of our daughters, our sisters, our lovers, and finally, our Mothers.

Author Donna Henes brings this entire discourse full circle with this clarion call:

> I do not think that it is a coincidence that just as the planet teeters on the very brink of total devastation, there comes along a generation of fiery, accomplished, clever, ambitious women at the height of our supremacy, to whip it back into shape. It is just a matter of connection. If we join together in a web of influence, the sheer enormity of our numbers means that we can actually achieve the critical mass necessary to make a real and lasting difference in the world. The future is in our very capable hands.[48]

> If the first woman God ever made was strong enough
> to turn the world upside down all alone, together
> women ought to be able to turn it right-side up again.[49]
> — Sojourner Truth

Indeed, "right side up"—and with the right kind of eyes, you will see the curtain lifting, you will witness a seemingly new but primordial light once again spilling into the world.

This time, the First Sex will write the tales.

4 The Longest War

Battles Against Black Freedom

Well into the second decade of the 21st century, when the corporate media or American politicians pronounced "the longest war" in the nation's history, they were invariably speaking about Washington's war on Afghanistan; Part One of the ill-fated, ill-begotten so-called War on Terror, that national temper tantrum that was launched in the dizzy aftermath of the 9/11 attacks; what the late Chalmers Johnson has dubbed (for spy-speak) "blowback." Deeper heads may opine that "the longest war" is a reference to the so-called War on Drugs—which began in 1971, with "Coplandesque" fanfare, by Richard Nixon, the man muckraker Pete Hamill dubbed "the Bela Lugosi of American politics"—and this "war" has lasted well into the 21st century. But even those eagle-eyed adherents would be in error.

We say "the longest war" is the war against Black Liberation.

If, as historians cite, African men and women mark their arrival in the so-called Americas in 1619 (an historical approximation, to be sure), then the war against Black Liberation has been raging for more than 400 years.

400 years!

In actuality, Africans had arrived on the shores of what would become the Americas centuries earlier than even the arrival of Christopher Columbus, as demonstrated beyond cavil by the late Ivan Van Sertima, Professor of Africana Studies at Rutgers University. However, these pre-Columbian African visitors came as travelers, not as conquerors, and they mixed with a people who, after all, were people like them. We will not explore Van Sertima's work here because, as those Africans came as voyagers, they were not part of the vast machinery of repression that the Euro-American transatlantic slave trade would become. They were not, as it were, called upon to be soldiers in the war for Black Liberation.

It was during the epoch of American slavery that Africans experienced a profound alienation that would mark generations to this very day, a period during which the State, as the centerpiece of American power, would protect, defend, and expand slavery to all corners of its national existence, and indeed, would fight lustily to extend it to the lands beyond its borders. For slavery meant money, wealth, and advancement in the world; and the machinery that made slavery possible was the doctrine of white supremacy. That is the heart of American growth and development, not the mythic mumblings about "liberty and freedom."

There can scarcely be an election in this nation without some politician claiming that "we founded this nation based on freedom" or "we were born as a nation of liberty," or the like. Few have been the politicians who have spoken (publicly) the simple, yet undeniable truth: "America began in slavery and these United States grew fat on the life-blood, the death-blood, of slavery."

Yet, who can honestly deny it?

And when Black people in this nation dared to fight for their freedom, they met the solid steel wall of WHITE SUPREMACY, against which generations of brains were dashed in that struggle. *Generations of resistors. Fighters. Freedom fighters.*

Indeed, let us pose this as a question: Which people have fought longest (or hardest) for freedom in America's long history? The answer, to paraphrase Lincoln, is "self-evident."

Africans. Blacks. Those today termed African-Americans. (This to the chagrin of some whites, who, in their nationalistic fervor, believe only in using the label "American" and who deny the reality of the retained Africanisms that are at the very heart of what the nation has become.)

Mary Frances Berry, both a historian and an historical figure in her own right, wrote in her 1971 work, *Black Resistance/White Law,* that the very presence of Africans in America has been to say the least, disturbing. In her preface, Berry notes:

> Black people have been a disgusting presence in America since the arrival of the first twenty Africans at Jamestown in 1619. To most blacks, their status, usually as slaves until 1865 and as second-class citizens thereafter, has been unacceptable; to some, it has been intolerable. Before 1865, in addition to aiding in the suppression of slave revolts, the national government ignored or approved—on constitutional grounds—white mob violence directed at blacks and their few white supporters even when local officials participated in the violence. Those blacks who did not become involved in conspiracy and rebellion before the Civil War were not necessarily "docile." They lived in the grip of a system of violent control institutionalized under the Constitution. The years since Reconstruction, when blacks became nominally free, are littered with incidences of white riots against blacks, burnings of black homes and churches, and lynchings, while federal and local law enforcement agencies stood idly by. And while federal law enforcement disregarded white violence, pleading lack of jurisdiction under the Constitution, it endorsed and contributed to rigorous campaigns of surveillance and control of rebellious blacks, using "constitutional" military force against them with impunity.[1]

Berry, a constitutional law professor for many years at the University of Pennsylvania, argues that the "law," as reflected in the Constitution, was but an "instrument" for the maintenance of "a racist status quo."[2] What this meant in real life was that the "law" could rarely be relied on to right social wrongs, to protect Black life or property, and, more often than not, it was an enemy of those aspirations. Of the sheer scale of the transatlantic slave industry, Berry, along with fellow historian John Blassingame, write:

> The first Africans arrived in the New World in 1502; by the time the slave trade ended in the 1860s, more than 100 million blacks had either been killed or transplanted from their homeland. Although statistics on the trade are imprecise, it appears that from 400,000 to 1 million of the 10 to 50 million Africans forcibly transported to the Americas came to North America between 1619 and 1808, when the legal slave trade ended. Thousands more, captured in wars fomented by Europeans, were smuggled in illegally until 1860. Eventually, the raids of such groups such as the Ashanti and Dahomey so disrupted

> and depopulated West African states that rulers began to protest against the trade. In the sixteenth century, for instance, the King of the Congo, Nzenga Merema, sent word to the Portuguese, "it is our will that in these kingdoms of Congo there should not be any trade in slaves nor any market for slaves." African rulers, unfortunately, were powerless to stop the trade.[3]

Upon arrival in what would be called America, Africans found an ever-present assault on their lives, their folkways, their religions, as well as their cultural life. They tried to resist in any way they could by escaping from bondage, by sabotage, by fire, and when pushed to the proverbial wall, by revolt. Some destroyed their "master's" property. Some stole relentlessly, and doing so diminished their master's property worth. Southern families, more aware than they pretended, lived in perpetual fear of being poisoned (for they often had their kitchens staffed by excellent Black cooks) as well as being wiped out by the "weapon of mass destruction" of the day: fires.

Same Old Devil

Indeed, if slavery was but legalized stolen labor and exploitation, then the deprivations and terrors of that system found a way to survive, even after the horrors of war. For after the Civil War had formally ended in 1865 and slavery was abolished by law, constitutional amendment, and arms, nevertheless it survived by means of political compromise, under new words, new terms, and new descriptions of the same old devil: convict leasing, sharecropping, and peonage. No matter the form, the essence remained the same—stolen, undervalued, exploited Black labor, used to enrich, feed, build, and preserve the White Nation. Even after the Civil War and its subsequent constitutional amendments, "free" Blacks discovered that what the law said on paper, and what it meant in real life, was a cruel deception. Berry and Blassingame stoke deep, Black memory to tell us that the law, even of the highest order, the Constitution, was surmounted by the deepest of hatreds and fears: national Negrophobia. The two scholar-historians note:

> The three enforcement acts passed by Congress in 1870-71, under the authority of the Fifteenth Amendment, seemed to ensure protection for blacks in the enjoyment of their political rights. The laws provided for extensive enforcement machinery, including authority for the president to call out the Army and Navy and to suspend the writ of habeas corpus if necessary. The acts permitted

> states to restrict suffrage on any basis except race or color. But between 1870 and 1896, when the bulk of this legislation was repealed, 7,372 cases were tried and hundreds of offenders, who were never brought to trial, were arrested. Despite this pre-1896 activity, the disfranchisement of blacks proceeded successfully. After 1874, enforcement efforts gradually declined altogether. The white South remained opposed, the white North was not interested, and the Supreme Court soon decided that most of the federal efforts to punish individual violations of voting rights were not used to enforce the law. Additionally, Congress failed to provide adequate funds to finance the federal courts and officials refused to undertake serious enforcement. Many federal officials disagreed with the effort and were not willing to attempt enforcement. The protection of black voting rights in the South was not a national priority.[4]

The U.S. government, despite the lofty words of the Constitution, continued to ignore white terrorism against Blacks. As a consequence, some—who were once the most stalwart of members of the Republican Party—spoke out against this mass betrayal. In the *Colored Citizen* newspaper (Fort Scott, Kansas) of October 1878 it is written: "The Democrats of the South are determined that the colored voters shall either be Democrats or not vote at all." In the *New York Globe* (October 1883), T. Thomas Fortune wrote bitterly, "we have the ballot without any law to protect us in the enjoyment of it. The Democratic Party is a fraud—a narrow-minded, corrupt, bloody fraud; the Republican Party has grown to be a little better."[5] Little wonder that the two capitalist parties were viewed with such derision, for the simple truth was that both parties had united under the broad banner of white supremacy, and Black votes—not to mention Black voters—were superfluous to those concerns.

In deep, Black memory, the era dawned after an all too brief Reconstruction period that has come to be called the "Great Betrayal." It would burn in Black memory for more than a century—from slavery, to imprisonment, to convict leasing, to peonage, to terrorism. For millions of Blacks, the law was a dead letter. Indeed, even in war, when Blacks took up arms to defend the White Nation, its soldiers were mistreated, ill-paid, and after every conflict, treated with contempt. Thus, for centuries, we see the maddening yin-yang of repression and resistance, revolving like a mad wheel of misfortune, right up until our present hour. Indeed, it was thus in every major (and some minor) colonies that would become the self-styled New World. For in each reigned the doctrine of white supremacy; and the converse of this was Black subjection.

The African fight for freedom was thus hemispheric, and soon, global.

So, for every society formed in the West (that is, every society created by European colonies), white supremacy was the rule that governed life; and Black subordination was its corollary. Thus, African languages were outlawed; as were African religion(s); similarly, African names and, indeed, memories of the ancient homeland, were banished. In many societies, marriages were forbidden; for how could "things" marry? Every indicia of humanhood was condemned as a violation of these new colonial laws. Laws enacted and enforced by outlaws.

Law became the foundation of a monstrous, inhuman Crime. That crime? Slavery, by whatever name or form it manifested itself—and the subsequent long, terrible war against Black freedom. In every area of American life, Black people had to struggle mightily in order to gain a foothold in this society. It mattered little which arena, for that battle too was global: education, law, commerce, housing, health, the military, and politics—all of it. In every realm of human endeavor (with the possible exception of the Black church), Blacks had to wage a long, costly, and dangerous struggle against the American tradition of exclusion and segregation.

To the uninitiated, words such as these may seem little more than rhetoric, for where, they ask, is the proof of these claims? What is its basis?

The Slaughterhouse Cases

We have written of the law's inherent defectiveness when it comes to the struggle for Black freedom. We need to look no further than the realm of the United States Supreme Court. Here, in the words of scholar/historian James MacGregor Burns (winner of the 1971 Pulitzer Prize in History), the Court exercised supreme duplicity when deciding what has come to be called "the Slaughterhouse Cases." In his examination of the Supreme Court's politically influenced decisions, Burns writes:

> A group of New Orleans butchers—all white men—had brought suit against a state-chartered monopoly of slaughterhouses. Louisiana had decided to centralize the city's chaotic system of private stockyards in a "grand slaughterhouse" to better regulate an unsanitary trade. Butchers objected that under the law they were forced to submit to the monopoly, paying the fees its

investors demanded, or go out of business. Their appeal rested on the Fourteenth Amendment. Louisiana, they said, had infringed their "privileges and immunities" as United States citizens, and by favoring the monopoly, the state had deprived them of "property" in their livelihoods without "due process" and denied them "equal protection of the laws."

In its first great test, the sweeping promise of the Fourteenth Amendment for liberty and equality was reduced to little more than empty words. Justice Samuel Miller, the Lincoln man who wrote for the court's majority in the *Slaughterhouse Cases,* acknowledged that the Civil War had "given great force to the argument" for a more powerful national government that would protect the rights of all Americans—and then he pushed that argument aside. The Supreme Court, he wrote, must maintain "the balance between State and Federal power." ...The rights Miller attached to national citizenship were meager—the right of access to Washington, D.C., and to coastal ports and navigable waters, as well as the rights to habeas corpus and to petition and assembly. Congress could impose no other constitutional "privileges and immunities" on the states; it could not bring within its power "the entire domain of civil rights heretofore belonging exclusively to the States." Those rights were not "embraced" by the Fourteenth Amendment. They must, Miller wrote, "rest for their security and protection where they have heretofore rested"—on the states.[6]

Judicial Terrorism

While this decision did not directly address the state or status of Blacks, it set the narrowly constricted perimeters of what national citizenship meant—and what it did not. It is one of those odd ironies of life that the day before *Slaughterhouse* was issued, a historic case was being born in another southern town, which would ripen into one of the most putrid fruits of the age. As did much in the American south, this case began with terrorism; and so it ended. With a cold form of *judicial* terrorism: the blindness, and crippled reasoning of white supremacy, encrusted over and into the law like a scabbed sore. Burns, turning to the case that would spell the doom and the false promise of Reconstruction, noted:

On that Easter Sunday [April 1873], the black community in a Louisiana county seat suffered what historian Eric Foner called "the

> bloodiest single act of carnage in all of Reconstruction." The Colfax massacre. In a bitter election dispute between black Republicans and white Democrats, blacks had been deputized to safeguard the courthouse in Colfax against a rumored white takeover. A mob of local whites used a cannon to blast open the courthouse and set it ablaze. Scores of fleeing blacks were mowed down. Amid outrage across the nation—and predictable inaction by state and local authorities—ninety-six men were indicted in federal court for violating the Ku Klux Klan Act, charged with conspiring to deny black men their constitutional rights. Of the ninety-six, only nine stood trial and only three were convicted. One of the three was William Cruikshank, and it was his name that would be attached to the epochal case presented to the Waite Court [for chief justice Morrison R. Waite, of Ohio] three years after the massacre.[7]

In order to decide this case, Waite and his colleagues had to do something that judges are uniquely qualified to do. They had to ignore the language of the Constitution, to do what they wanted to do, by the usage of legal legerdemain. They unanimously determined that the Reconstruction Amendments didn't apply, for as citizens of states, it was their duty, not that of the feds, to protect their lives and property. Burns quotes the *Cruikshank* opinion, linking it to *Slaughterhouse,* to show how the doors of the courthouse were sealed against Blacks who dared try to make the language of the Constitution real, by voting, running for office, or—heavens forfend!—actually winning offices. Burns noted:

> Conspiracy to murder, the chief justice held, could be no federal crime. It was "the very highest duty of the States," Waite wrote, to protect their citizens, neglecting the fact that Congress had passed the enforcement acts because states had been notoriously unwilling to prosecute whites for crimes against blacks, as the aftermath of the Colfax massacre itself had proved. But "sovereignty, for this purpose," Waite insisted, "rests alone with the States."[8]

The court went on to further shred the Fourteenth Amendment, further limiting the power of the federal government, but from a constitutional standpoint, the damage was, truly and surely, already exacted. For, if Blacks had to depend on the foxes to "protect" them, the jig was up. The message was clear. The Supreme Court could have written, just as honestly, "You niggers are on your own"—for that was its meaning.

It was the end of Reconstruction, slain by white terrorism.
It was the end of an era.
It was the end of a dream.

White Catastrophe, White Nightmares

In that great and foundational American novel, *The Adventures of Huckleberry Finn,* Mark Twain attempted, with greater candor than most white Americans, to reckon with the aftermath of emancipation and the profound failure of Reconstruction. As literature professor Neil Schmitz notes:

> Twain had rendered Jim's liberation in *Huckleberry Finn* at that precise moment in American history when barely realized liberties were being wrenched one by one from the grasp of the emancipated black man in the South. Between 1876 and 1883, the period during which he worked on the novel, the Reconstruction was nullified, the ambitious programs of the Radical Republicans abandoned and the fate of the Negro restored to the keep of his former master.[9]

Photo: Library of Congress (1907)

The controversial culmination of Twain's picaresque epic, in which the runaway white boy Huck, and the runaway slave Jim, who throughout the novel have done "that appalling thing—loaf on their raft with perfect equanimity,"[10] runs this unlikely friendship aground in the farce of white American catastrophe. Jim has been captured and is being held prisoner in a shed on the farm of the Phelps family in their anticipation of returning him to his owner and collecting the reward. But the Phelps' nephew turns out to be Huck's best friend, Tom Sawyer, and although Tom knows Jim has been legally freed from his bondage by his former mistress, he withholds this information in order to stage an elaborate prison break. These scenes show a comical, satirical novel devolving into bitter, satirical absurdity. Schmitz elaborates:

> In brief, Jim's situation at the end of *Huckleberry Finn* reflects that of the Negro in the Reconstruction, free at last and thoroughly

> impotent, the object of devious schemes and a hapless victim of constant brutality. What indeed was to be done with Jim, this black man whom Twain had so conscientiously humanized? "Murder, killing and maiming Negroes, raping Negro women—in the 80's and in the Southern South, this was not even news;" W. E. B. Du Bois wrote, recalling his years as a student at Fisk University, "it got no publicity; it caused no arrests; and punishment for such transgressions was so unusual that the fact was telegraphed North." This was the implacable reality that lay outside the shed on the Phelps farm, the historical context that made, then as now, the notion of Jim's "freedom" seem so obscene.[11]

But the flimsiness of Jim's legal freedom, and his actual physical bondage even under that freedom, mark only the edges of a deeper confinement imposed upon him, one that originates in the mind of both his white captors and his white liberators:

> In this new prison the first thing Jim must learn is that he has become a character in a fantasy. The white man who defined his slavehood now dreams and defines the experience of his liberation, and in both roles the black man must act his part or perish.[12]

So it was, that after the dream of Reconstruction was shattered, came the long season of nightmares. White nightmares. Nightmares born of the twisted logic and cold legalism of white supremacy, where terrorism became the tool, and Black bodies the objective.

Now, with the blindness of those most learned of men (the Supreme Court), the forces loosed wrought a terrible fate on Black people.

Lynchings. Seventy-six (that we know of) in 1919 alone.

For many, perhaps most, "lynching" is but a word: inert, bereft of depth, of meaning or color. Just a year before the historically infamous "Red Summer," in the spring of 1918, Walter F. White, the man who would later lead the NAACP, wrote of Brooks County, Georgia's terroristic lynching of Mary Turner, who was targeted for protesting the lynching of her husband:

> At the time she was lynched, Mary Turner was in her eighth month of pregnancy... Her ankles were tied together and she was hung to

> the tree, head downward. Gasoline and oil from the automobiles were thrown on her clothing and while she writhed in agony and the mob howled in glee, a match was applied and her clothes burned from her person. When this had been done and while she was yet alive, a knife... was taken and the woman's abdomen was cut open, the unborn babe falling from her womb to the ground. The infant, prematurely born, gave two feeble cries and then its head was crushed by a member of the mob, with his heel. Hundreds of bullets were fired into the body of the woman, now mercifully dead, and the work was over.[13]

(Today, when the world is appalled by the beheadings of ISIS, what do we make of such a brutal killing?)

A year later, race riots of white, rampaging mobs swarmed in twenty-five cities, burning churches, attacking homes and hounding Blacks walking in the streets. In 1919, Charleston, South Carolina; Longview and Gregg counties, Texas; Elaine, Phillips County, Arkansas; Washington, D.C.; and Chicago, Illinois, were all locales wracked by such violence. James Weldon Johnson (1871-1938), author, musician, co-composer of the Black national anthem, *Lift Every Voice and Sing,* and the first Black president of the NAACP, called that year "The Red Summer" and well it deserved the appellation. For that summer blood came down like rain.

World War I: "We return fighting"

This moment of heightened infamy would birth "the dream deferred"—a time when one could only dream of a day not yet dawned... of a future more hopeful than the grim present. Yet, who amongst us can predict the vagaries of fate? Who can truly tell what tomorrow may bring? It was not want, but need that brought America out of her inebriated stupor, drunk on the wine of white supremacy. For "war"—it has been said—"is the mother of all things." And war—a war of the world—would open doors long soldered closed, doors of opportunity, doors of the eternal lust for manpower, would burst open doors long considered closed, doors of a war-fed economic machine. For wars, even wars begun as white wars, needed bodies, even Black bodies, to win.

Veteran Black historian, Lerone Bennett, Jr., in his multi-edition *Before the Mayflower,* writes incisively of what forces converged to make this war go the way of the American Empire:

The First World War—the one that made the world safe for democracy—followed hard on the heels of the Black migrants and changed the meaning of race. There had been a general feeling before this war that the world belonged to the Europeans, and that the White West would go from progress to progress, from height to height. But the bloody carnage on the fields of Europe forced an agonizing reappraisal. It became clear in these years and afterwards that machines had loosed terrible forces and that history, a sly and capricious master, had unknown cards up her sleeves.

Of at least equal consequences was the fact that the war grew out of and reflected European struggles over colonial empires in Africa and Asia. Flowing from this fact was a new understanding, dimly perceived at first but constantly growing clearer, that the overwhelming majority of the peoples of the world were colored and that a belief of humanity, as Du Bois said, was a belief in colored people.

All this—the slaughter of tens of thousands of young men, the death of the idea of White progress, the rising tide of Afro-Asian color, the anarchy of a machine-world that required more machines, more colonial possessions, more weapons and more wars—changed the spiritual and social climate of the West. All over the world now, men grew anxious. They were not so sure, they would never again be so sure, of the divinity of their mission and the sanctity of their skin.

If all this was not clearly perceived in the first years of the war, it was dimly felt, even in black America, where there was a new gleam in the eye, a new spring in the walk, a new defiant tilt to the head. White Americans, perceiving this and feeling their world history was going down another road, responded with hysteria, intensifying repression and giving the war and preparations for the war an overcast of desperation.

Despite these signs, which were clear for all to see, Black Americans tried to entice the spirit of the occasion. There was patriotism in this, but there was also a clear understanding of the dialectic of Blacks and Whites and wars, a dialectic based on the fact that the greatest gains of Black America have been gifts not of the

> Constitution or White goodwill but of wars and catastrophes that forced their fellow citizens to recognize that they were stronger and more secure with Black Americans than without them.[14]

Some 370,000 Black soldiers and 1,400 commissioned officers joined up with the fight in World War I. More than half of them served in France, many earning distinguished medals fighting at Chateau-Thierry, Belleau Wood, Vorges, Metz, and St. Mihiel. Three of the four all-Black units fighting in France—the 369th, the 371st, and the 372nd—were awarded the Croix de Guerre for valor. But despite their sterling martial performance in defense of an American ally, France, the Americans went out of their way to remind French officials that they must apply Jim Crow rules when dealing with dark-faced men who were fighting for them. A secret memo from U.S. General John Pershing's headquarters, dated 7 August 1918, and entitled: "[To the] French Military Mission Stationed with the American Army–Secret Information Concerning the Black American Troops," gives, in its conclusions, the flavor of this nation-to-nation communiqué:

1. We must prevent the rise of any pronounced degree of intimacy between French officers and Black officers. We may be courteous and amiable with the last, but we cannot deal with them on the same plane as with the White American officer without deeply wounding the latter. *We must not eat with them, must not shake hands or seek to talk or meet with them outside of the requirement of military service.*

2. We must not commend too highly the American troops, particularly in the presence of [White] Americans...

3. Make a point of keeping the native cantonment population from "spoiling" the Negroes. *[White] Americans become greatly incensed at any public expression of intimacy between white women with black men.* [Emphasis added][15]

The war, despite its astonishing ferocity (for instance, some 600,000 deaths at the Battle of Verdun [Northeast France], February through July, 1916), was a relatively swift one [1916-1918]. For returning Black soldiers, who had seen war's awful face—and survived—the world seemed their oyster. Young men, full of strength and vigor, surely thought that their world would change—and for the better.

It was not to be—for they had not reckoned on white American anxiety, and their deep-seated Negrophobia. Black soldiers, many bedecked with French medals of honor and valor, left one war, only to walk into another—the war at home. The heady peals of their overseas triumphs would stonewall into the valleys of white supremacy. The aforementioned "Red Summer" would burn like a fever in 1919 America, where whites wilded on Black flesh, and riots and lynchings were the language of the mobs. This repression, coupled with the new energy of returning veterans who joined Black protest groups, like the NAACP, brought forth a militancy typified by the even-then renowned W.E.B. Du Bois, who, as editor of the NAACP organ, *The Crisis,* gave voice and coherency to this emerging Black mood. In the May 1919 edition, the editorial, penned by Du Bois himself, had a message as overt and distinctive as its editor:

> *We return.*
> *We return from fighting.*
> *We return fighting.*

The Crisis attracted the attention of the federal spy agency, the FBI, which visited the journal's offices in New York. Du Bois responded to this invasion as only he could do when the agents asked him what the organization was fighting for. Lerone Bennett's account is classic:

> Pulling himself to his full height, his eyes blazing with indignation, Du Bois answered: "We are seeking to have the Constitution of the United States thoroughly and completely enforced."[16]

That issue sold more than 100,000 copies (although it was held up by U.S. postal authorities for twenty-four hours).

"We build our temple for tomorrow"

In nature, where there are peaks, there are also valleys. It was equally so in the longest war of Black freedom. Terrorism swept though American cities like a white plague. A contagion of fear, designed to beat back the hearts, souls, and aspirations of Black millions, was the source of this national malady. And as Jews had once been hounded in European cities, Blacks were targeted in American cities, north and south.

This postwar period was, to be sure, an oddly American one. For it gave birth to hope kindled with dread. It marked the resurgence and national expansion of the Ku Klux Klan. It brought disillusionment to young Black veterans, yearning for a new world. Yet this period also birthed a new era of Black cultural expression—an era of historic proportion.

> *I, too, sing America.*
>
> *I am the darker brother.*
> *They send me to eat in the kitchen*
> *When company comes,*
> *But I laugh,*
> *And eat well,*
> *And grow strong.*
>
> *Tomorrow,*
> *I'll be at the table*
> *When company comes.*
> *Nobody'll dare*
> *Say to me,*
> *"Eat in the kitchen,"*
> *Then.*
>
> *Besides,*
> *They'll see how beautiful I am*
> *And be ashamed–*
>
> *I, too, am America.*
>
> **—Langston Hughes, 1926**

Photo: Carl Van Vechten, Library of Congress (1936)

Jazz broke out from its southern cradle, lighting the night skies of Harlem, Chicago, Philadelphia, and St. Louis. Black writers like Jean Toomer (*Cane*, 1923), Countee Cullen (*Color*, 1925), and the brilliant Langston Hughes (*I, Too*, 1926) lit up the literary firmament. Perhaps it was fitting that a poet like Hughes would emerge as the key voice of this movement that would later be called, "The Negro Renaissance," for it reflected a boldness, an openness, and an honesty that had heretofore been lacking in the realm of the Black arts. Hughes would expound: "We younger Negro artists who create now intend to express our individual dark-skinned selves without fear or shame. If White people are pleased, we are glad. If they are not, it doesn't matter. We know we are beautiful. And ugly, too. If colored people are pleased we are glad. If they are not, their displeasure doesn't matter. We build our temple for tomorrow, strong as we know how, and we stand on top of the mountain, free within ourselves."[17] It would take a poet, indeed, a master poet, a priest of the Word, like Langston Hughes, to capture the moment, and an era.

The theatre opened its gates to this new voice, and floorboards danced to new beats. Duke Ellington opened his show in Harlem's Cotton Club; Louis Armstrong recorded hot jazz on vinyl; and Fletcher Henderson, who broke the way of big bands, opened at the Roseland Ballroom on Broadway. Where real life was cribbed, constricted, and canalized by the strictures of law and the regimen of a white supremacist and provocative world, Black artists broke into the realm of the senses. It was as if they were suggesting, like the sirens of Odyssean myth, that life was sweeter on this beckoning, distant shore. That Black Life, amongst the most damned of men and women, was the wave of the future.

We build our temple for tomorrow.

World War II: Still Fighting on Two Fronts

Once again, the clouds thick with judgment and dark with despair, war would open the realms of the possible. For, as ever, once war broke, the nation would remember its dark stepchildren; those most rejected and dejected of men and women, to save them from the threatening embrace of chaos. For Germany, embittered by the humiliations of the post-World War I Treaty of Versailles, would, within a generation, rise again, and break through the limits of the treaty, by trying—and succeeding—to reclaim much of its territories lost after the war. This time, supported by corporate forces both at home and abroad (notably in America), the Germans would announce a new Rise (a new *Reich?*), an empire based on Nietzschean will and cold logic that would shake Europe, and much of the world, to its core: Nazism. They wanted their old lands back, to be sure.

But they wanted more. They wanted the world. And they almost got it as evidenced by art imitating life (almost) in Philip K. Dick's harrowing alternate reality novel *The Man in the High Castle.*

The array of forces put in their way included one million African-American soldiers, who struck fear in the hearts of the Aryans. And if World War I was horrendous, with its ten million military casualties, the growth of the technological arts of destruction revealed in World War II dwarfed the former, with its 45 million dead.

Before African-Americans would once again give their lives to a government that had a stark history of betrayal, the Black press launched the "Double V" campaign—for victory at home and abroad—against fascism, racism, and discrimination. Led by the *Pittsburgh Courier,* other Black newspapers joined the campaign—the *Chicago Defender, Atlanta Daily World, Norfolk Journal and Guide,* and the *Afro-American* among them—sending war correspondents abroad, not just to cover the carnage of war, but also the struggle against discrimination in the U.S. armed forces. The federal government's intelligence apparatus considered the prosecutions of Black publishers for impeding the war effort—then thought better of it.

Once again, Blacks gave their energies to organizations, understanding, as only history can teach, that people organized can achieve far more than people isolated into false individuality. They also remembered the lesson from their ancestor, Frederick Douglass: "If there is no struggle, there is no progress." 1943 bore an eerie resemblance to 1919, but with a significant difference: Black Americans were more organized, flexing more political power—and protest power. The NAACP, today seen as so tame and bourgeois in its orientation, was, for its time, the tip of a spear of radical organizing against the staid, rigid institutions of white supremacy. Their members were hounded by both the police and white vigilantes, and the legal establishment tried to destroy them with contempt of court citations amounting to more than a hundred thousand dollars for refusing to divulge their member lists.

In January 1947, an NAACP report labeled the previous year "one of the grimmest in the history" of the organization. It described "reports of blowtorch killing and eye-gouging of Negro veterans freshly returned from a war to end torture and racial extermination."[18] The report pronounced Black Americans "disillusioned" over the "wave of lynchings," and "brutality" they faced in the post-war period.

The war in defense of democracy, it seemed, did not include them.

Martin, Malcolm, and Counterintelligence

The riotous 1940s gave way to the post-war '50s, and just as creeks feed rivers, and rivers spill into oceans, the forces underlying this state of affairs, immense frustration and despair, gave voice and coherence to new forms of protest, both formal and informal, both legal and illegal, to attack the White Citadel of repression and state-borne terrorism. As young Black lawyers proceeded in the courts of law, younger Black activists took to the streets—in mobilizing, in boycotts, in great movements of considerable numbers of people—to give a face to the resistance felt in millions of Black breasts. A young, well-educated clergyman would return home, his Ph.D. in hand, and he would be drawn into a movement that would grant eloquence and power to the voices of the poor and the dispossessed. The emergent and influential medium of television would record and project the immediacy of these moments, and reach millions across the earth.

Born with the name Michael, the name of an archangel in Judaic, Christian, and Muslim belief, it was his second naming that would stick and become emblematic of an age: Martin Luther King, Jr. His titles, Reverend and Doctor, would further embellish his stature as a leader of significant consequence for an America, which was trying, desperately, fitfully, to run back to the safe "good old days" of legalized (U.S. Supreme Court-supported) segregation, repression, and terror. Lerone Bennett, from his book *Before the Mayflower,* illustrates the significance:

> Now, in 1955, Martin Luther King, Jr. fused these elements [i.e., nonviolent protests] and added the missing link, that which was sustained and bottomed Black America since slavery—the Black church. By superimposing the image of the Black preacher on the image of [Mahatma] Gandhi, by adding songs and symbols with concrete significance in Black America, King transformed a spontaneous local protest into a national resistance movement with a method and an ideology. "Love your enemies," he said, and tens of thousands of Blacks straightened their backs and sustained a year-long bus boycott which was, as King pointed out, "one of the greatest [movements] in the history of the nation." The movement brought together laborers, professionals, and students. More importantly, perhaps, it fired the imagination of Blacks all over America.[19]

Young, keenly intelligent, learned in the ways of both the Black church and white academia, titled and handsome, King came to symbolize a force greater than himself. He embodied the dark oppressed, striving for a livable future. He symbolized the grandchildren of slaves, and the inheritors of tortured, hellish yesterdays. He symbolized, perhaps more than anything, *change:* a change that the land that claimed "freedom" as its middle name, feared more than anything. Bennett's portrait of the era splashes the historical canvas of the Black church with the warm, golden glow of glory for its role in the Civil Rights Movement. Yet, on this score, we urge a certain caution. For the late scholar, activist, and historian Manning Marable has written that a significant sector of southern Black church leaders took umbrage with the young preacher's project, and stood, not with, but against the movement. Marable wrote:

> Since the Civil Rights Movement, it has become a standard myth that the black church was the central institution in the struggle to desegregate the South, providing essential resources and leadership. While it is certainly true that African-American clergy—including Dr. Martin Luther King, Jr., C.T. Vivian, James Lawson, Andrew Young, Hosea Williams, Ralph David Abernathy, Wyatt T. Walker, Fred Shuttlesworth, and many more—were major figures in the struggle for civil rights, the black church as an institution was deeply divided over the protest strategies and tactics of the desegregation campaign. The Reverend Joseph H. Jackson, the president of the National Baptist Convention, the largest African-American denomination, urged his ministers not to join King's new civil rights group, the Southern Christian Leadership Conference, in 1957. In 1961, King and 800 activist ministers were in effect forced out of Jackson's Baptist Convention... Many ministers who for years had been on the private payroll of white political and business elites had a financial interest in maintaining the Jim Crow status quo.[20]

It seemed that the white south wasn't the only entity that feared change. When Black protest groups demanded change, by fighting for it in the streets and occasionally even winning in the courts, those change-fearing forces staged counter-attacks of mad desperation and outright cold hatred. Across the South, in the wake of the breakthrough 1954 *Brown v. Board of Education* decision of the U.S. Supreme Court, outlawing segregation in education, units of the White Citizens Council sprang up across the region, a counter-force to the new legal decisions. Judge Tom Brady, a Yale-taught jurist working the bench in Mississippi, wrote a book that voiced stark resistance to both the court and the growing movement. In his work, *Black Monday,* Judge Brady wrote:

> [W]hen a law transgresses the moral and ethical sanctions and standards of the mores, invariably strife, bloodshed and revolution follow in the wake of its attempted enforcement. The loveliest and purest of God's creatures, the nearest thing to an angelic being that tread this terrestrial ball is a well-bred, cultured Southern White woman or her blue-eyed, golden-haired little girl.[21]

Circuit Judge Brady had a message for the Supreme Court, that body which the Constitution determined he was sworn to obey: "We say to the Supreme Court and to the northern world, 'You shall not make us drink from this cup... We have, through our forefathers, died before for our sacred principles. We can, if necessary die again.'"

Whoever suggested that change would be easy? These words were both echoes and precursors of war: echoes of the ruinous, savage Civil War that reduced southern cities to smoldering ash from northern military and industrial onslaught; precursors of the war to come, the war for social change. The war for freedom.

As the southern freedom movement rumbled through America's rural southland, the cities of the American North were also raging. For while it was true that Black folk felt a deep kinship with their relatives down south facing the violent madness of the U.S. apartheid, it is also true that things weren't exactly hunky-dory up North. With the ever-present specter of police violence hanging over dark heads, poor employment (if any at all), poor housing conditions and substandard education, not to mention damn-near nonexistent healthcare, all of it virtually haunting every sizable Black community, there was little that northern cousins could actually boast of to their southern kin. And while the good Rev. Dr. was the darling of the press (at least until his provocative Riverside Church speech delivered a year to the day before his assassination), urban life was an animal that King could neither fully understand, nor quite tame as he had done in the South.

In the northlands, the voice of Malcolm X rang like thunder, and quickened Black hearts with its urgency, its boldness, and its unrepentant Blackness. Where Martin was cultured, pedigreed, and manicured in the bouquet of the liberal establishment and the nascent Black bourgeoisie, Malcolm was the Other: brilliant in oration, but unlearned by the white man's schools, taught the underground lessons of the Nation of Islam in prison—yes, essentially born (or reborn!) in the bowels of imprisonment, uncompromising in his nationalism. While Martin appealed to church-going parents, Malcolm spoke to the impatient youth—especially those who sensed the illicit lure of the streets. Martin called for integration, democracy, and appealed to the American creed; Malcolm sought the establishment of a Black Nation, separate and independent of the USA, where Black sovereignty would reign. King spoke movingly of an American dream; Malcolm spoke forebodingly of an American nightmare.

Movements sprang up like mushrooms in the dark—nationalist, liberatory, radical, and revolutionary. Grassroots groups. National organizations. Student groups. And more. Black history became obligatory and "freedom schools" were established in Black communities north, south, east, and west. Groups as disparate as the Student Non-Violent Coordinating Committee (1960) and the Black Panther Party for Self-Defense (1966) organized and administered these "freedom schools." In the ranks of both groups, members and supporters tried to teach children lessons of Black history, literature, and other subjects. But what they really tried to teach was both simple and complex: *freedom.*

As ever, the question arose: which way to freedom? Integration? Separatism? Black Nationalism? What?

When questions such as these arise in any community, they usually find organized expressions of various ideologies trying to amass popular support. These questions evoked added salience after the assassinations of Minister Malcolm X (February the 21st, 19 hundred and a 65) and Rev. Dr. King (April the 4th, 19 hundred and a 68), for the removal of both leaders from the scene, especially in such violent fashion, spurred organizing across the national Black Community. Moreover, given the non-violent ideology of Rev. King, and the violent method employed to kill him, the trend quickened toward militancy. Groups like the Republic of New Afrika, the Junta of Militant Organizations (JOMO), the Revolutionary Action Movement (RAM), the US Organization, and the Black Panther Party (BPP) were formed, and grew like dandelions after a spring rain.

The blood of martyrs fed deep rivers of Black resistance.

There were national organizations and local ones, but no matter, all received the rabid attention of the state, its spies, and its agents. The notorious COINTELPRO (Counter Intelligence Program) files—made public by the 1971 break-in of an FBI agent document storage facility in Media, Pennsylvania—revealed government snooping, surveillance, and attacks on a variety of radical and moderate organizations as well as individuals across the American spectrum of politics. Not surprisingly, the greatest attention and interference was among Black groups, especially those dedicated to radical social change. Black nationalist groups (called "Hate Groups" in FBI files) were rarely too small for such government attention.

One example can be shown by the ill-use of marital discord exploited in the marriage of a leader of the St. Louis, Missouri-based group, the Black Liberators.

Learning from phone taps and inside informers of the separation between the leader and his wife, the FBI initiated a program that is diabolical in its intent and its perfidy. The text of the files explains itself:

> Enclosed for the Bureau are two copies and for Springfield one copy of a letter to "SISTER [surname blacked out]."
>
> The following counter intelligence activity is being proposed by the St. Louis Division to be directed against [Name deleted]. He is a former [deleted] of the BLACK LIBERATORS (Bufile 157-10356), [rest of sentence, roughly page in length, one line deleted]. The activity attempts to alienate him from his wife and cause suspicion among the BLACK LIBERATORS that they have a dangerous troublemaker in their midst.
>
> BACKGROUND:
>
> [Name of target deleted] is currently separated from his wife, [name deleted] who lives with their two daughters in [deleted]. He occasionally sends her money and she appears to be a faithful, loving wife, who is apparently convinced that her husband is performing a vital service to the Black world and, therefore, she must endure this separation without bothering him. She is, to all indications, an intelligent, respectable young mother, who is a member of the AME Methodist Church in [the rest of the page, except for routing notations at the bottom, is deleted and blanked out].[22]

As we have noted elsewhere, the rest of the memo has a handwritten copy of a note sent to his wife, complete with sloppy script, typos, and intentional misspellings, to imitate how the FBI perceived a Black Liberator member would write, to the leader's wife, stating that the leader was cheating on his wife with female Black Liberator members. The letter has two clear objectives: to exacerbate discord between husband and wife; and to create a split between members of the group. Indeed, we needn't guess what the objectives of the U.S. government were. They state it quite openly in the latter pages of the memo, which we here recite, *verbatim:*

> The following results are anticipated following the execution of the above-counter-intelligence activity:

1. Ill feeling and possibly lasting distrust will be brought between [blank] and his wife. The concern over what to do about it may detract from his time spent in the plots and plans of [deleted]. He may even decide to spend more time with his wife and children and less time in Black Nationalist activity.

2. The Black Liberators will waste a great deal of time trying to discover the writer of the letter. It is possible that their not-too subtle investigation will lose present members and alienate potential ones.

3. Inasmuch as Black Liberators strength is ebbing at its lowest level, in this action may well be the "death-blow."[23]

The foregoing was a proposal from the SAC [Special Agent in Charge] of the St. Louis office to the FBI Director, J. Edgar Hoover, in Washington, D.C. Within days a reply was sent from Hoover, approving the plot, only suggesting that it not be traced back to the Bureau. If this was so for a small, not very effective, local group, what of those who had organized more aggressive, more militant groups?

The answer is simple. They were treated as enemies of the state. Period.

Hyperbole? Hardly. The 1960s had more than its share of hyperbole. Movements were rich with such verbiage, especially given that much of this period was an intense, antiwar period, and people spoke with the passion of both youth and radicalism. But, when it came to those targeted by the state for COINTELPRO efforts, we mean, quite literally, "enemies of the state."

After the Media, Pennsylvania, file break-in, reporters across the country read, some for the first time, the lengths to which the state was prepared to go to stop, undermine, and destroy those who dared suggest "change in the American government." But, perhaps, for the sake of clarity, let us cite from the congressional record the testimony of the former Deputy Director of the FBI (and one of COINTELPRO's prime architects), William Sullivan, who testified before the famous Church Committee hearings and was asked if the FBI was "using techniques designed to destroy a person's family life?" Sullivan explained:

> [T]his is a common practice, rough, dirty, tough, dirty business...
> We are in it. To repeat, it is a rough, tough, dirty business and dangerous. *We have used that technique against foreign espionage agents, and they have used it against us.*[24] [Emphasis added]

Americans. Treated like "foreign espionage agents." Americans. Like the local leader of the Black Liberators. Like Malcolm X. Like Paul Robeson. Like comedian turned political activist Dick Gregory. Americans like Rev. Dr. Martin Luther King, Jr. (Not to mention Rev. Martin Luther King, *Senior!*)

Americans. Just like you.

For in truth, it had nothing to do with "national security," and everything to do with politics. Plain and simple: If you opposed the political status quo, you were deemed an enemy of the state. Once so deemed, well—anything goes. And it did.

Overstatement? If you dare think so, we invite you to read the following brief excerpt. Consider, as a long leitmotif, the case of Richard Claxton Gregory aka Dick Gregory, a brilliant and biting comedian of the 1960s, who was attracted to the Civil Rights Movement and to Martin Luther King. He transformed his performances from racially tinged comedy to socially insightful homilies—and once even dared to speak out against the violent criminality of the U.S. Mafia. In a Chicago speech, Gregory reportedly stated that the "syndicate" were "the filthiest snakes that exist on this earth." In light of the prominence of the FBI as a major U.S. law enforcement agency, one might think that the heads of the agency would wholeheartedly concur with Gregory's assessment and perhaps even applaud his anticrime sentiments. The Bureau's response, however, was telling. In an FBI memo dated 23 April 1968, Hoover directed the agent in charge of the Chicago office to:

> [D]evelop counter-intelligence measures to neutralize him... This should not be in the nature of an expose, since he already gets far too much publicity. Instead, sophisticated completely untraceable means of neutralizing Gregory should be developed...[25]

And just a few weeks later, another memo dated 5 May, again from Hoover and this time referring to Gregory as a "militant black nationalist," directed the Chicago agent in charge to:

> Consider the use of this statement ["filthiest snakes"] in developing a counterintelligence operation to alert [the crime syndicate] La Cosa Nostra (LCN) to Gregory's attack on LCN. It is noted that other speeches by Gregory also contain attacks on the LCN. No counterintelligence action should be taken without Bureau authority.[26]

Affixed to the May memo was a note saying that "Richard Claxton Gregory" had previously referred to the FBI in a derogatory manner (as well as the director, of course). Director Hoover promptly gave his OK to the operation, which consisted of anonymous letters routed to various Mafiosi in Chicago, Gregory's hometown. Did the FBI think the Mafia would boycott Gregory's speeches or stop laughing at his jokes?[27]

Nota bene: This is but one example, from one case, of what the government did to a *comedian.*

We learn from such an instance (as well as a myriad of others) that the true function of a so-called intelligence agency isn't to actually secure intelligence (for, if that were the case, we'd all have to admit that these agencies have failed miserably), but to function as a political police to protect the status quo (that is, the wealthy elite), no matter the rhetoric raised by any given administration. Their job is to instill fear, to retard resistance to government policy, to chill ideas, and most importantly to protect the imperium—not the people.

Their job is to police dissent, to thin the rabble, to make it appear that the people agree with the rulers.

Enemies of the State

That great observer of American life, Alexis de Tocqueville, famous still for his work, *Democracy in America* (1835), is regarded as the keenest student of the American system, and his works are used by many to support their positions, whether conservative, liberal, or radical. But, as used in the biblical example, activists quote de Tocqueville for their own purposes.

Perhaps least quoted, for reasons of fear and sensitivity, is his perspective on "negroes" in America. He predicted Black independence in the West Indies, and eventually here in the U.S., although not without a great struggle. He said that southern whites, although well-armed and skilled in military affairs, would lose due to the numerical strength of Blacks along the Gulf coast, due, in part, to "the agency of despair." This becomes possible, he foresees, if the north and south wage a war and emerge as two separate nations, the southern the weaker. Wrote de Tocqueville, again in a productive frame of mind: "If ever America undergoes great revolutions, they will be brought about by the presence of the black race on the soil of the United States—that is to say, they will owe their origin, not to the equality, *but to the inequality, of conditions.*"[28] [Emphasis added]

This gives us one glance at the centrality of Blacks to the American project, the linchpin around which the whole machine turns, one that requires a revolutionary change. That said, it is wholly reconcilable with early American thought.

And even after war, after nearly a century of state-supported terrorism, stolen labor (albeit by other names) and judicial, police, big business, and societal rejection of the fundamentals of citizenship (as in voting, serving in office, on juries, etc.), the State, through its most powerful agencies, continued to target Black figures of prominence. There were very few areas of social life among Blacks that weren't policed. Under the aegis of "fighting communism," the government intruded into the deepest crevices of Black life, and tried to destroy or discredit those they deemed "un-American."

As the Civil Rights Movement was picking up steam, and the Black Liberation Movement was beginning to stir, at the highest levels of government, targets were being drawn up in a secret plan of attack. In the spring of 1968, the FBI issued its now infamous "black messiah" memo, which listed the primary "goals" of its COINTELPRO operations. It is a telling look into the mind(s) of the State and declares clearly the precise objectives of the government. The memo, typed out on what appears to be an old beat-up manual Remington typewriter, states as follows:

> <u>GOALS</u>
> For maximum effectiveness of the Counterintelligence Program, and to prevent wasted effort, long-range goals are being set.
>
> 1. Prevent the coalition of militant black nationalist groups. In unity there is strength; a truism that is no less valid for all its triteness. An effective coalition of black nationalist groups might be the first step toward a real "Mau Mau" [Black revolutionary army] in America, the beginning of a true black revolution.
>
> 2. Prevent the rise of a "messiah" who could unify, and electrify, the militant black nationalist movement. [Name deleted] might have been such a "messiah;" he is the martyr of the movement today. [Names of several individuals listed and deleted from copy] all aspire to this position. [Name blanked out] is less of a threat because of his age. [Name deleted] could be a very real contender for this position should he abandon his supposed

"obedience" to "white, liberal doctrines" (nonviolence) and embrace black nationalism. [Name deleted] has the necessary charisma to be a real threat in this way.

3. Prevent violence on the part of black nationalist groups. This is of primary importance, and is, of course, a goal of our investigative activity; it should also be a goal of the Counterintelligence Program. Through counterintelligence it should be possible to pinpoint potential troublemakers and neutralize them before they exercise their potential for violence.

4. Prevent militant black nationalist groups and leaders from gaining respectability, by discrediting them to three separate segments of the community. The goal of discrediting black nationalists must be handled tactically in three ways. You must discredit those groups and individuals to, first, the responsible Negro community. Second, they must be discredited to the white community, both the responsible community and to "liberals" who have vestiges of sympathy for militant black nationalist [sic] simply because they are Negroes. Third, these groups must be discredited in the eyes of Negro radicals, the followers of the movement. This last area requires entirely different tactics from the first two. Publicity about violent tendencies and radical statements merely enhances black nationalists to the last group; it adds "respectability" in a different way.

5. A final goal should be to prevent the long-range growth of militant black nationalist organizations, especially among youth. Specific tactics to prevent these groups from converting young people must be developed.[29]

This memo is remarkable on several levels. First, it presumes to take the position that Blacks should have no say, either in who their own leaders should be (not to mention which organizations they should support), or in the important question of nationality. Presumably, Blacks should meekly let others choose leaders for them, and simply submit to the racist principles of white nationalism.

We respectfully urge you to re-read the salient points of the memo below; please note that this is the undeleted text, with the persons targeted for attention by the government now included. (Remember, these are the government's stated "Goals"):

1. Prevent a coalition of militant black nationalist groups…
2. Prevent the rise of a "messiah" who could unify and electrify the militant nationalist movement… *Malcolm X* might have been such a "messiah;" he is the martyr of the movement today. *Martin Luther King, Stokely Carmichael and Elijah Muhammed* (sic) all aspire to this position. *Elijah Muhammed* is less of a threat because of his age. *King* could be a very real contender for this position should he abandon his supposed "obedience" to "white, liberal doctrines" (nonviolence) and embrace black nationalism. *Carmichael* has the necessary charisma to be a real threat in this way.
3. Prevent violence on the part of black nationalist groups…
4. Prevent militant black nationalist groups and leaders from gaining respectability by discrediting them…
5. …prevent the long-range growth of militant black nationalist organizations, especially among youth.

This memo was dated 4 March 1968. Within one month of its writing, Martin Luther King, Jr., would be murdered and martyred in Memphis, gunned down on the balcony of the Lorraine Motel.

When was the last time you heard (or read) of anyone fearing the rise of a "messiah?" Why is it the role of government—*any government*—to "prevent the rise of a messiah?" This teaches us that the role of the U.S. government was quite similar to another empire, several millennia ago. It teaches us, in no uncertain terms, that the government's core function was to preserve white supremacy, by any means. As for "militants," it's clear as crystal that the nation's premier law enforcement agency was profoundly ignorant of the targets they were aiming at and simply misrepresenting reality—or they were high on crack. For the government identified people and groups like the Southern Christian Leadership Conference and the Student Nonviolent Coordinating Committee as groups with "radical and violence-prone leaders, members and followers."[30]

The Southern Christian Leadership Conference (SCLC) was, in essence, Rev. Dr. King's group. But, we guess, if Dick Gregory, the comedian turned civil rights spokesmen, could be targeted as a "militant black nationalist," why wouldn't the savages gleefully shredding the Constitution label the SCLC "radical," or "violence-prone"? By labeling and targeting groups such as these, the government could then act with impunity, sending agents hell-bent on violence, disruption, and chaos into groups that lived up to their skewed definition: enemy of the state. (Taking it a step further, we envision a day when a top U.S. government official—one sharpening his lifelong skills as a classic demagogue—will loudly define the press/media as the "enemy of the people.")

We have defined Martin Luther King as perhaps the leading civil rights figure of the 20th century. But we have only intimated how the FBI, in their loathing of King, targeted him—illegally wiretapping his phones, bugging his hotel rooms, reading his correspondence, and even attempting to push him to suicide. King, as we have said, was a handsome man, with the southern preacher's gift of gab. He attracted pretty women to him and he had difficulty abstaining from their advances as well as his own desires. The FBI, through its informers and its illegal surveillance of King and the places he stayed, knew this and sought to exploit it. When a highlight reel of these illicit recordings were presented to J. Edgar Hoover, he is reported to have exclaimed, "This will destroy the burrhead."[31] (A racial slur from a racist man leading "a racist outfit more concerned with persecuting civil rights activists than prosecuting organized crime figures."[32])

In November of 1964, King's wife, Coretta Scott King, opened a box delivered to the SCLC office in Atlanta to discover a version of this highlight reel along with a letter enclosed, which she initially thought was a copy of one of his many speeches. That is, until she read the following note:

> KING.
> In view of your low grade... I will not dignify your name with either a Mr. or a Reverend or a Dr. And, your last name calls to mind only the type of King such as King Henry the VIII...
>
> King, look into your heart. You know you are a complete fraud and a great liability to all of us Negroes. White people in this country have enough frauds of their own but I am sure they don't have one at this time that is anywhere near your equal. You are no clergyman and you know it. I repeat you are a colossal fraud and an evil, vicious one at that. You could not believe in God... Clearly you don't believe in any personal and moral principles.
>
> King, like all frauds your end is approaching. You should have been our greater leader. You, even at an early age have turned out to

be not a leader but a dissolute, abnormal moral imbecile. We will now have to depend on our older leaders like Wilkins, a man of character and thank God we have others like him. But you are done. Your "honorary" degrees, your Nobel Prize (what a grim farce) and other awards will not save you. King, I repeat you are done.

No person can overcome facts, not even a fraud like yourself... I repeat—no person can argue successfully against facts. You are finished... Satan could not do more. What incredible evilness... King you are done.

The American public, the church organizations that have been helping—Protestant, Catholic and Jews will know you for what you are—an evil abnormal beast. So will others who have backed you. You are done.

King, there is only one thing left for you to do. You know what this is. You have just 34 days in which to do this (this exact number has been selected for a specific reason, it has practical significant [*sic*]). You are done. There is but one way out for you. You better take it before your filthy, abnormal fraudulent self is bared to the nation.[33]

Although written in the voice of "a Negro," it is clear that this was written by high-level FBI agents (undoubtedly with the personal attention of Hoover, who hated King with a virulent passion), from a particular perspective of causing the most psychological damage to the idealistic young minister. It caused significant depression in the man, as no doubt intended. He later told a close friend (this, too, recorded by the FBI on a bugged telephone line), "They are out to break me."[34]

The recordings and nefarious letter also shocked and terrified Coretta, who would later claim that the two never discussed it. While this might sound unlikely, we must conclude that every relationship is different and that we will never really know the dynamics that animated that marriage. More to the point, this base attack on King, his marriage, and his mental wellbeing, were part of a vendetta against the Civil Rights Movement, not a federal investigation in pursuance of a criminal. "King, after all, had committed no crime. On the contrary, he was on his way to becoming one of the great Americans of our time and while, for sure, his personal morality was hardly conventional, it did not violate any federal law."[35]

Hoover, the man who specialized in the nation's secrets (especially its sexual ones), tried mightily to depose the hated Black figure from history's stage. But while the personality and world renown of the target may have been somewhat extraordinary, in truth it was but one battle in the ongoing war against the struggle for Black freedom. The government harassed him; they hounded him; they wiretapped and bugged him; they tried to destroy his marriage, and drove him to the depths of despair. But they did not stop him. He walked his walk. He preached the sermon spun from his very soul. His voice rang with the echoes of millions. And he was assassinated in Memphis, murdered while trying to ensure that Black garbagemen would be given a decent, living wage to do some of the most disagreeable work imaginable.

He did not stop, and the nation, and the world revel in his spirit. For, by not bowing to fear, to depression, to the hour of the wolf, he inspired millions and added another day to the long and ragged struggle for Black liberation.

While Martin Luther King, Jr., was many things, some positive, and some negative, he was hardly the totality of Black liberation—nor could he be. That war began long before his birth, and has continued long after his assassination. Nevertheless, given the sheer prominence of his person (few have national holidays named after them), his visage in stone upon the National Mall, the near-deification of his life (several church communities, including the Anglican Church, have named him a Saint), we think it noteworthy therefore, to give in some detail, a small portion of the literature and documents detailing this war against a man who would one day be a sainted figure.

Most Americans (and perhaps many around the world) are very familiar with King's "I Have a Dream" speech, delivered in the sweltering summer of 1963, on the site of Washington D.C.'s Lincoln Memorial, delivered before tens of thousands and broadcast globally. However, few are familiar with the FBI's reaction to King's speech, which gives us vital insight into how the power elites truly regarded King:

> We must mark [King] now, if we have not before, as *the most dangerous Negro in the future of this Nation...* from the standpoint of communism, the Negro, and national security... it may be *unrealistic to limit* (our actions against King) to *legalistic proofs* that would stand up in court or before Congressional Committees.[36] [Emphasis added]

The Rev. Dr. Martin Luther King was so "dangerous," it seems, precisely because he was growing in national influence, and could therefore, cause problems for the white supremacist status quo. The previous memo was distributed throughout the nation's intelligence agencies and to "the various military services," as well.

Who was "dangerous" to whom?

Dick Gregory, who knows a thing or two about government malfeasance, offers us unique insight on the elimination of the preacher from Atlanta's Ebenezer Baptist Church:

> You see King wasn't killed because of civil rights or integration. He was killed because he was the first black person in the history of America that got in the position to determine public policy. That had never happened before. Boom, take 'em out. And let me tell you, there will come a day a million years from now, if there's anyone left on this planet, the only reason America will get mentioned is because they will have to say that's where King was born. The only reason. No other reason.[37]

The War Against Black Political Power

Theoretically, in a democracy, a citizen is able to vote his or her public policy concerns into reality via the electoral franchise. We have seen how the U.S. and state governments have conspired, for the better part of a century, to deprive Black voters from the very franchise allegedly "guaranteed" by the 15th Amendment to the U.S. Constitution, which states, in part:

The right of citizens of the United States to vote shall not be denied or abridged by the United States or by any State on account of race, color, or previous condition of servitude...

When Black people in apartheid Mississippi tried to sit as a part of the 1964 Democratic Convention's state delegation, they faced the opposition of the administration, the Democratic Party, and—the FBI. Historians Ward Churchill and James Vander Wall have written:

> [T]he FBI helped to destroy the MFDP (Mississippi Freedom Democratic Party) initiative at Atlantic City, an entirely legitimate effort into which thousands had poured their best hopes for achieving some form of nonviolent "due process" change in

> American society—and for which [James E.] Chaney, [Michael] Schwerner, and [Andrew] Goodman and scores of others had died.
>
> Even though the MFDP delegation had received the required votes to be seated at the convention, replacing Mississippi's Jim Crow delegation altogether, party regulars (headed by President Lyndon Johnson) contrived to block these legal rights, preserving the segregationist status quo. In accomplishing this, Johnson utilized a special 31-person task force of FBI agents—who infiltrated the convention floor itself, utilizing phony NBC press credentials—commanded by Bureau Assistant Director [Cartha D.] DeLoach to wiretap and bug such civil rights leaders as Martin Luther King, and Fannie Lou Hamer, as well as CORE's [Congress of Racial Equality] James Farmer and Julius Lester, and SNCC's [Student Nonviolent Coordinating Committee] Stokely Carmichael, James Forman, Cleveland Sellers, and Ivanhoe Donaldson. Not only were the Johnson forces thus made privy to the MFDP's external communications with Democratic Party dignitaries such as Robert Kennedy, but with the group's internal communications—with each other, and with various new left advisers—as well. Needless to say, the political process was aborted under such conditions, a matter which inculcated an increasing sense of futility within much of the civil rights movement.[38]

Well. So much for "democracy," eh?

And if the State waged an ugly, subterranean war against the Civil Rights Movement's ability to freely participate in the electoral system (as in the case of the Mississippi Freedom Democratic Party), it unleashed an even uglier, more open war against those who dared to raise the red, black, and green flag of Black Liberation.

Among the many groups that tried to fight on that territory, the Black Panther Party stands virtually distinct from many of the era. For they sought—in the words of its founding member, Huey P. Newton, the organization's Minister of Defense—Black revolutionary political power. As such, it attracted the attention of the political police (aka the FBI), those forces of the state who fought to stifle, by means both foul and criminal, to extinguish such hopes, in furtherance of the national executive and the nation's central organizing tenet: white supremacy.

Organized initially as the Black Panther Party for Self-Defense in October of 1966, the Party attracted a plethora of supporters, especially among Black, ghetto youth and grassroots folks. It also attracted the enmity of the State—local and federal—which strove mightily to kill it in its cradle. Although the Black Panther Party, by name, had its genesis a month before and a coast apart from the Oakland example (see, for instance, Muhammad Ahmad's *We Will Return in the Whirlwind*), it was Oakland that resonated across the country, and sparked dozens of activists to organize similar offices in their communities.

Under the auspices of the Oakland core, offices quickly opened in cities as far-flung as Winston-Salem (North Carolina), Omaha (Nebraska), Seattle (Washington), Richmond (Virginia and California), Boston (Massachusetts), and Baltimore (Maryland). In a matter of months, more than forty chapters and branches sprouted from the Oakland example, north, south, east, and west. Where there were Black people, there was a Black Panther Party; and where there was a Black Panther Party, there was confrontation, conflict, and before long, state repression.

Quite unlike the Mississippi Freedom Democratic Party, the BPP wanted no part of the prominent, major political parties of the day, for they beheld them both as mere capitalist parties, designed to serve the interests of the economic elite. They considered themselves socialist in orientation, and, as such, they had little in common with the organized political process, and, with the exception of coalitions with other groups (like the California-based Peace and Freedom Party), initially seldom launched electoral projects.

In time, however, with the party's maturity, that option became a live one, which activated and energized the core membership of the organization. But no matter what phase the Party entered, there was never a time when the State apparatus, including its intelligence arm, did not seek nor attempt to obliterate it. They used means—*including criminal ones*—to "disrupt," "discredit," and "neutralize" the BPP, and indeed, all groups considered "black nationalist."[39]

Indeed, "black movements" were the bulk of the agency's work, and one group, the Black Panther Party, constituted the lion's share of the government's targets. Of the 295 documented actions taken by COINTELPRO designed to disrupt Black groups, 233 (that's *79 percent!*) were specifically directed toward the BPP's destruction. In fact, J. Edgar Hoover, the FBI's Director during this particularly Draconian period, publicly announced that the Black Panther Party constituted "the greatest threat to the internal security of the country."[40] With rhetoric such as this, almost anything was conceivable—and almost anything was possible. The FBI, along with other state and local agencies, outdid themselves in searching for creative techniques to destroy such targets. They utilized every tool imaginable—snitches, informants, provocateurs, drugs, media assassinations—and literal assassinations—to get rid of "the greatest threat."

The most pivotal case was that of Fred Hampton, a 21-year-old Panther out of the Chicago suburb of Maywood, who was a leader in his school and a member of the area's youth branch of the NAACP. He was attracted to the BPP's Chicago office—founded by a former SNCC organizer, Bob Brown—a year after Oakland began organizing. When Brown left in allegiance to the Africanist organizer, Stokely Carmichael, Hampton took over the office, and became Deputy Chairman of the state Party.

Hampton was, by all accounts, a gifted and creative organizer, a Panther who was viewed nationally as the next wave of Party leadership, and he was a shoo-in for the office of Chief of Staff of the national organization.

But that was not to be. For on the morning of 4 December 1969, the FBI supported and planned a raid on the Panther apartment on Monroe Street and that was the end of such high hopes. Given the federal nod of approval by the U.S. Attorney General, John Mitchell, and armed not only with automatic weapons but with a floor-plan drawn by the snitch/informant, William O'Neal (the Party's own "Chief of Security"!), about a dozen federal agents and the Chicago police hit the home, as Churchill and Vander Wall note:

> At about 4:30 [a.m], they launched an outright assault upon the Panthers, as Gloves Davis kicked open the front door and promptly shot Mark Clark point-blank in the chest with a .30 calibre M-1 carbine. Clark, who had apparently nodded off in a front room with a shotgun across the lap, barely had time to stand up before being killed more-or-less instantly. His reflexive response to being shot discharged the shotgun. It was the only round fired by the Panthers during the raid.
>
> Davis immediately proceeded to pump a bullet into eighteen-year-old Brenda Harris, who was lying (unarmed) in a front room bed; [CPD Sgt. Daniel] Groth hit her with a second round. [Joseph] Gorman, joined by Davis and his carbine, then began spraying automatic fire from his .45 calibre Thompson submachine gun

through a wall into the bedrooms. All forty-two shots fired by the pair converged on the head of Hampton's bed, pinpointed in O'Neal's floor-plan; one of the shots, fired by Davis, struck Hampton in the left shoulder, seriously wounding him as he slept. While this was going on, the second sub-team, firing as they came, crashed through the back door. This was followed by a brief lull in the shooting, during which Carmody and another (unidentified) raider entered Hampton's bedroom. They were heard to have the following exchange:

That's Fred Hampton...
Is he dead? ... Bring him out.
He's barely alive; he'll make it.

Two shots were then heard, both of which were fired pointblank into Hampton's head as he lay prone, followed by Carmody's voice stating, "He's good and dead now."[41]

Hampton, a young man destined to become a pivotal leader in the national organization, was slain in his sleep. One wonders, why did he not stir from his slumber when the sound of shotguns and machineguns burst through this relatively small apartment? Because, as later medical tests showed, he was under the influence of secobarbital, something he never indulged in. Party members believed he was given a "Mickey" by FBI agent/rat O'Neal, who probably laced his Kool-Aid with the drug.

As reported by Wes Swearingen in his 1995 work, *FBI Secrets: An Agent's Expose,* the ex-FBI agent reveals the revolting icing on the entire episode as described by FBI Special Agent Gregg York:

> There is a lounge at the FBI National Academy which sells low-alcohol beer in the evening after classes, but no hard liquor. Gregg York and I had finished a few pitchers of beer one night as we discussed old times. I don't recall just how the subject of the Black Panther Party came up. I may have started the conversation by comparing the work of the Los Angeles racial squad to the bag jobs Gregg and I had done in Chicago. I told York that some agents in Los Angeles had informants who had assassinated Black Panther members and I told him how Geronimo Pratt had been framed for murder and had been sentenced to life in prison.

> York grinned and said he had a better story than that.
>
> York told me about the December 1969 raid on the Chicago Panther headquarters in which Fred Hampton and Mark Clark had been killed by the Chicago police. He said the FBI had arranged for the raid by telling the police that the Panthers had numerous guns and explosives, and that they would shoot any police officer who entered the building.
>
> We did not speak for what seemed a long time. I kept thinking of how my old friend thought I was on his side when it came to killing African Americans. I felt sorry for Gregg York because he was still fighting Hoover's imaginary enemies: the communists, the Native Americans and the African Americans.
>
> We began to talk again, and York said, "We expected about twenty Panthers to be in the apartment when the police raided the place. Only two of those black nigger fuckers were killed, Fred Hampton and Mark Clark."[42]

As part of the longest war, several government agencies conspired to drug, then assassinate a young Black leader—one who steadfastly stood against the state's program and policy of white supremacy.

One of your authors later visited the crime scene. From the documentary film *Long Distance Revolutionary:*

> NARRATOR
> On December 4th, 1969, Chicago police raided the apartment of Black Panther Fred Hampton and then executed him while he slept—a sleep induced by a barbiturate cocktail courtesy of the Federal Bureau of Investigation. Local authorities claimed the Panthers opened fire on the police but clear-cut evidence later emerged that told a much different story—that the Chicago police along with the Cook County Attorney's Office and the FBI planned to assassinate the 21-year-old Hampton.
>
> Shortly thereafter, a delegation of Panthers from Philadelphia visited the crime scene. Mumia Abu-Jamal was part of that delegation.

TERRY BISSON (Abu-Jamal biographer)
There was a memorial service in a church in Philadelphia (Church of the Advocate) right after that and Mumia was actually one of the primary speakers. What Mumia said on that day I think was said in many memorial services across the country, which was that the police had just assassinated one of the bright lights of the Black Movement.

MICHAEL PARENTI (historian, political scientist)
There's no terrorist organization, there's no communist country, there's no jihadist or anybody else who has a record like the U.S. has in terms of imperial violence. So to focus on the Panthers and say they're violent, they're violent, they're violent... is kind of ridiculous.[43]

Soldiers

We have witnessed, in these brief pages, two sides of the war against Black freedom, where the tactics used were indistinguishable from those used against so-called foreign enemies or enemy combatants involved in espionage. For what else were they?

In 1851, in what historian Phillip Foner called a "major harbinger of the Civil War," in Lancaster County's little hamlet of Christiana, an act of rebellion against slave-catchers rocked both Pennsylvania and the nation like an earthquake. Christiana was where several escaped captives made their homes and lives, and when slave-catchers entered their community, they were given a stern invitation to leave, or be sent to the next world. These escaped slaves made good on their promise, running some off, and sending at least one to his grim reward. The words of the rebellion's leader, William Parker, spoken more than 200 years ago, had a ring of truth that still resonates with millions of Black Americans today when they honestly consider their place in the White Nation. Said Parker:

> [T]he laws for personal protection are not made for us, and we are not bound to obey them... [whites] have a country and may obey the laws. *But we have no country.*[44] [Emphasis added]

When your government tries to kill you, tries to make you commit suicide, or hires someone—or one of your *friends*—to drug you into a stupor, so that other agents of that government can kill you in your drug-assisted sleep, in what sense can one claim that the agents of such an entity are your government? It is far more accurate and honest to term such a body as an enemy of your person, your people, your community and, indeed, of most African people. It is equally as accurate to describe such efforts as a state of war against any hint of a true Black freedom struggle.

In sum, while Martin Luther King, Jr., and Fred Hampton, Sr. ("Sr" added posthumously as his child was also sleeping in the belly of his wife, Afua, who herself barely escaped being slaughtered in her sleep), were crucially distinct in their political outlook and orientation, both were avatars of the Black Freedom Struggle—and both were targeted by the United States government for liquidation precisely because both believed in Black Freedom.

Both are martyrs who died in service of Black Liberation, a struggle that did not end with their ultimate sacrifice, but that persists in the righteous and necessary assertion of the Black Lives Matter movement, a resurgence of this long, unbroken struggle born from the slain Black bodies of American citizens targeted and executed by weapons of the state, and at the hands of goons and thugs employed by the state.

So the longest war rages on, where the naiveté of liberal whites (and Blacks) conjuring the pipedream of a "post-racial" America is met with the blunt truth of the Empire and its history—a demagogic chant of "Make America WHITE Again" and a national campaign endorsed by the Ku Klux Klan that found a home, in 2016, at 1600 Pennsylvania Avenue. It also found a home (among other places) in Charlottesville, Virginia, on 12 August 2017, when neo-Nazi and white supremacist James Fields drove his Dodge Challenger from Maumee, Ohio, into murderous infamy on the downtown streets of Charlottesville, where he brutally murdered the peaceful civil rights activist, thirty-two-year-old Heather Heyer—and injured nineteen others—as he barreled through the crowd, his car a ferocious weapon.

The war for and against Black Liberation, the real longest war, is far from over.

Postscript:

Say their names: Ahmaud Arbery. Breonna Taylor. Sean Monterrosa. George Floyd...

MURDER INCORPORATED

empire \ genocide \ manifest destiny

5 Supreme Power in the Empire of the Law

When it comes to any discourse on the law, especially any exploration of the U.S. Supreme Court, remember this truism, chisel it into the sidewalk: *Law is politics by other means.*

27 May 1972.

America's genocidal war rages in Southeast Asia. Heretic George McGovern is close to winning the Democratic Party's nomination to run against the "cheap crook and merciless war criminal," Dick Nixon in the fall. Hunter S. Thompson (who the previous quotes belong to) publishes *Fear and Loathing in Las Vegas.* Perfect timing for counterculture comedian and social/political satirist, George Carlin, who is about to take the stage at the Santa Monica Civic Auditorium to record his epochal album, *Class Clown.* Ten years earlier, Carlin was arrested along with rocket fuel comedian and social critic (some say leper), Lenny Bruce, in Chicago's Gate of Horn club—Bruce on obscenity charges, Carlin for refusing to show the cops his ID.

Credit: Studio Photo/Unknown

George Carlin

So, on this distant night in La-La Land, as a Pacific breeze whips down lonely Main Street in the Peoples Republic of Santa Monica, George Carlin takes the stage with the same rocket fuel that jettisoned Lenny into a blacklisted orbit.

"Shit, piss, fuck, cunt, cocksucker, motherfucker, and tits." Those are the heavy seven. Those are the ones that'll infect your soul, curve your spine, and keep the country from winning the war. "Shit, piss, fuck, cunt, cocksucker, motherfucker, and tits," wow. Tits doesn't even belong on the list...[1]

(Listen to it today and hear the joyful laughter. It's fucking hilarious!)

Two months later, Carlin is arrested on obscenity charges at Milwaukee's *Summerfest.* In fact this arrest was one of numerous Carlin endured for performing his legendary "Seven Dirty Words."

About a year or so later, in 1973, "Shit, piss, fuck, cunt, cocksucker, motherfucker, and tits" floated through speakers inside John Douglass' car while the CBS executive and his teenage son are cruising along. Pacifica Network's New York City station, WBAI, was broadcasting Carlin's "Seven Dirty Words" routine from his new album, *Occupation: Foole.* It turns out that Douglass was also a member of a group called "Morality in Media," a haughty assemblage that sees themselves as a Cerberus guarding what is right and holy in the American zeitgeist. A month later Douglass filed a complaint with the Federal Communications Commission (the good old FCC).

Pacifica passionately defended the broadcast, comparing the importance of Carlin's work to that of Mark Twain's. Without fining Pacifica, the FCC issued a warning but the network didn't stop there—a Circuit Court in Washington, D.C. (by a 2-1 vote) declared that the commission did not have the legal authority to regulate the WBAI broadcast—one justice citing constitutional protection, the other citing the Communications Act's prohibition against censorship.

In 1978, the case reaches the proverbial "highest court in the land" where five justices added a nice tight broadcast schedule to the language of the First Amendment. By a 5-4 vote, the Court upheld the FCC's decision, finding that Carlin's act was indecent but not obscene (majority votes: Rehnquist, Stevens, Burger, Blackmun, Powell; minority votes: Marshall, White, Brennan, Stewart) and that the FCC had the authority to protect listeners against what they defined as an invasion of privacy. The Court writing: "[Broadcasters] cannot completely protect the listener or viewer from unexpected program content," because people are "constantly tuning in and out."[2]

Now here's the beauty part: the majority based their decision on this fact—because the Carlin broadcast was during the day (2pm), it didn't have as much constitutional protection as if the broadcast happened at midnight. *What?* Did they even look at the First Amendment? The language seems pretty clear:

> Congress shall make no law... abridging the freedom of speech

Justice William Brennan wrote one of the two dissenting opinions. He begins by writing:

> For the second time in two years, see *Young v. American Mini Theatres, Inc., 427 U.S. 50* (1976), the Court refuses to embrace the notion, completely antithetical to basic First Amendment values, that the degree of protection the First Amendment affords protected speech varies with the social value ascribed to that speech by five Members of this Court.[3]

With regard to the invasion of privacy issue, Brennan writes:

> Without question, the privacy interests of an individual in his home are substantial and deserving of significant protection. In finding these interests sufficient to justify the content regulation of protected speech, however, the Court commits two errors. First, it misconceives the nature of the privacy interests involved where an individual voluntarily chooses to admit radio communications into his home. Second, it ignores the constitutionally protected interests of both those who wish to transmit and those who desire to receive broadcasts that many including the FCC and this Court might find offensive.[4]

And then, having the audacity to use COMMON SENSE, Brennan writes:

> [F]or unlike other intrusive modes of communication, such as sound trucks, "[t]he radio can be turned off," *Lehman v. Shaker Heights, 418 U.S. 298,302* (1974) and with a minimum of effort.[5]

In 1971, Paul Cohen walked through the Los Angeles Municipal Courthouse wearing a jacket with the words "Fuck the Draft" boldly visible. Cohen was clearly protesting the depth of the Vietnam War and the draft. Cohen was later convicted of violating California Penal Code § 415, which prohibits "maliciously and willfully disturb[ing] the peace or quiet of any neighborhood or person... by... offensive conduct." The Court of Appeal held that "offensive conduct" means "behavior which has a tendency to provoke others to acts of violence or to in turn disturb the peace," and affirmed the conviction. The Supreme Court majority in *Cohen v. California* (1971) found this argument, along with their concurrent invasion of privacy argument (similar to the Pacifica/Carlin case) to be nothing more than excuses to suppress free speech and overturned the lower court's ruling. Reiterating the essence of *Cohen v California* in the dissent of *FCC v Pacifica,* Brennan writes:

> The ability of government, consonant with the Constitution, to shut off discourse solely to protect others from hearing it is, in other words, dependent upon a showing that substantial privacy interests are being invaded in an essentially intolerable manner. Any broader view of this authority would effectively empower a majority to silence dissidents simply as a matter of personal predilections.[6]

Justice Thurgood Marshall joined Brennan in the dissent on *FCC v Pacifica,* writing this short but stinging admonishment:

> I find the Court's misapplication of fundamental First Amendment principles so patent, and its attempt to impose its notions of propriety on the whole of the American people so misguided, that I am unable to remain silent.[7]

And then one final piece of COMMON SENSE from Brennan regarding the majority opinion:

> The opinion of my Brother POWELL acknowledges that there lurks in today's decision a potential for "'reduc[ing] the adult population . . . to [hearing] only what is fit for children.'"[8]

Dissenting opinions help and then every once in awhile the Court in its majority gets something right when it comes to protecting the country's citizens against the tyranny of the state or the cruelty of the corporatocracy (rather than being the habitual controlling tool and final arbiter for the rich, powerful, and the tyrannical). And let's not forget that most cases argued before the Court are technical, boring, and offer little meaning to the general public.

Over the decades-long life of the American Empire, a few cracks in the ivory tower have appeared and a few brave men and women have courageously fought the monster for enlightened social and political change. They've struck down discriminatory laws and actions and they've protected individual liberties—for instance, *Clay v. United States* (1971) was Muhammad Ali's appeal of his 1967 conviction for refusing to report for military induction based on his application as a conscientious objector. The Supreme Court, in a rare moment of great wisdom and constitutional courage, reversed the Fifth Circuit. We danced. *Float like a butterfly, sting like a bee, get up off that canvas, sucka, and call me Muhammad Ali.*

Unfortunately, if one were to write a chronicle of great moments in SCOTUS history, there could only be one title: *Even a Broken Clock is Right Twice a Day.* For every *Brown v Board of Education of Topeka* (1954) there's a long list of *Dred Scott(s) v Sanford* (1857). For every *Roe v Wade* (1973) there's a pile of *Korematsu(s) v. United States* (1944). And for every *New York Times Co. v. United States* (1971) there's darkness like *Citizens United v. Federal Election Commission* (2010).

Let's all say it together: "Law is politics by other means."

Indeed it is. Always has been. Including millennia-long religious law set in place for maximum control purposes. It was only 1831 and Alexis de Tocqueville, in his *Democracy in America,* already saw the graffiti on the wall, writing, "[S]carcely any political question arises in the United States that is not resolved, sooner or later, into a judicial question."[9]

Robert Dahl, the groundbreaking political scientist, understood the Court's political reality and underscored this certainty when he published "Decision-making in a Democracy: The Supreme Court as a National Policy-Maker" (1957). Dahl famously wrote about the Court's "most peculiar position" in American democracy:

> To consider the Supreme Court of the United States strictly as a legal institution is to underestimate its significance in the American political system. For it is also a political institution... Much of the legitimacy of the Court's decisions rests upon the fiction that it is not a political institution but exclusively a legal one.[10]

Prussian general and military theorist, Carl von Clausewitz (who died the year de Tocqueville famously came to America with prison reformer Gustave de

Beaumont), had many maxims, arguably the most famous: "War is the continuation of politics by other means." Clausewitz took the concept, around since humans crawled out of the primordial swamp, to its logical and bloody finish line.

The great American myth of judicial impartiality began where all the lies commenced—with the so-called Founding Fathers slash Framers. James Madison, smoking some colonial cannabis, had his own Lucy in the Sky with Diamonds moment framing SCOTUS as "an impenetrable bulwark against every assumption of power in the legislative or executive."[11] How's that worked out, Jim? Who buys this strain of American exceptionalism, you ask? Well, lots of people.

Attorney and author, Adam Cohen, sat down with journalist Amy Goodman on *DemocracyNow!* to discuss his book, *Supreme Inequality: The Supreme Court's Fifty-Year Battle for a More Unjust America.* Here's the opening exchange:

AMY GOODMAN: So let's go to the thesis of your book, that the Supreme Court has made America unjust in the last fifty years. Talk about what you call "supreme inequality."

ADAM COHEN: [O]ur society is becoming more and more unequal. The gap between rich and poor has been growing and growing to near-record levels. The question is: Why? The explanations we generally get are large forces like globalization and automation, or people look to the policies of the president and Congress. The point I make in this book is that the Supreme Court, which is an institution that we think of as the bastion of fairness, the advocate for the underdog, has actually been a major driver of inequality.[12]

The illusion all starts with THEATRICS

American musician and raconteur, Frank Zappa, once quipped, "Politics is a bunch of show and blow for people who don't understand." He then detailed the illusion:

> The illusion of freedom will continue as long as it's profitable to continue the illusion. At the point where the illusion becomes too expensive to maintain, they will just take down the scenery, they will pull back the curtains, they will move the tables and chairs out of the way and you will see the brick wall at the back of the theater.[13]

Any great dramatist will tell you the same thing. It's all done with smoke and mirrors. Aeschylus, Euripides, Sophocles. Rasputin. Houdini. Orson Welles. The Wizard of Oz.

The lights dim, the curtain opens, and for a moment the audience holds its collective breath... illusion becomes reality. SCOTUS plays on the same stage, creating the exact same mise en scène. We're surprised the justices don't enter swinging a thurible suspended from chains with incense smoking out from the metal censer—of course accompanied by distant church bells and monophonic Gregorian chant.

We are all trained and conditioned to see judges, clad in their dark and foreboding robes, as people who are superior to normal, average men and women. Gods and goddesses descending from Olympus. The robes lend an air of solemnity, wisdom, and certitude, similar to the vestments of priests, nuns, or monks. But in truth, they are not just like us—they are us, in every way that makes us human. They are angry, ambitious, biased and as base as are we all. Robes and theatrics change nothing.

When Chief Justice Roger Brooks Taney wrote, in the infamous *Dred Scot* case, "negroes have no rights that a white man is bound to respect," he was wearing a black robe.

When *Buck v. Bell* was decided, holding that it was legal to sterilize women who were deemed as "idiots," all of the judges making the ruling wore black robes—with the revered Oliver Wendell Holmes concluding his majority argument by pronouncing that "Three generations of imbeciles are enough." A big robe did he wear.

When the *Korematsu* case was decided, celebrating as legal the internment (read: imprisonment in concentration camps) of Japanese-Americans, simply because they were Japanese, all six justices who approved the ruling wore black robes.

Robes, no matter their color, are just robes. Like Joseph, the justices could have pranced out in Amazing Technicolor Dreamcoats and it doesn't change the fact that much injustice has been advocated, condoned, and validated by men wearing the uniform of a judge.

Photo: Collection of the Supreme Court of the United States

Justice Antonin Scalia

Which brings us closer to the present. 2018 to be precise—and as always: law is politics by other means. And this time it was gutter politics—just ask Christine Blasey Ford, Deborah Ramirez, or Julie Swetnick. Together, we watched a perverted carnival—the judicial senate hearings of one Brett Michael Kavanaugh: Georgetown Prep, Yale University, and most importantly a full-fledged fun-loving member of Delta Kappa Epsilon fraternity. Just ask Deborah Ramirez how much fun she had with Brett. Flash-forward to the aforementioned senate hearings with Kavanaugh in the hot seat—you saw the mask slip... you saw rage-fury-anger... and you saw political contempt.

U.S. Senate Hearings, Pool Photo

Brett Kavanaugh

You think a robe covers that?

The Three Musketeers

Harlan Fiske Stone was a Supreme Court justice from 1925 to 1946. He was chief justice for his last five years on the Court—the World War II years. Stone was a conservative Republican. "His brand of conservatism, grounded in the belief that the law is designed to protect the weak from the powerful," writes journalist Chris Hedges, "bears no resemblance to that of the self-proclaimed 'strict constitutionalists' in the Federalist Society who have accumulated tremendous power in the judiciary."[14] In fact, the Federalist Society has been gnawing away at individual rights and protection since its inception in 1982. How? By delivering Republican presidents well-groomed justices who are nothing more than "a naked tool of corporate oppression." Growing up alongside the so-called Reagan "revolution," and tutored in their embryonic stages by Antonin Scalia, the Federalists are responsible for the rise and placement of Neil Gorsuch, Clarence Thomas, John Roberts, and Samuel Alito.

Scalia, the architect of this corporate cabal, made "the United States a less fair, less tolerant, and less admirable democracy,"[15] according to attorney and author Jeffrey Toobin, writing in *The New Yorker.* For instance, Scalia's homophobia was off the charts out of control, especially for someone sitting with great power in the 21st century. When SCOTUS ruled in 2003 that gay citizens could no longer be tossed in jail for consensual sex, Scalia fumed:

> Today's opinion is the product of a Court, which is the product of a law-profession culture, that has largely signed on to the so-called homosexual agenda... Many Americans do not want persons who openly engage in homosexual conduct as partners in their business, as scoutmasters for their children, as teachers in their children's schools, or as boarders in their home. They view this as protecting themselves and their families from a life style that they believe to be immoral and destructive.[16]

Not all conservatives are hell-bent on viciously painting American society with a medieval brush. Scalia was—he helped to overturn the McCain-Feingold Act as well as other campaign finance regulations; he was instrumental in razing the Voting Rights Act; blocking climate-change regulations; and he was knee-deep in the rat shit also known as *Bush v. Gore.*

Harlan Fiske Stone was not. *Even a broken clock is right twice a day.* "Stone was wary of radicals and socialists," Hedges submits. "He could be skeptical of New Deal programs, although he believed the court had no right to reverse New Deal legislation. But he understood that the law was the primary institution tasked with protecting the public from predatory capitalism and the abuses of power."[17] Stone constantly voted with liberal jurists Louis Brandeis and Holmes, often breaking from the conservative majority—so much so they were nicknamed "The Three Musketeers." Hedges frames Stone's belief that the law, like society itself, needed to constantly evolve:

> He embraced what Oliver Wendell Holmes called "legal realism." The law was not only about logic but also about the experience of a lived human society. If judges could not read and interpret that society, if they clung to rigid dogma or a self-imposed legal fundamentalism, then the law would be transformed into a sterile constitutionalism. Stone called on judges to "have less reverence for the way in which an old doctrine was applied to an old situation." The law had to be flexible. Judges, to carry out astute rulings, had to make a close study of contemporary politics, economics, domestic and global business practices and culture, not attempt to intuit what the Founding Fathers intended.[18]

But as the 20th century passed into history, so did the promise of progressive and broadminded jurisprudence... and as Shakespeare wrote in *Hamlet,* there's the rub. Or as Tarantino wrote in *Pulp Fiction,* "I'ma get medieval on your ass"—in this instance, those words are uttered by a conservative and sadistic corporate Court, one that grows more aggressive by the day when it comes to destroying personal freedoms. In theory, the Constitution, the dusty document SCOTUS is charged with using when deciding a case, is written and designed ***to limit the behavior of the government against its citizens.*** Unchecked corporate and government power = tyranny and the death of any semblance of democracy.[19] As Brandeis wrote, "We can have democracy in this country, or we can have great wealth concentrated in the hands of a few, but we can't have both."[20]

From right here, right now... looking in the rear view mirror as well as looking far down the road toward an ominous horizon, America's Supreme Court (along with the executive and legislature) has firmly entrenched this pseudo-republic in a tyrannical corporate state—one that views a freethinking and compassionate democracy as the enemy, an enemy to destroy "with extreme prejudice." Hedges, along with so many others, believe that "the supposed clash between liberal and conservative judges is largely a fiction."[21] Hedges suggests that the numbers don't lie:

> The Alliance for Justice [a judicial watchdog group] points out that 85 percent of President Barack Obama's judicial nominees—280, or a third of the federal judiciary—had either been corporate attorneys or government prosecutors. Those who came out of corporate law firms accounted for 71 percent of the nominees, with only 4 percent coming from public interest groups and the same percentage having been attorneys who represented workers in labor disputes.[22]

This systemic corporatocracy, so well-entrenched across the judicial spectrum, continues to erode basic constitutional rights—the losses keep piling up, just like they did for the '62 Mets: right to privacy, habeas corpus, due process, probable cause requirements, fair trials, fair elections—they've "been erased for many, especially the 2.3 million people in our prisons, most having been put there without ever going to trial,"[23] writes Hedges, who goes on to stress that "Our judicial system, as Ralph Nader has pointed out, has legalized secret law, secret courts, secret evidence, secret budgets and secret prisons in the name of national security." Like bowling pins crashing about, we stand idly by as "constitutionally protected statements, beliefs and associations are criminalized."[24]

Nader once famously wrote (during the Kavanaugh hearings) that Brett Kavanaugh was a corporation masquerading as a judge. Nader's observation, albeit spot-on and accurate, is too limiting. In actuality, *the United States Supreme Court* is a corporation masquerading as a judge.

SIDENOTE (just for shits and giggles)
When did the acronym SCOTUS first appear? Here's a good probability: in the late 19th century when folks communicated via the telegraph, Walter Phillips (among others) published a book entitled, *The Phillips Telegraphic Code for the Rapid Transmission by Telegraph.* It was a codebook that allowed people to send secret or inexpensive messages, since pricing on telegraphs was based on length. SCOTUS appeared between the abbreviations (scndrl) for scoundrel and (scribl) for scribble.

In the Beginning: a "thoroughly undistinguished lot"

When Americans think of the Supreme Court, they imagine giants: legends of the law, as discussed, beings of a different and higher order, beings unmoved by the cauldrons of chaos boiling fiercely around them.

The modern-day media tends to support this grand view, often writing of the Court and its justices in subdued, neutral tones, rarely, if ever, engaging in criticisms that are commonly thought to abound in the political realms. Indeed, the 19th- and 20th-century press engaged more often in praise than in protest, no matter how outrageous or unjust the rulings rendered. In this sense, in the popular mind, the Court was projected as the very exemplar of rectitude. It was, therefore, right in its rulings; and its determinations, while seldom truly understood, were rarely questioned, much less challenged by American institutional bodies of opinion or eminence. This is all the more remarkable when we consider the origins of the institute that has grown into the behemoth that today stands as a central pillar of American law.

Most historians trace the Supreme Court's birth to the U.S. Constitution's Article III, which states in (pertinent) part:

> Section 1. The judicial Power of the United States, shall be vested in one Supreme Court, and in such inferior Courts as the Congress may from time to time ordain and establish. (U.S. Constitution, Art. I; Sect. 1)

The first Court session, held at the Royal Exchange building on New York City's Broad Street (February, 1790) was not an overwhelming success. Indeed, quite the contrary. So few justices showed up for work that it had to adjourn, as it lacked a quorum (back in 1790, the court had six members). And when it did field a quorum (4 of its 6 members), it did little for there were no cases on the Court's docket to hear or decide. The judges busied themselves with the adoption of rules of procedure, and admitted a few lawyers into its rarefied bar. This Court, named to the bench by the first president, George Washington, were, to a man, described by legal historian, Peter Irons, as a "thoroughly undistinguished lot."[25] As Irons explains:

> One spent time in debtors' prisons for defaulting on loans; one returned his commission after five days to serve in state office; one never attended a single Court session; one was impeached for political bias on the bench; one was insane; and another was senile.[26]

In the early years of the American republic, as many men refused politicians' invitations to join the Court as accepted. In fact, quite a few nominees accepted posts to the Court only to shortly thereafter accept more lucrative positions in state government. These Court positions were hardly sought out, for the pay was low, the Court was held in low esteem, and the process was known as "circuit riding," where justices spent months traveling to other parts of the country to hear and decide cases—often on horseback, or in coaches. This life was bitterly opposed by some. But as poor as the Court's reputation was, some members sought to bring it into even more disrepute. Justice James Wilson of Pennsylvania, a man of a fine Scottish education, an aristocratic mien, and "overweening" ambition, made history in ways he hardly intended. Irons writes:

> Wilson has a more serious flaw than ambition. He was also a reckless speculator in land and finance, which proved to be his downfall. Before and after he joined the Supreme Court, Wilson borrowed heavily to invest in bank stock and land grants from Pennsylvania to Georgia. Unable to pay his mounting debts and hounded by creditors, he became the first—and so far, only—justice to be jailed while serving on the Court, not once, but twice. Humiliated by his first term in debtors' prison, Wilson traded circuit-riding duties with Justice [James] Iredell in 1798 and took refuge in North Carolina, where another creditor had him jailed for two months. Wilson died shortly after his release, penniless and stripped of the power he once wielded on the Supreme Court.[27]

This early expression of a powerless, little-recognized, and lightly regarded court would eventually give way to a body that became increasingly central to the self-definitions and controversies of American life. For, never free of the political forces and politicians that chose and empowered them, the Court would nevertheless make choices about the directions to be taken by other societal forces, and whether their decisions were for good or ill, made in injustice or in wisdom, they did make their mark on the country and, beyond that, the world. Blown by the political winds of party, personal preference, or influenced by elections, they sought ways to entrench their power (as does every political body), to deepen their influence, and to raise their questionable prestige.

White Republic

The Supreme Court saw itself as the nation's elites saw itself: as primarily White, first. It should therefore not surprise us that one of the first congressional acts of the nation, the Naturalization Act of 1790, plainly limited nationalization to: "All free white persons."[28] And while this proved a lure to millions of Europeans, it proved a snare for the multitudes of color, both within and without the White Republic.

Within the borders of the U.S., the aboriginal peoples, the so-called Indians, saw what U.S. law meant firsthand. In essence, the law meant precisely what the dominant whites wanted law to mean: *whatever they wanted it to mean.*

As we shall see, it could mean one thing one day and a completely different thing on another. For the law was but an instrument by which they could achieve their own objectives: which usually meant the taking of Indian lands and territories.

Why is this important in a study of the Supreme Court's imperial rulings? The answer is actually quite simple. Imperialism didn't just spring into existence like Athena from the skull of Zeus. For imperialism, as Michael Parenti reminds us, is an economic reality, no matter the myths mouthed by media or academia. It is a relationship forged in force and maintained by terror, or, as Parenti explains:

> [I]mperialism is... the process whereby the dominant investor interests in one country bring to bear military and financial power upon another country in order to expropriate the land, labor, capital, natural resources, commerce, and markets of that other country... For centuries the ruling interests in Western Europe and, later on, North America and Japan laid claim to most of the planet

> Earth, including the labor of indigenous peoples (as workers or slaves), their incomes... their markets, and the abundant treasures of their lands.[29]

For Europeans who "discovered" this "new land" that they named America, the lands, holdings, and peoples of the wilderness lived in another country—indeed, they seemed to dwell in another world. In the pre-United States colonial period, and down into the opening centuries of the American republic, courts and commentators said openly and readily that Indian lands were not only sited in another country, but "sovereign" territories. While it is undisputed that the United States signed hundreds of treaties with Indian-governed polities, that fact alone tells us that treaties are pacts between sovereign nations. To read early (and indeed, later) Supreme Court opinions on Indian issues allows us to see the transition from recognition of sovereignty to newer, less independent categories of description, a measuring stick of one side's accretion of power, and another side's waning strength in relationship to the other.

Law, then, is an expression of power—not between equals—but between antagonists.

In *Johnson v. McIntosh* (1823), the Court announced a rather perverse opinion of the "right" of discovery and what results as a consequence. Thus, discovery is commingled with conquest; and conquest means—nakedly—that Americans could do essentially what they wanted to do with Indian lands, Indians "rights," and Indian sovereignty. In citing from the *Johnson* case, scholar David E. Wilkins writes:

> The United States, then, have unequivocally acceded to that great and broad rule by which its civilized inhabitants now hold this country. They hold, and assert in themselves, the title by which it is acquired. They maintain, as all others have maintained, that discovery gave an exclusive right to extinguish the Indian title of occupancy, either by purchase or by conquest; and gave also a right to such a degree of sovereignty, as the circumstances of the people would allow them to exercise.[30]

It is an odd kind of "sovereignty" that lies under the control of another who allows those deemed sovereign to exercise. It was not for naught that Indians said that, "white men speak with a forked tongue." Several years after *Johnson,* the Court decided a case brought by what was commonly called a "civilized tribe."

The Cherokees, dwelling in their ancestral lands in what later came to be called Georgia, were, by white, Western standards, an extraordinarily "civilized" people. After conversion by the Moravian Protestants, they adhered to Christianity, many lived in brick homes, and their leaders spoke English, as well as read and wrote the Cherokee language (by using an alphabet with 85 characters devised by the tribal sage, Sequoyah). They published their own newspaper, and translated the Bible into their tongue. They had a capital city for their nation: New Echota. Indeed, they were so close to the whites that they owned slaves—black people—and, with said labor, they grew prosperous in the land.

But prosperity sometimes breeds envy among neighbors.

The Cherokee, finding their lands seized by white Georgians, chose to put their faith in U.S. law to solve the problem. They took their case all the way to the Supreme Court—*and won!* In *Worcester v. Georgia* (1832), the Court ruled in favor of the Cherokees, upholding the sanctity of Indian treaties because tribes were "dependent domestic nations" that maintained their ancestral lands, which were neither ceded nor sold to the government. President Andrew Jackson chose to ignore this decision when he unleashed U.S. troops into the hills and vales of Georgia to remove Creek, Chickasaw, and Cherokee from their lands—treaties be damned. Under armed force, the "winners" of the *Worcester* case—some 17,000 men, women, and children—were marched across frozen ground to the West in what came to be called the "Trail of Tears" for the thousands who died en route. Thousands of their slaves also perished during the forced march—but few bothered to count those black bodies. What *Worcester* proved, unequivocally, was that there was law, and then there was *law.*

Law, formally, was that what was said in nice, neat opinions of white courts; *law* in reality was what was done in the actual and tangible world—to real people; and rarely did the twain meet. But if *Worcester* was not bad enough (in its lack of application), the Court would several years later announce a new rule of law, accompanied by a brand-new history! Chief Justice Roger B. Taney (yes—he of *Dred Scott* infamy), writing in the case *U.S. v. Rogers* (1846), would pen the following incredible passage:

Andrew Jackson
Slaveowner,
Mass Murderer,
Hero to America's
45th Resident of 1600
Pennsylvania Avenue

> The country in which the crime is charged to have been committed is part of the territory of the United States, and not within the limits of any particular State. It is true that it is occupied by the tribe of Cherokee Indians. But it has been assigned to them by the United States, as a place of domicile for the tribe, and they hold and occupy it with the assent of the United States, and under their authority. The native tribes who were found on this continent at the time of its discovery have never been acknowledged or treated as independent nations by the European governments, nor regarded as the owners of the territories they respectively occupied. On the contrary, the whole continent was divided and parceled out, and granted by the governments of Europe as if it had been vacant and unoccupied land, and the Indians continually held to be, and treated as, subject to their dominion and control.[31]

Wilkins has observed that such an "opinion" was but a "brazen fabrication" of, quite literally, hundreds of preexisting treaties with Europeans, and later the United States. It was written in the same venal spirit as *Dred Scott*: to assist the powerful and to oppress the powerless.

The law that governed here was White Nationalism—pure and simple—and it was written to legitimize land theft on a massive scale.

We have here cited Wilkins' work for the proper text of the *Rogers* decision, but he added italics to bring attention to the reader which sections of the opinion were the most blatant in their misrepresentations of history (the claimed basis for much of the opinion). Here, let us reflect on those sections to truly understand how lawless was this Supreme Court opinion—lawless in order to reach its preordained conclusion. Wilkins, in addition to being an Indian Studies professor, is also a member of the Lumbee Tribe (North Carolina), and notes in italics the following:

- *part of the territory*
- *assigned to them*
- *assent of the United States*
- *never been acknowledged or treated as independent nations*
- *whole continent was divided and parceled out*
- *subject to their dominion and control*

If this were a recitation of erroneous statements placed in a lengthy judicial opinion, perhaps there would be a little wiggle room—but in a paragraph with only five sentences? Wilkins demonstrated how erroneous the Court was in rendering its opinion, writing:

> The most inaccurate statements are as follows. First was the presumption that Cherokee land was actually territory belonging to the United States and that their territory had been "assigned" to them. As the Cherokee had been relocated from the Southeast to the West, these lands had been exchanged for the Cherokee's ancestral homes in "fee simple." In other words, the Cherokee merely transferred their aboriginal land rights from their eastern territory to territory in the west. The land clearly belonged to the tribe and was not "part of the territory" of the United States in the sense of property. It was patented to the Cherokee Nation by the President of the United States under the terms of the 1830 Removal Act and prior agreements: "The United States hereby covenant and agree that the lands ceded to the Cherokee Nation in the foregoing article shall, in no future time without their consent, be included within the territorial limits or jurisdiction of any state or territory."
>
> ...The individual property rights of the Cherokee citizens were to be respected and in the event they were interfered with, the federal government was bound to provide just compensation.
>
> The second inaccuracy was the idea that the Cherokee held title to their lands only with the "assent of the United States and under their authority." The only *authority* retained by the United States... involved the federal government's pledge to "protect the Cherokee Nation from domestic strife and foreign enemies and against intestine wars between the several tribes," and the promise to protect the Cherokee against "interruptions and intrusions from citizens of the United States, who may attempt to settle in the country without their consent..." The President of the United States had the "authority" and, more importantly, the duty to remove such interlopers.
>
> Third, Taney's most brazen fabrication was that tribes had "never been acknowledged or treated as independent nations" or regarded as "the owners of the territories they respectively occupied." This double assault on tribes as legitimately recognized nations

> and as property owners ignored the evidence of several hundred preexisting treaties that European nations (and later the United States) had negotiated with Indian nations. Further, ample evidence through Supreme Court case law—particularly the Marshall Court's Indian law decisions in *Worcester v. Georgia* and *Mitchell v. United States* (1835), which emphasized the fact that tribes were the possessors of a property title that was as "sacred as fee-simple"—documented the existence of a title that could be sold by the tribes to whomever they chose. This right is also evidence of a title that could be sold by the tribes in the Commerce Clause as separate polities.
>
> Finally, Taney inaccurately states that the lands of the United States had been effectively "divided and parceled out" as if there had been no prior human presence and the tribes thereafter were dealt with as "subjects" of the discovering European nations.[32]

Wilkins scuttled the last idea as easily as he did the prior two, but history is a poor retort to the law; for law is an instrument of power—and history is a creation of fact. Facts had little sway over the determinations of this imperial Court, which rewrote history to fit their opinions. But this is ultimately about far more than mere misstatements of law or fact. This is about Statements of Power—of imperial power, albeit of an internal colony. It is about law as Law—and law is ultimately about relationships.

For how else would the American Empire emerge if not through the powerful empire of its age: Great Britain. And how did Britain, or the imperial notion of Britain, come into being without subduing its closest neighbors—Wales, Scotland, and Ireland? These formerly independent nations were invaded, conquered, and dominated by foreigners from abroad. And the extinguishment of indigenous Irish nationalism (for example) under King Brian Boru (circa 1014) came by way of English invasion that presaged 700 years of conquest, repression, and reprisal. What the British learned over that seven-century period were the techniques of colonialism; what works and what doesn't work in the business of imperialism, capital extraction, and ideological domination.

Similarly, when the (future) Americans arrived in the Americas, they met great and sundry nations of considerable populations with incredible diversity. They could never have vanquished them all, so they waged war against those they could not subdue, made promises of peace to those who were too powerful to defeat, and then they used other techniques to achieve their ultimate aim: the seizure of indigenous lands—they wanted all of it, and they used the law to legitimize their efforts. In fact, "the law" was the simple instrument of another war: the war of words.

In *Rogers,* who could deny the implicit antagonism hiding in the honeyed prose of Taney as he announced the U.S. government's role in Indian affairs? Read, if you please, the following excerpt from *U.S. v. Rogers,* which would hide a world of sorrows:

> [F]rom the very moment the general government came into existence to this time, it has exercised its power over this unfortunate race in the spirit of humanity and justice, and has endeavored by every means in its power to enlighten their minds and increase their comforts, and to save them if possible from the consequences of their own vices.[33]

(Man, oh man! Weren't the Cherokees lucky to have such thoughtful Euro-Americans around to "increase their comforts" and "enlighten their minds?")

Hidden amongst the niceties are thorns adorning a poisonous rose, for this was a precursor to a judicial principle that would effectively bar most Indian questions from future judicial review for generations—the notion of political versus judicial questions. Once again, Chief Justice Taney in *Rogers:*

> But had it been otherwise, and were the right and the propriety of exercising this power now open to question, yet it is a question for the *law-making* and *political departments* of the government, and *not for the judicial.* It is our duty to expound the law as we find it...[34] [Emphasis Wilkins']

So, in the same opinion in which the writer and the court majority lauds itself for its "humanity and justice" toward "this unfortunate race," it announces a judicial principle that will ensure that its unenlightened tribal members will find greater difficulty obtaining judicial review. Ostensibly, this "political question" arose from the Court's reluctance to intervene into the powers and prerogatives of the executive and legislative branches of the government. In truth, when the winds seemed to blow in their favor, the Court's majority has ruled repeatedly on political questions. Indeed, there are few questions that do not present a political facet to be questioned or resolved. Simply put: Taney's rule allowed the Court to sound high-minded when they elected to close the doors to issues or claimants who might prove too controversial to the Court's prestige.

Yet, we are not done with Taney's perambulations into the law as instrument of central, state, White power. We've mentioned Taney earlier as the principal author of the *Dred Scott* decision, which found, among other things, that "negroes have no rights that white men [are] bound to respect," and we have seen his view in *Rogers* that denies sovereignty and nationhood to indigenous peoples in the U.S. environs. Yet, Taney, some years later, did have occasion to restate his views when he wrote *Dred Scott.* Deep in the heart of his lengthy opinion, he writes a revealing passage; he addressed Indian nationhood thusly, in stark contrast to African peoples:

> The situation of this [African-American] population was altogether unlike that of the Indian race. The latter, it is true, formed no part of the colonial communities, and never amalgamated with them in social connections or in government. But although they were uncivilized, they were yet a *free and independent people,* associated together in nations and or tribes, and *governed by their own laws.* Many of these political communities were situated in territories to which the white race claimed the ultimate right of dominion. But that claim was acknowledged to be subject to the right of the Indians to occupy it as long as they thought proper, and neither the English nor colonial Governments claimed or exercised any dominion over the tribe or nation by whom it was occupied, nor claimed the right to the possession of the territory, until the tribe or nation consented to cede it. *These Indian Governments were regarded and treated as foreign Governments,* as much so as if an ocean had separated the red man from the white; and their freedom has constantly been acknowledged, from the time of the first emigration to the English colonies to the present day, by the different Governments which succeeded each other. Treaties have been negotiated with them, and their alliance sought for in war; and the people who compose these Indian political communities have *always been treated as foreigners not living under our Government.*[35] [Emphasis added]

When one reads *U.S. v. Rogers,* one can hardly believe that the same writer penned the words that appeared in *Dred Scott.* The judicial hypocrisy is palpable and brain numbing. Yet, it was Taney, the Court's Chief Justice, who authored both opinions, both of which essentially achieved the Court's central objectives in each case: the truncation of rights of both communities. It was for this exigency that Taney employed the language and reasoning he needed to meet those ends—irrespective of the fact that they were diametrically opposed.

There is another element that springs from the language and logic of these cases that is rarely discussed: race. For here, in every inglorious line, the logic of racial hierarchy, indeed, of white supremacy, forms the buttress upon which this cribbed kind of law is written.

It would be but stating the obvious to say that Taney, perhaps the most historic of chief justices in American history (not much of an overstatement, as there have been only 17 of them since 1789!), was a dyed-in-the-wool racist. But such a comment is cheapened when we consider that while we may today perceive his views as outrageous, he formed a majority in many of the cases that we today look askance at. Taney wrote amidst a context in which the American republic was growing off the genocide and slaughter of centuries. He did not write alone. He also wrote for the powerful and the wealthy, who fully agreed with his views, for they gathered much of their wealth from such widely accepted exploitations.

From "noble savage" to "merely savage"

The Indians took the fatal fall from noble savage to merely savage. If we look back to the voices of journalism from the founding years of the U.S. republic, we find a rare and ugly kind of honesty that drew few objections from readers, and many hosannas in support. President George Washington was the first president of the Union. He therefore named, as we have seen, the first, albeit "undistinguished lot" of the Supreme Court. Less well known is his history as a warrior against the Indian clans, tribes, and nations. Historian Barbara Alice Mann, author of *George Washington's War on Native America,* writes that the destruction of the Iroquois, of their peoples, lands, foods, and tools, sent waves of jubilation throughout the Ameri-Anglo colonials.

The newspapers were no less jubilant, with the *Virginia Gazette* gloating openly on 30 October 1779 that the "Indians [we]re feeling all the calamities which follow from a savage and barbarous war. They are taught by severe experience, the power of the American empire."[36] That publicly stated and politically felt national self-apprehension, that of "empire," came naturally to the mind and lips, for had not this vast, "new" country defeated the most powerful empire of the age?

Had it not repeatedly humbled the "merciless Indian savages" of the wilderness? That idea, that national-self perception, spoken of within months of the founding of the Republic, and its Supreme Court, did not dwell in isolation. It lived in consciousness, and found its life in that unrelenting holocaust called Indian Wars, which, literally, expanded the U.S. empire, acre-by-acre; hectare-by-hectare. The empire's legal apparatus merely did its duty by waging wars of words, to further justify the *lebensraum* at America's heart, to denationalize the Indians, by treating them as (in the term used in *Rogers*) "this unfortunate race."[37]

It is a measure of the American national schizophrenia that the emerging nation—through the Court—denationalized "Indians" to further their exploitation, while early power brokers popularly, openly, in the highest rungs of national, political, and class life, defined the nation as White. Wilkins notes that the *Rogers*/racialization era of Indians was accompanied by the deep intrusions of Congressional forces designed to make *Rogers* real; for, if the Indians weren't nations, much less sovereign nations, then well-sounding interactions were needed to "civilize" these savages. Wilkins writes:

> In the summer of 1846, shortly after the *Rogers* pronouncement, the Senate Committee on the Judiciary convened and inquired into the "expediency," not the constitutionality, of extending federal criminal laws over the Indian territory. The committee said the subject was one of "great interest and importance" because the 1834 law had been ineffective in controlling "crimes of the most shocking character..." The committee instructed Commissioner[s] of Indian Affairs, William Medill, T. Hartley Crawford, and William Armstrong for their opinions on why the federal government had the "original power...to subject the Indian tribes within the limits of their sovereignty to any system of laws having for their object the prevention or punishment of crimes, of the amelioration and improvement of the red race..."
>
> "The correct doctrine on this point" was laid out, continued Medill, in the "views of the highest judicial tribunal of the land [and] must be deemed to be conclusive."
>
> Medill went further and said that his federal power of guardianship was essential to Indian "civilization" and the "improvement of their moral and intellectual condition." While acknowledging that the United States historically had not interfered with internal tribal

> matters, "as the guardians of the Indians, and responsible for their welfare and happiness... the United States [has] not, in any case, wholly divested itself of the power to *interfere,* when the laws of a tribe have been oppressive and unjust, or have been so enforced as to excite domestic strife and bloodshed."[38]

From equals to "guardians of the Indians" suggests a fall for the indigenous too grievous to be born. It is cosmic. It also denotes the mark of empire—using legalist terms that have no correlation to reality, yet are fine sounding, noble, even good. Indeed, the peoples of a newly made, quasi-colonial territory would experience many things from Taney's *Rogers;* but neither their "welfare," nor their "happiness" were among them. What these and a plethora of cases reveal are not so much what the cases were about, literally, as in the legal principles announced therein; but in the themes that swam beneath them, which would later rise to create some unexpected and unseen result.

Consider this: if two sovereign nation-states have a conflict, how do they usually resolve it? The first, of course, is diplomatic discussion and reasonable resolution to which both sovereigns agree. The second, barring peaceful resolution, is war. *But no sovereign submits to the judiciary of its sovereign opponent.*

In the post-World War II era, under the auspices of the United Nations, nations joined international pacts (called treaties) and agreed to submit to supranational entities, as, for example, the International Court of Justice (known popularly as the World Court). Similarly, the entity created under the Rome Statute is known as the International Criminal Court. Consider that international legal principle when you discover that the U.S. named itself as the final arbiter regarding the relationship of the two sovereignties: Indian nations and the United States. Which side would have an unfair advantage? Which side would be guaranteed to obtain its own objectives? How could such an entity (as the U.S. Supreme Court) claim to be a fair judicial arbiter given that scenario?

Remember: law is politics by other means.

After the Civil War

When the U.S. Civil War came to its conclusion, many Indian nations, especially those that sided with the Confederacy, paid a heavy price for their intervention on the side of the losers. The U.S. Congress used its highly militarized powers to wrest land from the tribes, their most precious possessions—the dwelling places of their ancestors. The short-lived Reconstruction era (circa 1865-1877) saw the gradual and then total withdrawal of U.S. troops from the South—and many of those troops (among them the famed "Buffalo soldiers") went west to subdue the Indian nations (tribes). But even open war had its limits, as shown by Ulysses S. Grant (the second president after Lincoln), who called for a "Peace Policy." Wilkins writes:

> President Grant, in an effort to eliminate abuses in the Indian office, and as part of the larger plan to assimilate the tribes, laid out his famous "Peace Policy." This policy assigned the Indian agencies scattered throughout the country to various Christian denominations. According to Grant, "No matter what ought to be the relations between such settlements and the aborigines, the fact is they do not harmonize well, and one or the other has to give way in the end."
>
> According to Grant, *"a system which looks to the extinction of a race is too horrible for a nation to adopt without entailing upon itself the wrath of all Christendom and engendering in the citizens a disregard for human life and the rights of others, dangerous to society."* It was not, however, merely the wrath of other "civilized nations" that propelled the Grant administration to seek alternatives to warfare with the tribes.[39] [Emphasis added]

Like most things that move nations, it came down to economic power: that is, money. Congress wanted to recoup vast sums of money spent on a ruinous, destructive war. And, according to Wilkins, it had the perfect solution:

> In the report issued by the Senate's Committee on the Pacific Railroad, Senator William Stewart (R., Nevada) wrote that tribes "can only be permanently conquered by railroads. The locomotive is the sole solution of the Indian question, unless the government changes its system of warfare and fights the savages the winter through as well as in summer."
>
> Furthermore, Senator Stewart noted that the past thirty-seven years of wars with tribes had cost the United States twenty thousand lives and more than $750,000,000. In fact, urged Stewart, "the chairman of the House Committee on Indian Affairs estimated recently that the present current [expense] of our warfare with the Indians was $1,000,000 a week—$144,000 dollars a day." Grant's "Peace Policy,"

it was believed, could do no worse and would undoubtedly be far less expensive and more morally defensible.[40]

When a "Peace Policy" becomes a synonym for war, then language has lost all meaning. For the objectives of both policies narrowed into the singular channel of white acquisition of Indian territories. War by other means is just war. And policy, which changes methodology yet retains the same objective, is but window-dressing.

Grant, apparently, didn't want the ugly imagery of "genocide," but while his gentle words seemed the essence of reason, reality was gnawing at the edges of the political stage. That reality was rooted in the rushes of the Indian Wars, 19th-century advances upon Native lands by the Americans, augmented by the new national energies unleashed by the close of the Civil War and the transfer of American troops into the Western theater after the collapse of Reconstruction.

The U.S. Supreme Court formed yet another theater of war—the war where words had one meaning, yet were but weapons advanced to accomplish the consolidation of the internal imperial project. It is interesting to note that this period was also the same time that the Congress passed and the president (Lincoln) signed into law the Homestead Act (1863), which opened up vast tracts of formerly Indian lands to white (and European) settlement. This Act granted public lands covering 160 acres (65 hectares) to any homesteader for a nominal fee along with a promise to reside thereon for five years. It had the effect of chomping up vast tracts of Indian lands, and despoiled the indigenous people of their ancestral homes along with the graves of their ancients. Writer and researcher Tim Wise has written of that period as the one in which millions of whites acquired land and its concomitant wealth:

> [T]he Homestead Act, passed in 1862, ultimately distributed nearly 250 million acres of land to 1.5 million homesteading families, virtually all of them white. Today, at least 20 million white Americans continue to benefit from those early land giveaways, either by virtue of still holding said property in the possession of their families, or by having been able to sell the land and reap the benefits of those sales intergenerationally. Other estimates place the number of living Homestead Act descendants at closer to *50 million,* with almost none of these being persons of color.[41]

We are reminded here that imperialism is, at bottom, exploitation, and here, Indian loss of land meant life, wealth, and expanded space for white Europeans.

David E. Wilkins has noted that the Supreme Court has treated the First Peoples of this continent by a variety of interpretations and terms that lessened their autonomy, sovereignty, and presumed ability to act in their best interests in the lands of their fathers. Citing the work of scholars and legal commentators (principally drawn from what has been termed the "Critical Legal Theory" school of interpretation, or those who perceive the hand of politics under the robes of the Court), Wilkins has characterized the writings and majority opinions of the Court as coming from a variety of perspectives, each further diminishing the life, liberty, and lands of the First Peoples. In summary, Wilkins has noted the following ways the Court has defined indigenous peoples here in the land we now call the United States:

- **Constitutional/Legal:** Or relations bound by Constitution or treaty right; or Congress as the party representing the Constitution, and Indians as outsiders under treaty.
- **Civilizing/Paternalistic:** Relations based upon the U.S. as "civilizer" of Indian savages, usually expressed as the former working to assimilate the latter.
- **Nationalism/Federalism:** The powers of the central government vis-à-vis those of states, and how powers are distributed not only between them, but according to a hierarchical code of power distribution, i.e., with whites at the top, and Indians, Asians and Africans below.[42]

While these three categories are, on their face, somewhat simplistic, they bear a wealth of strategic and methodological variation, which, over an extended period of time, worked to the dire detriment of the First Peoples, and enriched the White Empire. This analysis of Supreme Court case law and legal reasoning peels back the language used to reveal those interests being upheld and protected—and those concomitantly dismissed.

Much of the discussion of Indian life, culture, and folkways, was one of disparagement, as between "good" versus "bad" Indians, theoretically under the notion that good Indians were to be treated well, while "bad" Indians were to be subjected to the unrestrained fury of the military power of the United States government and denied any redress under its judicial institutions. Of course that depends on who is doing the defining, and when—and also where.

Good Indians initially meant the Five Civilized Tribes (Cherokee, Choctaw, Chickasaw, Creek, and Seminole), ostensibly because they were, at least nominally, Christians. But despite this appellation, each and all of them faced either removal, massive land-theft, and/or war when they resisted the American land-hunger that dishonored and stole their lands in violation of treaty.

The real tragedy is that the Supreme Court often aided or abetted these efforts, or when their rule was ignored by other branches (mostly the executive), they sat idly by, silent spectators to their national impotence in the face of arms. Wilkins explains that these theoretical constructs erected by the Court are but "masks" utilized not only to conceal the subterranean interests underlying Court action, but also to dehumanize the recipients of the Court's legal analysis, either by defining them as "savages" (and as such unworthy of "civilized" legal consideration), or "wards," a term which is, in a sense, worse than savage in that it infantilizes Native peoples by treating them as permanent children who need to be protected by American elites and U.S. institutions of power, who themselves function essentially as *guardians ad litem* over this ignorant child race. This way of thinking can only lead to, at the very least, flawed decision-making, for it recreates and falsely projects full human beings into uncivilized half-persons closer to the animal world, or eternal children, who need the perpetual tutelage of their white betters, until they not only learn, but transform, somehow (perhaps magically) into whites.

Among American elites these projections served several important functions. They justify almost any measure taken against indigenous peoples, as an aid to the dispossessed—by the dispossessor! In *Cherokee Nation v. Georgia* (1831),[43] Chief Justice John Marshall formed a majority to opine that the Cherokee, as a "domestic, dependent nation"—and not a sovereign state—was encroaching on state land. Marshall would describe Indian relations to the United States as "resemb[ling] those of a ward to his guardian." Moreover, he argued, this guardianship was within the "competence of Congress" as "these Indian tribes *are* the wards of the nation. They are communities *dependent* on the United States. Dependent largely for their daily food. Dependent for their political rights..."[44] [Emphasis added] Thus, it was the duty of Congress to protect and defend the aborigines.

Congress, as a political body, could hardly be asked to be "protective" of a community that could neither vote for them, nor financially support their campaigns. In a real sense, they could be no more protective of First Peoples than the President—or the Supreme Court. This was not just *un*constitutional—it was *non*constitutional—and it was a mask that did far more than conceal, or even disfigure. It was a mask that killed. And what was masked was the real role played by Congress, the President, and the Supreme Court. No matter what they said, even as they ostensibly acted as "protectors," "guardians," or "defenders" of their "wards," the truth was that they made sure that the First Peoples always seemed to come up holding the short end of the proverbial stick.

History has abundantly shown this to be so.

Zones of Application

Ironically, the Supreme Court strived mightily to protect and insulate the Constitution from any use to which they did not intend. Acting as if this document was the holy of holies sealed up in the Ark of the Covenant, the Court has a long jurisprudence of not only reading it narrowly, but of applying it even more sparsely, and well—niggardly. From the earliest years of the Republic, and echoing into the present era, we see that the Constitution is zoned off, interpretationally, just as the actual original copies that are extant remain under lock and key, walled off, sealed away from the very breath of those beings called citizens of the republic that is written of therein.

The Constitution reads like a treaty of significant promise and protection, but from its inception, what the words say, and what they mean, are two very different things. This is seen with utter clarity when we consider, not only how it has been (and continues to be) applied in cases involving "Indian country," but after America's projection abroad, in the last, waning years of the nineteenth century, when America, in the name of Anglo-Saxon racial duty, marched abroad to *civilize* those in Asia, the Pacific, the Caribbean, and beyond. Suffice it is to say that when the U.S. planted its flag on Cuban, Puerto Rican, Filipino, or Chinese soil, it made damn sure that its venerated Constitution was not included in its collective knapsack.

Indeed, through the Supreme Court, it was rendered illegal for them to do so!

Shortly after the turn of the last century (circa 1900), when Americans made their high-level trade incursions into China, they erected what used to be called "capitulations," or legal agreements (we hesitate to call them treaties, although they may be known by such designations officially), which extended to Americans (and other whites) personal and national immunity from all local, provincial, and national laws of China.

As the Chinese were regarded by Westerners as uncivilized, that contagion followed upon their barbarous laws, which could not be applied to Christians (read: whites). Indeed, the U.S., in imitation of their imperial tutors, the British, established what is known as "extraterritorial jurisdiction" in the form of the United States District Court for China, where Americans could be tried separately from Chinese law. However, while this extraterritoriality offered immunity to Americans from Chinese law, it also established a severely limited version of American law that did not include the application of the U.S. Constitution, including the right to a jury trial and due process. We would describe this scenario as the Supreme Court and the American government having their cake and eating it too.

The practice of imposing extraterritoriality on host nations, exempting foreigners from local or national laws, was common when Europeans entered foreign territories. The host nations, often bullied economically and militarily into such agreements, were resentful of this judicial imposition, hence the early usage of the term "capitulation" to describe these "agreements." It should not surprise us that these concessions were rarely, if ever, granted to foreigners (especially from non-Western [read: "nonwhite"] lands). And while international law professor Kal Raustiala tells us that extraterritoriality was a method by which some states could make foreign, undeveloped (read: "uncivilized") states a level, rational, and predictable place for trade, it is also true that it served to communicate a sense of general superiority and, perhaps worse, racial superiority over the vast populations of host states, often people of Asian, Middle Eastern, or African lineages.[45]

As noted above, many of the regions where such extraterritoriality was in place were sites where the Constitution had little or no practical application. When the U.S. District Court for China was established in 1906, it excluded fundamental constitutional guarantees based in part on precedents established by the Supreme Court in its ruling in the case of seaman John Ross. On 9 May 1880, while serving aboard the American vessel, the *Bullion,* Ross got into a fight with a fellow crewman, Robert Kelly, and knifed him to death. Under the laws of extraterritoriality at the time, Ross could not be tried by Japanese courts or officials for the crime, even though it occurred in the Japanese harbor of Yokohama. At the time it was common practice for Westerners living in Asia to be tried by consular courts of their own nationality. Even though Ross was actually British, because he lived and worked aboard an American vessel, this ship became the determinant of his extraterritoriality, and he therefore went before Thomas Van Buren, the

American consul serving in Kanagawa, Japan, where he was promptly convicted of murdering Kelly and sentenced to hang. Ross chose to appeal and his plea found favor with U.S. President Rutherford B. Hayes who commuted his sentence to life imprisonment. Not satisfied with this decision, Ross decided to challenge the jurisdiction of the consular courts on the basis of their unconstitutionality, in that they did not permit a jury trial, competent defense counsel, and other such constitutional guarantees.

The major obstacle for Ross, it seemed, was that the laws of extraterritoriality, as set forth within the U.S.-Japanese 1857 Convention of Yanagawa, declared, in part: "Americans committing offences in Japan shall be tried by the American consul, and shall be punished according to American laws."[46] But for Ross, tried by a consular court and initially sentenced to death, a challenge to the constitutionality of this ruling seemed a strategy designed to prevail, for how could an "American court"—even a consular one—ignore the very foundation of American law, the Constitution of the United States?

In his appeal to the U.S. Supreme Court, Ross argued that the Constitutional rights accorded to Americans should have effect no matter where an American faced charges. In his briefs, his arguments were as clear as they were simple, claiming "so far as crimes of felonious character are concerned, the same protection and guarantee against an undue accusation or an unfair trial, secured by the Constitution to the citizens of the United States at home, should be enjoyed by them abroad."[47] The Supreme Court was, to say the least, not persuaded by such an argument, and responded:

> By the Constitution a government is ordained and established "for the United States of America," and not for countries outside of their limits. The guarantees it affords... apply only to citizens and others within the United States, or who are brought there for trial for alleged offenses committed elsewhere, and not to residents or temporary sojourners abroad. *The Constitution can have no operation in another country.* When, therefore, the representatives or officers of our government are permitted to exercise authority of any kind in another country, it must be on such conditions as the two countries may agree...[48] [Emphasis added]

Ross lost, not because his claim didn't have logical appeal, but because his argument didn't resonate with the nine persons on the 1890 court. *In re Ross* was the result of the Fuller Court, under chief justice Melville Fuller, a man who, when nominated for the part, was called "the most obscure man ever [so] nominated," according to one newspaper.

In what certainly sounds odd today, Fuller's entire legal education consisted of six months at Harvard Law School, perhaps the equivalent of what paralegals study today. But perhaps he was nominated more for his political connections rather than his legal acumen, for he was a staunch Democrat in an age when that meant unbridled white supremacy, and a pronounced antipathy against Blacks. He was a supporter of Stephen Douglas against Abraham Lincoln, bitterly opposed the Emancipation Proclamation, and supported an Illinois constitutional amendment to bar Blacks from voting in the state. But where Blacks could expect little consideration under his jurisprudence, the same could not be said of the rights of corporations, for, as legal historian Peter Irons writes, his "loyalty to corporate interests was never questioned."[49]

Fuller would join and preside over a court that had recently decided, albeit in a slick, backhanded way, that corporations were entitled to the protections of the Fourteenth Amendment, as they were "persons" in constitutional analysis. Ironically, this was the same court that so caressed the interests of corporations in *Santa Clara County v. Southern Pacific Railroad Co.,*[50] by granting it corporate personhood under Morrison Waite (1886). The court would find that railroads were constitutionally permitted to abide by racial segregation on their trains, under the "separate but equal" theory in *Plessy v. Ferguson.*[51] Thus, to a court composed of corporate lawyers, the Fourteenth Amendment, the fruit of the bloodiest war in the nation's history, designed to protect and serve the freedom needs of Africans in America, was but a writ to protect, personalize, and promote corporate welfare above those of Black people. It was this narrow, hair-splitting, conservative court that upheld Ross' conviction, and tossed his claims aside.

Ross would stand for decades, closing the door to any claim of extraterritorial constitutionality, for the Constitution, it appears, could not swim; and it certainly couldn't pass beyond America's sacred borders. It is interesting that *Ross* arose in 1890, for it would not be long before a new wind would blow through the stodgy, oak and mahogany paneled walls of the court. Those winds would come, not from abroad, but from within; and they would emerge from the very ground that many members of the court, as former corporate lawyers, had struggled to serve and protect: growing business interests.

And the Supreme Court helped grease the skids...

The dawn of the twentieth century saw the standoffish Americans looking with something like lust at the burgeoning colonial acquisitions of their European cousins. By the leap into the 1900s, European states held vast swaths of African, Asian, and Pacific territories, from which raw materials were extracted, and economies fed. As the forces of capitalism sought new markets and new lands to conquer, it too looked at Asia as the new Promised Land. But Asia was not all.

The Spanish-American War of 1898-99 was less a real war than an imperial passing of the baton. For Spain, despite the immense riches suctioned from its colonial territories, was left spent, weakened, and a shell of its former self. To this tired entity came the United States: young, vital, fresh, and—let's face it—hungry for its share of this global booty. As two imperial states, they fought wars not so

Photo: United States Marine Corps (1930)

Smedley Butler cheerleading at a USMC football game

"In short, I was a racketeer, a gangster for capitalism" —Major General Smedley Darlington Butler

(about his imperial antics with the U.S. military)

much to beat each other, as to ensure that the Mestizo and Creole masses on the imperial periphery wouldn't get any uppity ideas about independence.

When the U.S. invaded Cuba, the indigenous rebels were on the brink of victory over their Spanish overloads. The U.S. dipped in, took Cuba as a Spanish cession, and inserted the infamous Platt Amendment (1902) into Cuba's constitution, ceding Guantánamo Bay to the U.S. in perpetuity, one of the last remnants of the "capitulations" discussed earlier.

U.S. success in Cuba led to colonial moves on Puerto Rico (1899), the Philippines (1898), and Guam (1899), with the latter two becoming doorways to Asia—and while this epic globe-hopping and these colonial wars were raging, Americans were seriously divided about this brave new world they were facing. But before long, the U.S. would be a nation among nations, or an empire erected above all. In 1900, the Democratic Party, with its populist (i.e., the "common man") rhetoric at hand, set into its party platform a statement of anti-imperialism that would seem bold today. In platform language the Democratic Party said the following:

> We hold that the Constitution follows the flag, and denounce the doctrine that an Executive or Congress deriving their existence and their powers from the Constitution can exercise lawful authority beyond it or in violation of it... *imperialism abroad will lead quickly and inevitably to despotism at home.*[52] [Emphasis added]

The race, between Williams Bryan Jennings (Democrat) and William McKinley (Republican), led to the Democrat being bested by the Republican. McKinley received a million votes more than his Democratic opponent. Whether or not, as the party platform had it, "the Constitution follows the flag," is debatable. What we cannot question is that it follows election returns. With McKinley's triumph and the failure of the Democratic Party's anti-imperialist campaign, we see a noticeable and distinct transformation in the U.S. Supreme Court's position on extraterritoriality and the reach of the Constitution.

Although still a deeply conservative, hidebound, and corporate-centric body, the Court had to be mindful of popular will as expressed and reflected in the national elections. This reflection found legal expression in what scholars and law professors have come to term "The Insular Cases," some fourteen rulings made in the opening decade of the 20th century, which, inch by inch, millimeter by millimeter, sketched out new powers as well as new limits to constitutional rights abroad.

As the U.S. acquired new territories in the Caribbean and the Pacific, the Court strived to create new rules, which enabled and empowered the executive branch by granting it wide latitude in these new American colonies and occupied lands. But, not surprisingly, these new borders and empowerments stretched to accommodate those in these colonial governments, while it disempowered the dark and teeming masses bristling under American-backed suzerainty. While trying to square two opposing positions, the Court kept in mind an overarching view that we would consider repugnant today (at least some of us). The first principle was whether the new territories could be "incorporated" within the States, and if so, how it could be justified; the second was whether or not the Bill of Rights applied to these new lands, and if so, to whom?

The Court accepted and decided over a dozen cases to address and reconcile these questions. They utilized what today seem crude prejudices about "uncivilized" peoples, to decide whether they were "ready" for such liberties as promised in the Bill of Rights. For instance, in *De Lima v. Bidwell* (1901), the Court decreed that the nation had the right to acquire new, overseas territories. In discussing Puerto Rico, it determined that as it was ceded to the U.S. by treaty from Spain, it was no longer foreign, and therefore, foreign duties imposed by statute did not apply to it when it imported goods to the American mainland. Curiously, under *Dooley v. United States* (1901), exports from the U.S. to Puerto Rico *were* taxed. In *Downes v. Bidwell* (1901) several justices decided that while Puerto Rico wasn't foreign, it was still "not part of the United States," as such a term referred only to states. In *Hawaii v. Mankichi* (1903) the court decided that only those rights considered "fundamental in nature" were protected by the Constitution. These did not include indictment by a grand jury, nor a unanimous jury. By 1904, the court announced an "incorporation" theory in *Dorr v. United States* regarding the rights of Filipinos. As the lands and peoples were not yet "incorporated" into the U.S. nationality, they were "not fit" for jury trials, and unless and until Congress so incorporated them into the United States, no such rights were forthcoming.

Legal scholar Walter F. Pratt, Jr., has described the insular cases as a matrix of "myriad justifications and tortured reasoning."[53] But he also writes that the Court was trying to find its way amidst great changes in national policies, especially in light of a fast changing political and electoral climate. So what makes (as Pratt avers) a legal reasoning "tortured?" Pratt does not explain. But we view it from another perspective: that the Court follows, not only election returns, but (more importantly) BUSINESS concerns (after all we must not forget that many of the Court's leading members cut their legal eyeteeth as corporate counsel).

We must therefore read many of the Court's decisions with a sharp eye toward whom did it help and whom did it not? In other words, whose interests did they protect—the wealthy, the established, the well heeled? Or the "common man" (or woman), the worker, the peasant, the citizens who were not moneyed?

Many of the Insular Cases dealt with tax policies, and whether duties could be applied to exports or imports. The Court went to great lengths to protect the burgeoning growth in international trade, as well as America's place in what was fast becoming its informal empire of far-flung and vast territories around the Caribbean, the Pacific, and points east (toward Asia). When laws conflicted with capital accumulation or ease of shipment, they were generally leveled to assist this emerging business practice. However, when foreign nationals or "foreign, but domestic" populations tried to activate the Constitution on their behalf, they were, more often than not, turned away from the rights "guaranteed" by the precious Constitution.

When Puerto Ricans or Filipinos or Guamese or Chinese immigrants tried to access the rights written in the Constitution, they were determined to be insufficiently civilized to utilize such gifts as trial by jury, grand jury indictments, or assistance of counsel. In many cases, they were simply informed that they were not "citizens" and thus had no right to such lofty promises. Shortly after the passage of the thirteenth, fourteenth, and fifteenth amendments, these rights applied more often to the needs of corporations than they did to human beings. Nor could it be said that the Court acted in good faith when it sought to isolate the term "citizen" to mean *white people,* when so many people tried to be included in the "any persons" texts of the Constitution's Fourteenth Amendment regarding Due Process of law.

On 9 July 1868, the following text of Amendment XIV was ratified by Congress:

> Section 1. All persons born or naturalized in the United States, and subject to the jurisdiction thereof, are citizens of the United States and the State wherein they reside. No State shall make or enforce any law which shall abridge the privileges or immunities of citizens of the United States; nor shall any State deprive any persons of life, liberty, or property, without due process of law; nor deny to any person within its jurisdiction the equal protection of the laws.

Sounds pretty good. But in practice it has been either disobeyed or ignored by many (perhaps most) states of the Union from the day it was signed into law, and for more than a century thereafter. That's because the guiding principle of the United States has always been White Supremacy—and the letter of the law be damned.

For Black people, this statement can hardly be challenged.

As we have seen, as Reconstruction waned, during which whites half-heartedly tried to apply the Constitution's promises to Black Southerners, and the old order began reasserting itself through vigilantism and terrorism, one southern editor praised Reconstruction's demise. He said of the Fourteenth and Fifteenth amendments, they "may stand forever, but we intend... to make them dead letters on the statute-book."[54] And so they did.

At the same time Reconstruction was dying on the vine (the latter period of the 19th century), other national minorities, most notably the Chinese of the newly acquired (from Mexico) West Coast, were experiencing virulent and unrelenting repression at the hands of California's white majority and its majoritarian officialdom. In *Baldwin v. Franks* (decided in 1887), the Court's chief justice and a majority of its members decided the following question: Are Chinese aliens, lawfully residing and working in the U.S., protected by the terms of the Chinese-U.S. Treaty of 1880-1881, and is the same constitutional?

First, some background: a number of Chinese persons, living in and around the environs of Nicolaus, Sutter County, California, were attacked, assaulted, and forced by armed men to leave their places of legal business and homes and were placed aboard a steam-boat barge and sent elsewhere. Under the terms of the 1881 Treaty, signed by the President of the United States and the Emperor of China, the safety and wellbeing of Chinese subjects was protected by the host country (the U.S.) from violation. Under said treaty, a number of Chinese filed complaints against the violations of the terms of the rights of such persons, and local officials held a number of accused assailants in custody under a warrant issued by the commissioner of the circuit court, holding, among them, Thomas Baldwin, Bird Wilson, William Hays, and others for violating the protected rights of Sing Lee and other plaintiffs. Baldwin and several of the accused sought habeas corpus relief, and dismissal of the charges. First, the terms of the treaty as signed by both parties, and relevant articles numbers two and three:

> Art. 2. Chinese subjects, whether proceeding to the United States as teachers, students, merchants, or from curiosity, together with their body and household servants, and Chinese laborers who are now in the United States, shall be allowed to go and come of their own free will and accord, and shall be accorded all the rights, privileges, immunities, and exemptions which are accorded to the citizens and subjects of the most favored nation.
>
> Art. 3. If Chinese laborers, or Chinese of any other class, now either permanently or temporarily residing in the territory of the United

> States, meet with ill treatment at the hands of any other persons, the government of the United States will exert all its power to devise measures for their protection, and to secure to them the same rights, privileges, immunities, and exemptions as may be enjoyed by the citizens of the most favored nation, and to which they are entitled by treaty.[55]

Again, what the Supreme Court seemed to resolve were two key and interlocked questions posed by *Baldwin: "Are Chinese nationals protected by the terms of the treaty?"*; and intimately tied with this, the subsidiary question, *"Are state government officials bound by the terms of a treaty signed by the national Executive?"* Legal scholar Walter F. Pratt earlier called the court of the time one torn by "tortured reasoning." We shall see here an excellent demonstration of that quality.

For, in a legal, diplomatic, and political sense, treaties such as these could hardly be held to be exceptional. We should be mindful that at the very time that Chinese laborers were seeking a peaceful and unmolested work environment, whites in China and Japan were protected by capitulations: treaties forced on Asian nations exempting them from the "uncivilized" courts of the Orient. In fact, Americans, British, and other European nationals could only be tried by white consular courts. They were thus immune from the local, host-country judiciaries.

The excerpts from the 1881 treaty were consolidated and placed under the Revised Statutes of the United States, and hence, *a part of U.S. law.* Chief Justice Morrison Waite, writing for the majority, threw the case thusly:

> The real question to be determined, therefore, is whether what is charged to have been done by Baldwin constitutes an offense within the meaning of its provisions. The section is found in title 7, c. 7, Rev. St., embracing "Crimes against the Elective Franchise and Civil Rights of Citizens," and it provides for the punishment of those "who conspire to injure, oppress, threaten, or intimidate any citizen in the free exercise or enjoyment of any right or privilege secured by him by the Constitution or laws of the United States, or because of his having exercised the same;" and of those who go in companies of two or more "in disguise on the highway, or on the premises of another, with intent to prevent or hinder his free exercise or enjoyment of any right or privilege so secured." The person on whom the wrong to be punishable must be inflicted is described as

> a *citizen*... [130 U.S. 691]... [I]t is apparent that the great purpose of Congress in its enactment was to enforce the political rights of citizens of the United States in the several states.[56]

Waite seems to have intentionally ignored the terms of Article VI of the Constitution that he was sworn to protect and defend, to wit (at Clause 2):

> This Constitution, and the Laws of the United States which shall be made in Pursuance thereof; *and all Treaties made, or which shall be made,* under the Authority of the United States, *shall be the supreme Law of the Land;* and *the Judges in every State shall be bound thereby,* anything in the Constitution or Laws of any State to the contrary notwithstanding. [Emphasis added]

Often referred to as "The Great Dissenter" because of his many dissents, especially in cases that restricted civil liberties, including *Plessy v. Ferguson,* Justice John Marshall Harlan would dissent from Waite's and the majority view:

> By the treaty of 1880-81 with China, the government of the United States agreed to exert all its power to devise measures for the protection, against ill treatment at the hands of other persons, of Chinese laborers or Chinese of any other class, permanently or temporarily residing at that time in this country, and to secure them the same rights, privileges, immunities, and exemptions to which the citizens or subjects of the most favored nation are entitled, by treaty, to enjoy here. It would seem from the decision in this case that if, Chinamen, having a right, under the treaty to remain in our country, are forcibly driven from their places of business, the government of the United States is without power, in its own courts, to protect them against such violence, or to punish those who in this way subject them to ill treatment. If this be so as to Chinamen lawfully in the United States, it must be equally true as to the citizens or subjects of every other foreign nation residing or doing business here under the sanction of treaties with their respective governments. I do not think that such is the present state of the law, and must dissent from the opinion and judgment of the court.[57]

Harlan added later in his dissent this observation:

> My brethren hold that section 5508 [of the Revised Statutes] describes only wrongs done to a "citizen;" in other words, that congress did not intend, by that section, to protect the free exercise or enjoyment of rights secured by the Constitution or laws of the United States, except where citizens are concerned. This, it seems to me, is an interpretation of the statute which its language neither demands nor justifies. Observe that the subject with which congress was dealing was the protection of "any right or privilege" secured by the Constitution or laws of the United States...
>
> The rule of interpretation which the court lays down, if applied in other cases, will lead to strange results.[58]

Baldwin, which came eleven years after *Cruikshank,* came down to the same, narrow channel: the berserkers and white terrorists who committed violence against Blacks and Chinese people would be protected. The violated men, women and, children were simply out of luck.

Gunboat Jurisprudence

How do you think such a court would rule when it came to people overseas—those dark, swarming millions who tried to breathe free under white American gunboats and bayonets? We need not wonder. For, as in any occupation, there was one law for the conquerors and another for the conquered. When the U.S. invaded Cuba, ostensibly to help them fight against the fading power of Spain, they introduced two kinds of law, in complete complicity with imperial Spain.

In the 1901 *Neely* case, the Supreme Court made it abundantly clear what "rights" the Cubans (whom the Americans claim they came to help liberate) were entitled to. Law professor Kal Raustiala notes:

> The *Insular Cases* also reinforced the notion that military occupation by the United States was not tantamount to sovereignty. In *Neely v. Henkel,...* handed down in 1901, the justices held that although Cuba was occupied by and governed by the United States, it was nonetheless "foreign territory" because the United States was not a successor in title to the island (as had been the case with Puerto Rico). As a result Cuba "cannot be regarded, in any constitutional, legal, or international sense, a part of the territory of the United States." As a result, the writ of habeas corpus, trial by jury, and

> other constitutional protections for the accused did not apply. These provisions, said the court, "have no relation to crimes committed without the jurisdiction of the United States against the laws of a foreign country." Military government, in short, might mean complete American control, but it did not mean constitutional control.[59]

Was the Constitution so fragile, its hallowed rights so sacred and pure, that it could not "protect" the rights of Others, both within and without the territory of the United States? Or was it so strikingly exclusionary, so full of promise without production, that it was never actually intended to "protect" the rights of the majority of the People? Or was it a document meant to "protect" the white, rich elites, those who had a Baron's Revolt against their British colonizers, so that they could keep the lion's share of the spoils of war, genocidal domination, and centuries of slave labor? Was this a document handed down from Mt. Sinai, writ with the hand of God, or was it a contract, between the wealthiest, most connected powdered wigs in the country, designed to ensure that they came out of the revolution well-situated and positioned in order to continue exploiting, slaving, and genociding?

These questions are not merely rhetorical, for institutions, like nations, given their power and prominence over the lives and minds of men and women, have at their roots, truths that gnaw, like mice, at their founding myths. How often do we hear, daily it seems, pundits who shout to the rafters, "America was founded on freedom!"? Similarly, how often are we taught, from the cradling knees of our parents and teachers, that the Supreme Court granted such and such freedoms, for so and so? We rarely think of such things, for they are the stuff of our consciousness, rarer still are they ever questioned.

Speaking of myths, one of the great misnomers inherent in the longstanding national dialogue regarding the so-called "rights and freedoms granted by the Constitution" is just that—the Constitution (and by extension the government) doesn't "grant rights and freedoms to the citizenry" like a candy-filled vending machine or generous Santa Claus, but rather the Constitution *limits the behavior of the government.* We wrote this earlier in the chapter but it bears repeating. This is a fundamental misunderstanding and basic flaw in the hearts and minds of the many and, at the same time, it is a corrupt position deliberately exploited and perpetrated by the elite—in both the corporate media and, of course, in the halls of power. And why would they operate any differently? The masses are sleepwalking, anesthetized by a myriad of distractions and manipulations. Ignorance is not bliss. Ignorance leads to tyranny.

Bottom line? It's about the balance of power and power concedes nothing.

And yet. And yet... When we peer past the mists and clouds, the shouted glories of Founders and Giants, we see the raw viscera of the State and its accommodations with Power. We see that the burdens of Empire, though quested for by business and corporate interests and sold by the political elites who were purchased for such purpose, are but aided and abetted by the highest judicial minds of the age; politicians in black robes, who manipulate words and deeds to deny the most fundamental rights of humankind, who structure sentences to bind, fetter, betray, and flimflam the heart prayers of millions. The victims. For them... for us... it's a swindle, a confidence game, one that involves skillful persuasion and the clever manipulation that can make politics sound like law.

This Supreme Court, sworn to protect, defend, and uphold the Constitution, sought, more often than not, to sacralize the document, enshrine it in gold, and place it afar and away from the rabble, the great unwashed both within and without the Empire. It became, far too often, a Proclamation of Promises—promises unfulfilled.

Policing the World—one "Shithole"[60] country at a time

Earlier, we discussed *In re Ross,* the case where a British man seeks to have the U.S. entertain his claims under the guarantees of the Constitution. His efforts were unsuccessful, as the Court sought to limit the reach, scope, and breadth of the Constitution and its Bill of Rights. The Ross case arose in 1890, and stood as a barrier to American citizens abroad seeking constitutional protections for more than sixty years, until the post-World War II years, when the Court decided several cases in 1957, among them *Reid v. Covert.*[61] These cases came to be known as the cases of "the murdering wives" (according to Supreme Court justices) and dealt with two American woman who accompanied their husbands to military bases abroad. When Clarice Covert and Dorothy Krueger Smith killed their husbands, they were subjected to court-martials, convicted, and sent back to American prison to serve their life terms.

When the women pressed their appeals up to the Supreme Court, which, under *Ross,* denied their appeals to the Constitution's extraterritoriality, a funny thing happened. The Court abruptly reversed itself, and ordered briefs in the two cases, over the strong objections of the Eisenhower administration, which argued that "the rule of the *Ross* case has never been questioned, and we think it is not seriously questioned here."[62] Fortunately for Madames Covert and Smith, however, this was precisely what the Court was doing, as it reexamined a precedent that had stood for more than six decades. In *Reid v. Covert* and *Kinsella v. Krueger,* the court announced a new rule for the day. It decided that Status of Force Agreements (or treaties setting the rights and immunities of military forces and their dependents abroad, called SOFAs) could not deprive U.S. citizens abroad of their rights to a jury trial (as opposed to court-martial). As the process employed did not comport with the Constitution or Bill of Rights, their convictions could not stand.

As such, these cases marked the emergence of the U.S. as a global post-war power, and one with an unprecedented reach of military bases the world over. And as this quasi-imperial infrastructure took root in hundreds of places around the planet, the Supreme Court, which arguably didn't follow the flag, did, however, march after the troops. It had to incorporate this global structure into its formerly narrow, bordered, territorial constitutional framework.

As U.S. influence expanded after World War II, its reach grew in commensurate scope as did its power. Working through the United Nations, the U.S. extended its jurisdiction through notions of extraterritoriality that would have shocked earlier generations of lawyers and even presidents. One instrument of its expansion of police power was in pursuit of the ephemeral "drug war." Indeed, it is often difficult to determine where the imperialist, intrusionist efforts of agencies like the CIA ended, and where its narcotics-related efforts began. Even bodies like the FBI, historically and strictly territorial in nature, developed a global presence, as Raustiala notes:

> The FBI often played a central role in extraterritorial policing, particularly from the 1990s onward. Between 1990 and 2000 the FBI tripled its overseas legal attaché of offices. The FBI's overseas work increasingly involved investigating terrorist attacks, and associated investigations often straddled the line between intelligence work and policing. Prior to the 9/11 attacks, the preferred strategy of the federal government was to prosecute terrorists in ordinary criminal court. To ensure that prosecutions could effectively move forward in American courts without compromising vital classified

intelligence, the FBI investigatory teams increasingly were divided into two: a "dirty," or "dark," team and a "clean," or "light," team.[63]

Truth be told, we can trace a robust extraterritoriality by U.S. government agencies before the events of 9/11 came to pass. When the Khobar Towers in Saudi Arabia were bombed, killing some nineteen Americans, more than 500 FBI agents were sent to investigate the attack. When the USS Cole was bombed on the coast of Yemen, some 100 FBI agents were soon to arrive to investigate the attack. The events of 9/11 have only served to kick that trend into maximum overdrive, clearly demonstrating the institutional conflicts between the judiciary and the executive, especially as the administrations tried to reassert old theories of territorial limits to create what some critics have called a "legal black hole" in Guantánamo, Cuba.

Leading actors in the White House and the Justice Department sought out Guantánamo precisely because it was not part of the U.S. territory, and, as such, safe haven from the interventions of the U.S. courts. In fact, the nation's federal judiciary had said exactly that when, during the 1990s, Haitians escaping the political violence tied to the right-wing coup against President Jean-Bertrand Aristide, were seized by U.S. Naval personnel and sent to Guantánamo as detainees. These Haitians, protesting their treatment at the hands of the Americans, as well as their continued detention, sought judicial review by way of the Haitian Refugee Center—a U.S.-based advocacy group. The Refugee Center sued seeking access to the refugees under the First Amendment to the Constitution. The Eleventh U.S. Circuit Court of Appeals rejected their complaint, arguing that the First Amendment didn't apply. As for the Haitians, the court said that they "had no recognized substantive rights under the laws of the Constitution of the United States."[64] That's largely because, even post-*Reid v. Covert,* some judges still believed that the Constitution stopped at the water's edge, for the U.S. Navy, by interdicting Haitians before they set foot on American soil, and interning them on Cuban soil (Guantánamo Naval Base), kept them beyond the jurisdiction of American courts.

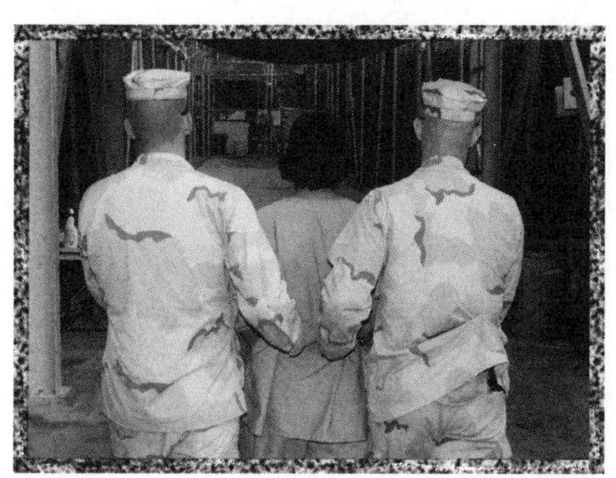
Photo: U.S. Navy, taken by Navy Petty Officer 1st Class Michael Billings

Guantánamo military guards escort a prisoner

The more things change…

Yet, Guantánamo's more recent usage, as a mass prison where torture and illegal interrogations are conducted, elicited more concern and sympathy than the travails suffered by the Haitians. Indeed, an American presidential candidate won (Mr. Obama), in part, by promising to close the Guantánamo brig down. By the end of his eight-year term, the gulag remained open for business with cell space expanding. But while Arabs, Pashtuns, and Uyghurs may be many things—they were not Haitians. Thus, the imperial court made room for them to enter the realm of the Law.

Absolute Security

In the wake of the national mania stirred by the 9/11 strikes on lower Manhattan and the Pentagon, the nation's security and intelligence officials, struck dumb by the hubris of the act, embarked on a mission to achieve the unachievable: *absolute security.* They launched into a war (initially, by tying Iraqi President Saddam Hussein to the attacks) that the vast majority not only opposed—but also actively demonstrated against in numbers that far exceeded protests against the Vietnam War in the 1960s and '70s. Literally, millions of people took to the streets in loud, colorful, spirited protests. Calling them a "focus group," Mr. Bush promptly ignored them by essentially stating that, "leaders must lead." Bush stated:

> First of all, you know, size of protest, it's like deciding, "well, I'm going to decide policy based upon a focus group." The role of a leader is to decide policy based upon the security—in this case, the security of the people.[65]

Whaaaa??? "Focus group?"

Activist and academic Robert Jensen describes the composition of this so-called focus group:

> The worldwide antiwar actions on February 15, 2003, were the single largest public political demonstration in history. Millions of people all over the globe poured into the streets to try to derail the Bush administration's mad rush to war.[66]

In addition to unleashing the dogs of war, Bush sent detainees from the Afghanistan War to Guantánamo Bay Naval Station brigs, based explicitly on the theory that it was beyond the reach of the nation's judiciary, as it was on foreign soil. One Bush administration insider stated the case quite badly, by writing that U.S.-based military bases were:

> Relatively easy targets for terrorists to attack. They would frighten and possibly endanger U.S. civilians. And detentions there were more likely to be subject to legal challenges since they were on U.S. soil. GITMO [military-speak for Guantánamo], by contrast, was isolated and well defended. And because it was technically not a part of U.S. sovereign soil, it seemed like a good bet to minimize judicial scrutiny.[67]

In the long aftermath of 9/11 and the smoldering holocausts of war, the Court would give its legal stamp on cases that seemed to limit the reach of the national executive. In what one day may be called, "The Terrorist Cases," or perhaps, "The Guantánamo Cases," the Supreme Court has decided a number of related cases, and in almost all of them, has issued a stunning rebuke to the Executive's power to do what [s]he will in time of war.

In *Hamdi v. Rumsfeld* (June 2004), the case of Yaser Esam Hamdi was decided by a confusing flurry of judicial opinions, each stepping on the other. Plurality opinions are rare and court watchers have struggled to intuit the court's meaning, delivered in seven, eight, or nine separate opinions, thus close readings are required to determine some principles of agreement. Despite the judicial din of distracting voices, Sandra Day O'Connor's memorable line has risen to the top of public consciousness. Said the now-retired justice: "[A] state of war is not a blank check for the President when it comes to the rights of the nation's citizens."[68] Predictably, liberals reacted to O'Connor's turn of phrase with swoons of delight, presumably because it beat back a president that they detested, or it seemed to make so much sense about the limits of presidential power. But, lost in the sauce were the other findings made by the court's plurality. O'Connor's additional words are worthy of repeating here:

> There is no bar to this Nation's holding one of its own citizens as an enemy combatant. In [*Ex parte*] *Quirin,* [(1942)] one of the detainees, Haupt, alleged that he was a naturalized United States citizen... We held that "[c]itizens who associate themselves with the military arm of the enemy government, and with its aid, guidance and direction enter this country bent on hostile acts, are

> enemy belligerents within the meaning of... the law of war."... While Haupt was tried for violations of the law of war, nothing in *Quirin* suggests that his citizenship would have precluded his mere detention for the duration of the relevant hostilities... Nor can we see any reason for drawing such a line here. A citizen, no less than an alien, can be "part of or supporting forces hostile to the United States or coalition partners" and "engaged in an armed conflict against the United States,"... such a citizen, if released, would pose the same threat of returning to the front during the ongoing conflict.[69]

From the era when the rights of Americans were too precious to share with those lesser beings who did not have the divine foresight to be born American, now the repression that was once used only on the uncivilized outsiders (with the exception of Blacks, of course) can now be visited upon Americans. As O'Connor's plurality opinion reflects, Hamdi was indeed a citizen, for he was born on U.S. soil, in Louisiana, of Saudi parents. His family returned to Saudi Arabia when he was three years old. Hamdi and his lawyers argued that he was not an enemy combatant, but a victim of the program of the Northern Alliance (anti-Taliban U.S. ally in Afghanistan), who were paid bounties for each "Taliban" turned in. Eventually Hamdi was quietly released from Guantánamo, on the condition that he renounce his American citizenship and return to Saudi Arabia with severe travel restrictions.

Hamdi accepted with alacrity and left for his home and family in Saudi Arabia in September 2004—three months after the *Hamdi* decision. After *Hamdi,* a slew of cases rose and fell at the Court like a line of ducks. *Rasul v. Bush,* as well as *Boumediene v. Bush,* held that non-citizens, held under the jurisdiction of the United States, had the right of habeas corpus to review and challenge their detentions.[70] These cases represented the complete collapse of the administration's theory of why Guantánamo was selected as a detention site, free of any meaningful judicial review. The *Rasul* and *Boumediene* cases didn't just represent a defeat for the executive, but a rejection of the legislative power as well, for it rejected congressional attempts to evade federal judicial intervention, not only by placement of the alleged combatants on Guantánamo, but by enacting statutes that explicitly denied the rights of civil and habeas review by the federal judiciary. The Court, often narrowly (*Boumediene*: 5-4 vote; *Rasul*: 6-3 with one concurrence and several dissents) abrogated these congressional attempts to deprive aliens of habeas corpus review of their detentions. It is noteworthy that both Rasul and Boumediene lost their appeals at the District and appellate court levels.

The central theme of both cases was one of extraterritoriality—whether Guantánamo Bay Naval Base was under Cuban or U.S. sovereignty. As the terms of the Platt Amendment retained nominal Cuban sovereignty, the courts have previously ruled that it was outside of U.S. judicial reach (see, for example, the earlier Haitian cases and examples cited). But, as a matter of fact, the U.S. controlled entry, egress, and usage of the landscape, and there, the court reasoned, U.S. jurisdiction controlled. In this respect, the theory of extraterritoriality failed the U.S. administrations by opening up their prison camp to judicial, and therefore, journalistic review. It has been, and indeed continues to be, a bone of contention on a global scale, as it causes considerable consternation among Western and international elites.

The administrations may have failed in making their "black hole" an invisible interrogation and torture site, but it succeeded in the ultimate expression of extraterritoriality: war. It initiated a war, several in fact, which are still causing repercussions around the world. Iraq will be recovering for generations after massive death and destruction, and Afghanis will long remember the U.S. invasion—replete with a murder spree courtesy of cruise missiles, drone strikes, and a good ol' fashioned ground invasion. The consequences of these wars (along with god-knows what the CIA and mercenary contractors have done in the shadows), with regard to the damage inflicted back on the U.S. Empire, may also not be known for generations.

And despite the many rulings of the Supreme Court in the Terrorism Cases (as of this writing), there are still men encaged in Guantánamo, some who have been imprisoned (the polite, judicial, and military euphemism is "detained") for nearly a decade or more, charged with nothing, convicted of less—and some even cleared by American military and intelligence forces. (Note: since 2002, there have been approximately 780 individuals sent to the Guantánamo Bay prison.) On these questions, as of this writing, the nation's highest court has been virtually silent. For what is the worth of judicial review, if it doesn't lead to freedom?

After the Play Has Ended...
John Paul Stevens Reexamines the Law

We have developed the theme of the U.S. "Supremes" as a theatre of sorts, where democracy games are played on the fields of the Law. But what happens to a Justice who is no longer a Justice?

John Paul Stevens (1920-2019) retired from the Court in 2010 after 34 years on the bench. In his vanishing years he showed the world how to make a contribution after the curtain went down on showtime. Stevens served as a Circuit Court judge prior to joining the Supremes, and after more than thirty years of a judicial career, he still couldn't put down his pen. Or turn off his mind.

In 2014, Stevens published *Six Amendments,*[71] a remarkable yet short work where he advocated for a fundamental re-thinking of the U.S. Constitution. Stevens, now writing his opinions from outside of one of the world's most influential judicial bodies, called for basic revisions to six areas of the law, using history and logical arguments to support his appeal.

Photo: Steve Petteway, SCOTUS

U.S. Supreme Court Justice
John Paul Stevens

Specifically, Stevens addressed the following areas of modern legal practice:

- Death Penalty
- Campaign Financing
- Sovereign Immunity
- Political Gerrymandering
- "Anti-Commandeering Rule"
- 2nd Amendment (aka gun control)

Stevens, now off the Court, still felt the rhythms and pulses of the bench and suspected that he could resolve some nagging issues that he believed he left undone and unsaid during his long and rich career at the State's highest court. In fact, once a Justice departs the Court, s/he has a host of public options available: one may sit on lower benches, such as one or several of the twelve U.S. Courts of Appeal. Another may visit Europe and lecture at various law schools to give a wider understanding of U.S. law. Some justices write, as did the former Justice Sandra Day O'Connor, on the arcane history of the Court.

Justice Stevens chose the latter. In his last near-decade of life, he penned two books: *Five Chiefs* (a memoir of five U.S. Chief Justices), and the aforementioned *Six Amendments.* In this last book, we see Stevens reexamining some of the themes that arose during his years on the bench. Stevens wrote of his former colleagues with unerring politeness, and rarely critiqued them. But this didn't mean that he was free from deep disagreements with what he considered errors of logic or law.

Let's examine his six amendments.

The Death Penalty

On the simmering controversy of the American death penalty, Stevens—who entered the Court as a conservative appointee of the appointed-President, Gerald Ford—voted early as a Justice to bring back the death penalty in America in *Gregg v. Georgia* (1976), which reversed the earlier ruling calling the American death penalty unconstitutional in *Furman v. Georgia* (1972). In *Gregg*, Stevens announced the 7-2 decision defending and reimposing the American way of death. But in the 5-4 *Furman* case, Stevens actually concurred, which found the death penalty "wantonly and freakishly imposed" and constituted an intolerable risk in a free society, and thus was "intolerable" under the Eighth Amendment.

After years of trying to make it less "wanton and freakish," Stevens would later decide in his writings to opt for its abolition, by suggesting a simple supplement to the Eighth Amendment, adding the words: "such as the death penalty" to the "cruel and unusual punishment" phrase.

> Excessive bail shall not be required, nor excessive fines imposed, nor cruel and unusual punishments inflicted, **such as the death penalty.**

How "freakishly" easy was that?

The Anti-Commandeering Rule

Although this rule is little known, it has an exaggerated and distorted impact on American state and federal law. Stevens apparently believed that early political influences set the law on erroneous paths, and the retired justice did not hesitate to note these treks as deeply flawed. He begins his text with perhaps the least-known objection, such as the "Anti-Commandeering Rule." This refers to early trends in U.S. law, which conceived the federal government and state governments as separate sovereigns, often at odds with each other. As such, the Court decided that the feds could not demand that state officials assist them in their efforts to enforce the law, but they could make requests, which, of course, the states could freely refuse.

In interpreting the Supremacy Clause of the Constitution (Article VI), the Court, in a 5-4 ruling, interpreted the clause narrowly, as Stevens explained:

> . . . (1) in *Printz v. United States* (521 U.S. 898) (1997), . . . the Court announced what has come to be known as the anti-commandeering rule—a rule that prohibits Congress from requiring state officials from performing federal duties.

This rule, Stevens now argued, was not only wrongly decided, but it endangered modern society by preventing states and the federal government from protecting their people. In his dissent from *Printz,* Stevens wrote:

> Since the ultimate issue is one of power, we must consider the implications of it in times of national emergency. Matters such as the enlistment of air raid wardens, the administration of a military draft, the mass inoculation of children to forestall an epidemic, or perhaps the threat of an international terrorist, may require a national response before federal personnel can be made ready to respond.

Stevens called on Congress to amend the Constitution's Article VI, by adding the words, "and other public officials" to the Supremacy Clause, thus ending the controversy, once and for all. Like this:

> This Constitution, and the laws of the United States which shall be made in pursuance thereof; and all treaties made, or which shall be made, under the authority of the United States, shall be the supreme law of the land; and the judges **and other public officials** in every state shall be bound thereby, anything in the Constitution or laws of any State to the contrary notwithstanding.

Perhaps Stevens had more faith in Congress than the People have.

Sovereign Immunity

When most Americans use the term "sovereign" one thinks it refers to the notion, or idea, that what is being discussed is state or federal government power. There is also a nascent sovereign movement in the land that regards citizens as sovereigns of the self, and as such, not subject to governmental authority. But that is not the usage to which we refer here.

Here, "sovereign" is used in its oldest sense, to refer to the inherent power(s) of the crown, and its limits on state and, indeed, constitutional power. The roots in Anglo-American law may be traced to jolly old England and the Latin phrase, Rex Non Potest Peccare, or "The King can do no wrong." But what can such a thing mean in America, after the Revolution—a revolution based upon a Declaration of Independence, which expressly states that the King (George III) had committed numerous wrongs and sins against the American colonists.

Stevens wrote of early Supreme Court justices and political figures of that period using the common law British-derived notions "sovereign immunity" to bar suits against states, as the State inherited the powers and immunities of the English kings. Stevens argued that a law does not remain a law simply because of its longevity. In the case of sovereign immunity (or the immunity of the State from suit), he cited Abraham Lincoln's 1861 State of the Union message, where the President said, "It is as much the duty of Government to render prompt justice against itself, in favor of its citizens, as it is to administer the same between private individuals."[72]

Stevens recommended that the Constitution be amended to say the following:

> Neither the Tenth Amendment, the Eleventh Amendment, nor any other provision of this Constitution, shall be construed to provide any state, state agency, or state officer with an immunity from liability for violating any act of Congress, or any provision of this Constitution.

Campaign Finance

The issue of money in politics arose several times during Stevens' tenure on the U.S. Supreme Court bench. The shifting political forces on the Court swung the issue from side to side, like a seesaw, one trying to prevail over the other. These swings of fortune also reflected which party held power over the U.S. presidency, for s/he who held the Oval Office determined who sat in the nation's highest tribunal.

For decades, Stevens submits, Americans have been very concerned about money in politics. He cites the words of President Theodore Roosevelt at his 1905 annual address to Congress:

> All contributions by corporations to any political committee for any political purpose should be forbidden by law; directors should not be permitted to use stockholders' money for such purposes; and, moreover, a prohibition of this kind would be, as far as it went, an effective method of stopping the evils aimed at in corrupt practices acts.

It has been more than a century since Roosevelt spoke those words, but the systemic problem of corporate money greatly influencing American politics—at all levels—is still the corrupt main circuit cable coursing through the entire organism, largely because the Supreme Court has vacillated and/or supported the corporate takeover of U.S. elections. Why? *The protection of predatory capitalism over the welfare and will of the People.* Stevens cited the prominent (and obscure) cases at issue, such as *Buckley v. Valeo* (1976) and the controversial *Citizens United v. Federal Election Commission* (2010)—a case Stevens described as a "giant step in the wrong direction."

Citizens United ruled that corporations were, like natural persons, protected by constitutional free speech rights, and thus couldn't be limited by campaign rules that set limits to such use in political campaigns. Stevens would propose a Constitutional Amendment that would freely allow Congress to write laws that limited corporate funds for political purposes, essentially overturning *Citizens United.*

Political Gerrymandering

Stevens offers us a history lesson on the arcane origins of the term, "Gerrymandering," which we will not recount here (read Stevens' book!).

Suffice it is to say, gerrymandering was (is!) a practice of creating voting districts designed to unfairly weight the areas of a political party or which intentionally weakens the representation for the out-of-power party. As Stevens instructed in his section on this issue, while racial gerrymandering is indeed unconstitutional, the same cannot be said about political gerrymandering.

Stevens would, by his proposed Constitutional Amendment, change this picture by equally outlawing this practice of political gerrymandering. While the Court found that racial gerrymandering was in violation of the Reconstruction Amendments (specifically, the 15th Amendment respecting the unencumbered right to vote by Black people), the right to engage in elections free from a politically gerrymandered process has not drawn the Court's support. Stevens, who argues that both forms are equally unfair, would submit the amendment striking down the practice as violative of the democratic political process.

The 2nd Amendment (aka "gun control")

Perhaps few issues raise the hackles of Americans more than the issue of gun control—in part due to the central role played by guns and violence in U.S. history, specifically the American Revolution, the vicious Indian wars, and the under-addressed and little-known slave rebellions.

The gun, as a symbol, is as much a part of American self-identity as was the sword for 19th-century Japan. This means that the struggle for an amendment that changes or transforms understandings of gun policy and ownership will not be an easy one.

Stevens cited the impact of the 2008 *D.C. v. Heller* decision, which, for the first time, protected individual rights of gun ownership for domestic self-defense. That case supercharged the anti-gun control movement and energized state legislatures across the country to enact laws that all but *required* gun ownership by eligible citizens. There is some hyperbole there, but not by much, for the gun culture in America has grown by leaps and bounds since *Heller* became the law of the land.

In recent years the incidence of mass shootings, in schools, theaters, malls, and other places of mass attendance has been symptomatic of a society in the process of serious entropy and utter collapse. This feature of American life has been one that is peculiarly American in its incidence and scope. When viewed against the gun death numbers of every other country on the face of the planet, the U.S. outdistances every single society by mathematical chasms so large as to be laughable if not appalling.

What engendered Stevens' interest in the Second Amendment? He writes that the grammar school massacre in Newtown, Connecticut, moved him to reexamine the issue. The event demonstrated the limits of the federal government to regulate the laws governing gun ownership and usage. Stevens recalled the words of former Chief Justice, Warren Burger, who, speaking on the MacNeil/Lehrer NewsHour on PBS, took the National Rifle Association (NRA) to task for its efforts to break away from all gun regulation. Burger, sitting in retirement, told his hosts that the Second Amendment activists had fooled Americans, and that the masses...

> had been the subject of one of the greatest pieces of fraud, and I repeat the word "fraud" on the American public by special interest groups that I have ever seen in my lifetime.[73]

Stevens would amend the Second Amendment to add the following insertion:

> A well-regulated Militia, being necessary to the security of a free state, the right of the people to keep and bear arms **when serving in the Militia** shall not be infringed.

This latter section completes Stevens' *Six Amendments,* but it is only fair to note that they came nearly a decade after he left the Court. It is telling that one heard nary a whiff of such subjects during the three decades of his high court service.

Such an observation suggests the limits of his judicial power while he sat on the Court, and how much relative freedom he experienced once he took off his robes. It also offers us a glimpse into how other justices, steeped as they are in their official duties, are refraining from giving voice to issues that are perhaps burning in their minds.

We have observed how Stevens was reluctant to speak of his colleagues, except in the politest, if not glowing terms. Over the decades, of course, it is only fair to suppose that some relationships were collegial and warm amongst such a small, odd lot of judges. But there's always an exception to every rule.

Stevens doesn't dwell on personalities so much as he disagreed with positions that threaten the democratic process. He illustrated the fact that a judge is often liberated after he leaves the judicial (political?) body and is able to think of the broader, historical ramifications of the Law on the nation, beyond the interests of his colleagues. Stevens provided historical perspective that may animate historians, surely, but also provided depth to legal thinkers, who tend to adopt legal positions from a narrow, static field.

There are lessons lurking in Stevens' consideration of *Six Amendments,* for it shows us how much broader the law can be, once the judge steps off the stage.

Occasionally a Justice Does Care When They Wear the Robe

Remember the opening tune from the old Andy Griffith Show? The whistling... the strange announcer telling us the names of the stars... Sheriff Andy Taylor (who never carried a gun) and his son Opie walking through the woods of North Carolina... Andy has their fishin' poles in tow and Opie pitches a rock toward a pristine lake, presumably filled with trout and catfish. It was Americana 101—and oddly enough the environment was in perfect balance with man (and his boy).

(What the hell does this have to do with the Supreme Court?)

It wasn't North Carolina but a reservoir near the top of Coldwater Canyon overlooking the City of Angels. Pine trees, dirt roads, fishin' hole, voilà—North Carolina, Hollywood style. Today, as it was in the early 1960s, the reservoir is surrounded by amazing acreage of mountains, forests, flora, and fauna and is known to the locals as "WODOC" or the William O. Douglas Outdoor Classroom.

See, even before it was hip to be environmentally conscious—or a necessity to be lest we allow the planet to fall into receivership and bankruptcy—some smart people actually cared about the kind of world they were going to leave their grandchildren. "Wild Bill" Douglas was one of those people.

Nominated to the bench by Franklin Roosevelt, William Orville Douglas served on the Supreme Court from 1939 to 1975. His thirty-six years is the longest term in the history of the Court. Douglas was famous for writing a host of dissenting opinions against the monstrosity of power. Republicans tried to impeach Douglas from the bench. Congressman Gerald Ford spearheaded one attempt, and among other attacks on Douglas, Ford cited his "liberal opinions."

> It was against a background poignant with memories of evil procedures that our Constitution was drawn.
>
> — "Wild Bill"

Unlike our frustration with the aforementioned John Paul Stevens (who paradoxically succeeded Douglas) and his inability to constitutionally fight for judicial change that benefits the citizens of the United States rather than the corporatocracy, Douglas fiercely battled for civil rights and civil liberties, against the war in Vietnam, as well as waging war for environmental justice while he wore the robe.

In fact, while on the bench, WOD was at the heart of a shift toward modern environmentalism. During his long tenure on the Supreme Court, he championed positions that sought national solutions to protect the air, water, and land that included fostering public involvement and safeguards of minority interests. WOD advocated and supported democratic action for conservation issues as well as public monitoring of governmental and corporate activities traditionally working against environmental integrity.

In 2018, Washington State Attorney General Bob Ferguson led a hike called "Save Our Coast"—an action to protest the federal government's offshore oil-drilling proposal. Ferguson was walking the twenty-two-mile coastal route that WOD hiked in 1958 in a similar protest to protect the beachhead on the Olympic Peninsula. "One thing is certain in today's environment," writes M. Margaret McKeown in the *Seattle Times,* "no Supreme Court justice will be joining the hike." McKeown believes that it would be "unthinkable" in this era to witness Douglas' veracity. "From his chambers at the Supreme Court," McKeown continues, "Douglas... was a one-man lobby shop for the environment. He cajoled and persuaded the secretaries of the Interior and Agriculture, badgered the Forest Service and the National Park Service, and inveigled members of Congress to support his causes."[74]

Sometimes they do fight. Sometimes the Constitution does matter. Sometimes a judge holds up their end of the bargain and protects the minority from the tyranny of the majority. And sometimes because your judicial opinions and behavior on the bench made a difference in a myriad of ways, like being known as "Nature's Justice," they name a land reserve after you in the Santa Monica Mountains that serves as an active classroom to more than 10,000 Los Angeles Unified School District children yearly. William O. Douglas—a legacy that matters.

Photo: Library of Congress

William O. Douglas

As nightfall does not come at once, neither does oppression. In both instances, there is a twilight when everything remains seemingly unchanged. And it is in such twilight that we must be most aware of change in the air— however slight—lest we become unwitting victims of the darkness.

—"Wild Bill"

Behold a New World

The Imperial Court—which sought to put the vaunted promises of the Constitution and its Bill of Rights beyond the reach of the First Peoples who lived here for tens of thousands of years before the European holocaust, beyond the utility of Africans who were born in the national territory (classic cases of intraterritoriality), beyond the use of Puerto Ricans, Filipinos, Haitians, and for a time, even beyond the reach of Americans abroad—was forced by changing imperial conditions to bestow at least sweet lip service of constitutional protections upon those who allegedly waged war against the Empire.

Before we depart this chapter, it is important to get some flavor of the Court's treatment of those on the outside of the imperial core. It's important for us to hear their voices, and to examine their thinking, especially when it came to others. In 1922, in the case, *Balzac v. Porto Rico* (yes, that's how the Court spelled it in their opinions back then), the court denied the right of jury trial to people on the island, and did so with the following reasoning:

> The jury system needs citizens trained to the exercise of the responsibilities of jurors. In common-law countries centuries of tradition have prepared a conception of the impartial attitudes jurors must assume. The jury system postulates a conscious duty of participation in the machinery of justice which it is hard for people not brought up in fundamentally popular governments at once to acquire. One of its greatest benefits is in the security it gives the people that they, as jurors, actual or possible, being part of the judicial system of the country, can prevent its arbitrary use or abuse. Congress has thought that a people like the Filipinos or the Porto Ricans, trained to a complete judicial system which knows no juries, living in compact and ancient communities, with definitely formed customs and political conceptions, should be permitted themselves to determine how far they wish to adopt this institution of Anglo-Saxon origin.[75]

It is hard to read words such as these without determining that its writers are essentially declaring "Porto Ricans" and Filipinos as too stupid, or perhaps too Latino (as in passionate and undisciplined), to handle jury trials. The imperial court can no longer state such Anglo-Saxon nonsense as displayed here. It must embrace a universality that it may not truly believe in, but they must act as if it's a central theme in their thinking.

The world the courts inherited is no more. Behold a new world.

The law must follow—or be left behind.

MURDER INCORPORATED

empire \ genocide \ manifest destiny

6 Stasi 2.0

We are all "Enemies of the State"

> *The right of the people to be secure in their persons, houses, papers, and effects, against unreasonable searches and seizures, shall not be violated, and no Warrants shall issue, but upon probable cause, supported by Oath or affirmation, and particularly describing the place to be searched, and the persons or things to be seized.*
> —Amendment IV
> Bill of Rights, Ratified on 15 December 1791

In early 2014, when discussing the U.S. Government's abuse of data mining and surveillance—actions that smacked of authoritarian privacy invasions—former president Jimmy Carter told NBC News that he believed his email communications were being monitored by the National Security Agency. To avoid Big Brother's incursion, Carter said he was going old school: typing his letters, buying stamps, and dropping them off at his local post office. Let's remember, this isn't an infamous anarchist targeted by the FBI for WTO actions or a former member of the Weather Underground looking to challenge the monolith of empire, but rather a former president and CEO of the Corporation *itself* sending private notes to other world leaders. Do you think the "Man from Plains" knows a thing or two about how his government operates? This was the same president who signed

the Foreign Intelligence Surveillance Act (FISA) into law—an act that was the direct knee-jerk reaction to the U.S. Government's domestic spying apparatus, one that was grinding the Constitution to a pulp, including but not limited to nefarious actions that stretched from COINTELPRO to the Nixon administration's gross abuse of power.

When Carter revealed his treks to the post office, General Keith Alexander, then the Director of the National Security Agency, offered the former president the expected patronizing and condescending reprimand. While sitting perched like a peacock on FOX News (aka The Cartoon Network), his chest decorated with shiny toy medals, looking like a goddamn Christmas tree, the hawkish Alexander was given the pulpit to set Carter straight: "Well, we're not." (Alexander and the stooge reporter from FOX snicker.) "He can now go back to writing emails." Alexander continued his Orwellian whitewash: "The reality is we don't do that, and if we did it would be illegal and we'd be held accountable and responsible."[1]

Apparently, if you embrace Alexander's word as gospel, there's nothing to even talk about: if the NSA says everything's groovy, then everything's groovy. The program was assessed at the time by Obama (in between murderous drone strikes), the U.S. Congress (a moribund collection of carpetbaggers), the Department of Defense (remember when Abbie, Jerry, and Ginsberg tried to levitate the fucking thing?), the Director of National Intelligence James Clapper (who will outright lie to anyone who's listening, they're not), and finally the Department of Justice, who together with all the abovementioned watchdogs of civil liberties, found that everything the U.S. intelligence community is engaged in is legal, above board, and rooted deeply in a firm base of constitutional integrity. And why shouldn't we take Alexander's word on this? The U.S. Government has never been involved in any disreputable actions. It's all lollipops and cotton candy. Jesus, that was a short chapter.

[Edward Snowden] is the quintessential American whistleblower, and a personal hero of mine. Leaks are the lifeblood of the republic and, for the first time, the American public has been given the chance to debate democratically the NSA's mass surveillance programs. Accountability journalism can't be done without the courageous acts exemplified by Snowden, and we need more like him.[2]
—Daniel Ellsberg, at one time "The Most Dangerous Man in America"

Photo: Susan Wood (1976)
Daniel Ellsberg

Photo: Laura Poitras / Praxis Films (2013)
Edward Snowden

Your authors concur with the man who was a hero himself when he turned a giant spotlight on the Vietnam War in 1971 with the release of the Pentagon Papers. But "hero" is not how the world's richest man characterizes Edward Snowden, the former CIA employee and NSA contractor who released a plethora of classified documents to the American people (their documents) that revealed the scope and operational details of the Empire's global surveillance programs.

In a 2014 interview with *Rolling Stone* magazine, Microsoft co-founder Bill Gates extolled the virtues of allowing the government somewhat free rein to gather information in a wholesale fashion. Gates waxed poetic about numerous possibilities—from cameras recording everything we do ("having cameras in inner cities is a very good thing") to the surveillance-aided apprehension of some nebulous monster ("gathering nuclear-weapons plans... to kill millions of people"). Gates also wished that "we were having more intense debates about these things." Where the hell has Bill been? Jeff Goddell, the *Rolling Stone* scribe conducting the interview, picked up on this: "Thanks to Edward Snowden, who has leaked tens of thousands of NSA documents, we are. Do you consider him a hero or a traitor?" Gates responds, "I think he broke the law. So I certainly wouldn't characterize him as a hero."[3] The inference is obvious: he would characterize him as a traitor.

And why wouldn't he? Snowden's courageous and massive revelations showed that Microsoft actively cooperated with the NSA to thwart the software giant's own encryption in order to intercept private communications belonging to Microsoft users. Snowden's leaks also revealed that Microsoft was the first to cooperate with PRISM, the NSA's massive surveillance data mining program. The documents, released by *The Guardian,* also revealed that Microsoft allowed the NSA and their clandestine data troll—PRISM—entrée to Hotmail, Live, and Outlook emails prior to encryption. Ryan Neal of *International Business Times* reports that, "Microsoft also worked with the FBI to help the NSA access the SkyDrive (now OneDrive), a Microsoft cloud storage service with more than 250 [now 450] million users."[4] In 2011, when Microsoft bought Skype, it allowed PRISM to gather video and audio conversations as well. *Smile... you're on Candid Camera.*

And it wasn't just Microsoft that rolled over and played dead with your privacy; other co-conspirators included Apple, Google, Facebook, Yahoo, and AOL. Referring to this collaboration between government snoops and corporate turncoats like Microsoft, Neal concludes, "Perhaps most alarming, the data collected through PRISM was not limited to the NSA, but also shared with the FBI and CIA. One document called the program a 'team sport.'"[5] In fact, the document you're reading right now would go a giant step further, defining this exemplary teamwork model between government and its partner corporations as "totalitarian."

"But the enemy I see wears a cloak of decency"

None of this is really that surprising. Bill Gates is a global political figure because he is unfathomably wealthy—his fortune amassed by spearheading a company hell-bent on dominating every aspect of the technology playing field while not taking any prisoners. Bill Gates and Paul Allen's days in Redmond, Washington, resembled William Tecumseh Sherman marching through a smoldering Georgia. So massive was Microsoft and so powerful was their stranglehold on the industry that they were hauled into federal court over countless anti-trust violations. Microsoft made a deal with the Feds to change their behavior but the die was cast.

Today, billions upon billions of dollars in philanthropic endowments have bought him attention and, for awhile, hero worship—until, of course, a closer look revealed a ravenous wolf-capitalist in sheep's clothing. Fortunately, some courageous journalists weren't put to sleep by the Bill and Melinda Gates Foundation and their untold billions earmarked to help save the world.

A *Los Angeles Times* investigative team broke a major story in 2007 that revealed investments made by the Gates Foundation recouped millions from corporations specifically held responsible for problems the Foundation claimed they're committed to eradicating. For instance, in Africa, in the Niger Delta, Bill and Melinda financed programs to combat polio and measles while at the very same time pumping in excess of $400 million dollars into major oil companies (including Chevron, Exxon Mobil, and Shell). These same corporations bear much of the guilt in the region for the various forms of pollution responsible for a host of killer health problems the indigenous population is forced to live and die with everyday. Bill and Melinda invested in major American and Canadian polluters including the ill-famed Dow Chemical. Bill and Melinda also want to help wipe HIV and AIDS off the planet. That's sweet but the Foundation has invested in pharmaceutical giants who sell drugs that cost infinitely more than most AIDS patients around the globe can actually afford.[6]

A *Mother Jones* headline in late 2013 underscored this reality: "The Gates Foundation's Hypocritical Investments." The publication reports that the Foundation's endowment guidelines pronounce: *"[O]ur nutrition efforts focus on delivering proven interventions and developing better tools and strategies for providing pregnant women and young children with the foods and nutrients they need."* And then the Foundation invested more than $2 billion in Coca-Cola, McDonald's, Pepsico, Burger King, KFC, Taco Bell, and Pizza Hut.[7]

So much for fucking nutrition.

Bill Gates says that, "As a businessman, I believe the free market fuels growth. Unfortunately, the market often fails to address the needs of the poorest." Sounds promising, right? But then the Gates Foundation invested more than $1 billion in Walmart and the Arkansas junk dealer's continued assault on the workforce.[8]

The Gates Foundation promotes that Bill and Melinda *"have defined areas in which the endowment will not invest, such as companies whose profit model is centrally tied to corporate activity that they find egregious."* And then the Foundation invested almost $5 million in GEO (a private prison company) and G4S (a private UK company that operates juvenile detention facilities in the U.S.). In fact, in 2015, a Florida Grand Jury called G4S's facilities "a disgrace to the state of Florida" and called for one location to be shut down.[9] GEO, the private prison company—like all private prison companies—needs to continually foster mass incarceration to make money. *Mother Jones* reports that, "In its most recent annual report to investors, private prison company GEO Group listed some risks to its bottom line, including 'reductions in crime rates' that 'could lead to reductions in arrests, convictions and sentences,' along with immigration reform and the decriminalization of drugs."[10]

Bill and Melinda also want to overhaul the public education system. Now, we're not suggesting that this system doesn't need an utter and complete overhaul—a revolution of epic proportion is needed—but not from elite billionaires whose solutions remain completely market-based and accountable to no one. On MSNBC, journalist Joanne Barkan referred to this as "democracy deficit."[11] Discussing the base motivations of "the Big Three" so-called benevolent billionaire education funding sources (Bill Gates: Microsoft, Sam Walton: Walmart, Eli Broad: Sun America/KB Homes), Barkan writes that:

> [T]heir market-based goals for overhauling public education coincide: choice, competition, deregulation, accountability, and data-based decision-making. And they fund the same vehicles to achieve their goals: charter schools, high-stakes standardized testing for students, merit pay for teachers whose students improve their test scores, firing teachers and closing schools when scores don't rise adequately, and longitudinal data collection on the performance of every student and teacher.[12]

One final thought to ponder regarding Microsoft Bill, the Boy Scout who was quick to point the traitorous finger at Edward Snowden. Mr. Gates should look deeply into his own associations and behavior before making bogus pronouncements and casting stones. Jeffrey Epstein—the infamous (read: scumbag) convicted sex *offender* (that's journalism speak for "rapist" and "pedophile" when a rich guy exploits and viciously abuses *underage women*... more media-speak to rewrite the actual word for the real victims: "children")—lured millionaires, billionaires, captains of industry, politicians, and assorted other rich cocksuckers (that's the real word for "cocksucker") to his elite sphere of financial and debased influence. People you may have heard of like Bill Clinton and Donald Trump, to name just a couple in his collection of big cheeses. Now, we're positive and very sure that these upstanding men were not involved in Epstein's web of sex trafficking and the rape of young girls—hell, these are family men and church-going men who have lived lives of innocence personified. And then there was the "sweetheart" plea deal negotiated by rabid Harvard mouthpiece, Alan Dershowitz, along with the U.S. Attorney for the Southern District of Florida, Alexander Acosta, that essentially shut down the FBI's investigation as well as its 53-page indictment that was never presented to a Grand Jury. In fact, the investigation revealed a mountain of incriminating testimony from a bountiful victim pool—testimony that included illicit actions like twelve-year-old triplets flown in from France for Epstein's birthday. Happy Birthday, Jeff.

Bill Gates, the world's second richest person, began his relationship with Epstein AFTER Jeff was convicted of his sex crimes. "[B]eginning in 2011, Mr. Gates met with Mr. Epstein on numerous occasions—including at least three times at Mr. Epstein's palatial Manhattan townhouse, and at least once staying late into the night," reports *The New York Times,* based on interviews with more than a dozen people familiar with the relationship. *The Times* also reports that representatives of the Gates Foundation paid "multiple visits to Mr. Epstein's mansion," discussing a proposed multibillion-dollar J.P.Morgan charitable fund "that had the potential to generate enormous fees for Mr. Epstein." Bill and Jeff kept seeing each other and Jeff actually helped out with transportation costs like flying Gates on his private Gulfstream jet to his Palm Beach estate from Teterboro Airport in New Jersey—the same airport Epstein was arrested at in 2019 on additional sex trafficking charges.

Whatever Gates was up to is immaterial. The fact that he embraced a well-known gutter dirtbag degenerate like Epstein and then pointed his finger at a courageous political patriot like Edward Snowden, suggesting treason, should tell you all you need to know about William Henry Gates III.

So why undress money bags for 1,331 words regarding his comments on Snowden, surveillance, and whistleblowers? Because Gates is an operational cog in this predatory-capitalist paradigm that the Empire's surveillance machinery is designed to protect. His comments, his philosophy, and his anti-democratic actions in the corporate stratosphere are in service to protect the investments of the most powerful empire the world has ever seen. Obviously, George Orwell wasn't speaking about Bill Gates, but he was referring to Gates' predecessors as well as cementing a great universal truth, when he wrote: *The further a society drifts from the truth, the more it will hate those that speak it.*

And that's why Gates and the long line of government apologists behind him attempt to destroy the messengers, the whistleblowers, the truth-seekers, and the few journalists who dare question the status quo.

Americans in particular are very good at acting and voting against their own best interests. They are easily bamboozled into believing that Julian Assange is up to no good, that Chelsea Manning and Edward Snowden are traitors, and that Glenn Greenwald should hang for his treasonous actions. Accusing these gutsy individuals of being enemies of the state is tantamount to sucker punching your mailman in the face when he hands you a legal notice letting you know you've been swindled out of your inheritance.

Author and social critic Henry Giroux calls this current American disease "Totalitarian Paranoia in the Post-Orwellian Surveillance State." That is our current dystopian narrative: massive surveillance (backed up by ubiquitous military might) will protect the captains of industry, the houses of wealth, and the ever-revving engine of capital. Even the lie—that massive surveillance stands in duty to freedom, liberty, and democracy—is believed by very few individuals. It's no more than a zombie-like mantra spoken over and over because, for the anesthetized masses, it's easier than facing the truth. Ask yourselves and then someone should ask Bill Gates: *Who's the hero? And who's the traitor?*

Well-Connected

People who study and run predictive models about technology in the near future forecast that by the year 2025 there could be more than 75 billion electronic devices linked to the Internet: from the obvious, like your laptop, phone, and Kindle, to your refrigerator that will calculate food inventory and announce when your milk is about to go sour. The flow of personal data will be complete and omnipresent.[13]

Familiar with Big Pharma? Well, say hello to *Big Data,* your new best friend and a skyrocketing multi-billion dollar monster business. Passively named "data aggregators," these powerful and rapacious companies buy (your) data from almost any entity (banks, healthcare providers, retailers, travel/leisure companies, etc.) and then sell the analyzed and supersized "Big Data" to any third-party who wants to purchase it.[14] Alice Marwick, writing for *The New York Review of Books,* observes that a profound amount of information about your behavior, activities, even "who you are," both online and off, "are combined, analyzed, and sold to marketers, corporations, governments, and even criminals. The scope of this collection, aggregation, and brokering of information is similar to, if not larger than, that of the NSA, yet it is almost entirely unregulated."[15] In fact, much of the behavior of these Big Data firms is entirely unknown to the public.

Catherine Crump and Matthew Harwood from the ACLU argue that no, nothing is sacred. "What will come next?" they ask. "Will eating habits collected by smart fridges be repackaged and sold to healthcare or insurance companies as predictors of obesity or other health problems—and so a reasonable basis for determining premiums?"[16] Everything in your house—television, thermostat, and toilet—will connect to Al Gore's information highway, transmitting data to entities that all fancy a piece of your action. "[T]he Googles, the Facebooks—make money off their users' personal data and they want a cut of the spoils," warn Crump and Harwood. "Your home will know your secrets, and chances are it will have loose lips."[17]

As the American population gets sucked down into this rabbit hole, the matrix of our lives—what we do in our cars, our bedrooms, even in the far-reaches of our mind—"will be monitored and analyzed in ever more intrusive ways by corporations and, by extension, the government."[18] And therein lies the final nail driven into the ankles of liberty. Crump and Harwood discuss the logical next step:

> When everything is increasingly tracked and viewed through the lens of technological omniscience, what will the effect be on dissent and protest? Will security companies with risk assessment software troll through our data and crunch it to identify people they believe have the propensity to become criminals or troublemakers—and then share that with law enforcement? (Something like it already seems to be happening in Chicago, where police are using computer analytic programs to identify people at a greater risk of violent behavior.)[19]

History, together with the current American security state, screams out that the government will do (and has done) almost anything to get their hands on private information to utilize against anyone they deem dubious. "Law enforcement will exploit any database built, if it makes it easier to figure out what the rest of us are up to," Crump and Harwood suggest. They report that Experian, a major data aggregator, plainly told a Senate Committee that "government agencies" purchase information from them all the time.[20]

Predictive Pop Tarts

"Big Four" accounting conglomerate, Deloitte Touche Tohmatsu, outside of their general bean counting also makes mountains of dough "consulting" other makers of mountains of dough. Together with KPMG, Ernst & Young, and PricewaterhouseCoopers, "these four firms form a powerful cartel that wields tremendous clout in the finance, business and government circles worldwide," writes investigative reporter Bruce Livesey at Canada's *National Observer.* "Their influence seeps into every aspect of the economy."[21] And guess what? Deloitte (with $43.2 billion in revenue back in 2018 alone[22]) is boldly advertising to cliquey government eyes "Investigative Analytics—Leveraging data for law enforcement insights."[23] They warn their readers (read: prospective government clients flush with taxpayer cash):

> The digital world presents investigators with a massive, seemingly impenetrable wall of data. For example, in one year alone, a single FBI investigation collected six petabytes of data—the equivalent of more than 120 million filing cabinets filled with paper... Without effective data analysis, law enforcement agencies will struggle to counter the criminal actors they are charged with targeting.[24]

Have no fear, law enforcement agencies. Deloitte will partner with you and "deliver" (that's a great corporate buzz word) the necessary investigative tools and techniques to handle your maximum overload. Then they lower the bait:

> Artificial intelligence (AI), open source data management tools, predictive analytics solutions, and social media exploitation capabilities are helping many investigators and operators make sense of mountains of data.[25]

If one word in that fish food above didn't jump out and punch you in the face, please read again:

> Artificial intelligence (AI), open source data management tools, predictive analytics solutions, and social media exploitation capabilities are helping many investigators and operators make sense of mountains of data.

We wager you got it that time—*predictive.*

PREDICTIVE. PREDICTIVE. PREDICTIVE.

And this trend isn't new. The FBI as well as police departments across the nation have been implementing these programs and technologies "despite scant evidence of reliability, with little public debate or transparency, amid serious concerns about racial inequities."[26] Mountains of dough—again, taxpayers' dough—has been flowing into the coffers of these private corporations creating and/ or implementing *predictive police technology,* companies like IBM, Microsoft (of course), Hitachi, and yes, Deloitte, among others. Ezekiel Edwards of the ACLU (one of those pain-in-the-ass civil liberties organizations trying to defend the Constitution against these barbarians) warns:

> Data collected by police is notoriously bad (we don't even know how many people police kill every year), easily manipulated, glaringly incomplete, and too often undermined by racial bias. When you feed a predictive tool contaminated data, it will produce polluted predictions. *In fact, it appears predictive policing software is more accurate at predicting policing than predicting crime.* Rather than informing us where criminals will be and when they will commit crimes, these algorithms more reliably predict where the police will deploy.[27] [Emphasis added]

From Russia With Love (Part One)

Edward Snowden, from his memoir *Permanent Record—*

America's fundamental laws exist to make the job of law enforcement not easier but harder. This isn't a bug, it's a core feature of democracy. In the American system, law enforcement is expected to protect citizens from one another. In turn, the courts are expected to restrain that power when it's abused, and to provide redress against the only members of society with the domestic authority to detain, arrest, and use force—including lethal force. Among the most important restraints are the prohibitions against law enforcement surveilling private citizens on their property and taking possession of their private recordings without a warrant.[28]

Critics of policing by statistical prognostication strongly caution against the practice, suggesting that it's only as good as the intrinsic practices of the department or agency using it. That's actually generous of the critics because as history proves—beyond any shadow of any doubt—federal law enforcement agencies as well as big time city police departments (and community departments) have an appalling and scandalous record of mangling, circumventing, or sidestepping constitutional protections; and when they're not playing those games, **manufacturing guilt** has become an art form. "If a police department places a premium on over-enforcement of low-level offenses over reducing communities' entanglement in the criminal justice system," explains Edwards from the ACLU, "or if its mindset is characterized by militarized aggression and not smart de-escalation, or if it dispenses with constitutional protections against unreasonable searches and seizures and racial profiling when inconvenient, then predictive tools will only increase community harm."[29]

And, of course, the increased "community harm" will affect communities of economic disadvantage and of color significantly more than say Short Hills, New Jersey, or Highland Park, Texas. If measured visually, the difference would look like Sheriff Andy Taylor in Mayberry vs. Fort Apache, The Bronx. The hard facts have been clear since the beginning of time: the chasm between whites and blacks in the land of the free, especially when it comes to the criminal justice system (stops, frisks, searches, arrests, pretrial detentions, convictions, and sentencing) resembles the Grand Canyon on a clear northern Arizona morning.

Various forms of predictive policing have been growing since the 1990s with America's cops force-feeding data points into their slick new shiny software. Edwards posits that when you feed contaminated data into the monster, it will produce polluted predictions, "which will in turn result in predictions that will have nested within them those original racial disparities."[30] Or, garbage in garbage out… racism in racism out, the goddamn American way. "As sure as the sun rises," he argues, "police will continue to enforce laws selectively against communities of color."[31] And if we know anything about the codified nature of Big Data we know that the original social and political issues—classism and racism—will be articulated within the algorithms.

Kade Crockford is the Director of the ACLU's Technology for Liberty Program, working to protect and expand First and Fourth Amendment rights in a digital age and scrutinizing how these police technologies impact their primary targets: Muslims, immigrants, people of color, and dissidents. It's a fight for liberty that must be fought and eventually won. Crockford sees predictive policing as a "tech-washing of racially discriminatory law-enforcement practices" that does little more than perpetuate the existing system and is simply "tinkering around the edges [of the criminal-justice system] and calling it revolutionary reform."[32]

Back in 2009, *Police Chief Magazine* published a seminal article promoting predictive policing. Standing in the long dirty shadow of William Parker and Daryl Gates, the piece—entitled "Predictive Policing: What Can We Learn From Wal-Mart and Amazon About Fighting Crime in a Recession?"—was written by LAPD's Chief of Police, Charlie Beck, along with a self-proclaimed "evangelist" for embracing analytics "to prevent bad things from happening," Colleen McCue (at the time a consultant for MC2 Solutions).[33] Ingrid Burrington at *AlterNet* writes, "The article likens law enforcement to a logistics dilemma, in which prioritizing where police officers patrol is analogous to identifying the likely demand for Pop-Tarts."[34]

As the post-9/11 Orwellian "Minority Report" age grows more aggressive, so does law enforcement adoration—in the media, the movies, on television, and in the general zeitgeist of rising American fascism. Loading the cops up with leftover Pentagon toys inflamed by the technology god is like putting an AK-47 in the hands of a precocious young boy who's been off his Ritalin for a few days—and unfortunately we don't have to imagine how horrendous the situation can get: we're already there. Black men gunned down—with alarming regularity—in cold-blooded murder with the white cop triggerman walking away scot-free in what former Attorney General Eric Holder called "the greatest legal system the world has ever known."[35] Sure it is, just ask Tamir Rice, Rumain Brisbon, Michael Brown, Jr., Eric Garner... you know the long list of names.

In our society we have no major crimes...but we do have a detention camp full of would-be criminals.
—Philip K. Dick, *The Minority Report* (1956)

Expecting a historically corrupt, racist, economically twisted and shattered system to magically fix itself with software analytics is delusional and self-serving. It's a money-grab by the software companies and their pimp consulting firms... and a tyrannical play by the state and American law enforcement to exploit and implement what George Orwell called "thoughtcrime" in *1984,* and what novelist Philip K. Dick later coined as "pre-crime" in the aforementioned *The Minority Report*—where "bad guys" are apprehended based on foreknowledge by psychics known as "Precogs."

Life imitating art. Tyranny imitating constitutional rule.

In a roundtable discussion at The Marshall Project (a journalism watchdog of the U.S. criminal justice system), Mallory Hanora, the Executive Director of Families for Justice as Healing, framed predictive policing this way:

> It's incredibly frustrating in a national movement moment when we're actively confronting police brutality and state violence against people of color that we're simultaneously hearing messages "community policing" and also "predictive policing"—neither of which put any accountability on police, and both of which channel resources and trust to the police while expanding their scope of power.[36]

From Dick's short story, *The Minority Report:*

> Anderton said: You've probably grasped the basic legalistic drawback to precrime methodology. We're taking in individuals who have broken no law.
>
> But they surely will, Witwer affirmed with conviction.
>
> Happily they don't—because we get them first, before they can commit an act of violence. So the commission of the crime itself is absolute metaphysics. We claim they're culpable. They, on the other hand, eternally claim they're innocent. And, in a sense, they are innocent.

Privacy Sacrosanct Until We Say It's Not

In 2014, President Barack Obama left his uncle's cabin and sauntered in front of six perfectly folded and draped American flags, with another flag adorning his lapel, and then offered a dogmatic discourse on America's long trajectory of surveillance. It was a public relations spectacle that resembled a puppet leader addressing his banana republic. In fact, Obama's manipulative speech was a bizarre history lesson—one that attempted to weave Orwellian surveillance into the bedrock of American ideals. Obama's milky dreamworld positioned Paul Revere as the country's first NSA agent, and the president's goal was clear: make the illicit actions of surveillance—and the acceptance and approval of these actions by the American people—patriotic. He began:

> At the dawn of our Republic, a small, secret surveillance committee born out of the Sons of Liberty was established in Boston. And the group's members included Paul Revere. At night they would patrol the streets, reporting back any signs that the British were preparing raids against America's early patriots.[37]

"Audacious" doesn't even begin to describe the stretch marks on that one. Michael Ratner was president emeritus of the Center for Constitutional Rights. They represent Julian Assange and WikiLeaks along with other journalists and news organizations. Ratner wrote of Obama's ploy:

> Collecting the meta-data of billions of phone calls and 200 million text messages a day, as well as gathering data through the government's PRISM program and placing bugs in 100,000 computers all over the world seems significantly more extensive than monitoring British troop movement via horseback and candlestick—especially when you consider that the data being collected is in large part that of the American people, not a foreign enemy during war time.[38]

The American colonies rebelled against King George for a host of reasons. What Obama the history teacher conveniently leaves out was the "British Empire's use of general warrants—including 'writs of assistance,' that allowed agents of the king to search and seize colonial property, including letters and papers,"[39] Ratner reminds us. This unchecked exploitation of privacy and personal freedom was an abuse the framers of the new American constitution expressly addressed in the Bill of Rights, specifically the Fourth Amendment.

Throughout American history, the pendulum has rocked between civil libertarians who embrace the actual language and spirit of the Fourth Amendment regarding the absolute necessity for *probable cause* along with a *legitimate and very specific warrant*—and the various government factions who continually attempt to stage-manage the Constitution with aggressive, warrantless surveillance. For instance, it's laughable (and dangerous) how far off course the stated intent of the FISA court has swerved from its original creation in 1978 as an allegedly vital watchdog preventing U.S. Government agencies from trampling over constitutional rights. Ratner wrote that FISA—*from the beginning*—has had a "horrendous track record of authorizing a massive spying operation" on American citizens and is nothing more than "a rubber stamp... with a tendency to never say no."[40]

From Russia With Love (Part Two)

Edward Snowden, from his memoir *Permanent Record*—

The constitutional system only functions as a whole if and when each of its three branches works as intended. When all three don't just fail, but fail deliberately and with coordination, the result is a culture of impunity. I realized that I was crazy to have imagined that the Supreme Court, or Congress, or President Obama, seeking to distance his administration from President George W. Bush's, would ever hold the IC (Intelligence Community) legally responsible—for anything. It was time to face the fact that the IC believed themselves above the law, and given how broken the process was, they were right. The IC had come to understand the rules of our system better than the people who had created it, and they used that knowledge to their advantage.

They'd hacked the Constitution.[41]

In Obama's "surveillance is patriotic" harangue—one in which he painted glorious images of Union balloons soaring over Confederate campfires, code breakers deciphering Japanese war plans, and Truman's heroic creation of the NSA to combat the evil Soviet empire—the 44th president's solution to dealing with secret court was to create an advocacy group that would defend civil liberties and privacy issues. *Come again?* An advocacy group to argue and remind JUDGES about constitutional protections? Aren't these protections (albeit mythical) the bedrock of American jurisprudence? No, they're not. Never have been. And guess what—the powerbrokers in this country know it.

As you've no doubt noticed, when we want to get to the heart of the matter, we turn to the great American truth-teller George Carlin (the Samuel Clemens of his generation):

> Politicians are put there to give you the idea that you have freedom of choice—you don't. You have no choice. You have owners. They own you. They own everything… The table has tilted folks. The game is rigged and nobody seems to notice. Nobody seems to care… Continue to elect these rich cocksuckers who don't give a fuck about you. *They don't give a fuck about you.* They don't care about you at all—*at all*—and nobody seems to notice. Nobody seems to

> care. That's what the owners count on: the fact that Americans will probably remain willfully ignorant of the big red, white and blue dick that's being jammed up their assholes everyday.[42]

Thanks, George.

I was a constitutional law professor, which means unlike the current president, I actually respect the Constitution.
—Candidate Barack Obama (at a 2007 fundraiser)[43]

Obama's quote is every bit as funny as Carlin's except the comedy is not based in truth but in farce. His actions when president can only be seen as a mockery and willful disregard of the United States Constitution. But that's nothing new in the arc of American history. Shortly after Obama's 2014 NSA speech, another comedian and truth-seeker, Jon Stewart, framed Obama's embrace of tyrannical secrecy over democratic transparency:

> Basically, the rule is: *We will totally follow the rules until such a time that we determine that we will no longer follow the rules. But don't worry about it—you won't hear about it 'cause we're going to do it in secret.*[44]

As referenced earlier, the Foreign Intelligence Surveillance Act, or FISA, was introduced in 1977 after wide-ranging congressional investigations revealed belligerent and patently illegal Nixon-era domestic surveillance programs as well as massive federal resources utilized to spy on Americans, especially dissident political activists. FISA was enacted to provide congressional and judicial oversight of the U.S. government's covert surveillance activities, with special regard for curtailing spying on Americans. In the post-9/11 dystopia, all three branches of the U.S. government have gone hog-wild twisting FISA every which way but loose. Amendments to the Act were fast and furious:

- USA PATRIOT Act of 2001
- Terrorist Surveillance Act of 2006
- National Security Surveillance Act of 2006
- Foreign Intelligence Surveillance Improvement & Enhancement Act of 2006

- Electronic Surveillance Modernization Act of 2006 (this died in the Senate)
- Protect America Act of 2007
- FISA Amendments Act of 2008
- Foreign Intelligence Surveillance Act of 1978 Amendments Act of 2008
- USA Freedom Act of 2015

And then, the...

- FISA Amendments Reauthorization Act of 2017 (in force through 2023)

"By signing this Act today," writes Donald J. Trump from the White House in January of 2018 (or whichever ghostwriter knew where to put the commas and the periods), "I am ensuring that this lawful and essential intelligence program will continue to protect Americans for at least the next 6 years. We cannot let our guard down in the face of foreign threats to our safety, our freedom, and our way of life."[45] The insane clown president is referencing his signing of the FISA Amendments Reauthorization Act of 2017, which civil liberty watchdog groups warn that the government will use to continue their warrantless intrusions into Americans' private electronic communications. Just before the U.S. Senate voted on this controversial surveillance program, one that will fuel American spy operations and codify illegal practices into law, the ACLU shouted from the highest mountain:

> "No president should have this power. Yet, members of Congress just voted to hand it to an administration that has labeled individuals as threats based merely on their religion, nationality, or viewpoints. The Senate should reject this bill and rein in government surveillance powers to bring Section 702 in line with the Constitution."[46]

Of course the Senate voted overwhelming in favor of the measure, 65 to 34. "Today, the United States Congress struck a significant blow against the basic human right to read, write, learn, and associate free of government's prying eyes,"[47] wrote Cindy Cohn, Executive Director of the Electronic Frontier Foundation. No matter which amended FISA Act is used and/or abused, the government—either unintentionally or by design—collects and sifts through untold numbers of domestic communications by way of warrantless surveillance. "Goaded by those who let fear override democratic principles," Cohn stresses, "some members of

Congress shuttered public debate in order to pass a bill that extends the National Security Agency's unconstitutional Internet surveillance for six years." This newfangled FISA action gives the FBI open access to the massive NSA-collected data "for purposes of routine domestic law enforcement that stray far from the original justification of national security."[48] The United States Senate—enablers and promoters of great autocratic rule. In fact, the Don King on such matters.

In 1970, at the height of the Vietnam War, the Democratic senator from South Dakota stood naked in front of his "brethren" and rocked Capitol Hill, his words roaring through the cavernous hall: "This chamber reeks of blood"—the horrid truth ricocheting off the so-called hallowed walls and the red Levanto marble pilasters. In fact McGovern's words that day were a paraphrase of John Bright—the greatest radical orator in all of 19th-century England... and in many ways, the corrupt Washington barbarians, your spineless and gutless elected leaders, have never wiped the blood (literal or figurative) off their fucking walls.

The Empire's Planetary Panopticon

The American government has been spying on its citizens as well as the citizens of the world since the first days of the new republic. Echoing Thomas Jefferson's days at Monticello when he gleefully spied on his slaves from his own domestic panopticon high above Mulberry Row, surveillance—both domestic and foreign—has been a major component of the emerging nation's and then the growing Empire's DNA. It has been a tool and a weapon as important (or more important) than the drums of war, bombs bursting in air, and boots on the ground.

What was surmised and/or known in many quarters (even before Edward Snowden's revelations) was that Washington's massive surveillance complex was profoundly entrenched and growing deeper and more colossal by the day. The beast now borders on one frightening definition: all-seeing and all-pervading. It's a motherfucker of anti-democratic totalitarian rule. Whether the surveillance takes place domestically and targets individuals dissenting against their country's behavior, or looks in on foreign leaders (enemy or friend) in the supposed safe confines of their own office in their so-called sovereign nation, America's brazen globo-cop operates with complete impunity and with a level of hubris heretofore unseen. In fact, the National Security Agency has a favorite term, a catchphrase, and one they spread throughout their documents: "collect it all." The phrase is so fitting it should be their "don't leave home without it" advertising slogan.

From Russia With Love (Part Three)

Edward Snowden, from his memoir *Permanent Record*—

After a decade of mass surveillance, the technology had proved itself to be a potent weapon less against terror and more against liberty itself. By continuing these programs, by continuing these lies, America was protecting little, winning nothing, and losing much—until there would be few distinctions left between those post-9/11 polarities of "Us" and "Them."[49]

What's more, this bald-faced American surveillance apparatus gets great support from computer manufacturers as they fly stealth anywhere they damn well please. Reuters reports that Russian researchers uncovered a massive hard drive infiltration operation attacking hard drives on personal computers in thirty countries worldwide—penetration courtesy of stealth NSA spying software. How does Reuters know? Former NSA workers have confirmed the operation. And how did the NSA get in and infect personal hard drives? First of all, they would have needed access to "the proprietary source code that directs the actions of the hard drives." And where would one get this information? From the manufacturers themselves, of course—companies like Toshiba, Western Digital, and Seagate among others. This access gives "the agency the means to eavesdrop on the majority of the world's computers," Reuters reports.[50] Ultimately, unbridled cyberespionage.

University of Wisconsin-Madison professor Alfred McCoy argues that this technological maelstrom "fulfills an ancient dream of empire. With a few computer key strokes, the agency has solved the problem that has bedeviled world powers since at least the time of Caesar Augustus: how to control unruly local leaders, who are the foundation for imperial rule, by ferreting out crucial, often scurrilous, information to make them more malleable."[51] Life, liberty, and the pursuit of blackmail, dirt, and lies.

But the motivation behind the skyrocketing growth of this mechanized imperial steamroller is not solely the dramatic explosion of technological wizardry in the so-called information age, but something much more foundational and ordinary: *money*—the all-important bottom line.

Advanced technology (electronic, computer, and satellite) has no doubt fueled the sweeping and spectacular abilities of American surveillance. As expected, this growth industry comes with a price tag... but the cost is surprisingly low and a real bargain for an Empire that so cavalierly paid more than $3 trillion dollars for its recent slaughter of the Iraqi people in addition to hemorrhaging more of your money on recent wars throughout the Middle East and Africa. For a back-in-the-day example and comparison regarding American killing versus spying, the NSA's 2012 budget was a paltry $11 billion for cyberwarfare—such a deal compared to wholesale pillage and slaughter.

Professor McCoy suggests that America's imperial thirst has embraced and enjoyed "a cost-savings bonanza."[52] As the Empire slowly loses its share of the world's gross economic productivity, "the US will need to find new ways to exercise its power far more economically," McCoy argues. "As the Cold War took off, a heavy-metal US military—with 500 bases worldwide circa 1950—was sustainable because the country controlled some 50% of the global gross product."[53] But with America's diminishing economic strength (world output falling, domestic spending rising), McCoy writes that, "cost-cutting becomes imperative if Washington is to survive as anything like the planet's 'sole superpower.'"[54]

Shrouded in Secrecy

Lest we forget, the U.S. government proudly funds and then unleashes seventeen separate intelligence agencies on its own citizens as well as the citizens of the world. The budget for this seventeen-pronged operation is part of the overall "annual tally for war, preparations for war, and the impact of war" paid for by the American taxpayer—approximately $1.25 trillion (with a "T") dollars.[55]

This breakdown was researched and reported by the Project On Government Oversight (or POGO)—a nonpartisan independent watchdog that investigates and exposes waste, corruption, abuses of power, as well as when the government fails to serve the public or silences those who report wrongdoing. Their analysis of the Trump administration's 2020 budget is a "dollar-by-dollar tour of the National Security State." In fact the U.S. government's $1.25 trillion dollar annual tally for war and the National Security State is more than double the Pentagon's budget. "If the average taxpayer were aware that this amount was being spent in the name of national defense—with much of it wasted, misguided, or simply counterproductive," reports Mandy Smithberger and William Hartung from POGO, "it might be far harder for the national security state to consume ever-growing sums with minimal public pushback. For now, however, the gravy train is running full speed ahead..."[56]

Even researchers and analysts who study America's declared budgets (and black budgets) on intelligence spending "know remarkably little"[57] about the actual nature of the beast. For instance, in the 2020 budget statistics released by the U.S. government, the total for intelligence is more than $80 billion. "The bulk of this funding, including for the CIA and NSA, is believed to be hidden under obscure line items in the Pentagon budget," Smithberger and Hartung conclude. It's a goddamn 34th Street shell game—except this shell game offers "at least 10 separate pots of money dedicated to fighting wars, preparing for yet more wars, and dealing with the consequences of wars already fought."[58] Smithberger and Hartung then lower the boom:

> So the next time a president, a general, a secretary of defense, or a hawkish member of Congress insists that the U.S. military is woefully underfunded, think twice. A careful look at U.S. defense expenditures offers a healthy corrective to such wildly inaccurate claims.[59]

Lists are good for a few things: buying groceries, things to do at work, and of course listing your enemies a la Dick Nixon. Let's add one more excellent list, one that clearly defines the omnipresent nature of America's tyrannical spy network—the big seventeen:

1. Department of Homeland Security Office of Intelligence and Analysis
2. Federal Bureau of Investigation
3. Central Intelligence Agency
4. National Security Agency
5. Defense Intelligence Agency
6. State Department's Bureau of Intelligence and Research
7. Drug Enforcement Agency's Office of National Security Intelligence
8. Treasury Department's Office of Intelligence and Analysis
9. Department of Energy's Office of Intelligence and Counterintelligence
10. National Reconnaissance Office
11. National Geospatial-Intelligence Agency
12. Air Force Intelligence, Surveillance and Reconnaissance
13. Army Intelligence and Security Command
14. Office of Naval Intelligence
15. Marine Corps Intelligence
16. Coast Guard Intelligence

Where's number 17 you ask? It's the Office of the Director of National Intelligence—this agency dedicated to coordinating the activities of the other sixteen agencies. And let's not forget that this tangled labyrinth of privacy invasion has burrowed and bored its tentacles deep into the ubiquitous and all-pervading carnival that is the 21st-century communications maze. We now know that the U.S. government's track record of breaching privacy in this electronic wizardry is long, odious, and ongoing when it comes to their various spook agencies' (especially the NSA's) illegal intrusions and excursions into citizens' emails, phone calls, and social media connections. There are simply too many indisputable reported examples of breaking and entering to catalog here, but no matter, we all know the hard facts as revealed by many, including Edward Snowden, Glenn Greenwald, *DemocracyNow,* CNN, *The New York Times, Washington Post,* etcetera.

Here's a perfect case in point as reported by the Brennan Center for Justice at New York University and *The Intercept.* Hundreds of thousands of Americans (in more than 600 actions nationwide) protested the Trump administration's cruel and oppressive so-called immigration policy—in particular, family separation. The protests called out Trump's racist xenophobia and subsequently demanded the abolition of ICE (U.S. Immigration and Customs Enforcement) as well as the National Rifle Association. As we all know, social media remains a very effective tool when organizing people, protests, and actions. Citizens watch, listen, and galvanize. That's the good news. What's the illegal and unconstitutional bad news? So does the Department of Homeland Security.

In early 2019, a Virginia-based private intelligence contractor (Looking-Glass Cyber Solutions) used copious Facebook data to gather intel on the 600 actions protesting family separation—and shared its findings with Homeland Security "where the data was disseminated internally," and then was "shared with the FBI and national fusion centers,"[60] writes Rachel Levinson-Waldman, Senior Counsel at the Brennan Center. "[T]hese centers, which facilitate data sharing among federal, state, local, and tribal law enforcement, as well as the private sector, have been heavily criticized for violating Americans' privacy and civil liberties while providing little of value."[61] Ryan Devereaux, award-winning journalist covering immigration enforcement for *The Intercept,* has revealed that, "In the last two years, law enforcement agencies executing the Trump administration's immigration agenda have cracked down on critics of the president's policies."[62] Other great leaders have also embraced this stratagem: Mussolini and Stalin come to mind.

Here's how it unfolded with the immigration protests. Homeland Security Investigations (HSI) is a division of ICE that was created to combat (according to their website) "criminal organizations." HSI was not charged with gathering intel on protesting Americans, but nonetheless "assembled and shared a spreadsheet of the New York City demonstrations, labeling them with the tag "Anti-Trump Protests,"[63] reports Levinson-Waldman. As the Central American refugees continued toward the promised land boldly advertising *Give me your tired, your poor, Your huddled masses yearning to breathe free,* "DHS's Customs and Border Protection **drew on Facebook data to create dossiers on lawyers, journalists, and advocates—many of them U.S. citizens**—providing services and documenting the situation on the southern border."[64] [Emphasis added]

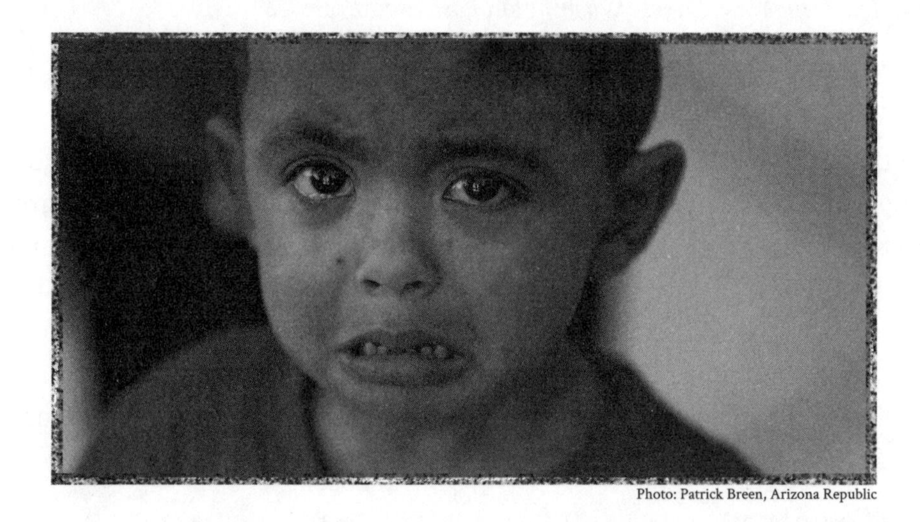

Photo: Patrick Breen, Arizona Republic

It's especially concerning given that these protests were basically thousands of moms and their kids, thousands of families, and that the Trump administration's response to that was to put them on a watch list.[65]
—Jess Morales Rocketto, co-chair of Families Belong Together

As discussed briefly in Book One of this series, the "Panopticon" is an architectural concept created by the English thinker Jeremy Bentham. He devised the concept of a secretive circular structure that would allow a single watchman the ability to survey almost every inmate in a prison or institution. Albeit extremely difficult to watch every inmate at every moment, the shrouded Panopticon forces those being watched to assume they are being scrutinized at every moment. In fact, the name derives its meaning from the Greek mythological figure "Panoptes"—a giant with one hundred eyes, making him one helleva watchman.

Sound familiar?

Control Everything

Neither a man nor a crowd nor a nation can be trusted to act humanely or to think sanely under the influence of a great fear.
—Bertrand Russell
(philosopher, mathematician, social critic, anti-imperialist, and antiwar activist)

Like "Panoptes," the tentacles of American state surveillance are countless and far-reaching. The Empire's insatiable craving for information-gathering centers around its drive for ultimate control of, well, *everything.* It's about consolidating power on both the domestic and foreign fronts. The ability for Washington to achieve this goal also depends on its ability to control, twist, warp, and fabricate the ongoing message—political manipulations always underwritten by fear and designed to force the body politic to acquiesce and gladly submit to any intrusion by the state. "To hell with privacy. To hell with the Constitution, the Bill of Rights. Take my wife, please, anything... Just keep me safe!"

"Philosophers have long noted the utility of fear to the state," writes Northwestern philosophy professor Peter Ludlow. "Machiavelli notoriously argued that a good leader should induce fear in the populace in order to control the rabble."[66] A major component of this fear mongering is pitting the "rabble" against one another. Create suspicion and paranoia throughout America: *"the other" may lurk among you. There's an enemy within.*

The red herring becomes real. Surveillance becomes salvation.

In fact, the groundswell of panic that rumbles through the country, like rolling thunder, also allows the Empire to carry out brutal actions on foreign shores without the threat of significant dissent, let alone domestic insurrection. War, torture, extraordinary rendition, secret detention, assassination of foreign leaders, assassination of American citizens, proxy wars and regime change all become necessary realities of a nation, as Russell warned, "under the influence of a great fear."

Lest you believe the national security state has not escaped from the laboratory like Victor Frankenstein's monster, digest this analysis by none other than Erik Prince—former Navy SEAL, the founder of the malevolent mercenary outfit Blackwater (aka Xe Services, aka Academi), and the absolute crown prince of darkness:

> America is way too quick to trade freedom for the illusion of security. Whether it's allowing the NSA to go way too far in what it intercepts of our personal data, to our government monitoring of everything domestically and spending way more than we should. I don't know if I want to live in a country where lone wolf and random terror attacks are impossible 'cause that country would look more like North Korea than America.[67]

Those words are not from Noam Chomsky or Naomi Klein… but *Erik Prince*—one of the coldblooded and terrifying faces of the American war machine, loaded on steroids and Jesus. Turn out the lights and shut the door. Cue the fat lady. It's over when Erik Prince starts making sense.

But just in case it's not over and we actually stand a chance of reclaiming our birthright, here is a brief and somewhat unruly look at the American surveillance apparatus and the various programs stomping on the rights of man.

❖ Federal Bureau of Investigation

The FBI grew in leaps and bounds throughout the 20th century. The ringleader and chief architect of Washington's top cop shop was J. Edgar Hoover, who Franklin Roosevelt gave immense authority to when he authorized this noxious and racist goon to wiretap phone lines with impunity. From that moment on, Hoover's clandestine empire was forever secure. In fact, more than any other single person in recent American history—from his vile attack campaign on Rev. Dr. Martin Luther King, through the dark and filthy shadows of COINTELRPO—he personally built the giant water slide funneling everyone into the national security state. "The FBI, since its founding, has generally steered clear of major crime like the Mafia," writes Gore Vidal in his book *Imperial America.* "In fact, much of its time and energies have been devoted to spying on those Americans whose political beliefs did not please the late J. Edgar Hoover," he continues, "a man who hated Commies, blacks, and women in, more or less, that order."[68] Vidal also reminds us that America's top cop positioned the Bureau as a willing and "collaborating tool" for slime-ball politicians as they destroyed the lives of targeted opponents—what Vidal described as "a nasty talent for amusing presidents with lurid dossiers on their political enemies."[69]

The ACLU reports that the FBI "has robust powers to peer into the lives of American citizens. But the FBI claims even broader authorities when acting in the nebulous realm of 'national security' [and] 'domestic intelligence,' where its actions are largely hidden from public view and the procedural checks and balances that apply in criminal investigations are all but non-existent."[70] (More on this to come.)

❖ Department of Homeland Security

As a knee-jerk reaction to the blowback that slammed into the Twin Towers, the Pentagon, and Shanksville, Pennsylvania, in 2001, the Department of Homeland Security was created and launched into our lives and consciousness. This behemoth federal agency actually incorporates and oversees twenty-two separate entities with vast intelligence and law enforcement powers. Incompetence and power-hungry aggression has consistently plagued this heavy-handed entity, implicating innocent victims every step of the way, especially when dealing with immigration and border security. On a roll, Vidal turns his sharp and scornful eyes on this anti-democratic monstrosity of a federal agency:

> For one thing, we no longer live in a nation, but in a Homeland... Now, when we have ceased to be a nation under law, but instead a homeland where the withered Bill of Rights, like a dead trumpet vine, clings to our pseudo-Roman columns, Homeland Security appears to be uniting our secret police into a single sort of Gestapo with dossiers on everyone to prevent us, somehow or other, from being terrorized by various implacable Second and Third World enemies.[71]

"Welcome to the American Gestapo." The quotation belongs to political scribe Doug Thompson, founder and publisher of *Capitol Hill Blue,* but the spirit of Thompson's salutation now enfolds all of us. Shortly after 9/11 the Bush Crime Family settled on "Homeland Security" as the moniker for the mammoth agency filled with career bureaucrats and spies, paper-pushers, cyber-geeks on a mission from God Almighty, as well as their shadowy minions ready to enforce Constitution-free zones. When asked about the etymology of the term, former Pentagon spokesman Kenneth Bacon admitted, "It does sort of have Germanic implications to it, and from that standpoint, it may carry unfortunate baggage, but I think it's descriptive."[72] Tom Ridge, the first head of Homeland Security and a guy who at one time attempted to execute one of your authors, pleaded ignorance when asked about the origins of Homeland Security: "Etymology unknown, don't have a clue."[73]

In 2002, when it wasn't popular, Doug Thompson read the totalitarian writing on the wall and offered this prescient warning:

> This new Department of Homeland Security has the power to wiretap any American it wants, without a court order, without cause and without justification to any higher authority. Homeland Security goon squads will have the power to enter any American home, without a search warrant, without probable cause, simply because someone somewhere says "hey, this guy might be a threat." No checks and balances, no due process. Nothing.[74]

Photo: Department of Homeland Security

Tom Ridge
(tough guy governor, likes to play god and pull the switch... three men murdered by the State of PA under his watch, signed more than 200 execution warrants— in 1999, he tried to kill one of your authors)

Early on, as "Vaterland Security" slithered and spread its tentacles from sea to shining sea, retired FBI Agent Franklin Postel agreed with Thompson's analysis: "We are entering a new era of domestic surveillance, one where the Constitution is secondary to the cause. The new department has the power to document the day-to-day actions of any American it chooses."[75]

Creeping Fascism: Ghosts of the past. For almost three decades, former CIA officer and intelligence analyst Ray McGovern had his finger on the pulse of the intelligence gathering apparatus of the U.S. government. In the 1980s he prepared the President's daily briefing on intelligence. Since his retirement, Ray McGovern has been a staunch and outspoken critic of American policy and actions—from the state's oppressive surveillance operations to torture and imperial warfare. McGovern understands the power of historical reference as a way to grasp the present and define the future. He reminds us of a young German lawyer and writer, Raimund Pretzel, known better by his pen name Sebastian Haffner, who documented the German people's reaction to the burning down of the Reichstag, Germany's parliament building, in 1933. "It was Germany's 9/11," McGovern writes, "after which (and you've heard the words a thousand times) 'everything changed!'"[76]

"Pretzel was there in Berlin to describe what he called the 'collective, limp collapse,'" McGovern continues, "'the nervous breakdown' of the German people.'"[77] Preztel/Haffner recalls:

> There are few things as odd as the calm, superior indifference with which we watched the beginnings of the Nazi revolution... With sheepish submissiveness, the German people accepted that, as a result of the fire, each one of them lost what little personal freedom and dignity was guaranteed by the constitution, as though it followed as a necessary consequence. No one saw anything out of the ordinary in the fact that, from now on, one's telephone would be tapped, one's letters opened, and one's desk might be broken into.[78]

The ICE-men cometh. Sometimes the Department of Homeland Security—and their ICE component—doesn't necessarily need dossiers or "intel." They just shoot and ask questions later. Actually, most of the time, they don't even bother to ask questions—shooting works out just dandy.

You've probably never heard the name José Antonio Elena Rodriguez. He *was* a resident of Nogales, Mexico—a town just across the imaginary line from Arizona. José was sixteen years old when U.S. Border Patrol agents fired multiple rounds across the border (firing from desert landscape stolen decades before by their employer—the U.S. government). The agents were retaliating because Mexican citizens were throwing rocks over the border and, as we all know so well, American exceptionalism dictates that you retaliate with guns blazing... *Just like in them Hollywood westerns... paint the town red!* Disproportionate deadly force? *Nah... just shoot the little spics. Fuck 'em, it's Miller Time... return to HQ and turn Ted Nugent up real fucking loud.*

José Antonio Elena Rodriguez was shot eleven times; seven of the shots hit him in the back. "The boy," writes Fernanda Santos of *The New York Times,* "collapsed and died on a cracked sidewalk blocks from his home, under a sign that read 'emergencias médicas.' The police in Nogales, Mexico, reported that he had been carrying only a cellphone."[79] In fact, from January 2010 through mid-2013, U.S. Border agents killed fifteen people and "not a single agent has been criminally charged in cases of lethal use of force."[80] The Department of Homeland Security began to review their policies (aka bullshit bureaucratic tap-dancing) only after sixteen members of the U.S. Congress condemned the agents as exhibiting "appalling behavior."[81] We guess Charlie Manson, David Berkowitz, and John

Wayne Gacy also exhibited "appalling behavior."

The whole aim of practical politics is to keep the populace alarmed by menacing it with an endless series of hobgoblins, all of them imaginary.
—H.L. Mencken

Under the heading of "politics shaped by fear and paranoia," operations by both the FBI and Department of Homeland Security stretch far beyond their own autocratic mission statements. "Securing the Homeland" and "National Security" triggers almost any excuse for a despotic operation. One typical example surrounds the 2011 meteoric rise and subsequent demise of the Occupy Movement. Profoundly redacted government documents secured by the Partnership for Civil Justice Fund through their Freedom of Information Act request detail how the FBI and Homeland Security defined Occupy as a criminal and terrorist threat "even though the agency acknowledges in documents that organizers explicitly called for peaceful protest and did 'not condone the use of violence' at occupy protests."[82]

The documents, although heavily edited, reveal that government agents were well engaged in major surveillance operations even before Occupy Wall Street moved into Zuccotti Park in lower Manhattan. After studying the illuminating documents, Mara Verheyden-Hilliard, the Executive Director of the Partnership for Civil Justice Fund stated that, "This production, which we believe is just the tip of the iceberg, is a window into the nationwide scope of the FBI's surveillance, monitoring, and reporting on peaceful protestors organizing with the Occupy movement."[83] Tip of the iceberg, indeed... imagine what has not been revealed. Remember, these are documents made public *by the government.*

Investigating the U.S. government's actions against constitutionally protected dissent, journalist Chris Hedges sees this severe attack on freedom as a classic byproduct of fear—an ongoing narrative (this one orchestrated by Barack Obama) "that has empowered the FBI and the Department of Homeland Security to silence the voices and obstruct the activity of citizens who question corporate power."[84] Verheyden-Hilliard agrees:

> These documents show that the FBI and the Department of Homeland Security are treating protests against the corporate and banking structure of America as potential criminal and terrorist activity. *These documents also show these federal agencies functioning as a de facto intelligence arm of Wall Street and Corporate America.*[85] [Emphasis added]

This behavior of massive and oppressive U.S. surveillance operations should only surprise those who either discount the arc of American history or those who suffer from severe bouts of amnesia. Or both.

❖ Department of ~~Defense~~ War and the NSA

The National Security Agency is the intelligence-gathering arm of the Department of War. Once again, the blowback on 9/11 proved to be a watershed moment for the intelligence community as they and others somersaulted into action. Baby Bush authorized the NSA, through executive order, "to conduct warrantless surveillance of American's e-mails and telephone calls in blatant violation of a federal statute which prohibited the practice (the Foreign Intelligence Surveillance Act)."[86] By 2006, the cat ate its way out of every bag as headlines announced the NSA's goal of collecting and logging EVERY CALL EVER MADE throughout the United States. That's a staggering admission. *USA Today* reported that the massive data mining was facilitated by the major telecommunications companies, including AT&T, Verizon, and BellSouth.[87] In fact these three giants were all under contract with the NSA. It was a very cozy relationship, and remains a very cozy relationship, with your privacy (read: liberty) hanging in the balance.

ACLU: FISA Gives NSA Almost Unchecked Power.[88] Since 2013 when *The Guardian* published documents provided by Edward Snowden that revealed the NSA's massive dragnet of international communications (which also acted as a masquerade to collect untold numbers of Americans' calls, emails, and text messages), it's been a parlor game trying to keep track of the NSA's gymnastics regarding what they collect, what they dump, and how the Congress, Courts, and Executive play along on the trampoline. For instance, in 2018, *The New York Times* reported:

> The National Security Agency vacuumed up more than 534 million records of phone calls and text messages from American telecommunications providers like AT&T and Verizon last year—more than three times what it collected in 2016...[89]

Then a year later, in 2019, the NSA "announced" that it may stop or curtail its controversial phone data surveillance program because of technical problems that led to the gathering of metadata records on Americans that it didn't have the authority to collect. Hmmmm...

Then a few months after that the Trump administration re-embraces the open drain—the headline in *Common Dreams:* "Alarm as Trump Requests Permanent Reauthorization of NSA Mass Spying Program Exposed by Snowden."[90]

Like we suggested: a parlor game. Get used to it. It's (more than likely) here to stay.

Besides the gross illegality of these actions as well as the flagrant bludgeoning of the Bill of Rights, the American military is financed by taxpayers' dollars for one thing: defend the citizenry from foreign aggression. That's it. Everything else is extracurricular and patently illegal. But as clichéd as it sounds, Big Brother and the Holding Company can employ at will the wherewithal of the U.S. military as they cast out a giant all points bulletin that consumes every piece of data Americans generate. Professor McCoy suggests that with supercharged technology at their disposal, the NSA "can now capture the kind of gritty details of private life that J. Edgar Hoover so treasured," stressing that this glut of private information provides "the sort of comprehensive coverage of populations once epitomized by secret police like East Germany's Stasi."[91]

There's no doubt that the growth of technology far outdistances the attempts to protect civil liberties. Using a vast arsenal of weapons (with fear always fueling the engine), the government—like Pac Man—gobbles up whatever they can, eroding the rights of man at every juncture. And that's the job of the state. We recognize and acknowledge their recurring playbook. Then, of course, it's the mission of concerned citizens, journalists, and revolutionaries to fight back and slow the erosion. It's a tough fucking job, akin to shoveling sand against the tide. McCoy details this historical ebb and flow:

> First comes the rapid development of stunning counterintelligence techniques under the pressure of fighting foreign wars; next, the unchecked, usually illegal application of those surveillance technologies back home behind a veil of secrecy; and finally, belated, grudging reforms as press and public discover the outrageous excesses of the FBI, the CIA, or now, the NSA. In this hundred-year span—as modern communications advanced from the mail to the telephone to the Internet—state surveillance has leapt forward in technology's ten-league boots, while civil liberties have crawled along behind at the snail's pace of law and legislation.[92]

As we enter the third decade of the 21st century, Americans have been beaten to a pulp, not unlike Jake LaMotta resembling ground chuck after being viciously pummeled by Sugar Ray Robinson. The body politic cowers and shudders like the bridge at midnight trembles. Rebellion is as far from reality as the constellation Corona Borealis is from your corner bodega. Battered by fear, ongoing warfare, and the increasing lies that generate the purported need for a "police presence," freedom is smashed, the will to organically fight back extinguished. Chris Hedges reminds us of Orwell's admonition regarding well-oiled totalitarian states: "[C]reate a climate in which people do not think of rebelling, a climate in which government killing and torture are used against only a handful of unmanageable renegades."[93] Hedges takes the warning to its logical conclusion, writing that the state "ceaselessly peddles fear to keep a population traumatized and immobilized. It turns the courts, along with legislative bodies, into mechanisms to legalize the crimes of state."[94]

Good morning, America.

❖ Central Intelligence Agency

Back in 1986, fifteen activists were arrested on the campus of the University of Massachusetts Amherst and charged with trespassing and disorderly conduct for declaring their fervent disapproval of CIA recruitment practices on college campuses. Among those arrested were a recharged Abbie Hoffman and former President Jimmy Carter's daughter Amy—then nineteen years old. Months later a jury acquitted the activists of all charges. Attorney Leonard Weinglass led the defense and convinced the jury to acquit based on what is known as "a necessity defense"—positioning a minor offense as a necessity to prevent a worse crime, especially one that poses a clear and present danger. During Weinglass' defense, numerous CIA crimes and nefarious actions were exposed under a bright spotlight. The jury was obviously affected. One 64-year-old woman was crystal clear in her reaction: "A lot of us were not aware of what the CIA was into. It was shocking and alarming, the things we heard from witnesses."[95]

Hooray for Hollywood. When Michelle Obama awarded Ben Affleck the Best Picture Oscar for *Argo* in 2013 it seemed clear that the long courtship between Hollywood and Washington power brokers was finally consummated in a royal and very public wedding. In the case of *Argo*—and its fellow Best Picture nominee, *Zero Dark Thirty*—the CIA was actually the big winner, not the films' producers. Along with a barrage of popular television shows like *Homeland, Alias,* and *24,* numerous big time, big money studio productions over the past two decades depict the Agency as ethical and necessary, with their actions proving to be very effective when fighting the proverbial bad guys. Similarly, the men and women who work for the Agency are portrayed as honorable, moral, and tough as nails—but ultimately caring; their hearts are always in the right place. It's all very heroic... and therefore very American. In fact the star of *Alias,* Jennifer Garner, was so committed to the Central Intelligence Agency that she made an unpaid CIA recruitment promo. Talk about a team player.

Washington's goal with Hollywood has been the same since George Eastman began shoving film into one of Tom Edison's cameras: propaganda. From Woodrow Wilson's Committee on Public Information, to the hype and evangelism to sell World War II, to the CIA buying the rights to Orwell's *Animal Farm* to ensure an anti-Soviet spin,[96] right on through to Kathryn Bigelow's two and a half hour commercial, *Zero Dark Thirty,* Washington has actively enlisted the help of its left coast partner. In fact, Bigelow's narrative drifts off into Never-Never Land as the film celebrates the absolute effectiveness of torture in gathering the intel necessary to catch Osama bin Laden. This wasn't artistic license but, rather, as we now know, pulp fiction. So much so that the acclaimed screen actress and long-time human rights activist, Susan Sarandon, felt compelled to release a statement, which said in part:

> [Y]ou should know that the movie has generated controversy because it leaves a mistaken impression: that the CIA's torture of prisoners "worked" by providing information that led to bin Laden. Some will use the movie to argue that the CIA's torture program was justified.[97]

Sarandon's point is not the ravings of a so-called Hollywood radical. Her evaluation was backed up by three U.S. Senators on the Intelligence Committee—all war hawks to varying degrees: the late John McCain, Diane Feinstein, and Carl Levin. Remember, these are three major cogs right at the heart of Murder Incorporated who concluded that torture did not lead to the capture and murder of bin Laden. These senators reported that, "The use of torture in the fight against terrorism did severe damage to America's values and standing that cannot be justified or expunged. It remains a stain on our national conscience."[98]

As important as Bigelow's indifference to the facts about torture leading to bin Laden, was her disregard for the fundamental reality that torture is demonstrably illegal and immoral. In fact the United States signed and ratified the "Convention Against Torture and Other Cruel, Inhuman or Degrading Treatment or Punishment" treaty. U.S. ratification makes it U.S. law—period. The treaty language is abundantly clear: "No exceptional circumstances whatsoever, whether a state of war or a threat of war, internal political instability or any other public emergency, may be invoked as a justification of torture."

That's the law. When stacked against the behavior of recent U.S. administrations, it becomes clear the rank level of thuggery inherent in the Empire's arsenal. "Torture is illegal in all circumstances," writes law professor Marjorie Cohn. "The prohibition of torture is absolute and unequivocal. Torture is never lawful."[99]

Ben Affleck's film *Argo,* writes investigative journalist Robert Parry (best known for covering Iran-Contra for *AP* and *Newsweek),* is replete "with strong propaganda overtones, feeding into the current hostility between the United States and Iran over its nuclear program."[100] They must have been giddy with laughter out at Langley as they watched Affleck's cartoon-like narrative. The director offers an obligatory nod to Washington's brutal coup of Iranian Prime Minister Mohammad Mossadegh in 1953 as the CIA orchestrated the overthrow of his democratically elected government, followed by installing the Shah and his twenty-five year reign of terror on the Iranian people. "*Argo* quickly descended into a formulaic tale of sympathetic CIA officers trying to outwit nasty Iranian revolutionaries," writes Parry, "complete with a totally made-up thriller escape at the end."[101]

Affleck's work of fiction also disregards how the Reagan presidential campaign illegally interfered with the Carter administration's hostage negotiations as a way of destroying their November opponent with their "October Surprise"—the cloak-and-dagger dealings between Khomeini and Reagan's inner circle (dealings detailed by Iranian President Abolhassan Bani-Sadr).[102] Parry concludes that these "bookend stories around *Argo* would get to more important truths," but when has Washington and their media myth-making machine ever been about truth? "The two stories would show how America has manipulated politics abroad," Parry stresses, "and how that practice has come home to roost."[103]

We can hear the naysayers now: *"It's only a movie."* Actually it's not. It's high-powered, high-pressure, big budget manipulation of the American people—the very people responsible for paying the tab on the Empire's imperial intrigues. Noam Chomsky and Edward Herman famously defined it as "Manufacturing Consent."

Whether it's the skewed illusions of *Argo, Zero Dark Thirty,* or *Charlie Wilson's War* (which portrays the CIA-sponsored jihadists in Afghanistan as freedom-fighters), these highly effective tools are a tightly knit collaboration between Washington kingmakers and their studio fixers creating celluloid heroes. But it wasn't always as cozy as the agitprop we witness today.

During the Cold War years, the CIA wasn't so involved with shaping a public image. The development of their mission wasn't as evolved as it is right now, smack dab in the middle of a massive security and surveillance state. Their actions were more about winning hearts and minds and shaping foreign policy behind the scenes. They wanted American movies (and novels and television shows) to underscore mythical American values like freedom, fairness, and liberty, but it was all about portraying America as the good guy in the arm wrestle that was the Cold War. Ted Gup, journalism professor at Emerson College, said in an interview with Public Radio International that as the Cold War ended the CIA knew they needed to craft a substantial public image of an essential agency necessary to the security and success of America. "It's come to recognize that without public support, its budget is in jeopardy. And its very activities are in jeopardy."[104]

Al Gore's old Harvard roomie and acting legend Tommy Lee Jones has a cousin, Chase Brandon, who the CIA hired as their entertainment and publication liaison in 1996. Prior to this, Hollywood depicted the spy and assassin agency as the heavy (go figure), but those days appear to be long gone. Author Tricia Jenkins (*The CIA in Hollywood: How the Agency Shapes Film and Television*) documents the hard right turn in high-definition, mythmaking since the late 1990s, taking the CIA from ruthless killers to necessary protectors of the American Dream. "Now it's a much more favorable presentation," Jenkins told PRI, "frequently being depicted as a moral organization that is highly efficient. It rarely makes mistakes, it's needed more than ever."[105]

That's the game plan, as evidenced once again by a big time American television show, this example *Jack Ryan*—a drama relying on steroid-fueled nationalistic tropes and produced with bold xenophobic flair by Amazon Studios along with the show's producers and stars. The narrative is pure American party line. During the first half of 2019, Trump and fellow acid-laced space traveler, John Bolton, unleashed Washington's "diplomatic" forces and backed an attempted coup against Venezuelan President Nicolas Maduro—complete with the requisite embargo and sanctions aimed at punishing the people of Venezuela. This time U.S. imperial actions were in support of the self-proclaimed presidency of Juan Guaidó. Enter

Tom Clancy's fictional character Jack Ryan. "Historian Gary Alexander pointed to the president's national security advisor John Bolton," writes Eoin Higgins of *Common Dreams,* "who endorses a bellicose foreign policy toward nearly every country in the world, as the ideological godfather of this season of 'Jack Ryan.'"[106] After viewing the series trailer for *Jack Ryan,* Alexander tweeted:

> No matter how cynical you might be about propagandistic American media, you are not prepared for how much watching this trailer is like snorting 100% pure John Bolton.

The storyline is a laughable political scenario, and as usual, one rooted in fear. "Central to the plot is the idea that Venezuela, once armed with nuclear weapons," Higgins explains, "would bomb the U.S.—a country with enough firepower to use a fraction of its weapons to flatten the Latin American country."[107] Besides being a ridiculous political scenario, it's cartoon gibberish masquerading around as real political drama, but that's never stopped Hollywood before. An undereducated American public, one gullible enough to continuously buy the fairytale myths regarding America's past and American exceptionalism absorbs this tripe as reality all the time—just look around.

Loveable lead man, John Krasinski (Pam's heartthrob in *The Office*), offers this bombshell as Jack Ryan:

> A nuclear Venezuela you will not hear about in the news, 'cause we'll already be dead.

In response to *Jack Ryan,* journalist Alex Rubinstein tweeted: "American propaganda is so over-the-top and ridiculous." Sunjeev Berry, the Executive Director of the Freedom Forward project at the Center for International Policy, tweeted: "Hollywood producers may identify as liberals, but their 'products' keep scaring us into neocon fantasies of war." Adam Johnson, the co-host of the podcast "Citations Needed," tweeted with tongue in cheek: "A nuclear Venezuela! Man I'm so glad we don't have state media propagandizing us in this country."

Snorting 100% pure John Bolton. Yuck.

There is no doubt that this snug relationship between the government and their powerful collaborators in the entertainment business raises hard-boiled ethical and legal questions, not unlike the similar relationship between government entities and the corporate media/press.

But the bottom line is clear: all of this well-financed and well-produced movie lore facilitates the fact that this coldblooded covert intelligence agency is busy wiping away the boundaries between foreign and domestic surveillance, along with the help of the Grand Wizard: the DNI (Director of National Intelligence)—the FBI-run Joint Terrorism Task Force (more than 600 state, local, and federal agencies, including the military and CIA[108]). Also involved in the assault is the ever-expanding ISE (Information Sharing Environment)—a colossal bureaucratic union that would shock and amaze even Big Brother.

The Hollywood makeover lulls the "rabble" to sleep as their privacy and civil rights are eviscerated. The propaganda is high octane and, unfortunately, it's working. And the really ironic part, the "beauty part" in Hollywood parlance, is that conservatives and right-wing pundits are constantly screaming about Hollywood radicals undermining American values and security. Yeah, sure.

Posse Comitatus Act

In 1878, after Reconstruction, Congress passed the Posse Comitatus Act, which effectively limited the president's power as well as that of the federal government to deploy the U.S. military in domestic situations. This act built upon the limitations set forth in the Insurrection Act of 1807. The framers of the Constitution clearly understood the kind of threat a domestic standing army posed to liberty (especially *their* liberty) and therefore established a government that demanded civilian control over the armed forces. But in recent years, Congress—as well as various administrations—has slowly weakened the Posse Comitatus Act as the U.S. military has been authorized for various domestic operations including drug enforcement, border control, and high-profile so-called domestic terrorism situations such as the 1993 murderous government assault on the Branch Davidians in Waco, Texas. When Bill Clinton nuzzled up to and signed the "Antiterrorism and Effective Death Penalty Act" in 1996, he not only triggered selective suspension of Habeas Corpus but he gave himself and future executives in the White House the power to use "all necessary means, including covert action and military force" internationally as well as domestically, effectively overriding Posse Comitatus entirely.

According to the ACLU, as the American police state grows stronger and becomes more entrenched, "the number of domestic missions the military is accepting and the number of troops it is deploying inside the U.S. is drastically increasing."[109]

❖ Local Spooks and Fusion Centers: "A bunch of crap"

Barney Fife is also violating your privacy...

There are even more "secret agents" interested in your stuff, maybe even poking around in your garbage, and they're employed by state and local governments. Throughout the 20th century, "red squads" were infamous for abusing citizens' rights by infiltrating groups and spying on individuals they deemed dangerous—you know the usual groups: labor, antiwar, civil rights, and any organization where the membership's primary skin color isn't white. In fact, these intelligence-gathering units went far beyond collecting information; infiltration and sabotage were common tools. The American Civil Liberties Union reports that state and local agents "sabotaged numerous peaceful groups" and "amassed detailed dossiers on political officials and engaged in 'disruptive' activities targeting political activists, labor unions, and civil rights advocates, among others." The legal watchdog group emphasizes the fact that, "Abuses of intelligence powers are not limited to federal authorities."[110] The Boston Police Department offers a perfect, albeit ridiculous example.

Under the heading "Criminal Act–Groups-Extremist," a secret Boston PD "intelligence report" was initiated to monitor the dangerous association of a Boston peace group with various subversive and treasonous speakers set to gather in a congregational church in Jamaica Plain. Former Boston city councilor Felix Arroyo was listed, along with crazed vicious terrorists like Boston University Professor Emeritus Howard Zinn and Gold Star mother Cindy Sheehan.[111] The Boston PD was also staying on top of the potential guest list, which included more dangerous minds like Sean Penn and Susan Sarandon. This incredibly treacherous information was gathered and logged in searchable electronic reports under ominous headings like "Groups—Civil Disturbance," or "Groups—Extremists." Some select intel was categorized below the banner "Criminal Act."[112] "Under what interpretation of the US and Massachusetts Constitutions," writes Nancy Murray of the ACLU, "can the non-violent First Amendment activity of groups like Veterans for Peace and United for Justice with Peace be routinely classified as a criminal act?"[113]

Set up shortly after 9/11 under the auspices of the DHS (and expanded greatly under Obama's watch), Fusion Centers are multi-jurisdictional surveillance centers sharing what is listed as "terrorism-related" intel between federal, state, and local cops and spies. But here's the kicker: private sector and military participation exists freely within the framework of the Fusion Centers. The involvement of corporations and the military is troubling on numerous levels, including the ability to sidestep privacy laws (not to mention the Constitution) as well as legislation in place that protects the citizenry from the Armed Forces controlling domestic life. In particular, Fusion Centers allow the Federales to dodge Posse Comitatus as well as other restrictions on military intelligence gathering in the United States. Antiwar activists, community organizers, and citizens mobilized against militarization have been popular targets, with peace groups infiltrated by moles—clearly violating not only Posse Comitatus but the First and Fourth Amendments.[114]

Of course, after the stealth approach by Obama, here comes Donald J. Trump—the cretinous anthropoid whose major foray into the sanctity of American law was his vicious white supremacist money-fueled lynching of Yusef Salaam, Korey Wise, Kevin Richardson, Raymond Santana, and Antron McCray—an attack by this New York Klansman in a thousand dollar suit that was ultimately counterfactual, amiss, erroneous, fallacious, and completely fucking wrong. After racist America elected this talentless TV slime king, he—this pillar of American justice—sends Attorney General Jefferson Beauregard Sessions across the Potomac to Alexandria to address the National Fusion Center Association—a collection of state and local cops high on cheap coffee and rock-hard on xenophobic Viagra. Jefferson Beauregard Sessions ambled up to the podium, stood on eight or nine phonebooks, and then thanked the rabble from nearly all the Fusion Centers who traveled there "from New England to Guam." *Guam?* Then the Attorney General, who was named after JEFFERSON DAVIS (for God's sakes), offered a message from his boss, who he said was a strong supporter of law enforcement and that he charged Jefferson Beauregard Sessions to "back the blue" and to ensure we are "a force multiplier."

> Coming of age in a fascist police state will not be a barrel of fun for anybody, much less for people like me, who are not inclined to suffer Nazis gladly and feel only contempt for the cowardly flag-suckers who would gladly give up their outdated freedom to live for the mess of pottage they have been conned into believing will be freedom from fear.
>
> —Hunter S. Thompson, *Kingdom of Fear* (2003)

A significant amount of this eye-in-the-sky monitoring across the country is also designed to intimidate lawful First Amendment activity, forcing the public to shy away from questioning the government as well as participating in Constitutionally protected dissent or civil disobedience.

Mike German was a veteran FBI agent specializing in domestic terrorism and covert operations. He left law enforcement and joined the ACLU as a way to reveal to Congress and the American public the "continuing deficiencies"[115] in FBI operations. Discussing fusion centers and cells, German says the ACLU released a report "warning of the potential dangers that these multi-jurisdictional centers had, because it was unclear whose rules applied. Were we using federal rules? Were we using state rules? Local rules?"[116] German also stressed that the report questioned the deep-rooted role of the U.S. military as well as the various private companies employed, forcing us to ask: *what rules govern their conduct?*

Critics categorize five distinct ways DHS Fusion Centers put civil liberties and citizens' privacy at constant risk:

✓ **Ambiguous Lines of Authority**
Who's in charge here? Wait... those rules exist where?
Who approved this shit?

✓ **Private Sector Involvement**
Well if you don't work for the government,
who do you work for? Who's that?

✓ **Military Participation**
Private Pyle, why exactly is the military here?

✓ **Data Mining**
Do you really need a miner's helmet working
on a PC? How do you know I like porn?

✓ **Excessive Secrecy**
(knock, knock) *Is there anybody in*
there? C'mon, we can hear you!

No doubt this labyrinth of domestic spying follows in the footsteps of COINTELPRO and past reprehensible and illegal actions and how deep, far, and wide it stretches is anyone's guess. What is known, according to German, is that the Department of Homeland Security recognizes as operational the vast majority of these fusion centers. German adds, "[T]hese things are rapidly growing, without any sort of proper boundaries on what activities happen within them and without really any idea of what it is the military is doing in these fusion centers and what type of access they have to U.S. personal information."[117]

As of this writing, a Fusion Center has not uncovered a single terrorist plot. The ACLU reports that, "Their output is often, in the words of one government official, 'a bunch of crap.'"[118]

❖ Suspicious Activity Reporting Programs

"If You See Something, Say Something"

Suspicious Activity Reporting Programs or SAR programs encourage every man, woman, child, small dog, or rat to report suspicious behavior. Originally implemented in New York City by the Metropolitan Transportation Authority, the citizens of Gotham were instructed to "tell a cop or an MTA employee" if they saw something "suspicious." The program has been licensed to the DHS and expanded nationwide. Cities everywhere are rapidly adopting the program.

Photo: Steven Lek

In a de facto manner, federal-state-and-local law enforcement has deputized everyone to spy on everyone, or as they put it, ensuring that citizens "remain vigilant and play an active role in keeping the country safe."[119] But the Empire wants more as it continues to manufacture its technological tyranny.

❖ Domestic Drones: Surveillance Weaponized

"That's the signpost up ahead—your next stop, the Twilight Zone."

It's a cool, hazy day in the city Herb Caen dubbed "Baghdad by the Bay." You're sitting outdoors at a small bakery café near the corner of 19th and Ocean Avenues, just down the street from the San Francisco Islamic School. There's a weird feeling in the air... that calm before something bad happens. Maybe it's your imagination. Maybe not. Then you hear a growing whistle that quickly becomes more vicious as the nerves in your body quickly recoil. Your head whips north toward Sloat Boulevard and you see it clearly: on an 80° angle, a small streak of energy takes out a beat-up Chevy—turning the car into a smoldering wreck. People are screaming, running every which way.

Welcome to a domestic drone attack. Unbelievable? Of course we hope so...but to echo Abbie Hoffman once again:

> *This is the United States, 1968, remember. If you're afraid of violence, you shouldn't have crossed the border.*

A CNN headline during the Obama years read: "Holder does not rule out drone strike scenario in U.S." Civil liberty groups are emphatic that the use of drones domestically—in either a surveillance capacity or weaponized—is inevitable... and the inevitable has now become reality. Domestic cops already possess Predator drones, the same unmanned robot that launches hellfire missiles into wedding parties and villages across the Middle East. The *Los Angeles Times* reported way back in 2011 that police in North Dakota used a Predator drone for surveillance, enlisting the aircraft from a nearby Air Force base.[120]

The ACLU and other privacy groups have been gearing up for the inescapable reality of an aerial assault on U.S. soil, positioning the expected battle with the state as well as the powerful domestic drone lobby. Not surprisingly, "These efforts are being impeded by those who mock the idea that domestic drones pose unique dangers," writes former constitutional lawyer and current investigative journalist Glenn Greenwald. He then connects the governmental and corporate apologists to the outer limits of American exceptionalism:

> This dismissive posture is grounded not only in soft authoritarianism (a religious-type faith in the Goodness of US political leaders and state power generally) but also ignorance over current drone capabilities, the ways drones are now being developed and marketed for domestic use.[121]

From local cop to Rambo. Since the late 1960s, the militarization of America's civilian police forces has grown in unison with the expansion of the National Security State. Beginning in the City of Angels after the Watts Rebellion of 1966, infamous LAPD Inspector and chief goon, Daryl Gates, developed an elite police squad trained in military tactics. He named the unit SWAT—Special Weapons Attack Team. Later, the acronym was softened to Special Weapons and Tactics. At about the same time, ex-Marine Charles Whitman perched himself on the University of

Texas clock tower and opened fire for ninety-six minutes, killing fifteen people. This massacre increased the call for the proliferation of SWAT teams across the country. In San Francisco, the capital of the late sixties counterculture, Mafia-induced and testosterone-laden Mayor Joe Alioto took great pleasure in his violent battle against what the SFPD called "Hippieville," otherwise known as Haight-Ashbury. "He gave the SFPD's fearsome tactical squad full rein to run riot," writes David Talbot in his book *Season of the Witch.* Alioto viewed the neighborhood as "a war zone" and the kids living there as the enemy. The tactical squad, "high on its own testosterone and unhinged authority," reveled in "chasing down student protestors at San Francisco State and Haight hippies and beating them at will."[122]

The very first SWAT assault took place in Los Angeles on 6 December 1969 as Daryl Gates attacked the L.A. headquarters of the Black Panther Party. Six months later, Richard Nixon signed a bill that authorized "no-knock warrants," which allowed police in the D.C. area to bust into homes without alerting the inhabitants. Shortly thereafter, Nixon signed an omnibus drug bill that expanded no-knock warrants beyond District of Columbia city limits.

As expected, the SWAT-mentality was glorified on television and in dark theatres across America. The paramilitary approach to basic law enforcement—along with the necessary badass hardware—spread throughout the country. Late in 1981, the "Military Cooperation with Law Enforcement Agencies Act" became law. The act authorized the military to train civilian cops in the use of new military weaponry and support equipment. The act also paved the way for the military and local law enforcement to share vast amounts of information.

Three years later, the concept of "policing for profit" took root as local police departments working with federal agencies now earned a piece of the action, claiming a percentage of the assets seized during drug raids. In fact, so much of the subsequent growth and purported need for the U.S. security state over the past thirty years has been embedded and shrouded in the spurious "war on drugs."

Flash-forward to 1997: the "Law Enforcement Support Program" made it much easier to reassign military weaponry and equipment to local police departments. *Al Jazeera America* reports that U.S. government figures document more than $4.3 billion dollars worth of military equipment has been transferred to local police forces since the program began. The number continues to steadily rise.

Flash-forward again, this time to 2005: Professor Peter Kraska from Eastern Kentucky University offers a shocking statistical reality: between 50,000 and 60,000 SWAT raids took place in the U.S. *in 2005 alone*—doubling from just ten years before.[123]

Robo Cop—"Dead or alive, you're coming with me." We've all seen the images: robotic-like cops, dressed in riot gear and heavy-duty armament, tearing into civilians with a vengeance. Through their tinted shields, they don't see fellow Americans—they see the enemy. Investigative reporter Radley Balko captures the essence of this current dark chapter in the Republic's history in his examination of the beat cop-turned-soldier reality. He calls it the "Rise of the Warrior Cop"—clearly, a very accurate description. American politicians, in an effort to divert the public's attention away from their utter incompetence to effect positive change—as well as actions they initiate or endorse that they know run contrary to the best interests of the people—have waged diversionary wars on nebulous enemies like drugs, immigration, and of course terrorism. And with these "wars" comes a battlefield mentality, one that becomes increasingly more terrifying.

And battlefields need gear.

So, like morning follows night, drones are the perfect next generation for local law enforcement determined to fully embrace militarization. Drones are getting smaller and smaller, cheaper and cheaper, "more agile—but just as lethal," stresses Glenn Greenwald.[124] The drone manufacturers are actively hyping and flaunting their marketing business model based on domestic law enforcement utilizing weaponized drone technology. Most Americans can't fathom weaponized drones being used on U.S. soil and U.S. citizens—*but why not?* The history of federal, state, and local law enforcement is one of constant and brutal violence—not only on criminal activity but also a favorite tactic when dealing with citizen dissent, union organizing, antiwar and peace demonstrations, civil disobedience, as well as dealing with political groups the U.S. government considers "dangerous" (read: a threat to *das kapital*—and the wider the gulf between rich and poor becomes, the more intense the threats become).

"The belief that weaponized drones won't be used on US soil is patently irrational. Of course they will be," Greenwald warns. "It's not just likely but inevitable. Police departments are already speaking openly about how their drones 'could be equipped to carry nonlethal weapons such as Tasers or a bean-bag gun.'"[125]

Greenwald's detailed research reveals the following straightforward approach for local cops to embrace and utilize the violent flying robots: drones—weaponized or surveillance-equipped—are intended to be used in hazardous situations, protecting the users (the cops) and whacking the targets (the alleged bad guys). "Police agencies and the increasingly powerful drone industry will tout their utility in capturing and killing dangerous criminals and their ability to keep officers safe," writes Greenwald.[126]

And make no mistake about it: the mainstream media will do their usual rock-solid job of relying on elite and influential autocratic sources when peddling the effectiveness and necessity of drone technology. Law enforcement will be positioned as protectors of Christendom against the coterie of terrorists, killers, rapists, and political deviants looking to undermine mom and apple pie (and we're not talking about the terrorists, killers, rapists, and political deviants running the country).

Greenwald uses a 2011 report on National Public Radio's big time show *All Things Considered* as the perfect example of bias (and therefore salesmanship) toward ideological power and fortification of the powerful status quo. Listening to the report was like experiencing an infomercial for Ginsu knives. The military was lauded for their successful use of weaponized drones in the Middle East—the extensive number of murders (collateral damage) in the American assault on brown people was never mentioned in this "report." But Glenn Greenwald, the journalist the powerful would like hanging from a tree, reminds readers about NPR's domestic drone advertisement:

> [T]he potential for abuse is vast, the escalation in surveillance they ensure is substantial, and the effect they have on the culture of personal privacy—having the state employ hovering, high-tech, stealth video cameras that invade homes and other private spaces—is simply creepy. But listeners of NPR would know about virtually none of that. On its All Things Considered program yesterday, NPR broadcast a five-minute report from Brian Naylor that purported to be a news story on the domestic use of drones but was, in fact, much more akin to a commercial for the drone industry.[127]

Why? It's the mammon, stupid. One company in particular that's pushing the boundary of privacy encroachment and provides yet another example of the militarization of domestic police departments is called, we shit you not, Persistent

Surveillance Systems. PSS has built a system that uses a 192-megapixel camera that records giant swaths of life and geography—anywhere they want, any time they decide. Flying attached to small drone aircraft or positioned high above the population, this flying Cyclops generates "blanket" and suffocating surveillance for anyone who wants to pay. The ACLU's Crump and Harwood underscore the military's fingerprints in all of this: "The inventor of the camera, a retired Air Force officer, helped create a similar system for the city of Fallujah, the site of two of the most violent battles of the U.S. occupation of Iraq. It's just one example of how wartime surveillance technologies are returning home for 'civilian use.'"[128]

In 2011, eight American civilians died in terrorist attacks. During the same year, twenty-nine Americans died in lightning strikes. Since the Sandy Hook school shooting in 2012 when a gunman killed twenty children and six adults in Newtown, Connecticut, school shooting murders perpetrated by Americans as well as all killed by American gun violence numerically outdistance those killed in terrorist attacks by significant and prodigious measure.[129] In fact the mathematical evidence exists at different ends of the spectrum. But the guns keep flowing from gun manufacturers who should be prosecuted as accomplices to murder rather than rewarded with excessive treasure... and of course the NRA keeps pissing themselves silly—and nothing of substance changes. Ever.

Yet, the American Empire spends billions upon billions upon more billions on "patently absurd" domestic security projects.[130] Similar to the Military Industrial Complex, the security biz has major corporate winners positioned at the end of the rainbow, shoveling your cash, your healthcare, your retirement, your education, your infrastructure—into giant bags that get shipped back to Lockheed Martin, General Dynamics, Boeing, Northrup Grumman, and to all the usual suspects. When you factor in the Empire's ongoing foreign wars, occupations, the staggering defense budget, nuclear play-toys, and the myriad of private contractors sucking on the government's teat, the totals are beyond staggering. Analogous to the financial bailout of Wall Street thieves in 2008, the ongoing military/security budget swindle is nothing more than a yearly heist on the American treasury. It's grand larceny of epic proportion. "The decade's biggest scam," Greenwald laments, "trillions of dollars are transferred to the private security and defense contracting industry at exactly the time that Americans—even as they face massive wealth inequality—are told that they must sacrifice basic economic security because of budgetary constraints."[131]

Government watchdogs in the press, the few that actually dig beneath the surface of spin, report on the wastefulness and ineffectiveness of the budget dollars spent on security and surveillance, but Greenwald believes they "have the causation backwards: fighting Terrorism isn't the goal that security spending is supposed to fulfill; the security spending (and power vested by surveillance) is the goal itself, and Terrorism is the pretext for it. For that reason, whether the spending efficiently addresses a Terrorism threat is totally irrelevant."[132]

And they laughed. Former President Barack Obama at the White House Correspondents' Association dinner: "Jonas Brothers are here, they're out there somewhere. Sasha and Malia are huge fans, but boys, don't get any ideas. Two words for you: predator drones. You will never see it coming. You think I'm joking?"

No, we don't.

From Russia With Love (Part Four)

Edward Snowden, from his memoir *Permanent Record*—

My name is Edward Joseph Snowden. I used to work for the government, but now I work for the public. It took me nearly three decades to recognize that there was a distinction, and when I did, it got me into a bit of trouble at the office. As a result, I now spend my time trying to protect the public from the person I used to be—a spy for the Central Intelligence Agency (CIA) and National Security Agency (NSA), just another young technologist out to build what I was sure would be a better world.

Deep in a tunnel under a pineapple field—a subterranean Pearl Harbor-era former airplane factory—I sat at a terminal from which I had practically unlimited access to the communications of nearly every man, woman, and child on earth who'd ever dialed a phone or touched a computer. Among those people were about 320 million of my fellow American citizens, who in the regular conduct of their everyday lives were being surveilled in gross contravention of not just the Constitution of the United States, but the basic values of any free society.

The reason you're reading this book is that I did a dangerous thing for a man in my position: I decided to tell the truth.[133]

PENTAGON PLANS TO KEEP 20,000 TROOPS INSIDE U.S. TO BOLSTER DOMESTIC SECURITY[134]

The headline above and its associated story is from 2008 and it reported the Bush administration's stated goal of bolstering homeland security with regard to the amorphous threat of terrorist activity on domestic soil. Prior to 11 September 2001, the idea of deploying the forces of the U.S. military on American citizens "would have been extraordinary to the point of unbelievable," remarked Paul McHale, assistant defense secretary for homeland defense, during a speech at a Washington, D.C. think tank (Center for Strategic and International Studies).[135] *Extraordinary?* Maybe. *Unbelievable?* Oh, it's believable. But the operative question here should be: *Is it illegal?* And to that the answer is: *Yes, absolutely.* The action would clearly undermine the aforementioned Posse Comitatus Act—the long-standing federal law restricting the U.S. military's role in domestic law enforcement. And *morally?* Well, that's an entirely different discussion.

In fact, headlines like the one above in *The Huffington Post* and *The Washington Post* should send chills down the spine of most Americans—it doesn't but it should. The very idea of any president, along with the Pentagon, deploying troops on the streets of this nation will be the final stake driven into the heart of whatever liberty is left.

Flash-forward to June of 2020. The police killings (read: murders) of unarmed Black men and women finally set the country into a wholesale uprising. Fury and righteous indignation launched the body politic onto the streets of every major U.S. city, including of course Washington, D.C.

Enter Fuckface von Clownstick, the 45th CEO of the United States. After scurrying down into his bunker deep beneath the White House, scared shitless of the throng of peaceful Americans surrounding the joint, he emerged the following day to label the protests "acts of domestic terror" and then said this:

> If a city or state refuses to take the actions that are necessary to defend the life and property of their residents, then I will deploy the United States military and quickly solve the problem for them.[136]

Those words and the action they suggest underscore this stark reality: so-called American democracy is a myth. Oligarchs—in one form or another—have ruled the roost since time immemorial... and Trump, this unabashed authoritarian, left the podium after the screed above and ordered a goon and gas attack on the citizens outside—peaceful citizens clearly petitioning the Government THAT THEY OWN for a redress of grievances. The attack was ordered not only as a show of state force but as a way to clear a path so that he, a reincarnation of Benito Mussolini, could walk to a nearby church and hold up a Bible for a campaign photo opportunity. With the infamous and deranged Bull Connor pulsing through his veins, Trump threatened to invoke the Insurrection Act of 1807 to attack and overwhelm protestors. "The president's shameless, unconstitutional, unprovoked, and frankly criminal attack on protesters because he disagreed with their views shakes the foundation of our nation's constitutional order," said Scott Michelman, legal director, ACLU of the District of Columbia. "And when the nation's top law enforcement officer becomes complicit in the tactics of an autocrat, it chills protected speech for all of us."[137]

The American Stasi was on full display: the ongoing surveillance state bolstered in prime time by brute force—a sword and shield regime blatantly hellbent on absolute and undemocratic control. Behold: American fascism.

Our oft-cited comrade, Gore Vidal, recognized this reality in April 2002, as America was unraveling in the dark shadows of 11 September 2001. In his essay, "The End of Liberty," Vidal walked us down the newly minted 21st-century path leading to that place where we can all look up and hear the death knell of democracy ringing loud, ringing clear.

> Clinton, in his frantic pursuit of election victories, set in place the trigger for a police state which his successor is now happily squeezing.
>
> Police state? What's that all about? In April 1996, one year after the Oklahoma City bombing, President Clinton signed into law the Anti-terrorism and Effective Death Penalty Act... in which many grubby hands played a part including the bill's co-sponsor, Senate majority leader Bob Dole... But faced with opposition to anti-terrorism legislation—which not only gives the attorney-general the power to use the armed services against the civilian population, neatly nullifying the Posse Comitatus Act of 1878, but also, selectively, suspends habeas corpus, the heart of Anglo-American liberty—Clinton attacked his critics as "unpatriotic."

> Then, wrapped in the flag, he spoke from the throne: "There is nothing patriotic about our pretending that you can love your country but despise your government." This is breathtaking since it includes, at one time or another, most of us. Put another way, was a German in 1939 who said that he detested the Nazi dictatorship unpatriotic?[138]

Numerous U.S. executives, including Clinton, Bush, Obama, as well as the rabid Trump, have tried and have been somewhat successful at hammering away and circumventing the Posse Comitatus Act. The U.S. Constitution, which doesn't grant you rights like a vending machine but rather limits the behavior of the government, hangs perilously in the balance.

Citizens' Commission to Investigate the FBI

On 8 March 1971, one hundred and ten miles away from Media, Pennsylvania (a suburb of Philadelphia), Muhammad Ali and Joe Frazier were pummeling each other in Madison Square Garden. The eyes of the world were focused on "The Fight of the Century," but that evening, in Media—a sleepy hamlet residents call "Everyone's Hometown"—a daring break-in was underway at a small FBI field office. More than one thousand classified documents were retrieved by a small group of passionate American citizens who were active in both the civil rights and antiwar movements—ardent dissenters against the wanton murder in Southeast Asia as well as the domestic terrorist actions underfoot by a U.S. intelligence community hostile to the recently slain MLK, civil rights, black liberation, as well as other groups fighting for justice. This tight group—known as the Citizens' Commission to Investigate the FBI—knew "it was time to do more than protest."

As Ali peppered Smokin' Joe with a barrage of stinging jabs and Joe countered with a historic left hook that sent the Louisville Lip crashing to the canvas, the Bureau's malfeasance and corruption was about to be revealed by eight activists who broke into the tiny FBI office and gathered up every document they could find. "Among the documents," reports *DemocracyNow,* "was one that bore the mysterious word 'COINTELPRO.'"[139] One of the activist/burglars, John Raines, acknowledges the group consisted of whistleblowers before "whistleblower" had entered the lexicon. He also knew citizens had to do something bold, something intrepid because Hoover—besides being diabolical—was also untouchable. "He had presidents who were afraid of him," Raines explains. "Nobody was holding him accountable, and that meant that somebody had to get objective evidence of what his FBI was doing... get their files and get what they're doing in their own handwriting."[140]

At the time, Betty Medsger was a reporter for *The Washington Post.* Shortly after the break-in she received the cache of documents from "Liberty Publications" with a letter from the Citizens' Commission to Investigate the FBI explaining where, when, and why the stash of evidence was collected. Medsger was "shocked" and "stunned" by the trail of criminal behavior perpetrated by the Bureau and it quickly became apparent to the reporter that Hoover's FBI was especially fond of conducting "blanket surveillance of African-American people."[141] The documents detailed surveillance programs in nearby Philadelphia as well as various national programs.

The documents also revealed that the illicit spying and counterintelligence was ubiquitous throughout the community—"churches, classrooms, stores down the street, just everything." In fact, the FBI was grooming informants in every walk of life, all of them targeting domestic dissenters. The revelations also exposed the FBI's directive to "enhance the paranoia" of antiwar activists through harassment, intimidation, rumors, lies, and installing agent provocateurs everywhere. "The surveillance was so enormous," explains Medsger, "that it led various people, rather sedate people in editorial offices and in Congress, to compare it to the Stasi, the dreaded secret police of East Germany."[142]

The eight Media whistleblowers protected their anonymity for more than forty years, forcing the press and public to focus on the substantive content rather than the worn-out and predictable debate over whether the burglars were treasonous or not, as was the case with Daniel Ellsberg and the release of his Pentagon Papers just three months later.

On that fateful night, Frazier narrowly beat Ali—and while the two warriors nursed their wounds in a building anchored between 7th Avenue and 34th Street, eight other warriors set up shop in a Pennsylvania farmhouse and dropped a dime on the Bureau's ugly (and illegal) operation. The exposure of Hoover's massive and secretive COINTELPRO hijinks, along with his iniquitous violations of civil liberties, helped pave the way for the notable Church Committee (headed by Senator Frank Church of Idaho) that investigated the entire spectrum of U.S. intelligence operations. In fact, the Church Committee's damning report triggered various congressional intelligence oversight committees, including the House Select Committee on Assassinations, as well as the Foreign Intelligence Surveillance Court (FISA), which (as we've seen, sort of) kept U.S. surveillance in check for a short time. As expected, control by FISA waned as the various agencies kicked back, and then the subsequent reform measures dramatically dried up with the election of Ronald Reagan.

But on 8 March 1971, in the quiet suburbs west of Philadelphia, eight courageous men and women—with ice in their veins—decided, to hell with civil obedience, and put everything on the line in an audacious move to alert their fellow citizens that treachery was underfoot. In a move that defines self-sacrifice, these eight unexpected, swashbuckling activists bring to mind the essence of William Kuntsler's words when he spoke of the tragedy, courage, and death at Kent State University:

> *The four who died here, the nine who were wounded here... they did more for their country than all the Nixons and the Agnews and the Reagans could possibly do.*

"Meet the new boss, same as the old boss"

Journalist Glenn Greenwald interviewed whistleblower Edward Snowden in June of 2013. One of Snowden's most powerful remarks sums up the Groundhog Day-like history of U.S. surveillance programs: "The greatest fear that I have regarding the outcome for America of these disclosures is that nothing will change." In fact, that is the one constant regarding the American security state throughout history: no matter what bombshell disclosures hit the fan, or what Orwellian circumstance is deemed "Constitutional" by an obedient U.S. Supreme Court, democratic ideals and liberty are dragged out to the woodshed and beaten to a pulp.

Obviously, the Empire's security state did not simply materialize with the glorious opportunity afforded Washington's puppet-masters in a post-9/11 America. It began earlier, when fear and paranoia wreaked havoc on a population already oblivious to the criminal activity carried out or sanctioned by their government—activity that invited an international blowback scenario heretofore unseen in modern America.

And then it got worse.

With echoes of James Polk's provocation of war with Mexico, the purported sinking of the *USS Maine* in Havana Harbor, Joseph Goebbels' Reichstag Fire, Pearl Harbor, the Gulf of Tonkin "incident," and many other war pretext incidents dating back to the Roman Empire, Washington—under the reign of Bush and Cheney—kicked the current door wide open as fools and evil came rushing in. Together, holding hands, the war machine and the authoritarian surveillance state went for broke. If not for the bold actions of individuals like Julian Assange and WikiLeaks, Chelsea Manning, John Kiriakou, and Edward Snowden, the noose around the neck of privacy and liberty might be pulled rock tight and the chair beneath the body kicked over to the side.

It's no secret that this cauldron of autocratic surveillance and shredding of Fourth Amendment guarantees has been heating up for some time, building aggressively during the last century of the American Empire.

Alexander Graham Bell: *"Mr. Watson, come here... I want to see you."* It didn't take long: wiretapping sprang to life shortly after the invention of the telephone. Like porn became the first dark stepchild of the Internet, wiretapping has been endemic from the early days of electronic technology as private entities and the nation's cops began fishing for information. Forty-odd years after the first phone call from Bell to his assistant Watson, the U.S. Supreme Court approved wiretapping in the 1928 decision *Olmstead v. United States.* Four decades later in 1967, *Olmstead* was overturned in *Katz v. United States.*

Success: Surveillance in a Test Tube. In 1898, as William McKinley ushered in the so-called American Century, the new and expanding Empire occupied a distant outpost in barbaric fashion. In its eight-year war to dominate the Philippines, the U.S. slaughtered hundreds of thousands of Filipinos. Once in control, the new empire needed to track and control a still-rebellious population. What did they rely on? How did they do it? Professor Alfred McCoy, in his work documenting the history of the U.S. surveillance state, answers, "by fashioning the world's first full-scale 'surveillance state' in a colonial land."[143] The operation in the Philippines proved very successful and was the primer for Washington's next major step forward, "providing the basis for constructing America's earliest internal security and surveillance apparatus during World War I," explains McCoy.[144]

From the "Black Chamber" to the NSA. As the blood dried on the battlefields of Europe and the First World War receded into history, a predecessor to the NSA, branded the "Black Chamber," began intercepting and gathering telegrams from telegraph companies. This civilian operation, working in concert with the U.S. government as well as telecommunication companies, was violating the secrecy protections of the Radio Communications Act. The operation was disbanded after World War II, but decades later it resurfaced when Harry Truman signed the top-secret executive order in 1952 that established the National Security Agency.

Operation SHAMROCK. A few years before, in 1945, another predecessor to the NSA, the Armed Services Security Agency, initiated one of the most prevalent and aggressive intercept programs in American history—that is until recent NSA revelations. Furtively known as "Operation SHAMROCK," the government intercepted every telegram that entered or left the country. The blanket surveillance was "warrant-free" and the government spread the intel to all like-minded agencies. Reports reveal that, "The program, in its most active period, processes and analyzes up to 150,000 messages per month, an impressive figure, given the lack of data storage and processing available at the time."[145] Operation SHAMROCK operated for nearly thirty years and was uncovered in 1975 by L. Britt Snider, a 30-year-old Congressional investigator. The Church Committee's Chairman, Frank Church, made his interpretation of the findings abundantly clear: "The program certainly appears to violate section 605 of the Communications Act of 1934 as well as the Fourth Amendment of the Constitution."[146]

When investigative journalists from *Frontline* asked L. Britt Snider how the NSA got their hands on the massive number of telegrams throughout the SHAMROCK years, Snider simply replied, "They asked."[147] This was yet another clear-cut example of telecommunication corporations (entrusted with the public's expectation and right of privacy) caving in to government pressure and coercion. These SHAMROCK abuses as well as others investigated and revealed by the Church Committee in 1978 led Congress to enact the Foreign Intelligence Surveillance Act, which created a secret court and specific procedures aimed at managing domestic surveillance within the bounds of the Constitution. "What Congress said," explains Cindy Cohn, the aforementioned attorney at the Electronic Frontier Foundation, "is, 'Phone company, don't hand this stuff over to the government unless you have a warrant or other proper authority.'"[148]

Bugging MLK. For almost three years, and first ordered by (dig it) U.S. Attorney General Robert Kennedy, the FBI bugged Martin Luther King's home and his office. Paranoid government lackeys and henchmen suspected King of being a communist and of being Black. Today there's a world-renowned Martin Luther

King, Jr. Memorial situated in West Potomac Park overlooking the Tidal Basin in Washington, D.C. It's directly across the basin from the Jefferson Memorial—conspicuous acknowledgment that America knows no bounds when it comes to piling the bullshit high. We wonder if the statue is also bugged.

Shortly after King's assassination in 1968, Congress passed the Omnibus Crime Control and Safe Streets Act. On the surface the bill curbed wiretapping, but clearly maintained and bolstered the President's authority to order domestic surveillance when "national security" is at stake—once again, "national security," like grandma's nightshirt: it covers everything.

Operation CHAOS. In what was arguably one of the worst years in American history, 1968 ended with the election of Richard Milhous Nixon. A year that began with the Tet Offensive, which stunned American forces throughout Vietnam, a year that witnessed the assassinations of Martin Luther King, Jr., and Robert Kennedy, and a year that saw the violent debacle at the Democratic National Convention in Chicago when Richard Daley's goons went medieval on peaceful protestors, 1968 also ushered in a new era of surveillance—the Nixon era, when illegal domestic intelligence gathering went into overdrive.

Operation CHAOS was an illegal domestic surveillance program conducted by the Central Intelligence Agency from 1959 through 1974. Up to that point, CHAOS was one of the most extensive domestic surveillance programs in American history. CHAOS operatives and the CIA spied on thousands of U.S. citizens. Verne Lyon, a former CIA undercover operative, writes, "The CIA went to great lengths to conceal this operation from the public while every president from Eisenhower to Nixon exploited CHAOS for his own political ends."[149] CHAOS, on orders from Eisenhower, extended its early operations into the Cuban exile community recruiting for operatives to be used against Fidel Castro. Lyndon Johnson jumped onboard after Kennedy was whacked and expanded CHAOS onto college campuses looking to ferret out antiwar activists and dissidents organizing against the growing storm in Southeast Asia.

It was a glorious time for spooks as the CIA and FBI worked both sides of the street (international and domestic) and infiltrated domestic political entities everywhere. "[The CIA] used its contacts with local police departments and their intelligence units to pick up its 'police skills' and began in earnest to pull off burglaries, illegal entries, use of explosives, criminal frame-ups, shared interrogations, and disinformation," writes Lyon. "CIA teams purchased sophisticated equipment for many starved police departments and in return got to see arrest records, suspect lists, and intelligence reports."[150] Lyon reveals that within the framework of Operation CHAOS, the CIA and various police departments "carried out illegal, warrantless searches of private properties, to provide intelligence for a report requested by President Johnson, later entitled 'Restless Youth.'"[151] During this time, the CIA's domestic surveillance operation was managed and expanded by Deputy Director Richard Helms. Johnson desperately wanted intelligence on the radicals making his life miserable and making his war difficult to prosecute. According to Verne Lyon, Johnson's governing guidelines to Helms on intelligence gathering was fairly simple: "don't get caught."[152]

But then came Tricky Dick.

For the first year and a half of Nixon's presidency, Operation CHAOS continued unabated with Richard Helms working hard to keep the illegal activities under wraps. In June of 1970, a month after the massacre at Kent State, and with the murderous war in Indochina still raging and fueling antiwar thunder in cities and on campuses across the country, Richard Nixon instructed Richard Helms, J. Edgar Hoover, NSA Director Admiral Noel Gaylor, and Lt. General Donald Bennett to increase their domestic surveillance and counterintelligence programs on domestic dissent. To coordinate this effort, the little lost boy from Yorba Linda who would grow up to be king—an American monarch echoing Richard III—created the Interagency Committee on Intelligence, which was headed by Hoover.[153]

A few months later, the agency recommended bold new "black bag operations," including wiretapping and a physical mail-opening program. "Even Helms began to have second thoughts about how large CHAOS had grown," reports Verne Lyon, "but Nixon made it clear to him that the CIA was a presidential tool he wanted at his disposal."[154]

The tentacles of the operation were everywhere. For instance, the CIA was fond of employing moles in the press as well as academics on college campuses. They positioned their own agents to masquerade as independent businessmen who would then assist in their dirty work from strategic vantage points. The Agency denied the allegations, but the assertions later became fact as revealed by Oswald Johnston of the *Washington Star* and further confirmed by numerous other news organizations. It was revealed that some forty full-time and freelance reporters were on the CIA payroll. "And in 1974," Lyon reveals, "the CIA admitted that over two hundred CIA agents were operating overseas posing as businessmen."[155] In his 1977 landmark expose, "The CIA and the Media," Carl Bernstein detailed the Agency's relationship with the media and how the Church Committee actually helped to cover up the surreptitious relationships. Bernstein reports that the cover-up also extended to its association with slime-ball professors. "A similar decision was made to conceal the results of the staff's inquiry into the use of academics," Bernstein stressed.[156] At the time, Senator Gary Hart also made it abundantly clear: "It hardly reflects what we found... There was a prolonged and elaborate negotiation [with the CIA] over what would be said."[157]

Then came Watergate—and that's when the presidential portraits hanging in the White House started barking at Nixon. "The web of deception, misinformation, lies, and illegal domestic activities began to unravel with speed in the summer of 1972," Verne Lyon writes, and Helms knew the jig was up. He grabbed fellow CIA leader, William Colby—one of Washington's top-notch serial murderers who spearheaded the notorious Phoenix Program in Southeast Asia, and together they began to distance themselves from the Agency's lowdown operation against American citizens. As the Watergate revelations destroyed Nixon, his administration, as well as Washington's intelligence community, Helms was sacked and Colby pulled the plug on Operation CHAOS—but the heavy carnage was already inflicted.

Lyon's research cites the Center for National Security Studies' report on Operation CHAOS. From the late 1960s to 1974, the CIA assembled more than 13,000 personality files that included some 7,000 American citizens; they also compiled files on more than 1,000 domestic groups; and the CIA handed over intel to their brethren in law enforcement on more than 300,000 individuals.

"War is over if you want it." One of the individuals counted as a historical statistic belonging to Operation CHAOS was John Winston Lennon, who was simply trying to give peace a chance, but instead was targeted by the CIA and FBI as conspiring to spark revolutionary acts of terrorism and/or engage in so-called criminal activity. It was 1972. Lennon was in New York City organizing protests against the war. Nixon, along with the INS, were trying to deport the ex-Beatle because, well, you know, killers hate being called out for their murderous actions—especially by longhaired freaks endangering the world with their treacherous "Bed-Ins for Peace."

Under surveillance by both the CIA and FBI, Helms sent Hoover a coded communiqué with the subject line: *John Lennon and Project "Yes"*—as well as an ominous warning that Mr. Lennon was involved in a movement "which will include the use of video tapes, films, and special articles."

Robin (yells): *Holy mashed potatoes, Batman!*
Batman (jumps): *Quick. To the Batmobile!*

The FBI documents also disclosed a myriad of subversive actions on Lennon's part, actions that apparently were threatening the very bedrock of American life. One document stated that the man who penned "Mean Mr. Mustard" promised to help "finance a left wing bookshop and reading room in London." *Jesus Christ, he's a goddamn madman!* In another document, the FBI uncovered this bombshell of bloodthirsty rebellion: "Lennon emphasized his proletarian background and his sympathy with the oppressed and underprivileged people of Britain and the world." *This Liverpool louse knows no bounds!* The Bureau's top-notch undercover work also revealed that while in the U.S., Lennon and his wife "made a public appearance along with Jerry Rubin, on the Mike Douglas Television Show." *That's it. Give the Navy Seals their orders: execute John and Yoko right in their bloody bed!* When the documents were released, *Mother Jones* had it right:

> For all the unintentional humor that pervades these documents, they convey a far more sobering message: how willing the government has been at times to spy on, intimidate, and harass those whom it regards as its most effective critics.[158]

But who will watch the watchmen?

As Nixon waved goodbye from the South Lawn of the White House and was whisked away to Andrews for his rotation back to the sunny beaches of Southern California, his successor and pardoner, Jerry Ford—the man who granted Dick his writs of indulgence—was already in cahoots with Nixon's attorney general, William Saxbe. A recently released top secret memo dated 19 December 1974 reveals that Ford authorized Saxbe and his successors sanction "to approve, without prior judicial warrants, specific electronic surveillance within the United States which may be requested by the Director of the Federal Bureau of Investigation."[159] Hoover, like horseshit, was everywhere.

At the time, the intrepid muckraker Seymour Hersh was digging deep and broke a major front-page story in *The New York Times* that detailed the CIA's long-standing illegal domestic operation. It was clear: all of these surveillance programs shared the ever-present excuse for their existence and trumped-up legality: *national security*—it was (and remains) their chronic and open-ended authority under the rubric of protecting America. Presidents and federal spy agencies invoked "national security" for any reason... and through design the incantation has only grown more absurd.

As the 1970s rolled on, feathers were ruffled; spooks covered their asses, but Washington weathered the congressional storm known as the Church Committee (was it the fox watching the henhouse?). And then the Empire's police and security state returned to normal.

Once the unelected Jerry Ford was replaced by Jimmy Carter—and in historical convergence with the Church Committee's disclosures and subsequent restrictions set in motion by the Foreign Intelligence Surveillance Act—illegal government activities were somewhat curtailed. But as Reagan and his posse rode triumphantly into town, carnival-barking about a return to conservative values, the trend was dramatically reversed. Any gains achieved at reining in unbridled and illegal government operations were vanquished with Reagan's coronation.

In 1988, nearing the end of his two terms, a headline in *The New York Times* blared: F.B.I. PAPERS SHOW WIDE SURVEILLANCE OF REAGAN CRITICS. The Center for Constitutional Rights disclosed government records that document an orchestrated campaign of "extensive surveillance" on thousands of American citizens and hundreds of groups. The FBI's incursion began with groups critical of Reagan's death squads in Central America, as well as groups organizing peace demonstrations, but over time it expanded to a long list of groups. Among many caught in the net were the Council of Churches, the Southern Christian Leadership Conference, the Roman Catholic Maryknoll Sisters, the United Auto Workers, the National Education Association, the Sisters of Mercy Generalate in Baltimore, as well as a Women's Rape Crisis Center at Norfolk, Virginia.[160]

Early in Reagan's administration the term "counterterrorism" and "the war on drugs" started a long *pas de deux* that neatly connected local, state, and federal agencies. This rapport became the perfect foundation for what loomed on the horizon: an omnipresent and suffocating surveillance state.

For the moment, let's set aside illegal warrantless surveillance by the American Empire and briefly look at what Washington does consider "legal"—and this encompasses judicial warrants obtained by U.S. government agencies through the Foreign Intelligence Surveillance Court, a body of federal judges selected and impaneled by the Chief Justice of the Supreme Court *without,* we repeat *without* U.S. Senate approval. The court's hearings are secret and conducted *ex parte.* This is troubling on a number of counts, most obvious is its apparent violation of the Fifth Amendment: "No person shall… be deprived of life, liberty, or property, without due process of law." This basic foundation of American law is erased when it comes to *ex parte* legal proceedings, which take place without notice and without the presence of the affected parties.

You can't help but to ask yourself, "is this legal?" Surely no judge, nobody sworn to "protect and defend the Constitution" can allow this, right? And then, in places like between these pages, you learn the grim and bitter truth.

National Security reporter James Bamford has written quite a few books on the subject, among them *The Shadow Factory.* In one particularly striking passage, he writes of a prominent, well-known judge in D.C. and the role he played when confronted at the height of the hijinks of the Bush Crime Family. Bamford writes of the White House decision to embark on NSA warrantless surveillance and how a sitting federal judge responded to such a lawless act:

> Except for the presiding judge, Royce Lamberth, the FISA court was also kept in the dark about the NSA's warrantless program. But rather than being asked for his view on the pro-legality of the operation, Lamberth, probably the most experienced person in the country on the topic, was simply told that this was a presidential decision, period. The meeting… took place in the office of Attorney General John Ashcroft. During the meeting, which lasted nearly an hour, Lamberth said little and agreed to keep his fellow judges uninformed.[161]

If that quaint example doesn't tell you all you need to know about the FISA "court," we don't know what will. This is more than a secret "court." It is a silent "court." It's there, but it ain't there. Not for you. Hell, not for themselves!

The numbers don't lie. From 1978 (right after the creation of this cloistered body) through 1992, three presidents submitted more than 7,000 surveillance warrant applications to the court. All of them were approved as submitted. *All of them.*

From 1993 to 2000, Clinton's Justice Department submitted more than 6,000 warrant applications. The court modified one and rejected one. That's it for the first two-plus decades. One rejection. Simple math = rubber stamp… and the rubber stamp has continued to this day in unrelenting fashion. The vast majority of "hearings" take place behind locked doors and the rulings remain unpublished with the rare exception of a heavily redacted release every now and then. Will the highest court in the land ever step in on the side of privacy? The answer is doubtful and, until that happens, the Fourth Amendment will remain a sham, artifice.

William Barr & Robert Mueller's Cozy Love Nest

In 2019, America was treated to an Off-Broadway production of "Russiagate and Other Fantastic Tales." This was a co-production of the U.S. Justice Department along with MSNBC, CNN, *The NYT, WAPO,* and other mainstream associate producers. The "Special Counsel Investigation" held viewers, readers, and the mentally delusional captive waiting for justice to prevail with Trump being carried off to ADX Florence, the United States Supermax Penitentiary in Florence, Colorado.

Every day, Americans chewed on the morsels and breadcrumbs doled out by the myriad of players in this so-called investigation—the mainstream media twisting itself into a pretzel with confirmation bias. "It represents a massive abdication of responsibility to cover stories that were in front of us, that were glaring, that required huge amounts of digging about corruption, about conflicts of interest with this very dangerous presidency,"[162] author and journalist Naomi Klein told *The Intercept.* And then suddenly during this spectacle, the media turned the CIA, FBI, NSA, and Director of National Intelligence into the good guys wearing white hats, galloping over the ridge to save the republic from the orange scourge—with Robert Mueller, who they painted as Marshal Dillon keeping the streets of Dodge City safe for women and children. All of a sudden these historic liars, thieves, and killers were the saviors. "This has been an utterly colossal media failure and it reveals how little things have actually changed with the broader press since the Iraq War lies,"[163] writes *The Intercept's* Jeremy Scahill. "The starting point should be, to quote I.F. Stone, all governments lie. That is the biggest common denominator between the Iraq war media failures and the ones we have seen here with Russiagate."[164]

So as Americans settled back to watch the Trump morality play unfolding on a national stage, one starring their new knight in shining armor, Robert Mueller, up against Trump's mouthpiece, Attorney General William Barr, the play-by-play announcers in the press box seem to have forgotten the reality of the past—that these two characters slithered through nefarious backgrounds and were linked by one joint whopper, walking arm-in-arm together into dark surveillance. Luckily, Mueller's background wasn't forgotten by some, like the journalists at *The Hill,* one of their headlines blaring: "Robert Mueller's Forgotten Surveillance Crime Spree."[165]

As Director of the FBI, Mueller was backbone operational support for George W. Bush's AG Alberto Gonzales, who pronounced the president had the inherent authority to order the NSA to wiretap Americans as well as perusing millions of American's emails without warrants—the same operation that triggered one of the articles of impeachment against Nixon.[166] Mueller continued as the dutiful Bush surrogate demanding that ALL American's telephone records were germane to terrorism investigations. "Mueller signed orders to the Foreign Intelligence Surveillance Court," *The Hill* reports, "swaying it to continually renew its order compelling telephone companies to deliver all their calling records (including time, duration, and location of calls) to the National Security Agency."[167] Even though the Rachel Maddows of the press put the former FBI Director on a pedestal and portrayed Mueller as a non-partisan straight arrow and the greatest public servant since Mr. (Jefferson) Smith went to Washington, *The Hill* concludes that "during his 11 years as director of the Federal Bureau of Investigation, Mueller's agency *routinely* violated federal law and the Bill of Rights."[168] [Emphasis added]

And then Mueller became obsessed with one, Edward Snowden, as he attempted to negotiate with Russian officials for the whistleblower's extradition back to the U.S. "According to a former official," reports Carlos Ballesteros at *Newsweek,* "Mueller would call his Russian counterpart, Alexander Bortnikov, 'starting at 3 a.m. in Washington' every day for at least a week, 'begging to talk to the guy.' Bortnikov reportedly never answered the phone, and Snowden was granted asylum in Russia soon after."[169]

Enter William Barr… one shady character. In fact if you called Central Casting and requested the perfect actor to play Richard Milhous Nixon, a window-tinted Cadillac would pull up on set and William Pelham Barr would step out of the backseat, jowls and all—no make-up necessary. "I'm ready for my close-up, Mr. DeMille." Barr remains a key participant in the Iran-Contra scandal cover-up, securing pardons for six top defendants (read: criminal thugs) including former Defense Secretary Caspar Weinberger. Along with his boss, George H.W.

Bush, they completed the Iran-Contra cover-up on Christmas Eve 1992. Greg Walters at *Vice* reports that, "Barr's defense of the first Bush administration was seen as so robust at the time he was dubbed the "Coverup General" in 1992 by William Safire, the former Nixon speechwriter turned columnist for The New York Times."[170]

1992. The same year Barr and his then-deputy, Robert Mueller, hooked up to pull the trigger on the NSA's mass phone surveillance program, authorizing the Drug Enforcement Agency to begin gathering phone call data in bulk, "ordering telephone companies to secretly hand over the records of all phone calls from the U.S. to countries—which eventually grew to be well over 100 nations—where the government believed drug traffickers were operating."[171] In 2015, *USA Today* revealed that the "U.S. secretly tracked billions of calls for decades." This secret and illegal Barr/Mueller operation (later carried on by Janet Reno and her deputy Eric Holder) "was the government's first known effort to gather data on Americans in bulk, sweeping up records of telephone calls made by millions of U.S. citizens regardless of whether they were suspected of a crime."[172] Clearly this massive surveillance without warrant program became the NSA model for the colossal and unconstitutional sweep of data and concurrent invasion into Americans' privacy post-9/11 (see Patriot Act—342 pages Barr thought didn't go far enough). In fact Barr worked overtime to make it easier for Verizon and other phone companies to turn over mountains of their customers' private information. The ACLU reports:

> In the George W. Bush era, during which Barr served as executive vice president and general counsel at Verizon, the telecom giant participated in a massive, warrantless surveillance program known as Stellar Wind. Under Barr's watch, Verizon allowed the NSA to intercept the contents of Americans' phone calls and emails and to vacuum up in bulk the metadata associated with Americans' phone calls and internet activities.[173]

Barr and Mueller. Perfect bedfellows. If James Brown and Wilson Pickett are "the godfathers of soul" then these two remain "the godfathers of ____________"—well, you fill in the blank, there are many correct answers. Food for thought as you ponder: these two American "lawmen" have violated or fueled violations of constitutional rights for decades, "leaving a disastrous legacy of warrantless spying and government abuse."[174]

The Man from Hope (and other fairytales)

Regarding the current surveillance stranglehold gripping the American people, a fallacy exists in the body politic: that the long slippery slope to an Orwellian nightmare began after 9/11 with Cheney pulling the strings on Bush. There's no doubt that after eight long years of hegemony by Bush, Cheney, Rice, Ashcroft, Gonzales, Ridge, and the other caporegimes and foot soldiers in the Bush Crime Family, the Constitution was treated like a dangling piñata during Las Posadas. But first there was ECHELON.

The code name for a global system of data interception, ECHELON grew out of a World War II agreement between the United States, Great Britain, Canada, Australia, and New Zealand known as the "UKUSA Agreement." The program matured and gained traction during Cold War escapades with the Soviet Union, monitoring and gathering military and diplomatic intelligence. The program was first revealed in 1988 by British investigative journalist Duncan Campbell in his classic exposé "Somebody's Listening." Others broke similar stories in the mid-to-late 1990s: New Zealand journalist Nicky Hager (who went on to testify at the European Parliament when they investigated ECHELON) revealed his country's role, and *Nine Network* in Australia revealed the Australian government's participation. But the NSA skated by unfettered, and Clinton? Well, he had his hands full with blowjobs and blue dresses as the American press did their best impression of the *National Enquirer.*

"[M]ass surveillance systems operated by the U.S. and certain of its allies were in place and operating long before 2001," writes Maria Bustillos in *The New Yorker.*[175] In fact, when the European Parliament caught wind of the massive surveillance program they advised members to encrypt all communications. Their subsequent investigation stated, "in no uncertain terms that the Echelon network was being used to intercept private and business communications, not only military ones," Bustillos reports.[176] Clearly, ECHELON was being used for corporate and economic espionage. Wholesale surveillance on the American public was not far behind.

The UKUSA Agreement and ECHELON had another, more appropriately spooky name, "Five Eyes" (or FVEY), which worked overtime in the fifteen years prior to 9/11 and beyond. Some highlights through the years:

- The BBC reported that Prime Minister Margaret Thatcher ordered surveillance on two cabinet ministers in 1983.
- During Bill Clinton's first term, the NSA secured communiqués between the French manufacturer Airbus and the Saudi Arabian national airline suggesting bribes by Airbus to win the contract. The CIA, acting this time as the whistleblower, blew Airbus' cover. "Apparently this (and a direct sales pitch from Bill Clinton to King Fahd)," reports *The Economist,* "swung the aircraft part of the deal Boeing's and McDonnell Douglas' way."[177]
- In 1995, Clinton trade representative Mickey Kantor received NSA and CIA intel support as the U.S. was strong-arming Japan over trade negotiations. Kantor was receiving analysis of private conversations between Japanese bureaucrats and Nissan and Toyota executives, as well as conversations emanating from Japan's Trade Minister, Ryutaro Hashimoto. *The New York Times* headline said it all: "Emerging Role For the C.I.A.: Economic Spy."[178]
- The NSA spied on and gathered a giant classified file on Princess Diana until the fateful day in 1997 when the Mercedes W140 she was riding in piled into a concrete pillar going 70 miles per hour. The NSA denied releasing the file "because their disclosure could reasonably be expected to cause exceptionally grave damage to the national security."[179] Really?
- The BBC reported that British agents recorded the phone conversations of U.N. Secretary General Kofi Annan.
- *The Guardian* reported that U.S. diplomats, under a directive from Secretary of State Hillary Clinton, were ordered to spy and collect DNA info on the U.N. leadership, including Secretary General Ban Ki-moon.

Along with rapidly growing technology on all fronts, the program plainly became more pervasive during the 1990s as the NSA engaged in more aggressive and invasive domestic surveillance operations. This massive and secretive program, the forerunner to the current day PRISM "Big Data" operation, was part and parcel of Bill Clinton's NSA, but the mainstream American press was just sniffing around the edges, dramatically under-reporting the scope and danger of the NSA's operation with ECHELON. A CBS *60 Minutes* broadcast marked a rare exception when the news program aired an investigative piece on ECHELON in February of 2000:

> Everywhere in the world, every day, people's phone calls, emails and faxes are monitored by Echelon, a secret government surveillance network. No, it's not fiction straight out of George Orwell's 1984. It's reality, says former spy Mike Frost.[180]

Former Canadian intelligence agent, Mike Frost, explains to correspondent Steve Kroft, "It's not the world of fiction. That's the way it works. I've been there. I was trained by you guys," (referring to the National Security Agency).[181]

When the European Parliament investigated and then reported on the ECHELON operation, the report offered an opening salvo, a prescient warning from Juvenal—the second-century satirical Roman poet, who wrote:

Sed quis custodiet ipsos custodes.
(But who will watch the watchmen.)

I want to deliver a warning this afternoon: when the American people find out how their government has secretly interpreted the Patriot Act, they will be stunned and they will be angry.
—Senator Ron Wyden
Democrat of Oregon, during a debate about reauthorization of certain provisions of the Patriot Act[182]

In 2006, surveying the infirmed state of the union, Gore Vidal made it abundantly clear: "Eavesdropping without judicial warrants... This is what we call dictatorship."[183] Vidal was livid as he watched his country transition from a slippery slope of dangerous Constitutional struggles to an outright freefall into an authoritarian death grip. It was COINTELPRO-like programs all over again. The pendulum had swung all the way back, this time with a vengeance.

On 26 October 2001, forty-five days after the boomerang of blowback whacked the American Empire and killed almost 3,000 of its citizens, George W. Bush—with fear as his god and autocratic power as his nirvana—signed the USA Patriot Act into law. Author, activist, and reluctant politician Peter Camejo wasn't disinclined to take on the contentious act:

> It was, it is, an illegal act. The Congress, the Senate and the president cannot change the Constitution. And no one in their right mind can say to me with a straight face that the Patriot Act has not abrogated the Fourth Amendment... every Democrat or Republican... who voted for it, knew they were carrying out an illegal act in violation of the law.[184]

Not only were the legislators knowingly carrying out an illegal act that effectively superseded the Constitution, *THEY DIDN'T EVEN READ* the monstrous 342-page act that saw little if any debate. The totalitarian rubber stamp brings to mind Congressman John Conyers explaining to Michael Moore (in *Fahrenheit 9/11*) how Congress could pass the Patriot Act without reading it: "Sit down, my son. We don't read most of the bills."

The ACLU stated that the Patriot Act undermined and compromised the First, Fourth, Fifth, Sixth, Eighth, and Fourteenth Amendments. That's all. The Patriot Act also greatly bolstered the Executive Branch with sweeping powers that threatened the Bill of Rights, including new Attorney General guidelines that authorized the FBI to spy on political and religious groups without evidence of a crime, as well as making it legal for the government to monitor communications between federal detainees and representation, wiping out attorney-client privilege and thereby endangering the basic right to counsel.[185]

When it comes to surveillance, the Patriot Act empowers government agencies and government cops to carry out secret searches on a whim, conduct massive data sweeps on telephone and Internet communications and, with token judicial oversight, the new "law" gives agencies access to personal and private information including medical and mental health records, as well as financial reports. The Act also relaxed FISA restrictions, ensuring that wiretaps were made easier, such as "roving" wiretaps that blanket an individual person and not just a specific electronic device. The ACLU also outlines three additional areas where the Patriot Act grossly encroaches on Constitutional foundations:

- Expands terrorism laws to include "domestic terrorism" which could subject political organizations to surveillance, wiretapping, harassment, and criminal action for political advocacy.
- Allows FBI Agents to investigate American citizens for criminal matters without probable cause of crime if they say it is for "intelligence purposes."

- Permits non-citizens to be jailed based on mere suspicion and to be denied re-admission to the U.S. for engaging in free speech. Suspects convicted of no crime may be detained indefinitely in six-month increments without meaningful judicial review.[186]

PNAC

The ratification of the USA Patriot Act was a crowning glory for the boys who formed the neoconservative think tank in 1997 known as the "Project for the New American Century " (PNAC). In fact, the founders of this group, whose offices are situated adjacent to the Gates of Hell, conveniently morphed into George W. Bush's administration and included Dick Cheney, Scooter Libby, Donald Rumsfeld, Elliot Abrams, Richard Perle, and Paul Wolfowitz. In fact, as these neocons were regaining their positions of power in Washington, former CIA analyst Ray McGovern famously quipped, "When we saw these people coming back in town, all of us said, 'Oh my God, the crazies are back.'"

In 2000, the PNAC group released a report that outlined an empire-expanding game plan and suggested a roadmap for the United States to follow that would position and secure American global domination as well as controlling necessary resources throughout the 21st century. In the infamous PNAC report, the group called for the aggressive rebuilding of America's defenses in the very near future to ensure an ongoing and dominant global force. Ultimately, the goal was (and remains) global military hegemony. The report anticipated a long, uphill battle unless...

> The process of transformation, even if it brings revolutionary change, is likely to be a long one, absent some catastrophic and catalyzing event—like a new Pearl Harbor.[187]

Well, one year later they got one—and the floodgates exploded wide open. The ensuing invasions of Afghanistan and Iraq were orgasmic for "the crazies"—both in treasure accumulated and for what our friend George Carlin used to call "the bigger dick foreign policy theory at work"—power and dominion over others. Some dare call it rape.

And then of course came the USA Patriot Act, as "the crazies" turned inward on the sheep, focusing their madness on the masses—the ones they need to keep in chains so the flow of taxpayer dollars keeps gushing into *their* coffers, enabling the inevitable: more wars, more security, more contracts, more power... ultimately, mo' money.

The design and subsequent unleashing of the Patriot Act "betrayed the confidence the framers of the Constitution had," declares the ACLU, "that a government bounded by the law would be strong enough to defend the liberties they so bravely struggled to achieve." The ACLU concluded that, "the Patriot Act eroded our most basic right—the freedom from unwarranted government intrusion into our private lives—and thwarted constitutional checks and balances."[188] Journalist Chris Hedges, who studies the American landscape with a razor-sharp historic and legal eye, believes that atrocities like the Patriot Act and other assaults on the Bill of Rights, have undoubtedly jettisoned the nation into "a post-constitutional era." As 21st-century America continues to steamroll down oil-slicked hills to a constitutional wasteland, and right-wing politicians pack the federal courts and justice department with fascist ideologues, Hedges' assessment remains rock-solid and true.

Regardless of what Washington's politicians and their barking pundits say about sunset provisions and similar clauses that were allegedly designed to unplug the Patriot Act (as well as other legislation), in reality, they mean next to nothing. Congress continually pushes back and extends these expiration dates with alarming regularity. They're basically kicking the can down the road and manipulating the already-corrupt rules as they go along.

Sunset provisions are a way for the powerful to offer the capitulating masses a feel-good insurance policy. *Don't worry*—the current sales pitch goes—*let us get this situation with these dirty fucking Muslims under control, rough up the sumbitches, and then we'll go back to being the good ol' US of A, maybe even make 'Merica great again.* It's a convenient political catholicon, a blithe panacea. But the damage is done... the lid blown off Pandora's box... that crafty genie has slithered out of the bottle.

You know, if they just didn't stain the universe with their ugly embrace of the terror known as American slavery, these "founding fathers" said some decent shit every now and then. Here's James Madison:

> The means of defence agst. foreign danger, have been always the instruments of tyranny at home.[189]

A Surveillance State of Mind

It's a dangerous cocktail that's been shaken and stirred by Washington powerbrokers over the past century, and recently their nefarious and unconstitutional actions more resemble a mad scientist dashing around a laboratory in an alchemist's rapture. And no doubt, the cocktail has various ingredients.

For the citizenry, who are guilty of glad-handing over the Rights of Man, it's been equal parts mortal fear, blind jingoism, and outright amnesia regarding their own government and history. Zombified, they walk clueless over the cliff's edge.

For the corrupt powerbrokers, the grand manipulators, it's been what it's always been since Neanderthal One bashed Neanderthal Two over the head with a club and seized his spouse, children, food, and shelter: the elixir of power and the power of gold. "The state's wholesale intrusion into our lives and obliteration of privacy are now facts," Chris Hedges points out. "The most radical evil... is the political system that effectively crushes its marginalized and harassed opponents and, through fear and the obliteration of privacy, incapacitates everyone else."[190]

How will this repressive archetype of mass surveillance finally choke the life out of what's left of American liberty? At the precipice of this reality, Hedges builds the scenario:

> If we do not immediately dismantle the security and surveillance apparatus, there will be no investigative journalism or judicial oversight to address abuse of power. There will be no organized dissent. There will be no independent thought. Criticisms, however tepid, will be treated as acts of subversion. And the security apparatus will blanket the body politic like black mold until even the banal and ridiculous become concerns of national security.[191]

For the media, the professed Fourth Estate, their lack of responsibility as a watchdog over the corrupt nature of power has been damn near criminal. Journalist Amy Goodman calls it the "access of evil"—their fondness of exchanging their guts, courage, and responsibility for simple access to "the club." It's destructive enough on hard-hitting journalism that the corporate hierarchy and ownership of media outlets continually trade everything for the flow of advertising dollars, but when the scribes succumb, there's nothing left. Which brings to mind Jefferson's determination that "The press is the only tocsin of a nation."

Even when there are trenchant warnings and damning reports from powerful mainstream outlets, they come with caveats, loopholes, and embarrassingly pathetic behavior. Case in point was the exposé in *The New York Times* in 2005 divulging massive NSA warrantless wiretapping on American citizens dating back to 2002. America's "paper of record" buried the story and delayed its publication *for a year* based on immense pressure from Bush's White House. It was a workmanlike performance that would have made *Pravda* proud.

For the corporations—especially the telecommunication giants entrusted with the sanctity of the population's privacy—their capitulation to government agencies has been ongoing and comprehensive, making these monopolies complicit in the assault on the Constitution. Reports document that the NSA is paying "hundreds of millions of dollars a year to U.S. [telecom] companies for clandestine access to their communication networks."[192] In fact, documents released by Edward Snowden reveal voluntary cooperation from the giant telecoms dating back to the 1970s under the code name BLARNEY. The telecoms are required by law (politics by other means) to cooperate with so-called "lawful" surveillance orders issued by the rubber-stamp FISA court. But government payola clearly creates a bottom-line profit motive for Verizon, AT&T, and all the others to not only comply with requests but also become active and willing participants in the Big Brother abuse and molestation of the American people. Oligarchy 101.

A Really Special Relationship: The NSA and AT&T—*Perfect Together... consider them "the big eight."* We refer here to the eight fortress-like structures spread across the U.S. that operate as hubs for Ma Bell's efforts to work in partnership with the National Security Agency. AT&T calls these sites "Service Node Routing Complexes" and the NSA refers to them as "peering link router complexes." We call them "facilities with which to fuck the American people" (that's a technical term).

> The NSA considers AT&T to be one of its most trusted partners and has lauded the company's "extreme willingness to help."[193]

The enigmatic facilities stretch from coast-to-coast: Los Angeles, San Francisco, Seattle, Atlanta, and Dallas... there's an earthquake-resistant windowless skyscraper at 10 South Canal Street in Chi-town... there's also a citadel in D.C., close to the Capitol at 30 E Street, Southwest (that the NSA does not confirm nor deny they use the building nor do they acknowledge its very existence)... and then in Manhattan's Hell's Kitchen, there's a very special facility—this one sans windows and the damn thing is nuclear blast resistant. So when the apocalypse comes to New York City, the only things left alive will be the cockroaches, the Don Pepi pizza joint in Penn Station, some lucky AT&T snoops, and of course the NSA. "The horror..."

Once again, follow the money—it is the power of gold and the protection thereof. "It is capitalism, not government, that is the problem," Chris Hedges stresses.

"The fusion of corporate and state power means that government is broken. It is little more than a protection racket for Wall Street."[194]

Internet and social media giants are no better. Ironically, this tweeted from @Snowden:

> Businesses that make money by collecting and selling detailed records of private lives were once plainly described as "surveillance companies." Their rebranding as "social media" is the most successful deception since the Department of War became the Department of Defense.

Comfortable relationships between U.S. government spy operations (CIA, NSA, et al.) and multinational technology companies like Google exist (usually in plain sight) beneath the din of American and worldwide societies caught in a whirling technological maze of social and Internet media. For instance, Recorded Future is a company backed by both the Central Intelligence Agency and Google Ventures. This Internet tech company monitors the web "in real time" and then uses the information to provide—here it comes again—predictive analytics to forecast the future. The company, *Wired Magazine* reports, "scours tens of thousands of websites, blogs and Twitter accounts to find the relationships between people, organizations, actions and incidents—both present and still-to-come." The CIA/ Google venture advertises that it utilizes a "temporal analytics engine" that does magical things, way beyond your normal search engine, one that looks for "the 'invisible links' between documents that talk about the same, or related, entities and events."[195]

Invisible links? Don't you want the government and corporations filling in the blanks?

Parting Shot: In Defense of Snowden, Assange, Manning, et al.

It's actually very simple: there are heroes and there are villains.

For the most part, heroes always dwell in the minority—and it's usually the tiniest of minorities. For the most part, heroes stand up to the monolith of power in any milieu and say "no, not me, not now, not anymore." For the most part, and against all odds, heroes decide to take on the monster because the ogre in question is usually suffocating, corrupting, bending, or breaking the helpless, the defenseless, the meek, and the honorable.

And, for the most part, heroes take on these Goliaths, these bullies, at great peril to themselves. In early 2014, our oft-quoted correspondent Chris Hedges opened a debate at Oxford University arguing in favor of the proposition that, "This house would call Edward Snowden a hero." This was his inspiring opening salvo:

> I have been to war. I have seen physical courage. But this kind of courage is not moral courage. Very few of even the bravest warriors have moral courage. For moral courage means to defy the crowd, to stand up as a solitary individual, to shun the intoxicating embrace of comradeship, to be disobedient to authority, even at the risk of your life, for a higher principle. And with moral courage comes persecution.
>
> The American Army pilot Hugh Thompson had moral courage. He landed his helicopter between a platoon of U.S. soldiers and 10 terrified Vietnamese civilians during the My Lai massacre. He ordered his gunner to fire his M60 machine gun on the advancing U.S. soldiers if they began to shoot the villagers. And for this act of moral courage, Thompson, like Snowden, was hounded and reviled. Moral courage always looks like this. It is always defined by the state as treason—the Army attempted to cover up the massacre and court-martial Thompson. It is the courage to act and to speak the truth. Thompson had it. Daniel Ellsberg had it. Martin Luther King had it. What those in authority once said about them they say today about Snowden.[196]

The reigning American autocracy would have you believe that the whistleblowers are sneaks, snakes, vermin, and above all else—traitors. To the despotic and powerful, truth and justice remain irrelevant. Their motivations are fueled by power, more power, control, and unbridled avarice. Their attacks on the whistleblowers and the truth-tellers are to be expected, especially when their bubble-like world feels threatened. And that's when the elite watchdogs drop the hammer—stifle dissent and crush opposition movements with widespread surveillance and harassment. Keep the pressure heavy and, when necessary, use character assassination on individuals and groups and aim for the jugular. Journalist and constitutional scholar Glenn Greenwald suggests that when it comes to keeping the government and their apologists in check, the U.S. mainstream media is "neutered, impotent, and obsolete"—except when they utilize their vast resources to generate spin and mass propaganda to keep the masses blissfully misinformed. Power concedes nothing.

In American political theatrics, it's also defined as "inverted totalitarianism," as coined by political scientist and professor Sheldon Wolin.[197] "It is not derivative from 'classic totalitarianism' of the types represented by Nazi Germany, Fascist Italy, or Stalinist Russia," explains Wolin. "Those regimes were powered by revolutionary movements whose aim was to capture, reconstitute, and monopolize the power of the state."[198] Out with the old and in with the new. In these classic totalitarian models, Wolin also identified the fact that these revolutionary movements were personified by an incendiary firebrand, a tyrant to rally around. In America, where the tyranny is inverted and operating out of the shadows, it's all about sleight of hand—selling style over substance. It's about getting the masses to believe the bullshit.

Americans are told ad infinitum that the Constitution is sacrosanct and gospel, except, as Hedges suggests, it's been "steadily emasculated through radical judicial and legislative interpretation." Americans are told that their elections are as pure as the new driven snow and that these elections represent the glorious opportunity for change. They are perpetually told that the Bill of Rights protects all Americans equally, that the press is free, that their privacy is protected by Jesus himself, and that the check is in the mail. But then reality creeps in and heroic voices say "wait a second... not only does the emperor have no clothes, he's stark-raving mad." Hedges describes the American Mandarins with their hands on the paradigm of inverted totalitarianism:

> They so corrupt and manipulate electoral politics, the courts, the press and the essential levers of power as to make genuine democratic participation by the masses impossible. We have been left with a fictitious shell of democracy and a totalitarian core. And the anchor of this corporate totalitarianism is the unchecked power of our systems of internal security.[199]

But then here comes WikiLeaks... and a wrench is heaved into the works when the revelations reinvigorate the ideals of democracy. The government's dank and dirty laundry is now strung across the line in broad daylight, giving Americans a clear view of how their so-called leaders think and carry out policy—decisions that run contrary to what the people have been led to believe. Many times the reality is a refutation of the stories they've been told all their lives—from grade school through their latest foray into cable news and presidential press conferences. If American rhetoric actually existed on face value, the WikiLeaks disclosures would be boldly embraced. Instead, WikiLeaks and their founder

Assange are barraged by a torrent of ridicule and denunciation, not to mention legal indictment and even threats of death. As Noam Chomsky famously said, "Julian Assange shouldn't be the subject of grand jury hearings. He should be given a medal."

It's also a clear-cut case of blaming the messenger. Disregard the illegal, nefarious, diabolical—and many times murderous—behavior, and instead focus on and denigrate the men and women who shine a light in the darkness, usually at great risk. American journalists and media outlets should have rallied around Assange and WikiLeaks for breaking these colossal transgressions and crimes. The whistleblowers are doing exactly what is expected of the Fourth Estate: keeping power in check, being "the only tocsin of a nation."

Of all the WikiLeaks exposures, none rattle the cage more than the release of a 2007 military video that stars U.S. forces indiscriminately firing on Iraqi civilians from AH-64 Apache helicopter gunships. The murdered on the ground included Reuters news agency photographer Namir Noor-Eldeen and his driver Saeed Chmagh. The video reveals U.S. soldiers casually hunting down the civilians and then blowing them to pieces in sterile yet chilling fashion. Laughter and good ol' boy pats on the back conclude a fine day of shootin'—like poppin' black-tailed jackrabbits in a hot west Texas sun. A van pulls up in an attempt to save the wounded. One of the gunships opens fire again, killing more and badly wounding two children, again unleashing 30mm rounds, like shooting fish in a barrel. It's a sickening and horrific scene. It's exactly the brand of reality that the masters of war want to keep hidden from their cheerleading taxpayer bankers back home. Operation Iraqi Freedom looks a little different when U.S. gunships chase down and decimate unarmed civilians.

This is why WikiLeaks, Julian Assange, Edward Snowden, Chelsea Manning, as well as old school heroes like Daniel Ellsberg are so vital and essential if the truth is to ever make a difference. They love democracy. The United States Government and their instruments in the media hate democracy. Near the end of his life, gazing out of his living room window in the Hollywood Hills with that million mile stare, Gore Vidal told us he was brought up in the ruling class and that those in power "hate the people... the American people are an obstacle..." to everything power does, to everything power wants. Chomsky argues that surveillance and the classification of information is rarely done to protect the state or society from so-called enemies. Most of the time it's to protect the state from its own citizens.

When NSA technical contractor Edward Snowden released highly classified documents to *The Guardian* and *The Washington Post,* he knew in his gut that this revelation had to happen. Despite his critics' claims of treason, Snowden carefully released only a cache of documents that would reveal and deter unchecked surveillance, not the entire operation. In fact he could have brought the entire house down. He had access to *everyone* at the NSA. Edward Snowden could have revealed every nook and cranny of the Empire's operation—from the agents themselves to specific locales and foreign facilitators. EVERYTHING. But he didn't take down the whole system, as he said he could do "in an afternoon." Snowden released exactly what American citizens and the AWOL press needed to know about how American surveillance was spiraling out of control with the NSA, CIA, and FBI creating an unaccountable mass surveillance security state—one that targeted everybody.

> *He should be prosecuted for treason. If convicted by a jury of his peers, he should be hanged by his neck until he is dead.*
> —Former CIA Director James Woolsey

> *Snowden committed treason, he ought to be convicted of that, and then he ought to swing from a tall oak tree.*
> —Former U.S. Ambassador to the U.N. John Bolton

Well, that settles that. Words of wisdom from a chief thug and spook and a vicious war pig.

And then there's the sophisticated and grand insight from President Caligula, the former failed real estate magnate, when asked about Edward Snowden on the Cartoon Network's *Fox & Friends* in 2015: "Well, first of all he's a terrible guy... he's really hurt us in terms of relationship... spies in the old days used to be executed... there is still a thing called execution."

It's ludicrous to take as serious government (and media) claims that Snowden's revelations damaged "national security," which as we know is always their go-to assertion. Snowden's release of documents has endangered only one thing: *the myth of American freedom and liberty.* In fact, along with its murderous actions as globo-cop, the Empire's corrupt heart is now on public display. It's why the minions are scrambling for cover.

Besides control and power, mass surveillance is also motivated by paranoia. "One of the leading principles of international affairs, much too little recognized, is what may be called 'the Mafia doctrine,'" explains Noam Chomsky. "The Godfather does not tolerate disobedience. It's too dangerous. Even the slightest departure from subordination might incite others to follow the same path, eroding the system of domination." Chomsky says it's like the "domino theory"—if we don't stop them now, America will be vulnerable and helpless in a hostile world. "The Godfather can also be brutal and vindictive," the famed dissident continues. "One dramatic and revealing case is US policy towards Cuba... The US reacted almost at once with subversion, aggression, large-scale terror, and savage economic warfare... Cuba must be punished for what US planners fifty years ago described as its 'successful defiance.'" Chomsky concludes that, "The same principle applies to whistleblowers, though the Obama administration has gone far beyond its predecessors in seeking to control exposure of government actions."[200]

So, when is state surveillance okay?

The answer to this query is so incredibly straightforward it may sound cavalier and trite... but it's not. The answer simply embraces the United States Constitution as well as various domestic laws and international treaties. Those in favor of unbridled mass surveillance demand that aggressive spying is imperative to American security and that "some spying is always necessary," explains Greenwald. "But this is a straw man... nobody disagrees with that."[201] Greenwald then gets to the heart of the matter:

> The alternative to mass surveillance is not the complete elimination of surveillance. It is, instead, targeted surveillance, aimed only at those for whom there is substantial evidence to believe they are engaged in real wrongdoing.[202]

That's called erring on the side of the Constitution.

What's Really Scary

It appears even in the aftermath of bombshell revelations dropped by WikiLeaks and Assange, Snowden, Manning, William Binney, and the other courageous truth-tellers, that the spymasters and spooks are more resolute than ever. Let's recall that the publication of the Pentagon Papers did not immediately stop the Vietnam War—actually far from it. Journalist Danny Schechter (the "News Dissector") recalls that "There was four more years of carnage after Daniel

Ellsberg dropped the hidden history of our intervention in Vietnam showing how officials knew the truth even as they fed the public a litany of lies to keep a profitable if murderous enterprise going."[203] The long bloody saga of the Vietnam War was finally ended by the Vietnamese liberation army four decades ago and not by the actions of incensed Americans triggered by the Pentagon Papers. In fact, the current NSA juggernaut is rolling down hill and gaining thrust. "[T]he agencies seem to have the goods on the government as well as the rest of us," warns Schechter. "There is no American liberation army with the clout to shut them down."[204]

Former CIA analyst Ray McGovern reiterates the dire warnings: "Everybody is afraid. It's not just the journalists, it's people like Barack Obama, it's people like Dianne Feinstein—think about what the NSA has on Dianne Feinstein and her husband, who has made billions from Defense, and post office, and all kinds of nice cozy contracts... This goes back to J. Edgar Hoover."[205]

William Greider, the longtime National Affairs Editor at *Rolling Stone* and *The Nation,* takes the logical next step. In opining his love for the wicked political thriller *House of Cards,* Greider makes it clear that the spirit of the television series (that power rests with dark and powerful politicos) is pure fiction: "In the real world of Washington... politicians look more like impotent innocents compared to their true masters. It is the spooks and the spies who shuffle the deck and deal the cards."[206] When defining the netherworld of the American Empire, specifically the CIA and NSA, Greider underscores their supremacy and control based on his long association with Washington's elite: "The two clandestine agencies are the true puppet masters. It is elected politicians, even the president, who are puppets dancing on a string."

"Turnkey Tyranny"

Like a snowball rolling down Everest, American state surveillance has rolled through the last half-century with reckless abandon. And during the first twenty years of this century, America has been a dystopian oil-on-canvas that looks eerily similar to the final iconic frame of Franklin Schaffner's film *Planet of the Apes.* By any measure (this one defined by constitutional scholars gauging the crisis that is devouring the Framers intent, not to mention centuries of legal precedent), the U.S. government's overreach has actualized levels so inherently invasive as to put basic freedoms and society itself on the precipice of outright tyranny.

It's easy for us to sit here—Abu-Jamal locked in hell and Vittoria roaming free—and sound the alarm about the dark dangers of state surveillance. But it was not easy for Edward Snowden, who has risked life and freedom so that all of us might have a fighting chance to beat back the barbarians salivating at the gate. Snowden's living courage and dire words constantly remind us that we live in a time and place where the politics of fear drive the monster forward. In fact Snowden coined the term "turnkey tyranny" to underscore the very real possibility of the Executive Branch "flipping the switch." Snowden stresses that "[T]he systems are already in place. What happens tomorrow—in a year, in five years, in ten years—when eventually we get an individual [in the White House] who says, 'You know what? Let's flip that switch and use the absolute full extent of our technical capabilities to ensure the political stability of this new administration.'"[207]

Add to this harsh reality the fear-based coronation of the state's militarized police force (both federal and local) as compulsory... an untouchable and boilerplate necessity, and a complete totalitarian takeover is not farfetched—in fact it's right in our face, hiding in plain sight.

We end this chapter on the American surveillance and security state with words from Dick Gregory, speaking on a bullhorn in downtown Philadelphia—our beloved cradle of liberty. Dick was taking on Philadelphia's racist and corrupt police department and then turned his ire and wisdom on the entire state:

Wrong has always tried to spy on right. Right never spies on wrong.
There's something about light that wipes out darkness.

Photo: Unknown (circa 2010)

Richard Claxton Gregory

7 NO

Photo: Unknown

Diego Rivera

Diego Rivera, the great Mexican painter, proffered this clarion call: *The role of the artist is that of the soldier of the revolution.* When tyranny encroaches any society, as it has throughout history, without fail, the despots and autocrats always take aim at the artists and poets first. Tyrants know, they know full well that if they take away the words, the courageous words that question authority, the brave words that reveal the tyrants' nefarious underpinnings, if they take away the words as well as the images that stoke the people's mettle, that makes public the fact that the tyrants are building a Potemkin village around their launching pad, one ready to unleash the cruelty of their motives, the oppression of their power, the end of consensus, then they will clang the death knell, the final bells above the temple of democracy. They know like you know the sky is blue and the grass is green, that if they take away the words, the spirit, the inherent creative audacity of any society, you take away the power for people to communicate.

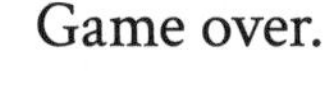

Game over.

Bomb Hugger
Artist: Banksy

And stifle they will, shutting down the Eduardo Galeanos... the Arundhati Roys... the John Lennons... the James Baldwins and Nikki Giovannis... the Betye Saars... and, of course, Banksy—imagine a world without the power of the *Bomb Hugger,* produced on a wall in East London. *Can love and peace overwhelm hatred and violence?* Banksy's arms of the child suggest yes. This artist, this visual poet challenges the very essence of the organizing principle of any society, any government—"the authority of the state over its people resides in its war powers."

So whether it's an iconic Rivera mural attacking the ruling class/the church/ or capitalism in Mexico City... or the post-punk rock and roll band, *Green Day,* calling out George W. Bush's murderous mugging on Afghanistan and Iraq in America's post-9/11 insanity, the artists and the poets remain the soul and truth-tellers in any society, open or closed.

> *Don't wanna be an American idiot*
> *Don't want a nation under the new media*
> *And can you hear the sound of hysteria?*
> *The subliminal mind-fuck America*

The most free, the artists and poets, the psyche of the masses, are first ridiculed, additional character assassination if necessary, or worse if really necessary. Many times in this boiling cauldron of rightness, journalists/activists/and historians become deputized as de facto poets—take your pick, history is chock-full of their beleaguered bodies and tormented minds. Fighting the wicked is shitty work. That's why sometimes absurdity is required—like during the height of the Vietnam War, when black-white-brown-red-and-yellow bodies were piling up in the jungles of Indochina and the time was perfect for a waggish and inspiring "stunt" as some called it—but they were dead wrong marginalizing it as a "stunt"—instead we called it performance art par excellence. Abbie Hoffman was ready to perform an exorcism on the Pentagon, America's most unholy house, by attempting to levitate the five-sided polygon structure three hundred feet in the air. "Everybody knows that a five-sided figure is evil," Abbie told us, "The way to exorcise it is with a circle." And a circle they tried to form around the fortress, chanting Aramaic exorcism rites—the circle never completed because the military, as they are apt to do, used tear gas and were whacking American citizens with rifle butts. Real tough guys. Beating the shit out of dissenters armed with flowers, guitars, and ideas. *The subliminal mind-fuck America.*

Later when asked what they were expecting to accomplish, Hoffman and fellow performance artist, Jerry Rubin, gave their straight answer: the whole damn place would "rise into the air, turn orange, and vibrate until all evil emissions had fled. The war would end forthwith." America's great scribe was there as well, with words, magic words that described his mystical view of the Pentagon as he marched over the Arlington Memorial Bridge, words that lightnings would carry to the cosmos in his extraordinary work *Armies of the Night:*

> The Pentagon rose like an anomaly out of the sea from the soft Virginia fields, its pale yellow walls reminiscent of some plastic plug coming out of the hole made in flesh by an unmentionable operation.
> —Norman Mailer

See? Words? Poets/Artists/Writers. Words matter. Especially free words.

You see, that's what government barbarians fear most—and they especially fear one word more than all the others:

NO

And that's what the courageous ones scream from the mountaintops when they use their art to reveal that the emperor has no clothes.

Tupac knew it.

> *I see no changes wake up in the morning and I ask myself*
> *Is life worth living should I blast myself?*
> *I'm tired of bein' poor and even worse I'm black*
> *My stomach hurts so I'm lookin' for a purse to snatch*
> *Cops give a damn about a negro*
> *Pull the trigger kill a nigga he's a hero*
> *Give the crack to the kids who the hell cares*
> *One less hungry mouth on the welfare*
> *First ship 'em dope and let 'em deal the brothers*
> *Give 'em guns step back watch 'em kill each other*
> *It's time to fight back that's what Huey said*
> *Two shots in the dark now Huey's dead*
> *I got love for my brother but we can never go nowhere*
> *Unless we share with each other*
> *We gotta start makin' changes*
> *Learn to see me as a brother instead of two distant strangers*
> ("Changes" 1992)

John Lennon knew it when he declared revolution with a screeching Epiphone Casino guitar to wake the living dead.

You say you'll change the constitution
Well, you know
We all want to change your head
You tell me it's the institution
Well, you know
You better free your mind instead
("Revolution" 1968)

Metallica (James Hetfield & Lars Ulrich) knew it when their song *One* accompanied film clips from Dalton Trumbo's harrowing antiwar masterpiece *Johnny Got His Gun*—proving again that video killed the radio star:

Now that the war is through with me
I'm waking up, I cannot see
That there is not much left of me
Nothing is real but pain now
Hold my breath as I wish for death
Oh please God, wake me
("One" 1988)

In the music video, a simple conversation between Joe Bonham as a little boy and his father slips through, one of the great antiwar truths in the film:

Boy	What is democracy?
Father	It's got something to do with young men killing each other.
Boy	When it comes to my turn, would you want me to go?
Father	For democracy, any man would give his only begotten son.

Billie Holiday knew it in 1939 when she recorded Abel Meeropol's poem about the brutal 1930 lynching of Thomas Shipp and Abraham Smith—a song nobody wanted to record and distribute. Wonder why...

Southern trees bear a strange fruit
Blood on the leaves and blood at the root
Black bodies swinging in the southern breeze
Strange fruit hanging from the poplar trees
("Strange Fruit" 1937)

Nasir bin Olu Dara Jones (Nas) knew it with his album titled *Untitled* and accompanied by the image of a slave master's whip marks on Nas' back, creating the letter "N"—

> *Assassinations*
> *Diplomatic relations*
> *Killed indigenous people*
> *Built a new nation*
> *Involuntary labor*
> *Took a knife split a woman naval*
> *Took her premature baby*
> *Let her man see you rape her*
> *If I could travel to the 1700's*
> *I'd push a wheelbarrow full of dynamite*
> *Through your covenant*
> ("America" 2008)

So did NWA *Straight Outta Compton*—

> *They have the authority to kill a minority*
> *Fuck that shit, 'cause I ain't the one*
> *For a punk motherfucker with a badge and a gun*
> *To be beatin' on, and thrown in jail*
> ("Fuck Tha Police" 1988)

In 1819, a woman identifying herself as "Africus" wrote and published a poem entitled *The Tears of a Slave,* as a brave petition against slavery:

> *Adieu, to my dear native shore,*
> *To toss on the boisterous wave;*
> *To enjoy my kindred no more,*
> *But to weep—the tears of a SLAVE!*
> *By the sons of freemen I'm borne,*
> *To the land of the free and the brave;*
> *From my wife and children I'm torn,*
> *To weep—the sad tears of a SLAVE!*

One hundred and sixty years later, Joe Strummer from *The Clash,* who knows a thing or two about rabble-rousing, also said NO to racism and the associated violence in the streets of Great Britain...

All over people changing their votes
Along with their overcoats
If Adolf Hitler flew in today
They'd send a limousine anyway
("{White Man} In Hammersmith Palais" 1978)

Some folks don't like their artists "getting political" or their athletes "talking politics." Al Jourgensen (born Alejandro Ramírez Casas), the Cuban-American pioneer of industrial metal and front man for the band *Ministry,* has never hid behind his radical politics, and has this to say to those who wish he would scrub and sanitize their lyrics and their political resolve: "I'll tell you what, to the detractors of Ministry, I promise you, I will stop making music. You just make it a nice little utopian world. All right? Then I'll shut the fuck up."

I've got something to say to you
I'll back it up with my fist
Sick and tired of dealing with assholes
That's why I resist
We're not snowflakes
We are the antifa
("Antifa" 2018)

And finally, the ever-growing snare drum leading up to Edwin Starr wailing on the counterculture soul psalm that landed on Clear Channel's no-play list following 9/11, along with other "dangerous" songs like Cat Stevens' *Peace Train.*

War, whoa, lord
What is it good for
Absolutely nothing, listen to me
("War" 1969)

We end *Murder Incorporated* (as we started, if you're paying attention) with two poets, two troubadours, both of whom, in their inimitable and powerful way, said NO to the Neanderthals—robber barons who take without asking and will literally kill you if you dare stand up and say:

Hey, what the fuck?

Here are Woody Guthrie & Gil Scott-Heron.

This Machine Kills Fascists

Photo: Library of Congress (1943)

Woody Guthrie

In May of 2012, forty-five years after his death, the body politic sorely needed the devotional and forewarning voice of Woody Guthrie to remind us that this was indeed a world gone wrong, when Woody's bardic progeny—the man born Robert Zimmerman aka Bob Dylan, the man who penned the jackhammer of all antiwar anthems, "Masters of War"—meekly accepted the Presidential Freedom Award from Barack Obama, at the time the most recent American master of war. Linh Dinh, the Vietnamese-American poet, born a few short months before the Johnson Administration unleashed the dogs of hell on Indochina—the same murderous war that so moved Dylan to howl "even Jesus would never forgive what you do"—wrote of another evening when Dylan and Joan Baez serenaded Obama: "Dylan's old squeeze, Queen Jane, sang at the same soiree, and before crooning, Baez even gazed at Obama and cooed, 'Mr. President, you are much loved.' In our inverted country, grizzled peaceniks now serenade a war criminal."[1]

This was not irony, nor satire, nor a simple twist of fate. It was perverse. As Dylan embraced his Presidential Freedom Award, he did so in the long shadow of Obama's Nobel Peace Prize—another true perversion as the Empire and its subjects hurtled toward the sun.

> *I'm gonna tell you fascists*
> *You may be surprised*
> *The people in this world*
> *Are getting organized*
> *You're bound to lose*
> *You fascists bound to lose*
> —Woody Guthrie, "All You Fascists"

The early years of the 20th century began with a healthy dose of radicalism and dissent. Influenced by the revolutionary movements in Europe and fueled concomitantly by the drums of war, by horrendous working conditions, as well as abject poverty in U.S. cities and rural communities, major shifts in political thought and alternative social remedies were well underway across America. Powerful labor organizations, like the anarchist-influenced Industrial Workers of the World, known to the masses as "the Wobblies," drew hard lines in the sand that clearly defined the mushrooming class struggle taking place across America and the world. "The working class and the employing class have nothing in common," stated the IWW preamble to its Constitution. "There can be no peace so long as the hunger and want are found among millions of the working people, and the few, who make up the employing class, have all the good things in life."[2] It was the robber barons (the original 1%) wanting to own and control the whole enchilada against the people, the masses mobilizing to fight back. It was in this atmosphere and from this rumble in the (urban) jungle that the great socialist movement of the early 20th century sprang up. It was also the conditions that inspired a young Woodrow Wilson Guthrie, born in Okemah, Oklahoma, in July of 1912, to look beyond his provincial trappings. But the times also influenced Guthrie in ways that illustrate why he remains a complex character to this day. A year before his birth, Woody's father—Charles Guthrie, a land speculator and Ku Klux Klan sympathizer—attended the notorious lynching of Laura Nelson and her fifteen-year-old son Lawrence, two African-Americans gagged and hanged by their necks from a public bridge over the North Canadian River in Okemah.[3] Hundreds of sightseers witnessed the hangings and Charles Guthrie was one of them.[4] The local newspaper, the *Okemah Ledger,* described Laura Nelson as "very small of stature, very black, about thirty-five years old, and vicious." The *Okemah Ledger* went on to praise the lynching, crowing on the front page that it was "executed with silent precision." The article concluded, "While the general sentiment is adverse to the method, it is generally thought that the Negroes got what would have been due them under process of law."[5]

This was the backwater, racially hostile, and intolerant world Woody Guthrie was born into. It was a world that clearly shaped and molded his complex oeuvre that combined leftist protest songs with hillbilly-like tunes where "nigger" was casually tossed around like any other lyric. But Woody got lucky as those early and ugly racist references were never recorded (or some believe they were destroyed). His legacy never took the appropriate hit it should have, but we'd be remiss if we didn't offer a sampling of Woody's lyrics before he saw the light. In his book *A Race of Singers: Whitman's Working-Class Hero from Guthrie to Springsteen,* author Bryan Garman writes:

> In a newspaper article he planned to distribute to his fans at KVFD, he offered a racist representation of blacks who allegedly interrupted a picnic he and friends were having at Santa Monica

> Beach. Caricaturing the African Americans as "savages," Guthrie complains of an "Ethiopian smell" that pervades the air and grows frightened as he watches their "cannibal" dances.[6]

Veteran journalist Jonny Whiteside frames Woody's racial foundation in an article he wrote for *LA Weekly:*

> Broadcasting on Pasadena's KFVD, Guthrie often indulged in on-air employ of ebonics and was stunned when a black listener characterized the singer as "unintelligent" after hearing Guthrie perform songs with titles like "Run, Nigger, Run" and "Nigger Blues." Fortunately for Guthrie, recordings of these tunes do not survive. Guthrie apologists are quick to point out that "nigger" was then in common usage. But its intended meaning was pejorative then—and, yes, racist—just as it is now. Later, Guthrie said, "A young Negro in Los Angeles wrote me a nice letter one day telling me the meaning of that word [nigger] and that I shouldn't say it anymore on the air. So I apologized." He next "tore all the nigger songs out of his songbook."[7]

Later, when Guthrie moved to New York, Martha and Huddie Ledbetter "invited this disheveled vagabond to live in their apartment," which was a bustling hub for many blues and folksingers of the day. And it was in the home of the legendary black bluesman, Ledbelly, that Guthrie grew beyond the rank ignorance of his Oklahoma childhood. "[A]s he listened to lessons about racism and hunger," Garmen writes, "Guthrie 'could not tell where [his] own personal life stopped and Ledbelly's started.'"[8]

The Great Depression, coupled with the Great Dust Storm, wreaked havoc throughout the Great Plains on thousands of desperate unemployed workers and farmers. A twenty-something Woody, along with countless other "dustbowl refugees," hit the roads heading west in search of work and a new life. Guthrie's account in his autobiography, *Bound for Glory,* was the story of this migration, riding freight trains and hitchhiking toward a distant horizon. And along the way, Woody played guitar and sang in saloons. He paid his dues and generously offered his art to the service of those anti-racist and anti-fascist forces fighting for social and economic justice.

One day I heard a song by Woody Guthrie called "The Ludlow Massacre"—a dark, haunting, powerful song. And that led me to look in a library about this event, which nobody had ever mentioned in any of my history courses.[9]
—Howard Zinn

> *You struck a match and the blaze it started*
> *You pulled the triggers of your Gatling guns*
> *I made a run for the children but the firewall stopped me*
> *Thirteen children died from your guns*
> —Woody Guthrie, "The Ludlow Massacre"

This song about a brutal massacre at a Colorado miners' strike leaves no doubt that Woody Guthrie was a union man. His songs in support of unions protecting workers from repression remain relevant and widely sung by singers who care today. The legendary folk singer and celebrated activist, the late Pete Seeger, tells his firsthand account of working with Guthrie on one ballad in particular:

> I'm proud to say I was present when "Union Maid" was written in June, 1940, in the plain little office of the Oklahoma City Communist Party. Bob Wood, local organizer, had asked Woody Guthrie and me to sing there the night before for a small group of striking oil workers. Early next morning, Woody got to the typewriter and hammered out the first two verses of "Union Maid" set to a European tune that Robert Schumann arranged for piano ("The Merry Farmer") back in the early 1800s.[10]

> *There once was a union maid, she never was afraid*
> *Of goons and ginks and company finks*
> *And the deputy sheriffs who made the raid.*
> *She went to the union hall when a meeting it was called,*
> *And when the Legion boys come 'round*
> *She always stood her ground.*
> —Woody Guthrie, "Union Maid"

It's important to note that the Dust Bowl, not unlike Guthrie himself, was part myth created by newspapers and writers of the time. Of course the Dust Bowl was a genuine environmental catastrophe but wind erosion and over-cropping was only part of the saga. A mass migration from the east and Midwest was already choking the American southwest with an unsustainable population—one that had been growing larger since the late 19th century.

When Woody arrived in the Golden State in 1937, along with thousands of "Okies," the hatred and violence from the so-called "resident" Californians opposed to this Midwestern onslaught was well underway. The circumstances were ripe to welcome voices of resistance. Woody started singing old-time traditional folk and hillbilly songs on the aforementioned Los Angeles radio station KFVD. Guthrie's twang and storytelling rang true throughout the migrant camps that embraced his reflective and familiar sound. Itinerant life was brutal and Woody's tunes gave them a much-needed break from their daily hell. Not surprisingly though, as Woody evolved as a "protest" singer, his message was clearly far to the left of his Dust Bowl devotees.[11] In fact, his evolution as a songwriter is a laboratory study of an artist undergoing a tectonic shift in public courage—a voice of dissent and radicalism during a time populated by red-baiting hit men, led by the infamous reprobate Senator Joe McCarthy.

"Pastures of Plenty," Guthrie's great ode to migrant workers, was a song that seeped into the California groundwater, evidenced two decades later when the same spirit pumped through the veins of Cesar Chavez:

> *I've wandered all over your green growing land*
> *Wherever your crops are, I'll lend you my hand*
> *On the edge of your cities, you'll see me and then*
> *I come with the dust and I'm gone with the wind*

Woody's art and activism was not the work of a man happy with the passive and submissive comfort of those old-time spirituals. He was in motion, *ONAMOVE,* ready to battle injustice here on Earth rather than wait passively and accept a poor man's slice of heaven. Will Kaufman, the author of *Woody Guthrie: American Radical,* frames his spirit:

> Woody Guthrie spent his productive life on the warpath—against poverty, political oppression, censorship, capitalism, fascism, racism, and ultimately war itself. His commitment to radical struggle forced him to face head on—and sometimes celebrate—the violence inevitable to the tearing down and reconstruction of an oppressive system, whether fascism in Europe or capitalism at home.[12]

This brawl is clearly evident throughout his life and he punches it home with his last stanza of "All You Fascists"—

I'm going into this battle
And take my union gun
We'll end this world of slavery
Before this battle's won
You're bound to lose
You fascists bound to lose!

I Was Blind. Now I Can See.

Well known for his songs championing poor, white Dust Bowl migrants, Woody evolved quickly. He created a far-reaching body of songs that condemned Jim Crow segregation, race hatred, as well as racial fascism. Like the repulsive songs from his early body of work, these songs were also never recorded, but the surviving lyrics dramatically underscore Woody's own personal transformation from a careless and cavalier Oklahoma racist to a dedicated and steadfast civil rights activist. It was a powerful public conversion that reached full volume in the summer of 1949 in Peekskill, New York, when Guthrie led a band of petrified folk singers at an outdoor hootenanny supporting the Civil Rights Congress—an event plagued by racist anti-communist forces in what came to be known as the "Peekskill Riots." Nevertheless, the show went on and Paul Robeson and Pete Seeger joined Woody. After the performance, local police—in cahoots with Klansmen and racial hooligans from the local American Legion—led the musicians' vehicles and the audience crowd going home down a lonely country road. The ambush lay in wait and the caravan of civil rights activists were viciously attacked.[13] Scott Linford of UCLA, reviewing Will Kaufman's 2011 work on Guthrie, frames this moment in time and Woody's evolution as a political force:

> The Peekskill riots demonstrate the politically fraught atmosphere of Guthrie's time and the multivalent role that music played in cultural combat. To the local police, Guthrie and Robeson's music was a loud symbol of communism and racial equality, a sonic threat so potent it had to be countered by the sound of helicopters. To the violent protesters, it was an anti-American insult that inspired hatred. To the concert-goers, it was a locus of solidarity worth risking bodily harm to hear and, later, in the embattled cars and buses, a font of collective courage and a defense against flung stone. The incident also crystallized typical aspects of Guthrie's character in a time of crisis: his fierce commitment to the radical cause and the plucky folksiness he employed strategically in its support.[14]

After this politically defining moment and surviving the Peekskill riots, Woody penned the angriest and most rebellious songs of his life, songs like "Peekskill Golfing Grounds," which keenly evokes the depths of hatred:

> *I've never heard such cusswords as they spit from off their lips,*
> *I just stood and watched their eyes blare as they walked a dozen trips.*
> *Jew bastard. Wop. Hey nigger. Kike and Commy. And, their lungs*
> *Sounded like a boiling snake den with a million poison tongues.*

In the late 1940s and into the fifties, Woody continued singing and working alongside major black artists like Huddie William Ledbetter aka Lead Belly, the blacklisted and courageous Paul Robeson, the blind bluesman for the ages, Sonny Terry, and the Piedmont-picking blues genius, Brownie McGhee. What started out for Woody as casual, ignorant, and just plain run-of-the-mill good old American racism changed radically, categorically proving that racists can be made... and unmade.

They're taking a revolutionary and turning him into a conservationist.
— Irwin Silber, Journalist, Editor, Publisher

Woody Guthrie's most iconic song, "This Land Is Your Land," was co-opted almost as soon as he composed the song in 1956 and thereafter greatly misunderstood. In fact, the song remains the perfect mirror image of America's overall misunderstanding of Guthrie, along with the malappropriation and repackaging of his legacy.

On the one-hundred-year celebration of Guthrie's birth, Lawrence Downes, in *The New York Times,* discussed this legacy alteration: "Maybe that's what happens to dissidents who are dead long enough. They are reborn for folk tales and children's books and PBS pledge drives. They become safe enough for the Postal Service."[15] And that's exactly what happened in 1998 when the U.S. Postal Service released the Woody Guthrie 32-cent stamp, to which his son Arlo Guthrie quipped, "For a man who fought all his life against being respectable, this comes as a stunning defeat."[16]

"This Land Is Your Land" best expresses Guthrie's radicalism and scrap as an artist. Not unlike Bruce Springsteen's "Born in the USA," people and politicians have embraced the song for all the wrong reasons—reasons that Woody and Bruce never intended. Some say it is legend, some say it is fact, but when Woody wrote "This Land Is Your Land," many believe he wrote it as a direct rejoinder to

Irving Berlin's ultra-patriotic "God Bless America." Woody's experiences living with the victims of America's economic crush tell a much different story from Berlin's jingoistic fairytale. Guthrie's most well-known song embraces ideas that were considered rebellious in their time, ideas that questioned the ruling class' definition of individual rights, liberty, and of course property ownership. Larry Rohter, writing in the music section of *The New York Times* concludes, "But instead of the standard, sanitized lyrics taught to schoolchildren as a kind of patriotic bromide, it offers an alternate version with an extra verse that is a biting, defiant and subversive jab at what today would be called the 1 percent."[17] Usually omitted in written texts and covers by other musicians, this passage best illustrates Woody's ability to flip the coin on Berlin's myth-embracing piece of xenophobic apple pie (you know the tune):

As I went walking I saw a sign there
And on the sign it said "No Trespassing"
But on the other side it didn't say nothing
That side was made for you and me.

I AIN'T A GONNA KILL NOBODY

I took a bath this morning in six war speeches, and a sprinkle of peace. Looks like ever body is declaring war against the forces of force. That's what you get for building up a big war machine. It scares your neighbors into jumping on you, and then of course they them selves have to use force, so you are against their force, and they're aginst yours. Look like the ring has been drawed and the marbles are all in. The millionaires has throwed their silk hats and our last set of drawers in the ring. The fuse is lit and the cannon is set, and somebody is in for a frailin. I would like to see every single soldier on every single side, just take off your helmet, unbuckle your kit, lay down your rifle, and set down at the side of some shady lane, and say, nope, I aint a gonna kill nobody. Plenty of rich folks wants to fight. Give them the guns.[18]

—Woody Guthrie, (from "Woody Sez"), 1939

From the early days when Woody was writing a column called "Woody Sez" for the communist daily paper, *People's World,* through to his death from Huntington's Disease in 1967, the pious and the powerful have dismissed him for being a communist dreamer, a quaint and ramshackle hobo balladeer. They've celebrated the safe stuff and buried the substance. Lawrence Downes concludes that, "The sentimental softening and warping of Woody's reputation began early, even as he was dying, in the 1960s. But under the saintly folk hero has always been an angry vigilante—a fascist-hating, Communist-sympathizing rabble-rouser who liked to eviscerate his targets, sometimes with violent imagery. He was a man of many contradictions, but he was always against the rich and on the side of the oppressed. He wrote hard-hitting songs for hard-hit people."[19]

But beneath it all, especially during the mid-20th century, it was Communism that struck fear in the hearts of most Americans, and it's Communism that the fear-mongers used as their silver bullet… and Woody Guthrie was one of the targets, one of the dangerous ones Management® had in their crosshairs.

By the mid-1970s, Woody's writings and songs proliferated in publications everywhere. One gentleman—a fellow song and dance man—was motivated to write this short note to the Guthrie family:

> *Dear Whoever,*
> *Woody lives,*
> *And I'm glad!*
> *love,*
> *John Lennon '75* [20]

Public voices of dissent and radicalism, like Lennon and Guthrie, are needed now more than ever; and like John Lennon, Woody Guthrie's spirit will endure. His stance against cruelty and tyranny was defined by turning people's suffering into poetry and exposing the misery for what it was: terrorism. We summon the words of Steve Earle, who also felt the dire need to make this musical plea across the ages in his song "Christmas in Washington"—a plea for the return of the truly revolutionary Dust Bowl Balladeer:

> *So come back Woody Guthrie*
> *Now, come back to us now*
> *Tear your eyes from paradise*
> *And rise again somehow*

Gil—The Real

Soul of a Nation

Photo: Unknown

Gil Scott-Heron

> Gil set the template, it's as simple as that. He set the template for being able to put some sort of rhythm and opinion and expressive thought and a sense of voice and musicality together. As far as black people are concerned, Gil Scott-Heron is like Bob Dylan... they're equals.[21]
> —Chuck D, Public Enemy

Gil Scott-Heron, the baritone poet, musician, and proto-rapper who was later lauded as "the Godfather of Rap" (a label he wore with quiet discomfort), was, by chance, almost never born.

We don't mean that the living soul born into post-World War II America was almost aborted—heavens forfend—no. We mean the legendary name that proudly emblazoned some twenty album covers and scripted the spines of several novels almost never got taken. Gil's father—a celebrated fútbol player nicknamed "The Black Arrow," the first black man to play for the Celtic Football Club in Glasgow—upon his son's birth, announced that his name would be Gilbert Saint Elmo Heron. His Mama heard "Elmo" and said, "Hell, no!" She won and they quietly agreed on her maiden name (Scott) to fill the middle space, and Gil Scott-Heron took secure residence on the third rock pile from the Sun.

This pioneering poet with a masterful political voice was born in Chicago on 1 April 1949 of a Jamaican father and African-American mother (they were called "Negroes" back then), and he inherited strong and intriguing energy from both beings—Gil's father, the renowned soccer player also named Gil (Giles), and his mother Bobbie, a librarian as well as an opera singer who elegantly performed with the New York Oratorio Society. Elder Gil and Bobbie separated early in Gil's life, and for stability sent the youngster to live with his maternal grandmother, Lily Scott, in Jackson, Tennessee, a quiet railroad junction some seventy miles east of Memphis. Young Gil lived a life that encapsulated and echoed the travels and travails of his people: The Great Migration to the North. He loved his youth there, where he was known throughout the community as "Bob Scott's boy" (although he was actually Scott's grandson, Lily's husband, who died the year before Gil's birth, but whose aura still hung over the city like a gentle rolling fog).

Gone, but not forgotten. Bob Scott was a man of substance—ahem—a "Black" man of substance, who put all of his children though college, including Gil's mom. And like many Black families of the era, life in the South had become intolerable, and stories from the North professed the sweet Promised Land. Well, it wasn't, of course. But his mother Bobbie went in search of those dreams anyway, hitting Chicago before settling in New York—the Bronx.

Gil's grandmother, Lily—a musician and civil rights activist—raised him and taught him to read using the *Chicago Defender* newspaper, which, to his youthful delight, featured the brilliant writing of the poet, novelist, and dramatist, Langston Hughes, also reared in the Midwest. Hughes remained an influencing and important force throughout Gil's life and work. Perhaps back there, in the following daylight of youth, the ideas began; for what Langston Hughes was, Gil Scott-Heron would become, although he would utilize more tools to speak the thoughts, voices, and deep yearnings of his people. Discussing his grandmother in 1986, Scott-Heron explained:

> She was an issues woman, looking at things in terms of what's fair and not fair. It's a question of looking in your heart for the truth and not seeing whether your favorite politician goes for a particular issue. On a right and wrong type of basis, this is how my grandmother raised me, to not sit around and wait for people to guess what's on my mind—I was gonna have to say it.[22]

Lily Scott was an enormous force on all of Gil's days as evidenced years later when he wrote and recorded "On Coming from a Broken Home"—

I had no strong male figure right?
But Lily Scott was absolutely not your mail order room service
type cast black Grandmother
I was moved in with her;
Temporarily, just until things were patched,
'Til this was patched and 'til that was patched
Until I became at 3, 4, 5, 6, 7, 8, 9 and 10
The patch that held Lily Scott who held me and like them 4
I become one more and I loved her
from the absolute marrow of my bones

Lily bought Gil an upright piano from an undertaker. "It was either six dollars or eight dollars, I'm not sure," Gil told a reporter. "The story would change from time to time depending on how much she was trying to tell me that we didn't have no money."[23] Regardless of the comical price, Gil learns to play by ear and as he matures it's clear he has all the tools: a piano, Langston Hughes, a civil rights foundation, and the invigorating muse of the Harlem Renaissance.

At his junior high, Gil faced daily racial abuse. He was one of three Black children selected to help desegregate the school. These blatantly racial experiences fueled his first volume of poetry (unpublished) when Gil was only twelve.

Lily Scott passed away shortly thereafter and he moved back with his mother in The Bronx. They had to learn how to take each other, for they didn't know each other, and, perhaps more importantly, like each other. But she gave him room to be the being that was himself, and also gave a mother's advice—simple, direct, and clear. Like her father, she was an educated woman, who earned a Master's degree when it wasn't a common thing to do (for women, or for Black women). She allowed him room to blossom—to become. Gil made the choices, as do we all. Good ones. Bad ones. Brilliant ones. And like all of us, stupid ones.

Gil Scott-Heron attended the all-boys DeWitt Clinton High School on Mosholu Parkway and quickly impressed the English Department with one of his short stories (a detective story!) and earned a full scholarship to the exclusive Ivy-League preparatory school, the Ethical Culture Fieldston School in the Riverdale section of The Bronx. "As one of five black students at the prestigious school, Scott-

Heron was faced with alienation and a significant socioeconomic gap," writes Jonah Weiner in *Rolling Stone.* "During his admissions interview at Fieldston, an administrator asked him, 'How would you feel if you see one of your classmates go by in a limousine while you're walking up the hill from the subway?' And [he] said, 'Same way as you. Y'all can't afford no limousine. How do you feel?'"[24] Early on we see the brutally honest laser beam of a mind able to cut through bullshit, the very essence of his historic writings and recordings.

Gil graduates from Fieldston and heads to Langston Hughes' alma mater, Lincoln University, a historically Black university fifty miles east of Philadelphia. Gil meets Brian Jackson and the two men become lifelong musical compadres. After two years at Lincoln, Gil hits the bricks to write full time. He pumps out two novels, *The Vulture* and *The Nigger Factory* (published in 1970 and 1971), as well as a volume of poetry. *The Vulture*—a murder mystery injected with politics and a distinct portrait of the late 1960s—receives critical acclaim.

If there was a mainstay in his life, it was music—both as one who loved to listen (mostly jazz), but also as a player—pianist, singer, songwriter, and one of the first to record and capture the form now known as spoken word. "Bob Scott's boy" starts performing poetry in New York's jazz clubs and coffee joints and is hit up by record producer Bob Thiele of Impulse Records, who produced some remarkable work by Coltrane, Mingus, and Rollins (John, Charles, and Sonny). "Surprisingly, Scott-Heron's debut is a live recording of his poetry, including material from *The Vulture,*" writes music journalist David Dacks. "Even the title, *Small Talk At 125th and Lenox,* showcases a man of biting wit who is unafraid to righteously take issue with the fading promises of the civil rights era, the emptiness of consumerism and entrenched economic iniquities in America."[25] Conga drums and sporadic piano hits accompany Gil's "rapid-fire, didactic spoken word style, which reaches its peak with 'The Revolution Will Not Be Televised' and 'Whitey On The Moon.'"[26]

Given the times, when rebellion and, indeed, revolution was in the air, Gil Scott-Heron joined his voice to the freedom strivings of Black beings. His jazz-inflected style (and that of his band, *Midnight Band*) came along at a time when both listeners and radio programmers were seeking something new—different, challenging, *real.* His tenor/baritone—clear, smooth, and with a hint of its Tennessee origins flavoring his words—were the perfect accompaniment for an age of Black Rebellion, as the Civil Rights and Black Liberation movements that captured Black America were percolating through millions of Afric brains.

His music could be both sardonic and sweet depending on his mood, and of that of his fellow space traveler, Brian Jackson, the accomplished pianist and flutist.

Scott-Heron and his band composed, sang, and recorded songs that were voices of protest against U.S. foreign policy ("Johannesburg" aka "Let Me See Your I.D."), against the apartheid system there, against the coming of the "[Ronald] Reagan era," against poverty in the ghetto, and against ubiquitous government corruption. Equally, many of his songs were tender melodies about children, woman, alcoholics, and the poor. Those qualities are seen in a song that went on to become one of the band's biggest hits, and, in part, defined him for generations of lovers of this style: "Winter in America"—

From the Indians who welcomed the pilgrims
To the buffalo who once ruled the plains;
Like the vultures circling beneath the dark clouds
Looking for the rain, looking for the rain.
From the cities that stagger on the coast lines
In a nation that just can't take much more
Like the forest buried beneath the highways
Never had a chance to grow, never had a chance
to grow.

It's winter;
Winter in America
And all the healers have been killed or forced
Away.

It's winter; winter in America
And ain't nobody fightin' 'cause nobody knows
what to save.

The con-stitution was a noble piece of paper;
With Free Society they struggled but they died
In vain

And now Democracy is ragtime on the corner
Hoping that it rains, hoping that it rains.
And I've seen the robins perched in barren
Treetops

Watching last ditch racists marching across the
Floor

And like the peace signs that melted in our
Dreams

Never have a chance to grow, never had a
Chance to grow.

It's winter, winter in America
And ain't nobody fightin' 'cause nobody knows
What to save.

Scott-Heron and his band(s) utilized messages like this to speak out on a wide range of social issues, often with a depth and sensitivity that proved stunning.

Between 1970 and 1982, the revolutionary poet laureate recorded thirteen albums. In fact, in 1974, he was one of the first acts legendary music exec Clive Davis signed to his new label, Arista Records. Scott-Heron performed at Musicians United for Safe Energy's "No Nukes" benefit concerts at Madison Square Garden in 1979 and then in 1985, he played on Steven Van Zandt's all-star anti-apartheid album, *Sun City,* along with Keith Richards and Ronnie Wood from *The Stones,* Miles Davis, Grandmaster Melle Mel, Peter Wolf, Bruce Springsteen, Bono, Clarence Clemons, Herbie Hancock, Pete Townsend, and many others. The cut was "Let Me See Your I.D." ("Johannesburg") featuring Gil Scott-Heron and Miles Davis.

L.A.'s like Johannesburg
New York's like Johannesburg
Freedom ain't nothin' but a word
It ain't nothin' but a word

It is particularly remarkable to see what was considered Black music in the 1970s and '80s, and to see the nature of what passes for Black music today. For Scott-Heron reflected on a consciousness and appreciation from the work of poets like Langston Hughes, who used his art to damn racism and ignorance. And like his childhood hero, Scott-Heron also used humor to make a point, or lighten mood based on a heavy piece. In "Small Talk at 125th and Lenox," the form is light, colloquial, but the subject is anything but—well, "small talk"—

Tell me:
Didja ever eat corn bread an' black-eyed peas?
Or watermelon and mustard greens?
Get high as you can on a Saturday night
And then head for church on Sunday to set things
right?

'I seen Miz Blake after Willie yesterday.
She'd a killed anybody who'd a got in her way!
Hey look! I got a tv for a pound of the head.
Jimmy Gene got the bes' Panamanian Red.
No, I ain't got no underclothes,
But the Hawk got to get through this Gypsy Rose!
I think Clay got his very good points.
You say a trey bad ait' thirteen joints?
Who cares is LBJ is town?
Up with Stokely and H. Rap Brown!
I dunno if the riots is wrong.
But Whitney bean kickin' my ass fo' too long.
I wuz s'pose to baby but they hel' my pay.
Did you hear what the rumor wuz yesterday?
Junkies is all right when they ain't broke.
They leaves you alone when they high on dope.
Damn, but I wish I would get up an' move!
Shut up, hell, you know that ain't true!

Throughout his career, during the lows and the highs, Scott-Heron wrote, recited, sang, and co-produced works that reflected the sighs and moans of his people, as did Hughes. In an age of billion**$$$** spent on space exploration, or on the raging wars in Southeast Asia, the *Midnight Band* would perform works that questioned, ridiculed, and attacked these vast projects, which were launched amidst social misery and want. From the work, "Space Shuttle," the following admonition:

Space Shuttle
Raising hell down in the ground!
Space Shuttle
Turning the seasons upside down.
Space Shuttle

And all the hungry people known
All change sho' 'nuff ain't progress when you're poor.
No matter what man goes looking for
He always seems to find a war.
As soon as dreams of peace are felt
The war is raging somewhere else.

There, in one phrase, are concerns broader and deeper than the central theme of the piece—the excesses of government largesse, hunger, poverty, war, and peace. From the tender age of twelve through his later battles with addiction, pitch battles, as well as his struggles with being HIV-positive, the concerns of the poor and oppressed ran through his work and performances with bluster, nerve, and glory... and were reflected back with insight, tenderness, and a deep consciousness into the outer-verse, the world of the living. In "Alien," Gil Scott-Heron gives voice to the dispossessed of Mexico: refugees to el Norte.

Midnight near the border
Tryin' to cross the Rio Grande
Runnin' with coyotes to
Where the Streets are paved with gold.

You're diving underwater
When you hear the helicopters
Knowing it's all been less than worthless
(If you meet) the border patrol
Hiding in the shadows
So scared that you want to scream
But you dare not make a sound
If you want to hold on to your dreams.

Hold on! It may not be a lot
Hold on! 'Cause you know it's all you got
No matter the consequences
Or the fear that grips your senses
You have to hold on to your dreams.

City of Angels
With its bright light fascination
Only adds to the confusion
That your mind must now endure.
The 'Gringos' take advantage
When they know that you're illegal
But you avoid La Policia
Like a plague that can't be cured.

Paying the 'mordida'
Lets you know what 'police' means
But you dare not file complaints
If you want to hold on to your dreams.

Hold on! It may not be a lot
Hold on! 'Cause you know it's all you've got
No matter the consequences
Or the fear that grips your senses
You have got to hold on to your dreams.

Down at Western Union
Sending cash back to your family
Or drinking down 'cervezas'
Where the lights are very low
Your mind may start to wander
When you think about your village
Or the woman that you love so much
Who's still in Mexico.

At just two bucks an hour
There is little to redeem (this life)
Except that in your mind
You've got to hold on to your dreams

Hold on! It may not be a lot!
Hold on! 'Cause you know that it's all you've got
No matter the consequences
Or the fear that grips your senses
You have got to hold on to your dreams.

Scott-Heron and his band(s), performing in an age of radical and revolutionary action, when Black and revolutionary consciousness was at its height, gave their services to the many and various struggles of the times. Toward the end of the 1970s, Gil and the band did fundraisers for the Joanna Little case—that of a young Black woman raped by her North Carolina jailer, who slew him in self-defense. They also fought with superstars, like Stevie Wonder, to support efforts to have Rev. Dr. Martin Luther King, Jr., memorialized in a national holiday. (They succeeded—even during the height of the Reagan administration.) But that struggle and the times of high activism led Scott-Heron to thinking, deeply, about the costs of such activism—even (and perhaps especially) artistic activism. In his posthumously published autobiography, Scott-Heron addressed those as well as related issues in a passage that seems to predict the loneliness that pervaded his adult life:

> Since I have lived in the United States of America all my life, I have seen too many deliberate distortions of events and too many slanted pieces of our history and lives to feel I can correct them all or even put a good-sized dent into them. All I can say to you is that if the truth is important to you, understand that most things of value have to be worked for, sought out, thought about, and brought about after effort worthy of the great value it will add to your life.
>
> It will come at a great price. The time and sweat invested in that pursuit may cost you in hours and days you cannot use in other directions. It may cost you relationships that you would give almost anything to develop with someone who cannot stand to come in second to anything. The passion with which you commit yourself to something intangible may well turn away the very support that could sustain you.
>
> What you will need is help that exceeds understanding. There may be disruptions on every level by those you try to touch, who shy away from you because understanding is not what you are looking for. Your only hope for stability on the levels of togetherness beyond understanding is trust. Anyone who claims to love you knows they will understand every element of these things that you need and that is where trust must carry you two the rest of the way. The truth you are seeking to write about, to sing about, to make sense of for others is something that you pursue not because you have seen it but because the Spirits tell you it is there.[27]

His life as an artist was therefore impressive, and powerful. His influence upon a new generation reveals that the title "Godfather of Rap," while not his choice, was a mark of respect for an artist who became an elder, yet spoke truth to power on almost every note and tone of his songs. With jagged and cutting wit, he scoffed at America's imperial forces as well as the might at work on the culture's naïve residents; from "The Revolution Will Not Be Televised"—

The revolution will not be brought to you by Xerox
In 4 parts without commercial interruption
The revolution will not show you pictures of Nixon
Blowing a bugle and leading a charge by John Mitchell
General Abrams and Spiro Agnew to eat
Hog maws confiscated from a Harlem sanctuary

The revolution will not be televised

The revolution will be brought to you by the Schaefer Award Theatre and
will not star Natalie Wood and Steve McQueen or Bullwinkle and Julia
The revolution will not give your mouth sex appeal
The revolution will not get rid of the nubs
The revolution will not make you look five pounds
Thinner, because The revolution will not be televised, Brother

To himself, he was a poet, an artist, a novelist, who used music to tell stories and give vibrancy to his works. He was the country boy, from Tennessee, who went to the big city, and "made it." But in heart, in mind, in song; those many others who fell lower, were his constant companions. He sang for them. He wrote for them. He struggled, for THEM. This next passage... from the incomparable, the unparalleled, the undefeated heavyweight champion of the world, "Whitey on the Moon"—

A rat done bit my sister Nell.
(with Whitey on the moon)
Her face and arms began to swell.
(and Whitey's on the moon)

I can't pay no doctor bill.
(but Whitey's on the moon)
Ten years from now I'll be payin' still.
(while Whitey's on the moon)

The man jus' upped my rent las' night.
('cause Whitey's on the moon)
No hot water, no toilets, no lights.
(but Whitey's on the moon)

I wonder why he's uppi' me?
('cause Whitey's on the moon?)
I was already payin' 'im fifty a week.
(with Whitey on the moon)
Taxes takin' my whole damn check,
Junkies makin' me a nervous wreck,
The price of food is goin' up,
An' as if all that shit wasn't enough

A rat done bit my sister Nell.
(with Whitey on the moon)
Her face an' arm began to swell.
(but Whitey's on the moon)

Was all that money I made las' year
(for Whitey on the moon?)
How come there ain't no money here?
(Hm! Whitey's on the moon)
Y'know I jus' 'bout had my fill
(of Whitey on the moon)
I think I'll sen' these doctor bills,
Airmail special
(to Whitey on the moon)

Coming to age in an Age of Revolution, Gil Scott-Heron sought his place in the world, where his voice could be heard amidst the din of late capitalism burning hot and hard. He found it by becoming a thorn in the side of the White Nation's imperialist nightmares, their dreams of conquest, avarice, and war eternal. Like his childhood hero, he stood on the side of the People.

Gil Scott-Heron: 1949-2011. For every waking moment, the man said "NO" to the beast, the darkness, and ultimately to the violence, corruptions, and poverty of empire.

We opened with Chuck D and we'll close with Ta-Nehisi Coates:

> *Gil knew he wasn't bigger than hip-hop—he knew he was just better. Like Jimi was better than heavy metal, Coltrane better than bebop, Malcolm better than the Nation of Islam, Marley better than the King James Bible. Better as in deeper—emotionally, spiritually, intellectually, politically, ancestrally, hell, probably even genetically. Mama was a Harlem opera singer, papa was a Jamaican footballer (rendering rolling stone redundant), grandmama played the blues records in Kentucky. So grit shit and mother wit Gil had in abundance, and like any Aries Man worth his saltiness he capped it off with flavor, finesse and a funky gypsy attitude.*[28]

PARTING SHOT

Photographed by Charles Milton Bell, Washington, D.C., 1879
The Metropolitan Museum of Art, Gilman Collection, 2005

Hinmatóowyalahtq'it
(Chief Joseph)

5 October 1877
Montana Territory, Morning

Forty-two miles from the Canadian border. Windswept barren plains. There's new snow. The Bear Paw Mountains frame the horizon. Dead and wounded from both sides disfigure the landscape. Sitting Bull's help is close (but will never matter).

For more than a thousand miles, as they searched for a peaceful new home, the Nez Perce people fought and eluded the invaders—the United States Army. For Hinmatóowyalahtq'it (Chief Joseph), this was the end of the line. History defined it as his "surrender speech," but from his heart and intellect, it was not surrender. If myopic historians holstered their exceptionalism for one moment and came at it with another set of eyes, they would understand what his words truly exemplified: compassion, justice, mercy, and peace.

> *Tell General Howard I know his heart. What he told me before I have in my heart. I am tired of fighting. Our chiefs are killed. Looking Glass is dead. Toohoolhoolzote is dead. The old men are all dead. It is the young men who say yes or no. He who led the young men is dead. It is cold and we have no blankets. The little children are freezing to death. My people, some of them, have run away to the hills and have no blankets, no food; no one knows where they are—perhaps freezing to death. I want to have time to look for my children and see how many of them I can find. Maybe I shall find them among the dead.*
>
> Then he turned toward White Bird and Yellow Bull and Husis Kute and met their eyes with his.
>
> *Hear me, my chiefs. I am tired. My heart is sick and sad. From where the sun now stands, I will fight no more forever.*[29]

At some point, Hinmatóowyalahtq'it laid down his rifle.

Endnotes

Publisher's Introductory Note

1 John Africa, *The Power of Truth is Final;* https://onamove.com/john-africa/

2 Mumia Abu-Jamal and Noelle Hanrahan, *All Things Censored,* Seven Stories, New York, 2001, p. 21.

3 Ramona Africa, personal interview conducted by Noelle Hanrahan and Jennifer Beach, July 16, 1992.

4 Joy James, *Imprisoned Intellectuals: America's Political Prisoners Write on Life, Liberation, and Rebellion,* Rowman & Littlefield, Lanham, Maryland, 2003, p. 4.

5 Ibid.

6 Amnesty International, "United States of America, A Life in the Balance: The Case of Mumia Abu-Jamal," (February 2000); https://www.amnesty.org/download/Documents/136000/amr510012000en.pdf

7 *Abu-Jamal v. Kane,* 96 F. Supp. 3d 447 (M.D. Pa. 2015).

8 Congressional Record, Senate, May 17, 1994 (Legislative day of May 16, 1994, Statement of U.S. Senator Robert Dole), p. 10404.

9 Mumia Abu-Jamal, *Survival Is Still a Crime,* Friends and Family of Mumia Abu-Jamal Press, 1968.

10 Howard Zinn, "The Optimism of Uncertainty," *The Nation,* September 20, 2004; https://www.thenation.com/article/archive/optimism-uncertainty

Foreword

1 Linda Burnham, "No Plans to Abandon Our Freedom Dreams!"; https://portside.org/2017-02-13/no-plans-abandon-our-freedom-dreams

Prologue

1 Tim Barringer, "Thomas Cole's Atlantic Crossings," essay in *Thomas Cole's Journey: Atlantic Crossings,* by Elizabeth Mankin Kornhauser and Tim Barringer, The Metropolitan Museum of Art and Yale University Press, New York and New Haven, 2018, p. 20.

2 Ibid.

3 Shannon Vittoria, "'Raw nature is getting thinner these days': Ed Ruscha and Tom McCarthy on Thomas Cole," *Now at The Met,* May 10, 2018; https://www.metmuseum.org/blogs/now-at-the-met/2018/ed-ruscha-tom-mccarthy-thomas-cole-course-of-empire

4 Elizabeth Mankin Kornhauser, "American Citizenship and Consummation," essay in *Thomas Cole's Journey: Atlantic Crossings,* p. 195.

5 Ed Ruscha quoted in, "'Raw nature is getting thinner these days': Ed Ruscha and Tom McCarthy on Thomas Cole"

6 Margaret Carrigan, "Met's Thomas Cole Show Highlights How an Immigrant Shaped American Identity," *Observer,* February 1, 2018; https://observer.com/2018/02/review-mets-thomas-coles-journey-atlantic-crossings-exhibition/

7 Alexander Nazaryan, "Getting Close to Fascism with Sinclair Lewis' 'It Can't Happen Here,'" *The New Yorker,* October 19, 2016; https://www.newyorker.com/culture/culture-desk/getting-close-to-fascism-with-sinclair-lewiss-it-cant-happen-here

8 Chris Hedges, "Sheldon Wolin and Inverted Totalitarianism," *Truthdig,* November 2, 2015; https://www.truthdig.

com/articles/sheldon-wolin-and-inverted-totalitarianism/

9 Richard Kreitner, "Sheldon Wolin, 1922–2015," *The Nation,* October 30, 2015; https://www.thenation.com/article/sheldon-wolin-1922-2015/

10 Chris Hedges, "The Coming Collapse," *Truthdig,* May 20, 2018; https://www.truthdig.com/articles/the-coming-collapse/

11 Ibid.

12 Sheldon Wolin, "Inverted Totalitarianism," *The Nation,* May 19, 2003; https://www.thenation.com/article/inverted-totalitarianism/

13 Chauncey DeVega, "Donald Trump's 'inverted totalitarianism': Too bad we didn't heed Sheldon Wolin's warnings," *Salon,* November 23, 2016; https://www.salon.com/2016/11/23/donald-trumps-inverted-totalitarianism-too-bad-we-didnt-heed-sheldon-wolins-warnings/

14 Sheldon Wolin, "Inverted Totalitarianism," *The Nation,* May 19, 2003; https://www.thenation.com/article/inverted-totalitarianism/

15 Chauncey DeVega, "Donald Trump's 'inverted totalitarianism': Too bad we didn't heed Sheldon Wolin's warnings," *Salon,* November 23, 2016; https://www.salon.com/2016/11/23/donald-trumps-inverted-totalitarianism-too-bad-we-didnt-heed-sheldon-wolins-warnings/

Chapter 1

1 John Swinton, as quoted in Michael A. Kirchubel, *Vile Acts of Evil - Volume 1 - Banking in America,* CreateSpace Independent Publishing, 2009, pp. 225-226.

2 Amy Goodman, *Independent Media in a Time of War,* documentary film, Hudson Mohawk Independent Media Center, 2003, transcript.

3 I.F. Stone, as quoted in Myra McPherson, "The Importance of Being Izzy and the Death of Dissent in Journalism," foreword to *All Governments Lie,* Lisa Drew/Scribner, 2006, New York, p. xi.

4 Ibid., p. xvi.

5 Ibid.

6 Stephen Colbert, White House Correspondents Dinner, April 29, 2006, transcript.

7 John Bartlett, *Bartlett's Familiar Quotations,* 17th ed., Little, Brown & Co., New York, 1882-2002, p. 443, n.1.

8 Edward Herman & Noam Chomsky, *Manufacturing Consent,* Pantheon Books, New York, 2002 (1988), p. 1.

9 Amy Goodman, interviewed by Brian Lamb, "Booknotes," C-SPAN, June 6, 2004, transcript.

10 Anthony DiMaggio, *Mass Media, Mass Propaganda: Examining American News in the "War on Terror,"* Lexington Books, Lanham, MD, 2008, p. 140.

11 Dan Rather, as quoted in DiMaggio, *Mass Media, Mass Propaganda,* p. 141.

12 Peter Beinart, as quoted in DiMaggio, *Mass Media, Mass Propaganda,* p. 141.

13 Thomas Friedman, as quoted in DiMaggio, *Mass Media, Mass Propaganda,* p. 141.

14 Paula Zahn, as quoted in "Iraq and the Media: A Critical Timeline," *Fairness and Accuracy in Reporting* (FAIR), March 19, 2007; http://fair.org/take-action/media-advisories/iraq-and-the-media/

15 Ashleigh Banfield, as quoted in "Iraq and the Media: A Critical Timeline."

16 Jack Shafer, "Deep Miller: Did the New York Times just change the rules of journalism?" *Slate,* April 21, 2003; http://www.slate.com/articles/news_and_politics/press_box/2003/04/deep_miller.html

17 Judith Miller, "Illicit Arms Kept Till Eve of War, an Iraqi Scientist Is Said to Assert," *The New York Times,* April 21, 2003; http://www.nytimes.com/2003/04/21/world/aftereffects-prohibited-weapons-illicit-arms-kept-till-eve-war-iraqi-scientist.html

18 Shafer, "Deep Miller."

19 Amy Goodman & David Goodman, *Static: Government Liars, Media Cheerleaders, and the People Who Fight Back,* Hyperion, New York, 2006, pp. 90-91.

20 Ibid., p. 98.

21 Ibid., p. 99.

22 FAIR, "Iraq and the Media: A Critical Timeline."

23 Mara Liasson, as quoted in FAIR, "Iraq and the Media."

24 Tom Brokaw, as quoted in Oliver Stone and Peter Kuznick, *The Untold History of the United States,* Gallery Books/Simon & Schuster, New York, 2012, p. 525.

25 David Cromwell, *Private Planet: Corporate Plunder and the Fight Back,* Jon Carpenter Publishing, Charlbury, UK, 2002, p. 70.

26 Cokie Roberts, as quoted in Amy Goodman & David Goodman, *The Exception to the Rulers: Exposing Oily Politicians, War Profiteers, and the Media That Love Them,* Hyperion, New York, 2004, p. 207.

27 Ibid.

28 David Portorti, as quoted in Amy & David Goodman, *The Exception to the Rulers.*

29 Amy Goodman, "Booknotes," transcript.

30 FAIR, "Iraq and the Media: A Critical Timeline."

31 Amy Goodman, "Booknotes," transcript.

32 Robert McChesney, as quoted in Cromwell, p. 71.

33 Ibid.

34 Chris Hedges, "Bad Day for Newsrooms – and Democracy," *Truthdig,* July 21, 2008; http://www.truthdig.com/report/item/20080721_so_goes_the_newsroom_the_empire_and_the_world

35 Matt Taibbi interviewed by Eric Johnson, *Vox,* October 18, 2018; https://www.vox.com/2018/10/18/17992608/matt-taibbi-rolling-stone-fairway-substack-newsletter-donald-trump-steven-perlberg-media-podcast

36 Shuja Haider, "One Has to Take Sides," *Jacobin,* August 13, 2017; https://www.jacobinmag.com/2017/08/charlottesville-fascism-white-supremacy-antifa

37 Ibid.

38 Charlotte Ryan, as quoted in Glenn Garvin, "How Do I Hate NPR? Let Me Count the Ways," *Chicago Reader,* June 24, 1993; http://www.chicagoreader.com/chicago/how-do-i-hate-npr-let-me-count-the-ways/Content?oid=882237

39 Garvin, "How Do I Hate NPR?"

40 Ibid.

41 Noam Chomsky, from a speech delivered at the Emmanuel Church, Boston, as broadcast on *DemocracyNow,* "From Bolivia to Baghdad: Noam Chomsky on Creating Another World in a Time of War, Empire and Devastation," January 1, 2007, transcript; http://www.democracynow.org/2007/1/1/from_bolivia_to_baghdad_noam_chomsky

42 David Sirota, "When did PBS become the Plutocratic Broadcasting Service?" *Salon,* February 13, 2014; http://www.salon.com/2014/02/13/when_did_pbs_become_the_plutocratic_broadcasting_service_partner/

43 Ibid.

44 Glenn Greenwald, @ggreenwald, Twitter post, Sept 8, 2014, 7:18 AM; https://twitter.com/ggreenwald/status/508982701245071360

45 Alexis de Tocqueville, *Democracy in America,* Bantam Classic, New York, 2004 (1835), pp. 306-307.

46 Lerone Bennett, Jr., *Before the Mayflower: A History of Black America,* Penguin, New York, 1993, p. 138.

47 Ralph Ginzburg, *100 Years of Lynching,* Black Classic Press, Baltimore, 1988, p. 9.

48 David Stannard, *American Holocaust: The Conquest of the New World,* Oxford University Press, New York, 1993, p. 130.

49 Ibid., p. 144.

50 Amy Goodman, "The Power of Dissent," from *Stop the Next War Now: Effective Responses to Violence and Terrorism,* Medea Benjamin & Jodie Evans, editors, Inner Ocean Publishing, Hawaii, 2005, p. 128.

51 William McKinley, as quoted in James Bradley, *The Imperial Cruise,* Little, Brown and Company, New York, 2009, p. 72.

52 Bradley, p. 75.

53 Thomas Butler, as quoted in Bradley, p. 75.

54 Theodore Roosevelt, as quoted in Bradley, p. 75.

55 McKinley, as quoted in Bradley, p. 79.

56 Bradley, p. 79.

57 Ibid.

58 Ibid.

59 Chauncey Mitchell Depew, "Speech at the Meeting to Ratify the Nomination of McKinley and Roosevelt at Carnegie Hall, New York, June 26, 1900," from *Orations, Addresses and Speeches of Chauncey M. DePew,* Vol. 6, John Denison Champlin, editor, Pennsylvania State University, 1910, p. 51.

60 Susan Brewer, "Selling Empire: American Propaganda and War in the Philippines," *The Asia-Pacific Journal,* Vol. 11, Issue 40, No. 1, October 7, 2013.

61 Ibid.

62 Ibid.

63 Noel Jacob Kent, *America in 1900,* M.E. Sharpe, Armonk, New York, 2002, p. 151.

64 Ibid.

65 Ibid.

66 Ibid.

67 Brewer, "Selling Empire."

68 Ibid.

69 Alejandro R. Roces, "The Moro Crater Massacre," *The Philippine Star,* March 13, 2010; http://www.philstar.com/opinion/557105/moro-crater-massacre

70 Theodore Roosevelt, as quoted in Mark Twain, "Comments on the Moro Massacre," 1906, from *Autobiography of Mark Twain,* Vol. 1, Mark Twain Project, University of California Press, Berkeley, 2012, p. 286.

71 Twain, "Comments on the Moro Massacre."

72 "Women and Children Killed in Moro Battle," *The New York Times,* March 10, 1906.

73 Twain, "Comments on the Moro Massacre" from *Autobiography,* pp. 284-285.

74 Phillip Ablett, "Colonialism in Denial: US Propaganda in the Philippine-American War," *Social Alternatives,* Vol. 23, No. 3, pp. 22-28.

75 Aimé Césaire, *Discourse on Colonialism* (1955), translated by Joan Pinkham, Monthly Review Press, New York, 2000, p. 32.

76 Bob Dylan, "It's Alright, Ma (I'm Only Bleeding)," lyrics, Special Ryder Music, 1965.

77 Noam Chomsky, *Necessary Illusions: Thought Control in Democratic Societies,* South End Press, New York, 1989, p. 8.

78 Ibid.

79 Dan Rather, interviewed on BBC *Newsnight,* May 16, 2002, as quoted in Amy & David Goodman, *The Exception to the Rulers,* p. 165.

80 Gore Vidal, interview with the authors, "Murder Incorporated Sessions," Street Legal Cinema, 2007, transcript.

81 Ibid.

82 Noam Chomsky, *Media Control,* Seven Stories Press, New York, 2002, p. 35.

83 Ibid.

84 Ashley Lutz, "These 6 Corporations Control 90% Of The Media In America," *Business Insider,* June 14, 2012; http://www.businessinsider.com/these-6-corporations-control-90-of-the-media-in-america-2012-6

85 BillMoyers.com staff, "What Does Media Consolidation Look Like?" October 22, 2013; http://billmoyers.com/content/what-does-media-consolidation-look-like/

86 Dan Rather, Bill Maher, *Real Time with Bill Maher,* HBO, Episode #249, May 18, 2012.

87 Amy & David Goodman, *The Exception to the Rulers,* p. 290.

88 Chris Hedges, "The Day That TV News Died," *Truthdig,* March 24, 2013; http://www.truthdig.com/report/item/the_day_that_tv_news_died_20130324

89 Ibid.

90 Ibid.

91 Amy & David Goodman, *The Exception to the Rulers,* p. 291.

92 *The World Almanac & Book of Facts: 2012,* "Casualties in Principle Wars of the U.S.," Sarah Janssen, editor, World Almanac Books, New York, 2012, p. 138.

93 William Blum, *Killing Hope: U.S. Military and CIA Interventions Since World War II,* Common Courage Press, Monroe, ME, 2004, p. 120.

94 Ibid., p. 104.

95 Martin Luther King, "Beyond Vietnam: A Time to Break Silence," delivered at Riverside Church, New York, April 4, 1967, audio and transcript archived by Stanford University; http://mlk-kpp01.stanford.edu/index.php/encyclopedia/documentsentry/doc_beyond_vietnam/

96 Ibid.

97 Tom Wells, *The War Within: America's Battle Over Vietnam,* University of California Press, p. 129.

98 Edward P. Morgan, *The '60s Experience: Hard Lessons about Modern America,* Temple University Press, Philadelphia, 1991, p. 149.

99 "Dr. King's Error," *The New York Times,* Editorial, April 7, 1967.

100 "Dr. King's Tragic Decline," *The Pittsburgh Courier,* Editorial, April 15, 1967.

101 "Dr. King's Disservice to His Cause," *LIFE,* Editorial, April 21, 1967.

102 Jim Abourezk, interview for *One Bright Shining Moment: The Forgotten Summer*

of George McGovern, documentary film, Stephen Vittoria, writer-director, Street Legal Cinema, 2005.

103 Howard Zinn, *Declaration of Independence: Cross-Examining American Ideology,* HarperCollins, New York, 1990, pp. 210-211.

104 William Sturkey, "'I Want to Become a Part of History': Freedom Summer, Freedom Schools and the *Freedom News,*" *The Journal of African American History,* Vol. 95, Nos. 3-4, Summer-Fall 2010, pp. 348-368; also see Maisha T. Winn, "'We Are All Prisoners': Privileging Prison Voices in a Black Print Culture," ibid.

105 Matt Taibbi, "Hey, MSM: All Journalism is Advocacy Journalism," *Rolling Stone,* June 27, 2013; http://www.rollingstone.com/politics/news/hey-msm-all-journalism-is-advocacy-journalism-20130627

106 Ibid.

107 Clemencia Rodriguez, "From Alternative Media to Citizens Media," (2001) from *Communication for Social Change Anthology: Historical and Contemporary Readings,* Alfonso Gumucio Dagron, editor, Communication for Social Change Consortium, South Orange, NJ, 2006, p. 763.

108 Pierre Omidyar, "Social Media: Enemy of the State or Power to the People?" *Huffington Post,* February 27, 2014; http://www.huffingtonpost.com/pierre-omidyar/social-media-enemy-of-the_b_4867421.html

109 Ibid.

110 Ibid.

111 "Coffee-houses: The Internet in a Cup," *The Economist,* December 18, 2003; http://www.economist.com/node/2281736

112 Ibid.

113 Ibid.

114 Thomas Carlyle, *The French Revolution: The Bastille, Volume 1,* Bernhard Tauchnitz, Leipzig, 1851, p. 224.

115 Jules Michelet, as quoted in Tom Standage, *A History of the World in 6 Glasses,* Walker & Company, New York, 2005, p. 170.

116 Taibbi, "Hey, MSM: All Journalism is Advocacy Journalism."

117 Ibid.

118 Ibid.

119 William Blum, *America's Deadliest Export: Democracy; The Truth About U.S. Foreign Policy and Everything Else,* Zed Books, London/New York, 2013, pp. 136-137.

120 Chelsea Manning, as quoted in Blum, *America's Deadliest Export,* p. 136.

121 Leonard Downie, Jr., *The Obama Administration and the Press,* Committee to Protect Journalists; https://cpj.org/reports/2013/10/obama-and-the-press-us-leaks-surveillance-post-911.php

122 Chris Hedges, *Empire of Illusion: The end of Literacy and the Triumph of Spectacle,* Nation Books, New York, 2009, pp. 189-190.

Chapter 2

1 Richard Lawrence Miller, *Drug Warriors & Their Prey: From Police Power to Police State,* Prager, Westport, CT, 1996, p. 7.

2 *The World Almanac and Book of Facts,* Sarah Janssen, editor, World Almanac Books, New York, 2012, p. 54.

3 Vijay Prashad, *Keeping Up With the Dow Joneses: Debt, Prison, Workfare,* South End Press, Cambridge, MA, 2003, pp. 80-81.

4 Noam Chomsky, interviewed by David

Barsamian, *How the World Works,* Arthur Naiman, editor, Soft Skull Press, Brooklyn, NY, 1986-2011, pp. 61-62.

5 David Stannard, *American Holocaust: The Conquest of the New World,* Oxford University Press, New York, 1992, p. 157.

6 Anders Stephanson, *Manifest Destiny: American Expansion and the Empire of Right,* Hill and Wang, New York, 1995, p. 6.

7 David Gilbert, *Love & Struggle: My Life With the SDS, the Weather Underground, and Beyond,* PM Press, Oakland, CA, 2011, p. 98. (Gilbert is now an anti-imperialist prisoner of the U.S. government, held in part because of his actions in resistance.)

8 Gore Vidal, *Perpetual War for Perpetual Peace,* Clairview Books, Forest Row, UK, 2002, pp. 67-69.

9 *World Almanac,* p. 54.

10 Andrew Harris and Jef Feeley, "J&J 'Did Everything' to Push Opioids, Oklahoma Witness Says," *Bloomberg,* June 11, 2019; https://www.bloomberg.com/news/articles/2019-06-11/johnson-johnson-fueled-opioid-crisis-trial-witness-testifies

11 Katie Thomas and Tiffant Hsu, "Johnson & Johnson's Brand Falters Over Its Role in the Opioid Crisis," *The New York Times,* August 27, 2019; https://www.nytimes.com/2019/08/27/health/johnson-and-johnson-opioids-oklahoma.html

12 Ibid.

13 Mark Levine, "Mainstream Media: The Drug War's Shills," from *Into The Buzzsaw: Leading Journalists Expose the Myth of a Free Press,* Kristina Borjesson, ed., Prometheus Books, Amherst, N.Y., 2002), p. 258.

14 Ibid., p. 275.

15 Gary Webb, "The Mighty Wurlitzer Plays On," from "Mainstream Media: The Drug War's Shills," p. 298.

16 Omali Yeshitela, "The Wolf and the Blade: I.S. War Against the African Community," delivered to the Black Power Organizing Conference, Philadelphia, PA, May 31, 1998.

17 Ibid.

18 Levine, pp. 267-268.

19 James Bradley, *The Imperial Cruise,* Little, Brown and Company, New York, 2009, p. 272.

20 Carl Trocki, *Opium, Empire and the Global Political Economy; A Study of the Asian Opium Trade,* 1750-1950, Routledge, New York, 1999, p. 42, as cited in Bradley, p. 273.

21 Trocki, p. 94, as cited in Bradley, pp. 274-275.

22 Bradley, p. 275.

23 Ibid.

24 Sir John Francis Davis, as quoted in Bradley, p. 276.

25 Steven Sora, *Secret Societies of America's Elite: The Knights Templar to Skull and Bones,* Destiny Books, Rochester, VT, 2003, p. 5.

26 Ibid., p. 8.

27 Ibid., p. 7.

28 Ibid., p. 93.

29 Ibid., p. 247.

30 John Looney, *The Media's Social Responsibility,* Peace Grows, Akron, OH, 1986 p. 19.

31 Bradley, pp. 289-290.

Chapter 3

1 Ean Begg, *The Cult of the Black Virgin,* Arkana/Penguin, London, UK, 1996 (1985), p. 64.

2 Ibid., p. 136.

3 Marilyn French, *The War Against Women,* Ballantine, New York, 1992, pp. 19-20.

4 Abigail Adams, as quoted in Gary B. Nash, *The Unknown American Revolution,* Penguin, New York, p. 2006 p. 210.

5 Ibid., p. 203.

6 John Adams, as quoted in Nash, p. 205.

7 Nash, pp. 288-289.

8 Howard Zinn, *A People's History of the United States,* Harper Collins, New York, 2003, p. 123.

9 Ibid.

10 Thomas Jefferson, as quoted in Zinn, p. 110.

11 Frederick Douglass, *On Slavery and The Civil War: Selections from His Writings,* Dover, Mineola, NY, 2003, pp. 12-13.

12 Helen Keller, as quoted in Zinn, p. 345.

13 Emma Goldman, "Woman Suffrage" (1917), from *From Many, One: Readings in American Political and Social Thought,* Richard C. Sinopoli, editor, Georgetown University Press, Washington, D.C., 1997, pp. 142-148.

14 Ruth Shagoury, "Who Stole Helen Keller?" *Teaching A People's History,* Zinn Education Project, June 21, 2012; http://zinnedproject.org/2012/06/who-stole-helen-keller/

15 Nash, *The Unknown American Revolution,* p. 233.

16 Howard Zinn, *Howard Zinn Speaks,* Anthony Arnove, editor, Haymarket Books, Chicago, 2012, p. 139.

17 Ibid., pp. 133-134.

18 Ibid., p. 140.

19 Zinn, *A People's History,* p. 504.

20 French, pp. 12-13.

21 Ibid., pp. 19-20.

22 Ibid., p. 30.

23 Mariarosa Dalla Costa and Selma James, *The Power of Women and the Subversion of the Community,* 3rd ed., Falling Wall Press, Bristol, UK, 1975, p. 10.

24 French, p. 37.

25 Ibid., pp. 35-36.

26 Ibid., p. 104.

27 *Buck v. Bell,* 274 U.S. 200 (1927).

28 Ibid.

29 *Skinner v. Oklahoma,* 316 U.S. 535 (1942).

30 Michael Eric Dyson, *I May Not Get There With You: The True Martin Luther King,* Touchstone, New York, 2000, p. 195.

31 Ella Baker and Marvel Cooke, as quoted in Zinn, *A People's History,* p. 404.

32 Barbara Ransby, *Ella Baker and the Black Freedom Movement,* University of North Carolina Press, Chapel Hill, 2002.

33 Jeanne Theoharis, *The Rebellious Life of Mrs. Rosa Parks,* Beacon Press, Boston, 2013, p. 25.

34 Ibid., p. 204.

35 Muhammad Ahmed, as quoted in Theoharis, *The Rebellious Life of Mrs. Rosa Parks,* p. 204.

36 Ibid., pp. 228-229.

37 The term derives from Newton's view that, under imperialism, true sovereign nations did not, and indeed, could not exist, for all were under imperial hegemony. Thus, communities existed, under various degrees of the appearance of independence, but all at the sufferance of the empire. See Huey P. Newton, *The Huey P. Newton Reader,* David Hilliard and Donald Weise, editors, Seven Stories Press, New York, 2002, pp. 169-170.

38 Tracye Matthews, "'No One Ever Asks, What a Man's Place in the Revolution Is': Gender Politics and Leadership in the Black Panther Party 1966-71," in *The Black Panther Party [Reconsidered],* Charles Jones, editor, Black Classic Press, Baltimore, MD, 1998, p. 283.

39 Angela D. LeBlanc-Ernest, "'The Most Qualified Person to Handle the Job': Black Panther Party Women, 1966-1982," in Jones, editor, Ibid, p. 306.

40 Newton, *The Huey P. Newton Reader,* p. 313.

41 Carol P. Christ, *For Mothers of the Women's Spirituality Movement,* Edited by Miriam Robbins Dexter and Vicki Noble, Teneo Press, Amherst, New York, 2015, p. 30.

42 Ibid.

43 Lydia Ruyle, *For Mothers of the Women's Spirituality Movement,* p. 275.

44 Mary Mackey, *For Mothers of the Women's Spirituality Movement,* p. 267.

45 Vicki Noble, *For Mothers of the Women's Spirituality Movement,* p. 2.

46 Luisah Teish, *For Mothers of the Women's Spirituality Movement,* p. 117.

47 Mackey, *For Mothers of the Women's Spirituality Movement,* p. 266.

48 Donna Henes, *For Mothers of the Women's Spirituality Movement,* p. 203.

49 Ibid., as quoted by Henes, p. 203.

Chapter 4

1 Mary Frances Berry, *Black Resistance/ White Law,* Penguin, New York, 1994 (1971), p. xi.

2 Ibid.

3 Mary Frances Berry & John W. Blassingame, *Long Memory: The Black Experience in America,* Oxford University Press, New York/London, 1982, p. 7.

4 Ibid., p. 155.

5 T. Thomas Fortune, as quoted in Berry & Blassingame, p. 156.

6 James MacGregor Burns, *Packing the Court: The Rise of Judicial Power and the Coming Crisis of the Supreme Court,* Penguin, New York, 2009, pp. 86-87.

7 Ibid., pp. 87-88.

8 Ibid., p. 88.

9 Neil Schmitz, "Twain, Huckleberry Finn, and the Reconstruction," *American Studies,* Vol. 12, No. 1, Spring 1971, p. 60.

10 Ibid.

11 Ibid.

12 Ibid., p. 62.

13 Walter F. White, as quoted in Lerone Bennett, Jr., *Before the Mayflower: A History of Black America,* Johnson Pub. Co., Chicago, 2000 (1961), p. 553.

14 Bennett, Jr., pp. 320-321.

15 Ibid., pp. 322-323.

16 Ibid., 326.

17 Langston Hughes, as quoted in Bennett, Jr., p. 328.

18 Bennett, Jr., p. 579.

19 Ibid., p. 349.

20 Manning Marable, *The Great Wells of Democracy,* Basic Civitas, New York, 2002, pp. 282-283.

21 Judge Tom Brady, as quoted in Bennett, Jr., p. 348.

22 Hearings Before the Select Committee to Study Governmental Operations with Respect to Intelligence Activities of the U.S. Senate, 94th Congress, 1st Session, Vol. 6, Federal Bureau of Investigation;

Intelligence Activities Senate Resolution 21, Nov./Dec. 1975, U.S. Government Printing Office, Washington, D.C., 1976, p. 617.

23 Ibid., p. 619.

24 Ibid., p. 24.

25 Associated Press, "Comedian Says Hoover Made Plans To Kill Him," *The Lakeland Ledger,* March 11, 1978.

26 Ward Churchill & Jim Vander Wall, *The COINTELPRO Papers: Documents from the FBI's Secret Wars Against Dissent in the United States,* South End Press, Cambridge, MA, 2002 (1990), p. 104.

27 Mumia Abu-Jamal, *WE WANT FREEDOM: A Life in the Black Panther Party,* South End Press, Cambridge, MA, 2004, p. 157.

28 Alexis de Tocqueville, *Democracy in America, Vols I & II,* Bantam Classics, New York, 2004 (1835), pp. 793-794.

29 "Memorandum from Director, FBI to Special Agents in Charge, 3/4/68," as cited in Books II and III, *Final Report of the Select Committee to Study Governmental Operations with respect to Intelligence Activities, U.S. Senate* (widely known as the Church Committee Report), U.S. Government Printing Office, April, 1976. Reproduced in unexpurgated form in Brian Glick, *War At Home: Covert Action Against U.S. Activists and What We Can Do About It,* South End Press, Boston, 1989, pp. 78-79; https://archive.org/details/War_At_Home

30 Bennett, Jr., pp. 658-659.

31 J. Edgar Hoover, as quoted in Jules Boykoff, *The Suppression of Dissent: How the State and Mass Media Squelch USAmerican Social Movements,* Rutledge, New York, 2006, p. 23.

32 Richard Cohen, "As Long As We're Renaming..." *The Washington Post,* December 16, 1997, p. A-27.

33 David J. Garrow, *Bearing the Cross: Martin Luther King, Jr. and the Southern Christian Leadership Conference,* Harper Collins, New York, 1986, p. 373.

34 Ibid., p. 374.

35 Cohen, "As Long As We're Renaming..."

36 Churchill & Vander Wall, *The COINTELPRO Papers,* pp. 96-97. (Citing memo dated August 30, 1963, from W.C. Sullivan to Alan H. Belmont, captioned "Communist Party, USA, Negro Question, IS-C.")

37 Dick Gregory, interviewed in *One Bright Shining Moment: The Forgotten Summer of George McGovern,* documentary film, Stephen Vittoria, writer-director, Street Legal Cinema, 2005.

38 Churchill & Vander Wall, *The COINTELPRO Papers,* pp. 170-171.

39 Memo from Director, FBI to Special Agents in Charge, Albany, N.Y., Aug. 25, 1967, as cited in Ward Churchill & Jim Vander Wall, *Agents of Repression: The FBI's Secret Wars Against the Black Panther Party and the American Indian Movement,* South End Press, Cambridge, MA, 2002, p. 58.

40 J. Edgar Hoover, as quoted in Joshua Bloom & Waldo E. Martin, *Black Against Empire: The History and Politics of the Black Panther Party,* University of California Press, Berkeley, 2013, p. 210. (Bloom and Martin do an exhaustive job of sourcing this infamous quote, see their citation, endnote 45, p. 444.)

41 Churchill & Vander Wall, *Agents of Repression,* p. 72.

42 M. Wesley Swearingen, *FBI Secrets: An Agent's Exposé,* South End Press, Boston, 1995, pp. 88-89.

43 *Long Distance Revolutionary: A Journey with Mumia Abu-Jamal,* documentary film, Stephen Vittoria, writer-director, Street Legal Cinema, 2013.

44 William Parker, as quoted in Ella Forbes, *But We Have No Country: The 1851 Christiana Pennsylvania Resistance,* Africana Homestead Legacy, Cherry Hill, NJ, 1998, pp. 265, 110.

Chapter 5

1 George Carlin, *Class Clown,* Little David/ Atlantic Records, Los Angeles, 1972, Track 9.

2 *FCC v. Pacifica,* 438 U.S. 726 (1978).

3 Ibid., Dissenting, Brennan.

4 Ibid.

5 Ibid.

6 Ibid.

7 Ibid.

8 Ibid.

9 Alexis de Tocqueville, *Democracy in America—Volume 1, Chapter 16,* Saunders and Otley, London, 1835.

10 Robert A. Dahl, *Decision-Making in a Democracy: The Supreme Court as a National Policy-Maker,* J. PUB. L. 279, 1957, p. 1 (also here: http://epstein.wustl.edu/research/courses.judpol.Dahl.pdf)

11 James Madison, *The Papers of James Madison,* University of Chicago Press, Chicago, 1962-77, Volume 1, Chapter 14, Document 50.

12 Amy Goodman interviewing Adam Cohen, *DemocracyNow,* March 6, 2020; https://www.democracynow.org/2020/3/6/adam_cohen_supreme_inequality_supreme_court?utm_source=Democracy+Now%21&utm_campaign=a17a9d61ff-Daily_Digest_COPY_01&utm_medium=email&utm_term=0_fa2346a853-a17a9d61ff-190226689

13 Frank Zappa, as quoted in *Bloodthirsty Bitches and Pious Pimps of Power: The Rise and Risks of the New Conservative Hate Culture,* Gerry Spence, St. Martin's Press, New York, 2006, Chapter 12.

14 Chris Hedges, "The Corruption of the Law," *Truthdig,* August 20, 2017; https://www.truthdig.com/articles/the-corruption-of-the-law/

15 Jeffrey Toobin, "Looking Back," *The New Yorker,* February 29, 2016; https://www.newyorker.com/magazine/2016/02/29/antonin-scalia-looking-backward

16 *Lawrence v. Texas* (02-102) 539 U.S. 558 (2003).

17 Hedges, "The Corruption of Law," *Truthdig.*

18 Ibid.

19 Ibid.

20 Ibid.

21 Ibid.

22 Ibid.

23 Ibid.

24 Ibid.

25 Peter Irons, *A People's History of the Supreme Court,* Penguin, New York, 2006 (1999), p. 86.

26 Ibid.

27 Ibid., p. 90.

28 James Bradley, *The Imperial Cruise,* Little, Brown and Company, New York, 2009, p. 29.

29 Michael Parenti, *The Face of Imperialism,* Paradigm Press, Boulder, CO, 2011, pp. 7-8.

30 David E. Wilkins, *American Indian Sovereignty and the U.S. Supreme Court: The Marking of Justice,* University of Texas Press, Austin, TX, 1997, p. 32.

31 Justice Roger B. Taney, as quoted in Wilkins, pp. 42-43—citing *U.S. v. Rogers* 45 U.S. 567 (1846).

32 Wilkins, pp. 43-44.

33 Taney, as quoted in Wilkins, p. 45.

34 Ibid.

35 Taney, as quoted in Wilkins, p. 50—citing *Dred Scott v. Sandford,* 60 U.S. 393 (1857).

36 Barbara Alice Mann, *George Washington's War on Native America,* p. 170.

37 Wilkins, p. 45.

38 Ibid., p. 50.

39 Ibid., p. 52.

40 Ibid.

41 Tim Wise, *COLORBLIND: The Rise of Post-Racial Politics and the Retreat From Racial Equality,* Open Media/City Lights, San Francisco, 2010, p. 74.

42 Wilkins, pp. 10-15.

43 *Cherokee Nation v. Georgia,* 30 U.S. (5 Pet.) 1 (1831).

44 *U.S. v. Kagama,* 118 U.S. 375 (1886).

45 Kal Raustiala, *Does the Constitution Follow the Flag?: The Evolution of Territoriality in American Law,* Oxford University Press, New York/Oxford, 2009, p. 59.

46 Raustiala, p. 63—citing in *re Ross,* 140 U.S. 453 (1890).

47 Raustiala, p. 64.

48 Ibid., citing in *re Ross.*

49 Irons, p. 218.

50 *Santa Clara County v. Southern Pacific R. Co.,* 118 U.S. 394 (1886) (unanimous 9-0 vote).

51 *Plessy v. Ferguson,* 163 U.S. 537 (1896) (7-1 vote, 1 justice not participating).

52 Raustiala, p. 4.

53 Walter F. Pratt, Jr., "Insular Cases," in *The Oxford Guide to United States Supreme Court Decisions,* Kermit L. Hall & James W. Ely, Jr., editors, 2nd ed., Oxford University Press, Oxford/New York, 2009, pp. 161-162—citing *De Lima,* 182 U.S. 1 (1901); *Dooley,* 182 222 (1901); *Dorr,* 195 U.S. 138 (1904); *Downes,* 182 U.S. 244 (1901); *Hawaii,* 190 U.S. 197 (1903).

54 Irons, p. 211.

55 *Baldwin v. Franks,* 120 U.S. 678 (1887).

56 Ibid.

57 Ibid., Justice Harlan, dissenting.

58 Ibid.

59 Raustiala, p. 84—citing *Neely v. Henkel,* 180 U.S. 109 (1901).

60 Donald Trump to a group of U.S. senators at a White House meeting, quoted by NBC News, January 12, 2018; https://www.nbcnews.com/politics/white-house/trump-referred-haiti-african-countries-shithole-nations-n836946

61 *Reid v. Covert,* 354 U.S. 1 (1957).

62 Raustiala, p. 140.

63 Raustiala, p. 160.

64 Raustiala, p. 164 (citing *Haitian Refugee Center v. Baker,* 953 F.2nd 1498 (11th Cir. 1992).

65 George W. Bush, as quoted in Robert Jensen, *The Citizens of the Empire: The Struggle to Claim Our Humanity,* City Lights, San Francisco, 2004, p. xi.

66 Jensen, p. xi.

67 Jack Goldsmith, as quoted in Raustiala, p. 196.

68 *Hamdi v. Rumsfeld,* 542 U.S. 507 (2004) (Justice Sandra Day O'Connor, opinion.)

69 Ibid.

70 *Rasul v. Bush,* 542 U.S. 466 (2004); *Boumediene v. Bush,* 533 U.S. 723 (2008).

71 John Paul Stevens, *Six Amendments: How and Why We Should Change the Constitution,* Little, Brown and Company, New York, 2014.

72 Abraham Lincoln, "December 3, 1861: First Annual Message," *University of Virginia, Miller Center,* (Presidential Speeches, Abraham Lincoln Presidency, Transcript); https://millercenter.org/the-presidency/presidential-speeches/december-3-1861-first-annual-message

73 Nina Totenberg, "From 'Fraud' To Individual Right, Where Does The Supreme Court Stand On Guns?" *NPR,* March 5, 2018; https://www.npr.org/2018/03/05/590920670/from-fraud-to-individual-right-where-does-the-supreme-court-stand-on-guns

74 M. Margaret McKeown, "Supreme Court Justice William O. Douglas was not just a legal giant, but also a powerful environmentalist," *The Seattle Times,* August 17, 2018; https://www.seattletimes.com/pacific-nw-magazine/supreme-court-justice-william-o-douglas-was-not-just-a-legal-giant-but-also-a-powerful-environmentalist/

75 *Balzac v. Porto Rico,* 258 U.S. 298 (1922).

Chapter 6

1 Keith Alexander, as quoted in Ashley Alman, "Keith Alexander: NSA Isn't Spying On Jimmy Carter's Emails, So He Can Stop Using Snail Mail," *The Huffington Post,* March 25, 2014; http://www.huffingtonpost.com/2014/03/25/keith-alexander-jimmy-carter_n_5031701.html

2 Daniel Ellsberg, "Edward Snowden To Join Daniel Ellsberg, Others on Freedom of the Press Foundation Board of Directors," Board of Directors, Freedom of the Press Foundation Press Release, January 14, 2014; https://freedom.press/blog/2014/01/edward-snowden-join-daniel-ellsberg-others-freedom-press-foundations-board-directors

3 Jeff Goddell, "Bill Gates: The Rolling Stone Interview," *Rolling Stone,* March 13, 2014.

4 Ryan W. Neal, "Snowden Reveals Microsoft PRISM Cooperation: Helped NSA Decrypt Emails, Chats, Skype Conversations," *International Business Times,* July 11, 2013; http://www.ibtimes.com/snowden-reveals-microsoft-prism-cooperation-helped-nsa-decrypt-emails-chats-skype-conversations

5 Ibid.

6 Charles Piller, Edmund Sanders, and Robyn Dixon, "Dark cloud over good works of Gates Foundation," *Los Angeles Times,* January 7, 2007; http://www.latimes.com/news/la-na-gatesx07jan07-story.html

7 Alex Park and Jaeah Lee, "The Gates Foundation's Hypocritical Investments," *Mother Jones,* December 6, 2013; http://m.motherjones.com/environment/2013/12/gates-foundations-24-most-egregious-investments

8 Ibid.

9 David Pegg, "For-profit juvenile detention facility 'a disgrace to Florida', says grand jury," *The Guardian,* July 27, 2015; https://www.theguardian.com/us-news/2015/jul/27/g4s-florida-juvenile-detention-centre-grand-jury

10 *Mother Jones,* "The Gates Foundation's Hypocritical Investments."

11 Joanne Barkan on MSNBC February 2011, "Joanne Barkan on How Billionaires

Run Our Schools," YouTube video, uploaded by "DissentMag," February 10, 2011; http://www.youtube.com/watch?v=bat-ByGSWa8

12 Joanne Barkan, "Got Dough? How Billionaires Rule Our Schools," *Dissent Magazine,* Winter 2011; http://www.dissentmagazine.org/article/got-dough-how-billionaires-rule-our-schools

13 Statista, "Internet of Things (IoT)," November 2016, New York; https://www.statista.com/statistics/471264/iot-number-of-connected-devices-worldwide/

14 Catherine Crump & Matthew Harwood, "Invasion of the Data Snatchers: Big Data and the Internet of Things Means Surveillance of Everything," *TomDispatch.com,* March 25, 2014; http://www.tomdispatch.com/blog/175822/tomgram%3A_crump_and_harwood,_the_net_closes_around_us/

15 Alice E. Marwick, "How Your Data Are Being Deeply Mined," *The New York Review of Books,* Jan 9, 2014; http://www.nybooks.com/articles/archives/2014/jan/09/how-your-data-are-being-deeply-mined/

16 Crump & Harwood, "Invasion of the Data Snatchers."

17 Ibid.

18 Ibid.

19 Ibid.

20 Ibid.

21 Bruce Livesey, "How Deloitte masked scandals in business and politics," *National Observer,* Canada, March 5, 2019.

22 Deloitte Press Release, September 18, 2018, New York; https://www2.deloitte.com/global/en/pages/about-deloitte/articles/global-revenue-announcement.html

23 Deloitte Insights, "Investigative analytics, Leveraging data for law enforcement insights," February 21, 2019; https://www2.deloitte.com/insights/us/en/industry/public-sector/law-enforcement-investigative-analytics.html

24 Ibid.

25 Ibid.

26 Ezekiel Edwards, "Predictive Policing Software Is More Accurate at Predicting Policing Than Predicting Crime," ACLU, August 31, 2016.

27 Ibid.

28 Edward Snowden, *Permanent Record,* Metropolitan Books, New York, 2019, p. 195.

29 Ibid.

30 Ibid.

31 Ibid.

32 Ingrid Burrington, "What Amazon.com Taught the Cops — The Tech-Fueled Rise of Predictive Policing," *AlterNet,* June 2, 2015; https://www.alternet.org/2015/06/what-amazoncom-taught-cops-tech-fueled-rise-predictive-policing/

33 Data-Smart City Solutions, "Dr. Colleen McCue: Pioneer in Data Analytics," May 8, 2013; https://datasmart.ash.harvard.edu/news/article/dr.-colleen-mccue-pioneer-in-data-analytics-133

34 Burrington, "What Amazon.com Taught the Cops — The Tech-Fueled Rise of Predictive Policing."

35 Eric Holder, "Attorney General Eric Holder Delivers Remarks at the Annual Meeting of the American Bar Association's House of Delegates," The U.S. Department of Justice, August 12, 2013; https://www.justice.gov/opa/speech/attorney-general-eric-holder-delivers-remarks-annual-meeting-american-bar-associations

36 Mallory Hanora at The Marshall Project, February 25, 2016; https://www.themarshallproject.org/2016/02/25/highlights-from-our-justice-talk-on-predictive-policing

37 Barack Obama, speech on NSA reforms, delivered at the Justice Department, Washington, D.C., January 17, 2014, transcript.

38 Michael Ratner, "Obama's NSA Speech Makes Orwellian Surveillance Patriotic," *Truthout*, January 27, 2014; http://www.truth-out.org/opinion/item/21461-obamas-nsa-speech-makes-orwellian-surveillance-patriotic

39 Ibid.

40 Ibid.

41 Snowden, *Permanent Record*, pp. 232-233.

42 George Carlin, *Life is Worth Losing*, Eardrum/Atlantic, 2005.

43 "Obama A Constitutional Law Professor?" *FactCheck.org*, March 28, 2008; http://www.factcheck.org/2008/03/obama-a-constitutional-law-professor/

44 Jon Stewart, *The Daily Show*, Comedy Central, January 20, 2014.

45 Donald J. Trump, "Statement by the President on FISA Amendments Reauthorization Act of 2017," White House, January 19, 2018.

46 ACLU, "ACLU Condemns House Vote on Surveillance Bill," January 11, 2018; https://www.aclu.org/press-releases/aclu-condemns-house-vote-surveillance-bill-0?redirect=news/aclu-condemns-house-vote-surveillance-bill-0

47 Cindy Cohn, "An Open Letter to Our Community On Congress' Vote to Extend NSA Spying," Electronic Frontier Foundation, January 18, 2018; https://www.eff.org/deeplinks/2018/01/open-letter-our-community-congresss-vote-extend-nsa-spying-eff-executive-director

48 Ibid.

49 Snowden, *Permanent Record*, p. 205.

50 Joseph Menn, "Russian researchers expose breakthrough U.S. spying program," *Reuters*, Feb 16, 2015; http://www.reuters.com/article/2015/02/16/us-usa-cyberspying-idUSKBN0LK1QV20150216

51 Alfred W. McCoy, "How NSA Surveillance Fits Into a Long History of American Global Political Strategy," *Mother Jones*, January 24, 2014; http://www.motherjones.com/politics/2014/01/nsa-surveillance-history-global-political-strategy-domestic-spying

52 Ibid.

53 Ibid.

54 Ibid.

55 Mandy Smithberger and William Hartung, "Making Sense of the $1.25 Trillion National Security State Budget," Project on Government Oversight (POGO), May 7, 2019.

56 Ibid.

57 Ibid.

58 Ibid.

59 Ibid.

60 Rachel Levinson-Waldman, "How ICE and Other DHS Agencies Mine Social Media in the Name of National Security," Brennan Center for Justice, June 3, 2019; https://www.brennancenter.org/blog/how-ice-and-other-dhs-agencies-mine-social-media-name-national-security

61 Ibid.

62 Ryan Devereaux, "Homeland Security Used a Private Security Firm to Monitor

Family Separation Protests," *The Intercept,* April 29, 2019; https://theintercept.com/2019/04/29/family-separation-protests-surveillance/

63 Rachel Levinson-Waldman, "How ICE and Other DHS Agencies Mine Social Media in the Name of National Security."

64 Ibid.

65 Ryan Devereaux, "Homeland Security Used a Private Security Firm to Monitor Family Separation Protests," *The Intercept,* April 29, 2019; https://theintercept.com/2019/04/29/family-separation-protests-surveillance/

66 Peter Ludlow, "Fifty States of Fear," *The New York Times,* January 19, 2014; http://opinionator.blogs.nytimes.com/2014/01/19/fifty-states-of-fear/

67 Erik Prince, as quoted in Eli Lake, "Blackwater Founder Erik Prince: War on Terror Has Become Too Big," *The Daily Beast,* November 19, 2013; http://www.thedailybeast.com/articles/2013/11/19/blackwater-founder-erik-prince-war-on-terror-has-become-too-big.html

68 Gore Vidal, *Imperial America: Reflections on the United States of Amnesia,* Nation Books, New York, 2004, p. 8.

69 Ibid.

70 "Spy Files: The ACLU Campaign to Expose and Stop Illegal Domestic Spying," ACLU; https://www.aclu.org/spy-files

71 Vidal, *Imperial America,* p. 9.

72 Kenneth Bacon, as quoted in Elizabeth Becker, "Washington Talk; Prickly Roots of 'Homeland Security'," *The New York Times,* August 31, 2002; http://www.nytimes.com/2002/08/31/us/washington-talk-prickly-roots-of-homeland-security.html

73 Tom Ridge, as quoted in Becker, "Washington Talk."

74 Doug Thompson, "Welcome to the American Gestapo," *Capitol Hill Blue,* November 20, 2002.

75 Ibid.

76 Ray McGovern, endorsement to Heidi Boghosian, *Spying on Democracy,* City Lights Books, San Francisco, 2013, NP.

77 Ibid.

78 Raimund Pretzel/Sebastian Haffner, as quoted in, ibid.

79 Fernanda Santos, "Shootings by Agents Increase Border Tensions," *The New York Times,* June 10, 2013; http://www.nytimes.com/2013/06/11/us/shootings-by-agents-increase-border-tensions.html

80 Ibid.

81 Ibid.

82 "FBI Documents Reveal Secret Nationwide Occupy Monitoring," The Partnership for Civil Justice Fund (PCJF), December 21, 2012; http://www.justiceonline.org/fbi_files_ows

83 Ibid.

84 Chris Hedges, "State of Fear," *Truthdig,* January 7, 2013; https://www.truthdig.com/report/item/state_of_fear_20130107

85 Mara Verheyden-Hilliard, as quoted in "FBI Documents Reveal Secret Nationwide Occupy Monitoring," PCJF.

86 "Spy Files," ACLU.

87 Leslie Cauley, "NSA has massive database of Americans' phone calls," *USA Today,* May 11, 2006; http://usatoday30.usatoday.com/news/washington/2006-05-10-nsa_x.htm

88 ACLU, "NSA Surveillance"; https://www.aclu.org/issues/national-security/privacy-and-surveillance/nsa-surveillance

89 Charlie Savage, "N.S.A. Triples Collection of Data From U.S. Phone

Companies," *The New York Times,* May 4, 2018; https://www.nytimes.com/2018/05/04/us/politics/nsa-surveillance-2017-annual-report.html

90 Jake Johnson, "Alarm as Trump Requests Permanent Reauthorization of NSA Mass Spying Program Exposed by Snowden," *Common Dreams,* August 16, 2019; https://www.commondreams.org/news/2019/08/16/alarm-trump-requests-permanent-reauthorization-nsa-mass-spying-program-exposed

91 McCoy, "How NSA Surveillance Fits..."

92 Ibid.

93 Chris Hedges, "The Last Gasp of Democracy," *Truthdig,* January 5, 2014; http://www.truthdig.com/report/item/the_last_gasp_of_american_democracy_20140105

94 Ibid.

95 Sadie Roosa, "Abbie Hoffman and Amy Carter Protest CIA, 1986," Boston TV News Digital Library, March 21, 2013; http://bostonlocaltv.org/blog/2013/03/abbie-hoffman-and-amy-carter-protest-cia-1986/

96 Matthew Alford & Robbie Graham, "Lights, Camera... Covert Action: The Deep Politics of Hollywood," *Global Research,* January 21, 2009; http://www.globalresearch.ca/lights-camera-covert-action-the-deep-politics-of-hollywood/11921

97 Susan Sarandon, "Zero Dark Thirty, Secrecy, and Torture," ACLU Blog of Rights, January 15, 2013; https://www.aclu.org/blog/human-rights-national-security/zero-dark-thirty-secrecy-and-torture

98 Ibid.

99 Marjorie Cohn, "Zero Dark Thirty: Torturing the Facts," *Huffington Post,* January 11, 2013; http://www.huffingtonpost.com/marjorie-cohn/zero-dark-thirty-fact-check_b_2452721.html

100 Robert Parry, "The Shortsighted History of Argo," *Consortium News,* February 25, 2013; https://consortiumnews.com/2013/02/25/the-shortsighted-history-of-argo/

101 Ibid.

102 Robert Parry, "October Surprise and Argo," *Consortium News,* March 7, 2013; https://consortiumnews.com/2013/03/07/october-surprise-and-argo/

103 Parry, "The Shortsighted History of Argo."

104 Ted Gup, as quoted in Arun Rath, "The History of the CIA in Hollywood Movies," *Public Radio International,* January 11, 2013; http://www.pri.org/stories/2013-01-11/history-cia-hollywood-movies

105 Tricia Jenkins, as quoted in Rath, "The History of the CIA in Hollywood Movies."

106 Eoin Higgins, "U.S. Propaganda Doesn't Get More Shameless Than 'Jack Ryan,'" *Common Dreams,* September 6, 2019; https://www.truthdig.com/articles/u-s-propaganda-doesnt-get-more-shameless-than-jack-ryan/

107 Ibid.

108 FBI Website, "Protecting America from Terrorist Attack: Our Joint Terrorism Task Forces"; http://www.fbi.gov/about-us/investigate/terrorism/terrorism_jttfs

109 Michael German, "The Erosion of Posse Comitatus," ACLU, *Daily Kos,* September 15, 2009; http://www.dailykos.com/story/2009/09/15/782384/-The-Erosion-of-Posse-Comitatus#

110 "Spy Files," ACLU.

111 Martine Powers, "Boston Police accused of spying on antiwar groups," *The Boston*

Globe, October 18, 2012; http://www.bostonglobe.com/metro/2012/10/17/boston-police-accused-surveillance-antiwar-protesters/7P0iOs86Q637BGYxI1ARBJ/story.html

112 Nancy Murray, "When Boston Police Spy on Free Speech, Democracy Suffers," *The Boston Globe,* October 18, 2012; http://www.boston.com/community/blogs/on_liberty/2012/10/when_boston_police_spy_on_free.html

113 Ibid.

114 *DemocracyNow,* "Declassified Docs Reveal Military Operative Spied on WA Peace Groups," July 28, 2009; http://www.democracynow.org/2009/7/28/broadcast_exclusive_declassified_docs_reveal_military

115 ALCU Biography of Mike German; https://aclu-wa.org/library_files/MikeGermanbio.pdf

116 *DemocracyNow,* "Declassified Docs Reveal Military Operative Spied on WA Peace Groups."

117 Ibid.

118 Ibid.

119 "Department of Homeland Security Announces 'If You See Something, Say Something' Partnership with the City of Charlotte," DOHS Press Release, Office of the Press Secretary, May 21, 2012; http://www.dhs.gov/news/2012/05/21/department-homeland-security-announces-if-you-see-something-say-something#

120 Brian Bennett, "Police employ Predator drone spy planes on home front," *Los Angeles Times,* December 10, 2011; http://articles.latimes.com/2011/dec/10/nation/la-na-drone-arrest-20111211

121 Glenn Greenwald, "Domestic Drones and their unique dangers," *The Guardian,* March 29, 2013; http://www.theguardian.com/commentisfree/2013/mar/29/domestic-drones-unique-dangers

122 David Talbot, *Season of the Witch,* Free Press/Simon & Schuster, New York, 2012, p. 153.

123 Nikhil Swaminathan, "A history of police militarization," *Al Jazeera America/Fault Lines,* February 26, 2014; http://america.aljazeera.com/watch/shows/fault-lines/FaultLinesBlog/2014/2/25/a-history-of-policemilitarization.html

124 Greenwald, "Domestic Drones and their unique dangers."

125 Ibid.

126 Ibid.

127 Glenn Greenwald, "NPR's domestic drone commercial," *Salon,* December 6, 2011; http://www.salon.com/2011/12/06/nprs_domestic_drone_commercial/

128 Crump & Harwood, "Invasion of the Data Snatchers."

129 Linda Qui, "Fact-checking a comparison of gun deaths and terrorism deaths," *Politifact,* October 5, 2015; https://www.politifact.com/truth-o-meter/statements/2015/oct/05/viral-image/fact-checking-comparison-gun-deaths-and-terrorism-/

130 Glenn Greenwald, "The decade's biggest scam," *Salon,* August 29, 2011; http://www.salon.com/2011/08/29/terrorism_39/

131 Ibid.

132 Ibid.

133 Snowden, *Permanent Record,* pp. 1-3.

134 "Pentagon Plans to Keep 20,000 Troops Inside US to Bolster Domestic Security," Headline in *Huffington Post,* December 31, 2008, which redirected to story in *The Washington Post,* "Pentagon to Detail Troops

to Bolster Domestic Security," Spencer S. Hsu and Ann Scott Tyson, December 1, 2008.

135 Ibid.

136 Donald Trump Speech Transcript June 1, 2020: *Trump May Deploy US Military to Cities;* https://www.rev.com/blog/transcripts/donald-trump-speech-transcript-june-1-trump-may-deploy-us-military-to-cities

137 "ACLU, Groups Sue Trump for Firing Tear Gas at Protestors Outside the White House," ACLU, June 4, 2020; https://www.aclu.org/press-releases/aclu-groups-sue-trump-firing-tear-gas-protesters-outside-white-house

138 Gore Vidal, "The End of Liberty," September 2001, commissioned and later rejected by *Vanity Fair;* http://www.gorevidalpages.com/2001/09/gore-vidal-september-11-end-of-liberty.html; later published as "September 11, 2001 (A Tuesday)," in *Perpetual War for Perpetual Peace,* Thunder's Mouth Press/Nation Books, New York, 2002 pp. 1-42.

139 *DemocracyNow,* "'It Was Time to Do More Than Protest—Activists Admit to 1971 FBI Burglary That Exposed COINTELPRO," January 8, 2014; http://www.democracynow.org/2014/1/8/it_was_time_to_do_more

140 Ibid.

141 Ibid.

142 Ibid.

143 Alfred McCoy, "Surveillance Blowback: The Making of the U.S. Surveillance State, 1898-2020," *TomDispatch,* July 14, 2013; http://www.tomdispatch.com/blog/175724/

144 Ibid.

145 Joey Carmichael, Pavithra Mohan, "How Surveillance Has Evolved in the United States," *Popular Science,* June 19, 2013; http://www.popsci.com/technology/article/2013-06/timeline-wiretapping-united-states

146 Frank Church, as quoted in "The NSA and the Telecoms," Catherine Rentz Pernot, PBS, FRONTLINE: Spying on the Home Front, May 15, 2007; http://www.pbs.org/wgbh/pages/frontline/homefront/preemption/telecoms.html

147 Rentz Pernot, "The NSA and the Telecoms."

148 Cindy Cohn, as quoted in Rentz Pernot, "The NSA and the Telecoms."

149 Verne Lyon, "Domestic Surveillance: The History of Operation CHAOS," *Covert Action Information Bulletin,* Summer 1990; reprinted online at http://www.serendipity.li/cia/lyon.html

150 Ibid.

151 Ibid.

152 Ibid.

153 Ibid.

154 Ibid.

155 Ibid.

156 Carl Bernstein, "The CIA and the Media," *Rolling Stone,* October 20, 1977.

157 Ibid.

158 "Pacifism Rocks," review of Jon Wiener, *Gimme Some Truth: The John Lennon FBI Files,* in *Mother Jones* (Media Jones), November/December 1999.

159 Kim Zetter, "President Ford Approved Warrantless Domestic Surveillance," *Wired,* April 5, 2010; http://www.wired.com/2010/04/ford/

160 Philip Shenon, "F.B.I. Papers Show Wide Surveillance of Reagan Critics," *The New York Times,* January 28, 1988; http://www.nytimes.com/1988/01/28/us/fbi-

papers-show-wide-surveillance-of-reagan-critics.html

161 James Bamford, *The Shadow Factory: The Ultra-Secret NSA from 9/11 to the Eavesdropping on America,* Doubleday, New York, 2008, p. 116.

162 Naomi Klein interviewed by Jeremy Scahill, "The Day After Mueller," *The Intercept,* March 27, 2019; https://theintercept.com/2019/03/27/the-day-after-mueller/

163 Ibid., Jeremy Scahill

164 Ibid.

165 James Bovard, "Mueller's Forgotten Surveillance Crime Spree," *The Hill,* January 29, 2018; https://thehill.com/opinion/criminal-justice/371206-robert-muellers-forgotten-surveillance-crime-spree

166 Ibid.

167 Ibid.

168 Ibid.

169 Carlos Ballesteros, "Robert Mueller is a Hothead Who Can't Own Up to His Own Mistakes, Former Aides Say," *Newsweek,* November 26, 2017; https://www.newsweek.com/robert-mueller-special-counsel-russia-aides-criticize-722670

170 Greg Walters, "William Barr's been accused of a presidential cover-up before," *Vice,* April 17, 2019; https://www.vice.com/en_us/article/pajdb9/william-barrs-been-accused-of-a-presidential-cover-up-before

171 Neema Singh Guliani and Brian Tashman, "William Barr Helped Build America's Surveillance State," ACLU, January 9, 2019; https://www.aclu.org/blog/national-security/privacy-and-surveillance/william-barr-helped-build-americas-surveillance

172 Brad Heath, "U.S. Secretly Tracked Billions of Calls for Decades," *USA Today,* April 8, 2015; https://www.usatoday.com/story/news/2015/04/07/dea-bulk-telephone-surveillance-operation/70808616/

173 Neema Singh Guliani and Brian Tashman, ACLU.

174 Ibid.

175 Maria Bustillos, "Our Reflection in the N.S.A.'s PRISM," *The New Yorker,* June 9, 2013; http://www.newyorker.com/tech/elements/our-reflection-in-the-n-s-a-s-prism

176 Ibid.

177 "Airbus' Secret Past," *The Economist,* June 12, 2003; http://www.economist.com/node/1842124

178 David Sanger and Tim Weiner, "Emerging Role For the CIA: Economic Spy," *The New York Times,* October 15, 1995; http://www.nytimes.com/1995/10/15/world/emerging-role-for-the-cia-economic-spy.html

179 Vernon Loeb, "NSA Admits to Spying on Princess Diana," *Washington Post,* December 12, 1998; http://www.washingtonpost.com/wp-srv/national/daily/dec98/diana12.htm

180 CBS News Staff, "Ex-Snoop Confirms ECHELON Network," *CBS News/60 Minutes,* February 24/27, 2000; http://www.cbsnews.com/news/ex-snoop-confirms-echelon-network/

181 Steve Kroft, as quoted in *60 Minutes,* "Ex-Snoop Confirms ECHELON Network."

182 Ron Wyden, as quoted in Charlie Savage, "Senators Say Patriot Act Is Being Misinterpreted," *The New York Times,* May 26, 2011; http://www.nytimes.com/2011/05/27/us/27patriot.html

183 Gore Vidal, "Gore Vidal Delivers State of the Union," *DemocracyNow*, January 31, 2006; http://www.democracynow.org/2006/1/31/gore_vidal_delivers_state_of_the

184 Foxnews.com, interview with Peter Camejo, February 17, 2004; http://www.foxnews.com/story/2004/02/17/raw-data-foxnewscom-interviews-peter-camejo/

185 ACLU, "The USA Patriot Act and Government Actions that Threaten Our Civil Liberties," pamphlet; https://www.aclu.org/files/FilesPDFs/patriot%20act%20flyer.pdf

186 Ibid.

187 "Rebuilding America's Defenses: Strategies, Forces, and Resources For a New Century," A Report of The Project for the New American Century (PNAC), September 2000, Section V, "Creating Tomorrow's Dominant Force," p. 51.

188 Michael German & Michelle Richardson, "Reclaiming Patriotism: A Call to Reconsider the Patriot Act," ACLU, March, 2009, p. 7.

189 James Madison, "The Debates in the Federal Convention of 1787," June 29, 1787, archived by The Avalon Project, Yale Law School; http://avalon.law.yale.edu/18th_century/debates_629.asp

190 Chris Hedges, "The Last Gasp of Democracy."

191 Ibid.

192 Craig Timberg & Barton Gellman, "NSA paying U.S. companies for access to communications networks," *The Washington Post*, August 29, 2013.

193 Ryan Gallagher and Henrik Moltke, "The Wiretap Rooms," *The Intercept*, June 25, 2018; https://theintercept.com/2018/06/25/att-internet-nsa-spy-hubs/

194 Chris Hedges, "The Post-Constitutional Era," *Truthdig*, May 5, 2014; http://www.truthdig.com/report/item/the_post-constitutional_era_20140504

195 Noah Shachtman, "Google, CIA Invest in 'Future' of Web Monitoring," *Wired*, July 29, 2010; https://www.wired.com/2010/07/exclusive-google-cia/

196 Chris Hedges, "Edward Snowden's Moral Courage," *Truthdig*, February 23, 2014; http://www.truthdig.com/report/item/edward_snowdens_moral_courage_20140223

197 Sheldon S. Wolin, *Democracy Incorporated: Managed Democracy and the Specter of Inverted Totalitarianism*, Princeton University Press, Princeton, NJ, 2008, p. xiii.

198 Ibid.

199 Hedges, "The Post-Constitutional Era."

200 Noam Chomsky, interviewed by Stuart Allen Baker for the *Bangkok Post*, February 15, 2014; http://www.chomsky.info/interviews/20140215.htm

201 Glenn Greenwald, as quoted in Conor Friedersdorff, "No Place to Hide: A Conservative Critique of a Radical NSA," *The Atlantic*, May 14, 2014; http://www.theatlantic.com/politics/archive/2014/05/on-nsa-surveillance-glenn-greenwald-is-not-the-radical/370830/

202 Ibid.

203 Danny Schechter, "Can We Stop America's Surveillance State?," *Huffington Post*, May 16, 2014; http://www.huffingtonpost.com/danny-schechter/can-we-stop-americas-surv_b_5334572.html

204 Ibid.

205 Ray McGovern, as quoted in Schechter, "Can We Stop America's Surveillance State?"

206 William Greider, "Spy Agencies, Not Politicians, Hold the Cards in Washington," *The Nation,* March 24, 2014; http://www.thenation.com/blog/178959/spy-agencies-not-politicians-hold-cards-washington

207 Edward Snowden, "State of Surveillance," interview with Shane Smith, *Vice,* HBO, June 8, 2016.

Chapter 7

1 Linh Dinh, "Singing For Empire: Make Love, Then War," *Counterpunch,* April 28, 2012; http://www.counterpunch.org/2012/04/27/make-love-then-war/

2 Industrial Workers of the World (IWW), "Preamble to the IWW Constitution," http://www.iww.org/en/culture/official/preamble.shtml

3 James West Davidson, *They say: Ida B. Wells and the Reconstruction of Race,* Oxford University Press, New York, 2007, pp. 7-9.

4 Will Kaufman, *Woody Guthrie, American Radical,* University of Illinois Press, Chicago, 2011, p. 145.

5 Seth Archer, "Reading the Riot Acts," *Southwest Review,* September 22, 2006.

6 Bryan Garman, *A Race of Singers: Whitman's Working-Class Hero from Guthrie to Springsteen,* University of North Carolina Press, Chapel Hill, 2000, p. 118.

7 Jonny Whiteside, "Little Known Fact: Woody Guthrie Was a Big Ol' Racist," *LA Weekly,* July 13, 2012; http://www.laweekly.com/music/little-known-fact-woody-guthrie-was-a-big-ol-racist-2412272

8 Garman, p. 118.

9 Howard Zinn, from *You Can't Be Neutral on a Moving Train,* documentary film, Deb Ellis, Denis Mueller, directors, First Run Features, 2005.

10 Pete Seeger, as quoted in Stuart Maconie, *The People's Songs: The Story of Modern Britain in 50 Records,* Ebury Press, London, 2013, p. 141.

11 "Woody Guthrie's Biography" Woody Guthrie Publications; http://www.woodyguthrie.org/biography/biography1.htm

12 Kaufman, p. xxv.

13 Kaufman, pp. 158-164.

14 Scott Linford, review of Kaufman, *Woody Guthrie: American Radical,* Ethnomusicology Review, vol. 16, 2011; http://ethnomusicologyreview.ucla.edu/journal/volume/16/piece/467

15 Lawrence Downes, "As Woody Turns 100, We Protest Too Little," *The New York Times,* August 18, 2012; http://www.nytimes.com/2012/08/19/opinion/sunday/as-woody-guthrie-turns-100-we-protest-too-little.html

16 Arlo Guthrie, as quoted in Downes, "As Woody Turns 100, We Protest Too Little."

17 Larry Rohter, "'Your Land,' and Guthrie's, Preserved," *The New York Times,* July 11, 2012; http://www.nytimes.com/2012/07/15/arts/music/your-land-and-woody-guthries-preserved.html

18 Woody Guthrie, excerpted from "Woody Sez," a collection of articles written for *People's World,* Woody Guthrie Publications, copyrighted 1975; http://woodyguthrie.org/biography/woodysez.htm

19 Downes, "As Woody Turns 100, We Protest Too Little."

20 Geoffrey Himes, "Dead 40 Years, Woody Guthrie Stays Busy," *The New York Times,* August 2, 2007; http://www.nytimes.com/2007/09/02/arts/music/02himes.html

21 Richard Cromelin, "Gil Scott-Heron dies at 62; singer and poet 'set the template' for rap music," *Los Angeles Times,* May 29, 2011; https://www.latimes.com/local/obituaries/la-me-gil-scott-heron-20110529-story.html

22 David Dacks, "Gil Scott-Heron: Pioneering Poet," *Exclaim!,* February 20,2010; http://exclaim.ca/music/article/gil_scott-heron-pioneering_poet

23 Ibid.

24 Jonah Weiner, "Tribute: Gil Scott-Heron," *Rolling Stone,* June 23, 2011.

25 Dacks, "Gil Scott-Heron: Pioneering Poet."

26 Ibid.

27 Gil Scott-Heron, *The Last Holiday: A Memoir,* Grove Press, New York, 2012, pp. 119-120.

28 Ta-Nehisi Coates, "The Godfather of Rap," *The Atlantic,* June 2, 2011.

29 Kent Nerburn, *Chief Joseph & the Flight of the Nez Perce: The Untold Story of an American Tragedy,* HarperCollins, New York, 2005, pp. 267-268.

Index

D

E

I

J

K

L

M

N

O

P

R

S

T

U

Z